AMERICAN EDUCATIONAL GOVERNANCE ON TRIAL: CHANGE AND CHALLENGES

AMERICAN EDUCATIONAL GOVERNANCE ON TRIAL: CHANGE AND CHALLENGES

102nd Yearbook of the
National Society for the Study of Education

PART I

Edited by
WILLIAM LOWE BOYD AND DEBRA MIRETZKY

20 03

Distributed by THE UNIVERSITY OF CHICAGO PRESS • CHICAGO, ILLINOIS

National Society for the Study of Education

The National Society for the Study of Education was founded in 1901 as successor to the National Herbart Society. It publishes a two-volume Yearbook, each volume dealing with a separate topic of concern to educators. The Society's Yearbook series, now in its one hundred-second year, presents articles by scholars and practitioners noted for their significant work in critical areas of education.

The Society welcomes as members all individuals who wish to receive its publications. Current membership includes educators in the United States, Canada, and elsewhere throughout the world—professors, researchers, administrators, and graduate students in colleges and universities and teachers, administrators, supervisors, and curriculum specialists in elementary and secondary schools, as well as policymakers at all levels.

Members of the Society elect a Board of Directors. The Board's responsibilities include reviewing proposals for Yearbooks, authorizing the preparation of Yearbooks based on accepted proposals, and appointing an editor or editors to oversee the preparation of manuscripts.

Current dues (for 2003) are a modest $35 ($30 for retired members and for students in their first year of membership). Members whose dues are paid for the current calendar year receive the Society's Yearbook, are eligible for election to the Board of Directors, and are entitled to a 33 percent discount when purchasing past Yearbooks from the Society's distributor, the University of Chicago Press.

Each year the Society arranges for meetings to be held in conjunction with the annual conferences of one or more of the national educational organizations. All members are urged to attend these meetings, at which the current Yearbook is presented and critiqued. Members are encouraged to submit proposals for future Yearbooks.

American Educational Governance on Trial: Change and Challenges is Part I of the 102nd Yearbook. Part II, published simultaneously, is titled *Meeting at the Hyphen: Schools-Universities-Communities-Professions in Collaboration for Student Achievement and Well Being.*

For further information, write to the Secretary, NSSE, College of Education m/c 147, University of Illinois at Chicago, 1040 W. Harrison St., Chicago, Illinois 60607-7133 or see www.uic.edu/educ/nsse

ISSN: 0077-5762

Published 2003 by the
NATIONAL SOCIETY FOR THE STUDY OF EDUCATION

1040 W. Harrison St., Chicago, Illinois 60607-7133
© 2003 by the National Society for the Study of Education

First Printing
Printed in the United States of America

Board of Directors of the
National Society for the Study of Education
(Term of office expires in the year indicated.)

Contributors to the Yearbook

WILLIAM Lowe BOYD, Editor, Pennsylvania State University
DEBRA MIRETZKY, Editor, National Society for the Study of Education

SARAH ARCHIBALD, Wisconsin Center for Education Research
JAMES CIBULKA, University of Kentucky
BRUCE S. COOPER, Fordham University
JOSEPH M. CRONIN, Nellie Mae Educational Foundation
LUVERN CUNNINGHAM, Ohio State University
MARK FERMANICH, Wisconsin Center for Education Research
FRANCES FOWLER, Miami University, Ohio
JANE HANNAWAY, Urban Institute Education Policy Center
CAROLYN HERRINGTON, Florida State University
FREDERICK M. HESS, American Enterprise Institute
PAUL T. HILL, University of Washington
JACK JENNINGS, Center on Education Policy
CHARLES TAYLOR KERCHNER, Claremont Graduate University
MICHAEL W. KIRST, Stanford University
ALLAN ODDEN, Wisconsin Center for Education Research
KENNETH STRIKE, University of Maryland
MICHAEL D. USDAN, Institute for Educational Leadership
TYLL VAN GEEL, University of Rochester

v

Table of Contents

Section One

Why is Educational Governance on Trial?

Section Two

How to Fix the Educational Governance System

Section Three

Rethinking the Governance of School Districts

Section Four
Rethinking the State and Federal Roles in Educational Governance

Section One
WHY IS EDUCATIONAL
GOVERNANCE ON TRIAL?

CHAPTER 1

Public Education's Crisis of Performance and Legitimacy: Introduction and Overview of the Yearbook

WILLIAM LOWE BOYD

The governance of American public education is clearly on trial today. The future character of American education very much hangs in the balance. After decades of criticism and mounting discontent about the academic standards, performance, and moral order of public schools, especially in our large cities, both policymakers and the public are increasingly embracing radical measures to alter or reform the governance and operation of the education system. The rapid spread and adoption of once heretical ideas are breathtaking. At the same time, attempts by professional educators and their interest groups to defend public education (e.g., Berliner & Biddle, 1995; Bracey, 1997a, 1997b, 2002) seem ineffective and unpersuasive to the public and the media. Instead, the initiative and leadership for future directions in public education have come largely from actors external to the public education system. The wave of recent reports and recommendations for reforming the governance system mainly reflects the thinking of corporate leaders, policy analysts, foundations, and critics of public education. This yearbook analyzes the reasons for these far-ranging developments, and describes and assesses the startling range of measures and changes that are occurring.

The central thesis of this yearbook is that educational governance is on trial today because American public education is caught up in a

William Lowe Boyd is Batschelet Chair Professor of Educational Administration and Professor-in-Charge of Graduate Programs in Educational Administration at Pennsylvania State University.

double crisis of both performance and legitimacy. Part one of the year-book addresses how and why this twin crisis has put public education on trial. This introductory chapter discusses the reasons for the double crisis and provides an overview of the contents and principal themes of the yearbook. The fact that education was a major campaign issue in the 2000 presidential election, with both major candidates calling for tough accountability reforms, reflects public sentiment today. George W. Bush promised to close failing schools and divide their federal funding among parents to use for private school tuition, a promise almost accomplished in the No Child Left Behind Act of 2001. Despite relying on the support of the teacher unions, Al Gore pledged to close and "reconstitute" (i.e., reopen with a new staff and leadership) schools that were still failing after 2 years with extra federal funds, or allow them to convert to charter schools. Speaking of Gore's plan, the *Wall Street Journal* (Kronholz, 2000, October 13, p. A20) called reconstitution the "ultimate threat, the neutron bomb of school reform." Public education groups nevertheless continue to view school voucher plans—such as those favored by George W. Bush and his brother Jeb, the governor of Florida, and now bolstered by the Supreme Court's *Zelman* decision—as the real "doomsday machine." How did we get to the point that the once unthinkable—voucher plans, privatization, takeovers, and reconstitution—is not only thinkable but actually happening?

Pressures for increasingly radical reforms of public schools have flowed from a variety of social trends interacting with a growing perception—right or wrong—that the schools are performing poorly or are inadequate for meeting the demands of the new global economy. Since the 1980s and the influential report *A Nation at Risk* (1983), many reforms have been attempted, with limited evidence of real improvement, especially in the education of poor and disadvantaged children. As a result, support continues to grow, at the very least in elite circles, for more radical reforms that would dramatically alter or even privatize public education. Public educators increasingly recognize the threats they face, but have trouble grasping the opportunities these threats present because they challenge fundamental aspects of the paradigm and ideology of public education to which they are wedded (Boyd, 2000).

The difficulties schools face are compounded by a growing perception that schools now must not only provide high skills for the information age but also prepare students for what can be called "high citizenship" (Boyd, 2000) in societies battling poverty and inequality, escalating social problems, and the breakdown of civility. In the struggle to meet the twin challenges of high skills and high citizenship, one of the casualties in multicultural societies could well be support for large and socially inclusive public school systems. On the one hand, mounting accountability pressures on the public schools flow from a performance crisis, with a large majority of disadvantaged students far below acceptable achievement standards and allegations that many other students are being poorly prepared for the needs of a knowledge-based "information society." On the other hand, public schools face a growing crisis of legitimacy, because the highly standardized and bureaucratized public education system is committed to a democratic "common school" and hence is unable to accommodate the demands of an increasingly diverse society divided by "culture wars."

Ethnic and religious groups dissatisfied with the moral order and culture of public schools, and better educated parents wanting more quality and choice in services for their children, unite in demanding more choice among schools—public, private, and parochial. Just how much the world has changed was captured in a *New York Times* story about young blacks—traditionally supporters of public education—turning to school vouchers as a civil rights issue (Wilgoren, 2000, October 9). Religious rights are also a concern. Despite the *Zelman* decision (which ruled that voucher plans, if properly designed, may include religious schools) and George W. Bush's support of policies permitting faith-based groups to receive government funds for charitable ventures, the perception remains that the public schools are highly secularized and not just neutral but hostile toward religious beliefs. This view has been reinforced by a number of developments. For example, government mandates are perceived by some to be pushing public schools to side against traditional families in support of gay and lesbian rights and same-sex unions, a trend now driving a wedge between public schools and the Boy Scouts movement.

The range of alternatives being considered and adopted in response to the crisis of performance and legitimacy is extraordinary. A race is on among political leaders to see who can promote the toughest testing and accountability programs for schools. Plans for state takeovers and reconstitution of failing schools (sometimes, as in Baltimore and Philadelphia, under private, for-profit management) have proliferated. The separation of educational and municipal government in big cities is beginning to disappear, as mayors are moving rapidly to intervene in the reform and governance of failing urban school systems. Urban school superintendents are no longer automatically being replaced by other leaders from education. Increasingly, military leaders or executives from the private sector are being recruited for these jobs, a pattern especially prominent in the largest and most problematic urban districts. Corporate models of governance are being adopted, with chief executive officers presiding over chief academic and chief operating officers. Elected school boards, very often politicized and fractious in urban districts, are facing mounting criticism in the form of proposals that aim to pass laws to limit board powers to broad policymaking and long-term planning (Goodman & Zimmerman, 2000). Plans to break up big city school systems abound. More broadly, vocal and well-funded groups are advocating a massive shift to charter schools or voucher plans. By 1996, more than 40 privately-funded voucher plans had been established in cities across the U.S, raising the visibility of the voucher alternative in the eyes of the public and the media (Mintrom & Vergari, 2002). At the same time, home schooling is flourishing and capitalizing upon the new availability of cyber-schools and rich educational resources on the Internet.

In one high-profile response to these challenges, illustrative of the ferment today, the National Commission on Governing America's Schools, created by the Education Commission of the States, proposed two alternative models of governance (National Commission, 1999). Each model responds to the demand for higher standards and accountability by decentralizing decision making and shifting greater authority and responsibility for results to the school level. Each model would give parents more choice of schools, allow money to follow a student, give schools more control over their personnel and budget, and redefine labor-management relations. Each would move from a "school system" to a high-performing "system of schools." The bolder of the two models would transform local school boards into "chartering boards," creating a system of "publicly authorized, publicly funded and *independently operated* schools," including private and parochial schools that would choose to come into the system (National Commission, 1999, p. 3, emphasis in original). With a grant from the Joyce Foundation, the Education Commission of the States has created a National Center for Innovation in Governing American Education to follow up on this work and "help states and districts understand and put in place innovative forms of school governance" (Keller, 2000, September 20, p. 21).

Why Radical Change Now?

Social institutions are notoriously difficult to change, and public education is no exception to this rule. Indeed, public education's ability to absorb and deflect reform efforts is legendary and the subject of colorful metaphors, like Cuban's (1979) storm at sea that leaves the deep waters undisturbed. Scholars generally agree that education's resistance to change springs from its "deep structures" (Tye, 2000, 2002) as an institution—that is, widely shared beliefs, values, and assumptions about the character and essence of public schooling that are hard to change. These deep structures shape beliefs about what constitutes "public education" (Hess, 2002, 2003) or a "real school" (Metz, 1989) and contribute to what Tyack and Tobin (1994) called the "grammar of schooling."

The Ideology of Public Schooling

Public education has a remarkably well developed ideology, widely shared by members of the public as well as educators, that provides deep structures of beliefs about its character and how it should be organized and governed. This ideology, at times almost a "religion" of public schooling, is manifested vividly in the reactions of its advocates to proposals they view as "illegitimate," such as for-profit management of public schools. The ideology of the governance of public schools is deeply committed to a belief in a democratic system of "common" public schools, *operated* as well as *financed* by the government, that provides a standardized curriculum, treats everyone equally (irrespective of social class, culture, race, or religion), and is accountable to a publicly elected school board. As part of a nonprofit public service, public schools are (ideally) supposed to be insulated from both politics and competition. They should not compete with one another for students or resources, or use selective or "elitist" admissions policies, and all schools should be treated alike and provide a "one best system" (Tyack, 1974). This makes "magnet" schools, charter schools, and other departures from the norm problematic.

The Ideology of Public School Teaching

Public school teachers, as well, should not be expected to compete. Their rank and compensation should be based on seniority, and on the diplomas and certificates they hold, rather than on merit or "performance" pay. Further, in the interest of equal treatment, the existing supply and demand for teachers with specialties that are in short supply should be ignored. Apart from their seniority and paper qualifications, all teachers should be paid roughly the same salary, irrespective of their specialties or level of performance, the latter usually being viewed as undeterminable by any objective means. And after a brief probationary period, public school teachers should receive the protection of tenure in their jobs, so that they can be removed, with great difficulty, only for gross failures in their performance and behavior.

Those subscribing to these beliefs about how public schools should be organized and managed are not troubled by the fact that these arrangements create a quasi-monopoly with a highly circumscribed structure of incentives. Instead, they believe that public school teachers and administrators, as public servants, will not succumb to monopoly pathologies, and will be motivated by professionalism and altruism to "do the right thing" for all children.

Given the celebrated staying power of public education as an institution, it is natural to question why radical change should be occurring now in governance arrangements for public education. After all, reform has been on the agenda for decades, especially since the desegregation and civil rights era of the 1960s. Even prior to the release of *A Nation at Risk* (1983) and the subsequent 20 years of reform efforts, public education had been besieged for two decades. Indeed, Boyd and Crowson noted in 1981 that:

One of the great paradoxes of American education is how little, and yet how much, our schools have changed over the past two decades of unprecedented ferment, turbulence, and systematic efforts at reform. In many of their most obvious features, schools have scarcely changed at all ... [despite] a virtual revolution in authority relations in schools; a sense of crisis about the normative order of schools; a serious decline in public confidence in, and support for, the schools; and substantial changes in how schools are governed. (pp. 311-312)

What is different now that might account for the shift toward radical reforms? Boyd and Crowson (1981) further observed:

A cynical observer might ask: So what is new? Criticism of the public schools has for some time been one of the national pastimes. American public education, virtually since its inception, has moved continuously from one proclaimed "crisis" to another (Kirst & Walker, 1971). What seems new this time around is the increasing acceptance, particularly among the middle class, of the idea that the nonpublic schools are doing a better job than the public schools, and that there no longer may be any compelling civic reasons to continue to patronize and support the public schools. This viewpoint, already popularized in support of policy proposals for tuition tax credits and educational voucher plans, has been bolstered by the (hotly contested) findings of Coleman's new report. ... Unlike previous "crises" faced by public education, the present one could conceivably contribute to the adoption of polices that could transform or even dismantle public education. (p. 313)

Paradigm Shift and Transformation

The transformation did not occur in the 1980s, but the forces of change had been set in motion. Now, 20 years later, the policies that may transform or dismantle public education are truly upon us. But why now? Institutional theory and research on institutional change suggest that significant change occurs only when there is an unusual convergence of social, economic, demographic, and political trends that make change in deep structures possible (Powell & DiMaggio, 1991). Thus, within a context of political and demographic trends that challenge public education in the United States, a "paradigm shift" in public education has been developing over the past 20 years. This shift is marked by a change in focus from inputs *to* the system to the outcomes and accountability *of* the system; by a shift in the attitudes of key constituency groups; and by a critical reexamination of what public education means and how it can or should be delivered (Boyd & Immegart, 1979; Chubb & Moe, 1990; Cibulka, 1995; Coons & Sugarman, 1978; Hill, Pierce, & Guthrie, 1997; Olson, 2000). The circumstances promoting this paradigm shift deserve book-length treatment rather than the necessarily incomplete and circumscribed overview that space permits here.

To begin, demographic trends in the United States present major challenges for public education. Declining birth rates, an aging population, and soaring numbers of senior citizens are particular concerns. Senior citizens living on a fixed income tend to be tax resistant and less interested in education than young families. They are inclined to turn out and vote in large numbers, and have become a potent political force in the United States. Further, population growth in the U.S. is occurring mainly among nonwhites. Because of the inequalities in our society, this means that children are increasingly raised in poor, disadvantaged families of color. As a result, within the context of an increasingly diverse and multicultural society, the public schools are being challenged to successfully educate increasing numbers of minority children who have not benefited from the "hidden curriculum" of the middle-class home.

At the same time, the middle class has become more affluent, better educated, and more quality-conscious as consumers. With the increasing importance of education for the future success of their children, their expectation for quality and choice in services and goods within our market-driven society has created the basis for a "politics of excellence and choice in education" (Boyd & Kerchner, 1988). This development has intersected with, and been compounded by, a key sociopolitical trend since 1980: the neo-conservative trend critical of the welfare state, of government spending, and of the public services, including especially public education (Ball, 1990; Boyd, 1992).

The Neo-conservative Movement

Irving Kristol, one of the intellectual leaders of the neo-conservative movement in the United States, humorously defined a neo-conservative as "a liberal who has been mugged by reality." Indeed, the sentiments associated with the "Reagan Revolution" and the trend against "big government" have progressed to the point that most politicians cringe at being called "liberals." The term liberal, once associated with socially progressive positions, has become discredited and associated with the label "tax-and-spend liberals." Similarly, public education, once considered among America's proudest creations, has been repeatedly attacked over recent decades and often disparagingly called "the blob" by those who view it as a huge, inefficient, monopolistic bureaucracy.[1]

The prime leaders in mounting this very effective "discourse of derision" (Ball, 1990) have been a national network of conservative think tanks and policy institutes that produces a steady flow of conservative policy critiques, research reports, and op-ed pieces for newspapers that decry government's inefficiency and wastefulness, the inadequacies of the "failing" public school system, and so on. In a society permeated by capitalism and business values, this sustained publicity campaign helps explain how neo-conservative views, once limited to a small elite, became increasingly widespread and influential.[2] Of course, think tanks, policy institutes, and foundations of all persuasions understand that ideas and rhetoric matter in policy and politics. How policy problems are framed and viewed affects the kinds of solutions that are proposed and the analysis and advocacy of policy alternatives. Groups with differing views wage an ongoing struggle to win the hearts and minds of the public, the media, and policymakers.

The network of conservative think tanks—with one located by design in each state, and all linked to the national "mother ship," the Heritage Foundation—has been remarkably effective in influencing the media and public opinion with regard to public policy and the role of government (Easterbrook, 1986). Conservative think tanks appear to be substantially more numerous and more visible than liberal think tanks. Even so, concerns about the widespread influence of conservative think tanks are usually met with counterclaims about the "liberal bias" of the media and, in regard to the sphere of education, about the political power and formidable lobbying and public relations capabilities of teacher unions. Yet, the unions are nearly always viewed as biased and self-interested, while the conservative think tanks can more easily advance their analyses as based upon objective scientific research and the public interest.

The sophisticated and well-financed efforts of conservative foundations in campaigning for charter schools and voucher plans are the subject of an illuminating paper by Mintrom and Vergari (2002). They discuss and analyze these efforts at the national level, and with case studies of efforts in California and New York. Significantly, they emphasize that these foundations recognize that the school choice campaign is an attempt to change the character and governance of public education:

The school choice debate is a debate about the adoption of alternative institutional arrangements for educational governance. Those who support the traditional public school arrangements and those who support a market-based approach to educational delivery tend to bring incongruous policy "frames" to bear on the debate. As Schon and Rein (1994, pp. 28-29) have observed, "In a policy controversy ... two or more parties contend with one another over the definition of a problematic policy situation and vie for control of the policymaking process. Their struggles over the naming and framing of a policy situation are symbolic contests over the social meaning of an issue domain, where meaning implies not only what is at issue but what is to be done." (p. 1)

It needs to be recognized, of course, that the successful effort to propagate the neo-conservative critique of public education was facilitated by other socio-political trends and by public education itself, which provided plenty of ammunition for critics. The appalling failure and dropout rates in our big city school systems are undeniably real.[3] Further, numerous reports and studies have documented the extremely dysfunctional management and politics of many big urban districts, some suffering corruption on top of mismanagement. A forthcoming report for the Wallace-Reader's Digest Funds titled "Structured to Fail: The 'Impossible' Job of the Urban School Superintendent" reports that current and former urban district superintendents who were interviewed acknowledged the generally dysfunctional state of affairs, including a strong tendency for employees and board members to focus far more on adult issues and perks than on the educational needs of students (Center for Reinventing Public Education, 2002).

The movement for educational voucher plans, established intellectually by Milton Friedman in the 1950s and popular with neo-conservatives, received a critical push into the mainstream with the publication and widespread recognition of John Chubb's and Terry Moe's *Politics, Markets, & America's Schools* (1990). The charter school idea was successfully incubated in Minnesota, with the intellectual leadership and political savvy of Joe Nathan (1989) and Ted Kolderie, who argued for "withdrawing the exclusive franchise" for public education from school districts (Kolderie, 1990). With the enactment of charter schools legislation in 39 states, an ongoing campaign for educational voucher plans bolstered by state initiatives in Milwaukee and Cleveland, privately-funded voucher demonstration programs in several cities, and intellectual leadership and research (e.g., Coons & Sugarman, 1978, and Paul Peterson's Program on Education Policy and Governance at Harvard [Peterson & Campbell, 2001]), the stage was set for the Supreme Court's decision in the *Zelman* voucher case.

No Child Left Behind

At the same time, school choice has not been the sole focus of reform (Wang & Walberg, 2001). Indeed, even more attention has been given to the state-led standards-based accountability movement, which has transformed governance relationships between states and local school districts, and has redefined and raised the bar on expectations for performance of public schools. But very significantly, the key themes of standards-based reform *and* of attempts to redefine the character of public education all come together in the momentous No Child Left Behind Act (NCLB) of 2001. However commendable its goals, NCLB marks what Elmore (2002) and others view as by far the greatest intrusion ever of the federal government into the domain of state and local control of education (Dillon, 2003)—an intrusion ironically championed by a Republican president who had promised to protect local control.

Grave concerns have been voiced that the very ambitious and demanding requirements of NCLB may lead to a situation in which 50-60% of all public schools are labeled as failing schools (Dillon, 2003). Indeed, NCLB is increasingly viewed as a threat to the future of public schools, because it is likely to further erode their reputation and legitimacy (Draper, 2002; Fletcher, 2003). NCLB's requirement that students in "failing schools" be given the option of obtaining supplemental services or transferring to successful schools links NCLB's standards-based accountability to market-based reforms. Indeed, the combination of the No Child Left Behind Act with the Supreme Court's *Zelman* decision has created a radically new and more favorable environment for school choice. Cynical critics are even asserting that the real purpose of NCLB is to undermine public schools and promote market-based reforms.

Conclusions

It is clear that the twin crises of performance and legitimacy confronting public schools interact and reinforce one another. The legitimacy crisis arises from socio-political and multicultural trends in the United States. The disturbing social trends seen here, and in many westernized societies today, have been the subject of numerous reports, studies, and books. Authors draw attention to the myriad of modern morbidities that put children at risk of not reaching productive adulthood—poverty, crime, drugs, and other problems that make it difficult to obtain an education, successfully enter the workforce, or otherwise contribute to society (see, for example, Brabeck, Walsh, & Latta, 2003; Stringfield & Land, 2002). Irving Kristol summed up the social and political situation in the United States as follows:

The current breakup experienced by the American family is having a profound effect on American politics, as well as on American society. One can go further and say that the social problems we are confronting, problems either created or exacerbated by our welfare state, are making the welfare state a cultural issue as well as an economic one. The Christian Right understands this, as does the secularist left. The "culture wars" are no political sideshow. Today, and in the years ahead, they will be energizing and defining all the controversies that revolve around the welfare state. (1996, p. A16)

One can argue about the extent to which it is the *welfare* state or the *capitalist* state that has created or exacerbated the social problems and "culture wars" confronting us, but there is no doubt that the problems exist, and the increasing diversity of our society adds to the tensions that must be managed. Indeed, a new, and for many, problematic America is emerging: multicultural, multi-faith, with alarming inequalities and permeable borders penetrated by globalization, by immigration (often illegal), and by international terrorism. Globalization, demographic trends, and "culture" wars—both internal to the United States and as part of the gap between the affluent, westernized world and Islamic and underdeveloped nations—are challenging and transforming the character of U.S. society. The hegemony of white majorities and even of the English language is no longer assured; "minority majorities" are emerging in some states, and demographic trends indicate that this is the wave of the future. Most of the population growth is occurring in poor, disadvantaged families, and in families for whom English is a second language. As the United States becomes more diverse, multicultural, and multilingual, and at the same time more unequal, the character, values, and legitimacy of our society and of its public school system are increasingly called into question.

"Globalization," as Kymlicka (1995, p. 9) observes, "has made the myth of a culturally homogeneous state even more unrealistic, and has forced the majority within each state to be more open to pluralism and diversity." This important effect of globalization challenges the old paradigm of public education as a "neutral" vehicle for national unity based on *majority* values. Tensions mount as public education's universalistic "one best system" tries to accommodate cultural diversity without betraying its "common school" philosophy. Can the center "hold" in public education when, as Alan Wolfe (2000, p. A22) observes, "America is engaged in an experiment in moral federalism, as state and local governments take sides in the country's culture wars"? Whose version(s) of moral standards shall the public schools adopt?

In this context, and in view of accelerating controversies in the education sector, it is clear that the politics of education is intensifying as the multicultural and rapidly changing aspects of our society become more obvious. Put another way, there is less social consensus, more "pluribus" than "unum," and the "one best system" approach to public education (Tyack, 1974) has collapsed along with the "myth of the unitary community" (Salisbury, 1967). In this new American society, many perplexing questions arise. What are our shared values? Whose history and "common school" is it now, anyway? What should be the curriculum and character of public schools for the emerging "new" America? Which of the many solutions being proposed should be adopted (Hill & Celio, 1998)? These and other challenging questions underlie the analyses presented in this yearbook.

Overview of the Yearbook

This yearbook is divided into four sections.[4] The first section, "Why Is Educational Governance on Trial?" focuses on the discussion of governance issues begun in this introductory chapter. In chapter 2, Jane Hannaway presents a review and critique of performance-based accountability policies. She cautions that while state and federal policies that promote rewards and sanctions for performance appear to make sense and are politically fashionable, such policies are created from a limited research base and tend to hinder real understanding of what works. The technical and political challenges are significant, as issues of control and of measurement interfere with both performance and policy assessment. Hannaway offers suggestions for more effectively exploring the effects of accountability on practice—including research on instructional practice effects, resource allocation patterns, and student academic behavior—and proposes a new working relationship between federal and state structures to promote more effective use of existing knowledge as well as expanded research efforts.

In Chapter 3, Kenneth Strike examines legitimacy in public education through discussion of three relevant constructs: liberty, democracy, and community. While acknowledging that there is widespread agreement that community is a good thing, he argues that, in reality, it is very difficult for schools to be communities. Almost by default, public schools continue to be viewed as though they were banks, with the primary goal being the development of individual human capital, because of the complexity of reconciling liberal and democratic interpretations of constitutional norms like equal opportunity, pluralism, and political socialization. This persistent inability of schools to fulfill cherished goals contributes, fairly or unfairly, to the crisis of legitimacy for public education.

The second section of the yearbook, "How to Fix the Educational Governance System," offers broad-based solutions for repairing the governance system. Paul T. Hill (chapter 4) argues that big city schools are unduly burdened by school board politics, union contracts, and state-imposed rules, necessitating a rejection of the current structure of governance and the substitution, instead, of more "school-friendly" systems. He sketches the problems of "lingering" governance and describes the real "rules" of governance, in which those in charge and those who are best equipped to organize politically are most likely to have their needs met. The right governance systems will emphasize effective schools above all else, and Hill offers an outline of critical supports, incentives, capacity builders, and change strategies before describing some cutting-edge governance models.

In chapter 5, Allan Odden, Sarah Archibald, and Mark Fermanich provide an overview of the movement from equity to adequacy in school funding as a partial result of standards-based reform. They describe approaches to determining adequate levels of funding for educating students to high performance standards (including the critical need to address teacher compensation), outline avenues for district design of needs-based per-pupil funding formulas, and address effective use of adequacy-based funding. They believe that adequate levels of revenue are essential for supporting more powerful education strategies, and that states and districts must partner effectively to determine, allocate, and deploy these revenues.

In chapter 6, Frederick M. Hess addresses the choice-based and contractual reforms that are challenging the traditional structure of school governance, describing the arguments of proponents and critics of market-based alternatives like charter schools, vouchers, and school contracting. He examines the available evidence on the performance of students in choice schools compared to students in regular district public schools, as well as the performance of public schools affected by choice-induced competition. As of this writing, choice alternatives have done little to change the responsiveness or market behavior of most public school districts. However, Hess argues that the controversy surrounding choice reflects fundamental disagreements about what the character of public education should be in a democratic society, and concludes that choice reforms therefore have the potential to radically alter governance structures of the future.

In chapter 7, Tyll van Geel examines the momentous *Zelman v. Harris* decision, in which the Supreme Court ruled, in June 2002, that the Cleveland, Ohio voucher program including private religious schools did not violate the Establishment Clause of the Constitution. He discusses the implications of the ruling for schools and for states, concluding that voucher programs will continue to encounter legal and political barriers, not the least of which will be a difficult balancing act between political acceptance and free speech considerations.

The third section of the yearbook, "Rethinking the Governance of School Districts," focuses on school district governance from a variety of perspectives. Luvern Cunningham (chapter 8) takes the notion of governance beyond traditional boundaries as he discusses the emerging community context of the governance function. This community context is distinguished by a reliance on dialogue and reflection and is promoted by an increased interdependence between citizens and their institutions, technological advances in communication, and an increased demand for accountability. He calls for renewed support of public engagement in learning and governance issues as a means of strengthening the connections between citizens and schools and of reinforcing democratic ideals.

Joseph M. Cronin and Michael Usdan (chapter 9) describe the widening search for school leaders as they discuss the nature of the urban school superintendency today. The demands of this position—ranging from changing school populations to increased and competing expectations on the part of the community and business, and shrinking resources—take a tremendous toll, particularly on superintendents who are not equipped to juggle the expanding functions of the job.

Cronin and Usdan see cities rethinking the urban superintendency in response to this dilemma, employing such diverse strategies as mayoral involvement, appointed school boards, recruitment of superintendents from non-educational fields, and the teaming of administrators. They predict continued involvement of general purpose government in school management and see few good options for school governance that do not involve some form of distributed leadership or partnerships.

In chapter 10, Michael W. Kirst further examines the relatively recent phenomenon of mayoral interventions in urban school systems and their gradations from simple influence to outright takeover. While it is too early to assess whether mayoral involvement has a positive impact on student achievement, it is clear that the public and the business community are generally supportive of such restructuring. Kirst cautions that mayoral interventions are highly dependent on specific city contexts and political cultures—using Chicago and Boston, in particular, to illustrate high influence approaches and outcomes—and predicts further evolution of the relationship between schools and city government.

Charles Taylor Kerchner and Bruce S. Cooper (chapter 11) scrutinize teacher unions in their struggle to reconcile their role as defenders of the very educational structure they were created to challenge. The legitimacy of unions is under attack, largely as a result of their role in, and association with, what are perceived as failing urban public school systems. Challenges to four aspects of union identity—as advocates of teacher professionalism, as school reformers, as political forces, and as socializers of new teachers—are outlined. It remains to be seen whether "reform unionism" will carry the day, as well as how unions will respond to an expansion of choice options, but it seems clear that the challenges to union legitimacy will continue.

James G. Cibulka provides an overview of some of the more radical options in accountability policies—takeover of districts and reconstitution of schools by states—in chapter 12. He finds that research so far indicates that these options tend to be more successful in promoting administrative and funding reforms than in improving core educational functions. Cibulka argues that radical accountability policies are popular responses to public frustration with the performance of public schools, but that such changes are unlikely to have lasting effects on the very low-performing schools that tend to be the targets of such interventions. He calls for further research and "policy learning" to determine the right combination of incentives, consequences, and capacity building (focusing in particular on teacher quality issues) needed to improve our most troubled schools.

The final section of the yearbook, "Rethinking the State and Federal Roles in Educational Governance," examines trends in these levels of the educational governance system. In chapter 13, Carolyn Herrington and Frances Fowler describe a dramatic transformation undergone by states and state policymakers over the last three decades, chronicling a movement from the sidelines to the center. They frame their discussion around two state responsibilities, funding and academic standards, to show how states have conceptualized their new roles, as well as to illustrate the accompanying problems states experience with limited capacity, technical knowledge, and political will. Governance changes have come to be an increasingly popular option for states pursuing reform. The authors conclude that effective policymaking and improved academic achievement are more likely to result from state investment in systemic research and development initiatives than from the "window dressing" currently in favor.

In the concluding chapter, Jack Jennings reviews the increasing federal role in American education, up to and including a comprehensive look at the No Child Left Behind Act of 2001. He provides a framework for an analysis of this expansion, and maintains that NCLB represents a commitment to an ongoing and significant role in education on the part of the federal government, targeting not only student achievement but also teacher quality and state and district responsibilities. It remains to be seen, however, whether district, state and federal capacity will improve enough to effectively implement the far-reaching mandates of NCLB and sustain this extraordinary expansion of federal authority.

NOTES

1. It should be noted that in the report *A Nation at Risk* (1983), a milestone in the declining reputation of public schools, the public schools were blamed for the nation's economic problems in competing with the Pacific Rim nations. But when our economy later improved, no one gave the public schools any credit for this. This is symptomatic of their status in our society; they are readily blamed, but seldom acclaimed.

2. It also should be noted that business leaders have led and dominated the recent national "Education Summit" meetings. Education's vulnerability in our society to business values is, of course, the theme of Callahan's (1962) book, *Education and the Cult of Efficiency.*

3. See, for example, Greene (2002, pp. 4-5) who found that "five districts among the 50 largest districts in the U.S. [had] overall graduation rates [in 1993] below 50%: Cleveland (28%), Memphis (42%), Milwaukee (43%), Columbus (45%), and Chicago (47%). ... Sixteen of the 50 largest school districts failed to graduate more than half of their African-American students ... All but 15 of the districts for which rates can be computed have Latino graduation rates below 50%."

4. The author acknowledges with gratitude the assistance of Debra Miretzky in the preparation of this final section of this chapter.

REFERENCES

Ball, S.J. (1990). *Politics and policy making in education: Explorations in policy sociology*. London: Routledge.

Berliner, D.C., & Biddle, B.J. (1995). *The manufactured crisis: Myths, fraud, and the attack on America's public schools*. Reading, MA: Addison-Wesley.

Boyd, W.L. (1992). The power of paradigms: Reconceptualizing educational policy and management. *Educational Administration Quarterly, 28*(4), 504-528.

Boyd, W.L. (2000, September). The 'R's of school reform' and the politics of reforming or replacing public schools. *Journal of Educational Change, 1*(3), 225-252.

Boyd, W.L., & Crowson, R.L. (1981). The changing conception and practice of public school administration. In D. Berliner (Ed.), *Review of Research in Education*, (Vol. 9, pp. 311-373). Washington, DC: American Educational Research Association.

Boyd, W.L., & Immegart, G.L. (1979). Education's turbulent environment and problem-finding: Lines of convergence. In W.L. Boyd & G.L. Immegart (Eds.), *Problem-finding in educational administration: Trends in research and theory* (pp. 275-289). Lexington, MA: D.C. Heath.

Boyd, W.L., & Kerchner, C.T. (1988). Introduction and overview: Education and the politics of excellence and choice. In W.L. Boyd and C.T. Kerchner (Eds.), *The politics of excellence and choice in education* (pp. 1-11). New York and London: The Falmer Press.

Brabeck, M.M., Walsh, M.E., & Latta, R. (Eds.). (2003). *Meeting at the hyphen: Schools-universities-communities-professions in collaboration for student achievement and well being. The 102nd yearbook of the National Society for the Study of Education*, Part II. Chicago: National Society for the Study of Education.

Bracey, G.W. (1997a). *Setting the record straight: Responses to misconceptions about public education in the United States*. Alexandria, VA: Association for Supervision and Curriculum Development.

Bracey, G.W. (1997b). *The truth about America's schools: The Bracey reports, 1991-97*. Bloomington, IN: Phi Delta Kappa Educational Foundation.

Bracey, G.W. (2002). *The war against America's public schools: Privatizing schools, commercializing education*. Boston: Allyn and Bacon.

Callahan, R. (1962). *Education and the cult of efficiency: A study of the social forces that have shaped the administration of the public schools*. Chicago: University of Chicago Press.

Center for Reinventing Public Education (2002, October 25). *Structured to fail? The "impossible" job of the urban school superintendent*. Draft of report to the Wallace-Reader's Digest Funds. Seattle, WA: Evans School of Public Affairs, University of Washington.

Chubb, J.E., & Moe, T.M. (1990). *Politics, markets, & America's schools*. Washington, DC: Brookings Institution Press.

Cibulka, J.G. (1995). The reform and survival of American public schools: An institutional perspective. In R.L. Crowson, W.L. Boyd, & H.B. Mawhinney (Eds.), *The politics of education and the new institutionalism* (pp. 7-22). Washington, DC: Falmer Press.

Coons, J.E., & Sugarman, S.D. (1978). *Education by choice: The case for family control*. Berkeley, CA: University of California Press.

Cuban, L. (1979). Determinants of curriculum change and stability, 1870-1970. In J. Shaffarzick & G. Sykes (Eds.), *Value conflicts and curriculum issues* (pp. 139-196). Berkeley, CA: McCutchan.

Dillon, S. (2003, February 16). Thousands of schools may run afoul of new law. *New York Times*. Retrieved February 17, 2003 from http://www.nytimes.com/2003/02/16/education/16EDUC.html

Draper, N. (2002, December 15). Lofty goals may leave schools far behind; some educators say the "No Child Left Behind" federal law will punish the state's public schools. *Minneapolis Star-Tribune*, p. A1.

18   INTRODUCTION   AND   OVERVIEW

Easterbrook, G. (1986, January). Ideas move nations: How conservative think tanks have helped to transform the terms of political debate. *The Atlantic Monthly, 25*(1), 66-80. Available: http://www.theatlantic.com/politics/polibig/eastidea.htm

Elmore, R.F. (2002, Spring). Unwarranted intrusion. *Education Next, 2*(1), 31-35.

Fletcher, M.A. (2003, January 2). States worry new law sets schools up to fail. *Washington Post*, p. A1.

Goodman, R.H., & Zimmerman, W.G., Jr. (2000). *Thinking differently: Recommendations for 21st century school board/superintendent leadership, governance, and teamwork for high student achievement.* Arlington, VA: Educational Research Service and New England School Development Council. Available: http://www.nesdec.org/Thinking_Differently.htm

Greene, Jay P. (2002, April). High school graduation rates in the United States. New York: Center for Civic Innovation, Manhattan Institute [November 2001, revised April 2002]. Retrieved February 17, 2003, from http://www.manhattan-institute.org/html/cr_baeo.htm

Hess, F.M. (2002, November). Making sense of the "public" in public education. *Policy Report*, Progressive Policy Institute. Available: http://www.ppionline.org/documents/Public_Ed.pdf

Hess, F.M. (2003, January 8). What is 'public' about public education? *Education Week, 22*(16), 56, 32.

Hill, P.T., & Celio, M.B. (1998). *Fixing urban schools.* Washington, DC: Brookings Institution Press.

Hill, P.T., Pierce, L.C., & Guthrie, J.W. (1997). *Reinventing public education: How contracting can transform America's schools.* Chicago: University of Chicago Press.

Keller, B. (2000, September 20). ECS center to sort through new governance structures. *Education Week, 20*(3) 21.

Kirst, M., & Walker, D. (1971). An analysis of curriculum policy-making. *Review of Educational Research, 41*(5), 479-509.

Kolderie, T. (1990, November 1). *Beyond choice to new public schools: Withdrawing the exclusive franchise in public education.* Washington, DC: Progressive Policy Institute, Policy Report. Available: http://www.ppionline.org/ppi_ci.cfm?contentid=1692&knlgAreaID=110&subsecid=181

Kristol, I. (1996, September 9). The feminization of the Democrats. *Wall Street Journal*, A16.

Kronholz, J. (2000, October 13). Reconstitution is heavy artillery in Gore's education reform plan. *Wall Street Journal*, p. A20.

Kymlicka, W. (1995). *Multicultural citizenship: A liberal theory of minority rights.* New York: Clarendon Press, Oxford University Press.

Metz, M.H. (1989). Real School: A universal drama amid disparate experience. In D.E. Mitchell & M.E. Goertz (Eds.), *Education politics for the new century* (pp. 75-91). New York: Falmer Press.

Mintrom, M., & Vergari, S. (2002, September 20). Foundation engagement in education policymaking. Paper presented at conference on "Advancing the Institutional Research Agenda in Education." Albany, NY: University at Albany, SUNY.

Nathan, J. (1989). (Ed.). *Public schools by choice: Expanding opportunities for parents, students, and teachers.* St. Paul, MN: Institute for Learning and Teaching.

National Commission on Excellence in Education. (1983). *A nation at risk: The imperative for educational reform.* Washington, DC: U.S. Government Printing Office.

National Commission on Governing America's Schools. (1999). *Governing America's schools: Changing the rules.* Denver, CO: Education Commission of the States.

Olson, L. (2000, April 24). Redefining "public" schools. *Education Week, 19*(33), 1, 24-25, 27.

Peterson, P.E., & Campbell, D.E. (Eds.). (2001). *Charters, vouchers, and public education.* Washington, DC: Brookings Institution Press.

Powell, W.W., Jr., & DiMaggio, P. (Eds.). (1991). *The new institutionalism in organizational analysis*. Chicago: University of Chicago Press.

Salisbury, R. (1967). Schools and politics in the big city. *Harvard Educational Review, 37*(3), 408-424.

Schon, D.A., & Rein, M. (1994). *Frame reflection: Towards the resolution of intractable policy controversies*. New York: Basic Books.

Stringfield, S., & Land, D. (Eds.). (2002). *Educating at-risk students. The one hundred and first yearbook of the National Society for the Study of Education*, Part II. Chicago: The National Society for the Study of Education.

Tyack, D. (1974). *The one best system: A history of American urban education*. Cambridge, MA: Harvard University Press.

Tyack, D., & Tobin, W. (1994). The "grammar" of schooling: Why has it been so hard to change? *American Educational Research Journal, 31*(3), 453-479.

Tye, B.B. (2000). *Hard truths: Uncovering the deep structure of schooling*. New York: Teachers College Press.

Tye, B.B. (2002, September 20). Deep structure analysis: A tool for policy and practice. Paper presented at conference on "Advancing the Institutional Research Agenda in Education." Albany, NY: University at Albany, SUNY.

Wang, M., & Walberg, H.J. (Eds.). (2001). *School choice or best systems: What improves education?* Mahwah, NJ: Lawrence Erlbaum Associates.

Wilgoren, J. (2000, October 9). Young blacks turn to school vouchers as civil rights issue. *The New York Times*, p. A1.

Wolfe, A. (2000, March 29). Uncle Sam doesn't always know best. *Wall Street Journal*, A22.

CHAPTER 2

Accountability, Assessment, and Performance Issues: We've Come a Long Way ... or Have We?

JANE HANNAWAY

A political consensus is currently in place. Poor performance of American students relative to students in other industrialized countries, fairly flat performance of U.S. students over time on NAEP scores, despite significant increases in expenditures, large and persistent disparities in performance across student subgroups in the United States, and an awareness of the increased importance of education for the well being of individuals as well as that of the national economy have all combined to produce a consensus that K-12 education in the United States is in need of basic systemic reform. Republicans and Democrats agree. Education leaders largely agree. Unions are going along, and parents support reform, at least in spirit.

The linchpin of systemic reform is performance-based accountability. The underlying theory is straightforward: hold relevant parties (students, teachers, schools, districts) accountable for student achievement. If student performance improves, reward; if performance does not improve, apply negative sanctions. Sounds simple, and change in this direction is in the works. Recent assessment and accountability policies of states and the federal government herald a movement without parallel in this country. The policies create neat sound bite opportunities for politicians and, more importantly, provide hope for productive change, but is it as simple as it sounds? And if it is so easy and makes so much sense, why haven't we done it before? And how deep and stable, exactly, is the consensus? What I have tried to do in this chapter is identify some of the important challenges that lie ahead as performance-based accountability polices are put into effect. The challenges are both technical and political and, indeed, in practice the two are related, as I discuss. But before trying to speculate about what

Jane Hannaway is Director of the Education Policy Center at the Urban Institute in Washington, D.C.

accountability policies portend for education, it may be useful to review briefly the current state of such policies.

Where Are We Now?

Recent federal educational accountability policy is no less than astounding, given the tradition and constitutional standing of state and local control of education in the United States. The recently reauthorized Elementary and Secondary Education Act (ESEA), the No Child Left Behind Act of 2001, requires that states test all students in grades 3-8 annually in reading and math, that the tests be standards-based, and that tests produce results that allow comparisons across grades, schools, and districts. States must also establish adequate yearly progress (AYP) measures to demonstrate the progress of all students as well as subgroups of students (economically disadvantaged students, students from major racial/minority groups, students with disabilities, and limited English proficient (LEP) students) in math and reading. Simply reporting progress is not enough; there are consequences. Schools that do not make adequate progress in meeting their annual objectives for 2 consecutive years must allow students in those schools to transfer to a better performing public school, and the district must pick up the transportation tab. If a school fails to make adequate progress for 3 years, the students receive vouchers for federal money that can be used to pay for supplemental services outside the school. If a school continues to make inadequate progress, the district is required to take further corrective action, including replacing the staff and restructuring the school. The focus of state and federal policies on performance, and holding schools and districts accountable for performance, is in sharp contrast to the focus on procedural compliance that dominated the management of education for decades. This new accountability also implicitly challenges theoretical ideas about the "loose-coupling" of educational organizations that developed in the 1970s and 1980s (March & Olsen, 1976; Weick, 1976) and its cousin, institutional theory, which describes organizational structure and governance as "myths" that legitimize the organization to the outside world and protect its technical tasks from close scrutiny (Meyer & Rowan, 1977). It represents a fundamentally different view of the ways schools are run and may require us to rethink ideas about the structure of educational organizations.[1]

Almost every state has some kind of assessment program, and 30 states now rate the performance of their schools, up from 19 states in 1998 (Quality Counts, 2002). That is almost a 60% increase in just 4 years. At this point, the structure of assessment and accountability systems varies widely from state to state. Some states, such as Tennessee, use a value-added approach to evaluate schools, measuring the growth of students over the course of the school year. Other states, such as Texas, evaluate schools on the basis of the percentage of students scoring as "proficient." Still other states, such as California, use change in school test scores from year to year. Some states use norm-referenced tests, others use criterion-referenced tests, and still others use a mixed bag. Some track the performance of subpopulations of students, such as disadvantaged and ethnic minority students, and include the separate performance of these subgroups in judgments about the school's overall performance. The extent to which tests are aligned with a state's standards also varies across states, as do the stakes attached to performance measures, and whether sanctions and rewards fall on schools, teachers, and/or students.

Adding to the complexity is instability. While state-developed testing and accountability has been around for well over 100 years with the New York Regents, it is only within the last few years that states have turned to testing as a way to steer the education system. States are learning—learning what is technically feasible as well as what is politically feasible. As a consequence, policies change, and often change dramatically. Although they rarely agree on which systems represent "high quality," Quality Counts, the AFT, and the Fordham Foundation, among others, try to keep track of these policies on an annual basis.

California. California may be the poster state for instability. It was a leader in standards and accountability in the 1980s, but progress came to an abrupt halt in 1990 when the Governor vetoed funding for the California Assessment Program. Funding for a new testing system was approved the following year, but the CLAS (California Learning Assessment System) was not administered until 1993. It lasted only one year. The state then passed the ABC Bill of 1995, establishing a back-to-basics curriculum, and a modified off-the-shelf test was used beginning in 1998. In the last few years, California has gotten fairly aggressive in terms of accountability, with significant financial rewards for performance for schools and teachers. Some might argue that the cart is before the horse, since tests solidly based on the state's standards are only now (2003) becoming available. In any case, financial rewards have floundered in California in the face of budget woes, and the history of reform in California overall has been very much one of one step forward, one step backward.

Florida. There have been big changes in other states, as well, some happening in short periods of time. Florida, for example, received considerable national attention in 1999 when the Florida A⁺ for Education Plan, the state's accountability program, was passed into law. As part of the state's accountability plan, the law established the first statewide voucher system and criteria for grading schools—A to F—largely on the basis of the state's test, the Florida's Comprehensive Assessment Test (FCAT), in grades 4, 5, 8, and 10. Students in schools that received two Fs in any 4 consecutive years were eligible to receive vouchers that in 2001 were worth over $4,000. Vouchers, however, have ultimately not been a big part of the system. Until 2002, only two schools in the state had been deemed voucher eligible, and only 51 students from these schools took advantage of vouchers. The 76 schools that had one F on the books in 1999, and were therefore at risk of becoming voucher eligible, all improved their tested performance enough to avoid voucher eligibility for the subsequent 3 years. Whether these test improvements signal real educational improvement is discussed later.

New changes were introduced in Florida in 2002. Testing was expanded to all grades from 3 through 10, and the state is moving to a value-added measure for accountability. Weighting on the test has also changed. Originally equal weight was given to reading, writing, and math. Now reading is emphasized at the expense of writing. In 2002, 10 schools enrolling over 8,000 students were identified as voucher eligible. And while a recent court ruling decided that the voucher program violated church-state provisions in the state constitution, the courts are allowing the program to continue during appeals. Testing became a major issue in the last gubernatorial race, indicating the extent to which accountability issues in education are becoming a public and political concern.

Maryland. Maryland is another state where there have recently been significant changes in policies. Maryland was an early reform state in terms of performance accountability. The Maryland School Performance Assessment Program, which made its debut in the early 1990s, received high marks from many educators for its innovative focus; its concern about raising education quality through, for example, a focus on problem-solving skills; and its eschewal of a standardized norm-referenced format. In the spring of 2002, however, the state made the decision to phase out its testing program.[2] The ostensible reason for the decision was compliance with the new federal policies that require individual test scores[3], but even before the federal legislation, parents were protesting the amount of time and attention testing received and expressed considerable dissatisfaction that the testing program provided no information on the performance of individual children. Broad-based declines in the 2001 test scores, some of which were large and unexplainable, also created serious concern about the reliability and validity of the test. So, in some sense, the days of the test may have been numbered even prior to the federal legislation.

The content and rigor of state-developed academic standards and their associated tests vary widely across states, as do the cut scores that mark proficiency. Linn, Baker, and Betebenner (2002) compared test results in Texas and Maryland and found that the percentage of students meeting standards in 2001 in eighth-grade reading in Maryland was only 27%, while in Texas it was 91%. The improvement trends since 1994 for Texas were steeper than those for Maryland as well. Part of the reason for the differences is that the Texas tests focused primarily on basic skills, while the Maryland tests were more demanding. As a consequence, a smaller fraction of students scored well in Maryland, and it was more difficult to show gains.

Using levels of state test performance or even changes in test performance does not necessarily provide a good picture of performance differences or rates of improvement across states. The dichotomy has become more obvious under the new federal legislation. Michigan, for example, has the largest number of schools listed on the U.S. Department of Education list of schools "in need of improvement," even though its students score above average on NAEP and it was in the top three states in terms of achievement gains. Arkansas, in contrast, showed no "failing" schools and it ranks below average on NAEP.

The extent to which, and the ways in which, federal accountability policies will affect school behavior and outcomes are perhaps not as clear as the headlines imply. Only a handful of states have developed an assessment system that could actually comply with the federal law. Weaker accountability provisions in the 1994 federal legislation, the Improving America's Schools Act (IASA), never really took hold. The Clinton Administration's Department of Education generously granted waivers of the accountability provisions (Olson & Raphael, 2001; Raphael & McKay, 2001). The Bush Administration, however, claims it is serious. If so, the performance-based accountability policies will break new ground. But any predictions of effects are uncertain at best. The details of different policies are no doubt important, but apart from the details, there are two basic problems that make prediction difficult. The first is the relative independence of state and local authorities; the second is obtaining clear and solid measures of performance.

Two Key Problems

Problems of Control

The performance accountability movement is an attempt to improve schools through exerting top-down control, from the federal government to the states and from states to local districts, through accountability policies. But education is not a command and control system. First, we have a federal system where responsibility for education lies with the states. Second, we have standard problems of agency. Agency refers to the relationship between a principal—the authority with ultimate responsibility for some task or area of work—and the principal's agent, the party who actually carries out the tasks. Principal-agent relationships are common and they make good sense; agents often have special skills, information, or some other capacity that the principal does not have and, as a consequence, they can often perform at least some tasks better than the principals. The problem is ensuring that the agents—in this case, districts, schools, and teachers—actually act in the best interest of the principals—federal and state authorities. The underlying issue is one of control, and there is a growing literature in the economics of organization focused on the topic (Milgrom & Roberts, 1992; Putterman & Kroszner, 1996).

The usual ways to solve the control problem and ensure that agents act in the best interests of the principals are through monitoring agents' behavior and/or providing incentives for them to behave in preferred ways. Without such controls, agents are likely to pursue their own interests at least some of the time—for example, by working less hard than a principal might wish, or by spending time on aspects of the work preferred by the agent more than by the principal. In the case of education, monitoring is simply not feasible. There are too many districts and too many schools, spread out over too many states. So the agent has an information advantage; the principal has only a limited picture of what goes on operationally. Incentives based on performance might work, but only to the extent that (1) they are good indicators of performance; (2) the agents know how to achieve the desired performance targets; and (3) the principals know what is possible. Without these conditions, incentive-based control is likely to have weak effects at best, and at worst, to be counter-productive to the extent that teachers and administrators divert their efforts to achieve largely bogus measures of performance. And this brings us to the second key problem and the true crux of the situation.

Problems of Performance Measurement

The most appropriate measure of the performance of schools is far from obvious. So the fact that different states use different measures, as we note above, should not be surprising. Even if we do not consider wider goals, such as citizenship, and focus only on student academic skills, and we agree that we will use tests to indicate mastery of those skills, there are problems. Below I identify these problems and discuss their implications.

It is important first to remember that tests provide information only about what they test, and what they test is only a fraction of what students learn. Testing specialists refer to this as "domain sampling." The fraction of the knowledge that is tested may not even be a good random sample of what is taught, given the wide range of topics covered in classrooms and the discretion that teachers typically exercise. In some cases performance on tests could grossly underestimate the learning that has taken place in the classroom. Consider, for example, a teacher who focuses heavily on higher order skills in a classroom in a state that tests only more basic skills. Her students might score very well on the test, but the scores would present an imperfect and very limited picture of the learning that had taken place. Another teacher might narrow the curriculum and focus heavily on test preparation and score higher than otherwise. In this case, what students know and truly understand is likely to be overestimated, relative to students in other classrooms. In both cases, there would be some "measurement error" in test scores.

Perhaps a more serious problem is misalignment. The importance of aligning tests, professional development, and curriculum has been stressed since the advent of the standards movement and systemic reform. And while there has been progress, many states still use tests, often off-the-shelf tests, that are not strongly linked to the state's standards. Presumably there is a correlation between what is tested and what is in the standards, but questions about mixed messages and accuracy of measurement emerge if rewards and sanctions are instituted on the basis of test scores that are not clearly aligned to standards. In this situation, the standards risk appearing to be a sham, assuming schools orient their behavior to produce what is being tested and rewarded, which is not an unrealistic assumption.

Also of concern are the incentives that imperfect or limited tests produce when used for accountability purposes. Under these conditions, tests provide incentives for teachers to skew and narrow their instruction to emphasize what is tested. They distort instructional behavior from what it would be otherwise. Such skewing is one of the reasons for the "saw-tooth" effect, discussed below. And while a more focused curriculum may benefit some children, we can never be sure, because we are generally not testing what is *not* taught. In other words, we have no measures that indicate what the opportunity costs are, i.e., what kinds of things students may have learned if teachers had not diverted their attention to what was being tested.

Apart from questions about *what* is tested are questions about *when* to test in order to get good measures of effects. The important work of Dan Koretz (1988) and Bob Linn (Linn, Graue, & Sanders, 1990) warns us that performance on tests is likely to continue to improve over time as teachers and students become more familiar with a test's format and content. Figure 1 shows the steady increase in student performance with one test, a sharp drop when it is replaced with another version, and then another steady performance climb. This is what is known as the "saw-tooth effect." Improved test results, especially in the short run, may provide an inflated measure of student progress and can lead to very faulty conclusions about policy effects.

FIGURE 1
The Saw-Tooth Effect: Trends in Percentile Rank of State Means

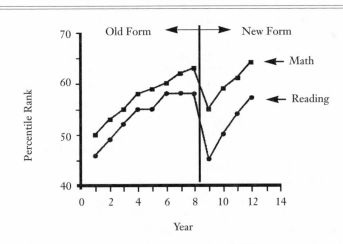

Source: Linn, R.L., Graue, M.E., & Sanders, N.M. (1990). Comparing state and district results to national norms: The validity of the claims that "everyone is above average." *Educational Measurement: Issues and Practice, 9*(3), 5-14.

The nature of the measurement—a level or value-added score—introduces a third area for discussion. States are moving to value-added and change scores as the basis of accountability systems. A strong and simple logic dictates the use of such measures. Policymakers want to reward schools for the improvement that they show, or the value they add to the performance of the students they serve. They don't want to reward schools for student performance that derives primarily, or even substantially, from what happens in families. Such scoring attempts to level the playing field for schools serving students from poverty backgrounds.[4] Students from affluent families are probably going to do well regardless of how good the school is or how much effort school actors exert. But there are serious technical problems that Kane and Staiger (2002a; forthcoming) and Linn and colleagues (Linn, Baker, & Betebenner, 2002; Linn & Haug, 2002) have identified.

One problem, for example, is that year-to-year changes are not reliable indicators of performance shifts because at least some significant part of test score fluctuation is due to factors beyond what happens in the classroom or the school.[5] Because differences across schools in valueadded measures are smaller than in level scores, change measures are particularly vulnerable. One aspect of the issue is sample size. Kane and Staiger (2002a) point out that the average elementary school in the U.S. has only 69 students per grade, a small number for statistical purposes. A handful of particularly bright students or particularly troublesome students could lead to big swings in year-to-year school performance, as could a lightning storm that distracted students during testing. Clearly, sampling variation or one-time shocks could lead to considerable year-to-year volatility. The problems are the most severe for small schools, which are considerably more likely than big schools to end up with large increases or decreases in performance simply as a consequence of their size. Indeed, Kane and Staiger (forthcoming) estimate that while North Carolina and Texas raised proficiency rates in math and reading by 2 to 5 percent per year—laudable, indeed—between 98 and 100 percent of the schools in those states would have not made adequate yearly progress, based on the original definitions of steady year-to-year progress in the No Child Left Behind legislation. Similar problems arise when separate test measures are calculated for small subgroups of students.

Another wrinkle in accountability is that effects may vary for different types of schools and for different types of students. There is evidence to suggest that the effects of accountability will be greatest for students at the bottom of the performance distribution, who generally are students from disadvantaged backgrounds (Grissmer & Flanagan, 1998). Results in Texas cities certainly suggest this (Hannaway & McKay, 2001).[6] At least two reasons might explain such a pattern. First, disadvantaged students might show the largest gains from formal accountability systems because the informal types of internal accountability found in more advantaged settings are not in play (Abelmann & Elmore, 1999). Middle class parents, for example, take a larger role in managing the daily operations of the schools their children attend, simply through the questions they ask of principals and teachers and through their general vigilance. Second, teaching the most disadvantaged students is clearly challenging. We might expect that in the absence of a formal accountability system, teachers would flounder, searching for effective strategies by jumping from one to another, perhaps too quickly. Accountability systems may provide not only focus but also the incentive to sustain that focus, which is crucial if immediate returns are not forthcoming.

We might also expect top students to learn less than they otherwise would under some formal accountability systems. In conducting case studies in Florida we were surprised to find that principals, teachers, and parents in schools rated "A" felt pressured to hold and/or improve their performance on state tests, even though a very large fraction of students topped the tests. They narrowed their curriculum, reduced their focus on more open-ended "project work," and even postponed all field trips until after the state tests in the spring (Goldhaber & Hannaway, 2001). The specter of a public reporting of test results that showed even a slight dip seemed to intimidate at least some high-performing schools into structuring themselves in ways that probably limited student learning. We should be concerned not only about the average effect of an accountability program on students, but also about interaction effects. Do various accountability systems affect some students or some schools differently than they affect others? Are there benefits for some and, indeed, costs to others?

The issues with measurement of school performance compound the control problems in perhaps obvious ways. To the extent that various agents prefer not to be held accountable, or perhaps rightfully question some of the bases for accountability, or are looking for grounds to de-legitimize the accountability system for other reasons, the potential for instability is there, in turn affecting the stability of assessment and accountability policies.

Even though individual states were developing accountability systems to improve school performance at the time the federal legislation was passed, they reacted to the legislation with complaints and concern. Education Secretary Rod Paige responded with a conciliatory letter, stressing the great flexibility states have for identifying schools not making "adequate yearly progress" and for determining what actions to take in dealing with these schools. But when states began, predictably, to exercise their discretion by lowering the bar for student achievement and changing their definition of "proficiency" in order to avoid federal sanctions, Secretary Paige changed his tone, calling those who tried to sidestep the legislation "enemies of equal justice and opportunity" (letter from Secretary Paige to Chief State School Officers, October 22, 2002). While the states and the federal government may have the shared objective of improving education, their operational objectives and the actions they actually take to achieve those objectives clearly differ. But attempts by the federal government to direct state behavior with sanctions may not work; indeed, they may have perverse effects, to the extent that states *lower* standards to avoid federal penalties.

But the problem is not simply our federal structure of education; it is more complicated. Gaming, or what some might consider gaming, can also go on at other levels—in districts, in schools, and in classrooms. As noted earlier, test-based performance is likely to direct attention and effort to that which is tested. In Florida, for example, the accountability system originally gave equal weight to math, reading, and writing, and a school had to fail in all three areas to receive an F. Every school that was at risk of receiving a second F quickly learned that it was easiest to achieve improved performance on the writing test, and indeed, with some extra attention, they all did. One principal explained that if students wrote three paragraphs, the first beginning with "first," the second with "then," and the final one with "finally," the student would receive a passing writing grade (Goldhaber & Hannaway, 2001). There may be some benefit to using such a rubric for some students and for some types of writing, but it is hard to justify as sufficient to demonstrate proficiency in writing. Using this framework, however, this school went from the lowest performing school in the state in writing to the most improved. Eventually, the state caught on and changed the system, giving less weight to writing in subsequent years. But in general, we should expect some level of gaming in accountability systems, whether it takes the form of diversion of effort, of coaching, or of outright cheating. The higher the stakes, the more likely the gaming will increase.

What Happens Next?

The technical problems described above indicate the degree of difficulty involved in determining not only good measures of school performance and improvement, but also the very efficacy of accountability policies based on student performance. It is important to recognize that the two—the various measures of performance and the value of performance-based accountability itself—are currently being tested simultaneously. As a consequence, it is possible to conclude that accountability policies do not work in education, perhaps because of the federal structure or because of agency problems and education politics, when in fact it is because *the performance measures are faulty*. Similarly, we could misdiagnose technical problems associated with performance measurement, not recognizing that the problem is a structural or political one.

Where do we go from here? Some analysts predict that the accountability movement will implode. They believe that the combination of rising political tensions and technical limitations will combine to weaken the movement into insignificance. And a growing choir of critics of the accountability movement would likely be pleased with this outcome. A good policy analyst, though, would pose the more relevant questions: Would *not* holding schools and teachers accountable result in even more undesirable effects? Would even *less* reliable instruments than standardized tests be used? Does exempting schools from accountability for performance result in "tacitly legitimizing a status quo that is grotesque and untenable for large numbers of students—especially the disadvantaged?" (Feuer, 2002)

Ideally, for real progress, we would want to disentangle the various elements of accountability policies and isolate their separate effects. But disentangling the effects of accountability and the problems of tested performance in standard ways is difficult, if not impossible. What is needed is a two-pronged analytic approach that keeps the separate areas of uncertainty in mind. The first prong would be an attempt to understand the effects of accountability policies, not only by looking at their relationship to student performance, but also by looking closely and systematically at their relationship to instructional behavior. Indeed, performance improvement on high-stakes tests should be considered tentative without some understanding of the behavior that produced it, or some confirmation of results with other measures of learning. The second approach would involve attempting to understand the merits and consequences of different measurement methods by enlisting new partners in the search for valid measures. Each of these approaches is discussed below.

Behavioral Consequences

Determining the contribution of various accountability systems to student achievement is, of course, the ultimate question of interest.

But for some of the reasons identified above, the task is not easy or straightforward, and undoubtedly any findings about effects will be disputed. Because of this, and because for purposes of replication it is always useful to understand the mechanisms by which policies affect outcomes, it is important also to track behavioral indicators of effects. Among other things, such indicators might prevent us from coming to false conclusions of "no effect." Accountability systems, for example, might affect school behavior in productive ways, but the performance measures may not be sensitive enough to capture the effects. Accountability measures may affect test scores, but in ways that do not affect real productivity or real learning by students. Indeed, imperfect measures could be "gamed" by schools, as discussed earlier, possibly even leading to *reductions* in educational productivity. Before drawing any conclusions about the beneficial effects of an accountability system, we should have some indication that the incentives implicit in the system lead to behavioral responses that have at least some measure of face validity as a contributor to student achievement.

Below I identify a few areas as examples of behavioral research that might provide a clearer picture of the effects of accountability on education—both the good and the not so good. Accountability systems introduce new incentives, and the question is to what extent and in what ways do schools respond.

Instructional practice effects. We have discussed the possible distorting effects of testing. Such effects might include teaching to the test, focusing on tested subjects at the expense of other subjects, and gaming the system through coaching. Some of these effects, as we have also suggested, may have different consequences for different types of students. Some accountability systems may lead teachers to give considerably more attention to particular students, perhaps the lowest achieving students, while other systems may lead to a form of triage. The costs of systematically observing behavior in the classroom are high, but teachers themselves are generally good reporters of what goes on in classrooms. Koretz, Barron, Mitchell, and Stecher (1996) found more than half the teachers in a Kentucky study reported that improvements in student performance were due to increased familiarity with the test and practice tests; only 16% of the teachers said improvement was due to "broad improvements in knowledge and skills" (cited by Kane & Staiger, forthcoming).

Resource allocation patterns in schools and school districts. In general, one might expect schools and school districts to adapt strategically to meet new performance demands. While resource allocation is only one type of response, patterns of findings can indicate whether and how the infrastructure of schools and districts is responding to performance accountability demands, and also might help explain why some states or districts or schools are more or less successful than others in meeting the demands. Identification of patterns could also help us pinpoint the types of districts and schools that are more and less adaptable, as well as whether certain conditions promote adaptability. Significant investment in professional development might be an example of such a condition. One recent study showed that accountability pressure alone had little effect on resource allocation, but accountability pressure in conjunction with new resources led to increased investment in instruction (Hannaway, McKay, & Nakib, 2002).

Student academic behavior. Student behavior and motivation might change as a result of accountability pressure on a school. Participation in after-school tutoring programs and in summer school, altered course taking behavior, and dropping out are examples of possible responses.

New research relationships. In the past few years, states have amassed a tremendous amount of new information on student achievement and at least some of the significant achievement determinants. These data present new opportunities to investigate the properties, technical and otherwise, of accountability systems based on student performance measures. Indeed, it is only because of the availability of these data that various technical issues with accountability have been identified. The federal structure of education in the United States also promotes variation in systems and measures across states, increasing possibilities for isolating different policy effects.

There is a clear federal role here. Rather than being the "policeman," the federal level could partner with states to develop new knowledge. Certain conditions, however, should be met to take greatest advantage of the research opportunities; most importantly, steps should be taken so that the political risk for state and local officials is minimized.

One way to expand knowledge and minimize political penalties is for the federal level to refrain from applying sanctions, so that the risk of states' losing control or losing resources is minimized. The higher the risks for the states, the more likely it is that states will protect themselves, and the less likely it is that accountability efforts will be transparent and open. Instead, the federal level should offer incentives for state officials to partner with federal authorities in research efforts. If states are publicly partnering in a research effort, what might otherwise be perceived as missteps in an accountability or assessment system could be reframed as "discovery" and "learning." Currently, we are establishing accountability systems that carry serious consequences for students, teachers, and schools, and we are operating from a limited research base. This is difficult to justify; in addition, by locking into policies prematurely, we lose valuable opportunities to learn and develop systems that fit the peculiarities of educational organizations and educational production.

Perhaps it is time to go back to some fundamentals of theory on educational organizations. Perhaps Jim March and Karl Weick had it right—there are well-articulated reasons why educational organizations have been described as "loosely coupled," and these characteristics are ignored at policymakers' peril. By forcing an accountability system on educational organizations without taking such characteristics into account, we can end up with a process with limited benefits and potentially perverse outcomes, as states and educational organizations attempt to fend off "forced coupling in ways that are difficult to observe and counter."

Notes

1. See, for example, Swanson, forthcoming.

2. We must note the irony that Quality Counts 2002 rated Maryland's standards and accountability higher than any other state, giving it a score of 98 out of 100 possible points.

3. The MSPAP is designed to yield school level, not individual student level, performance measures.

4. There is also considerable dispute and debate about how and whether to incorporate measures of student background into performance measures, even with value-added measures, because student background can affect learning rates as well as level. Some argue that if measures of student background are not taken into account, it gives an unfair advantage to schools with students from better off backgrounds. But if background measures are incorporated into the measure, we risk holding students from disadvantaged backgrounds to different standards (see Clotfelter & Ladd, 1996).

5. See Kane and Staiger (*Journal of Economic Perspectives*, forthcoming) on the signal to noise ratio of test results.

6. Because the Texas test focuses heavily on basic skills, many of the more advantaged students had "topped out," but the disadvantaged students still showed clear gains.

REFERENCES

Abelmann, C., & Elmore, R. (with J. Even, S. Kenyon, J. Marshall). (1999). When accountability knocks, will anyone answer? *CPRE Research Report Series, RR-42*. Philadelphia, University of Pennsylvania: Consortium for Policy Research in Education.

Clotfelter, C., & Ladd, H.F. (1996). Recognizing and rewarding success in public schools. In H. Ladd (Ed.), *Holding schools accountable* (pp. 23-64). Washington, DC: Brookings Institution.

Feuer, M.J. (2002). Accountability, testing, and unintended consequences. Dinner remarks, Brookings-Wharton Conference on Urban Affairs, October 24.

Goldhaber, D., & Hannaway, J. (2001). Accountability with a kicker: Observations on Florida vouchers. Paper presented at Annual Meeting of Association for Public Policy and Management (APPAM). Under review, *Educational Evaluation and Policy*.

Grissmer, D., & Flanagan, A. (1998). Lessons from the states: Exploring rapid achievement gains in North Carolina and Texas. Washington, DC: National Education Goals Panel. Available online http://www.negp.gov/reports/grissmer.pdf

Hannaway, J., McKay, S., & Nakib, Y. (2002). Reform and resource allocation: National trends and state policies. In W. Fowler (Ed.), *Developments in school finance* (pp. 57-76). Washington, DC: U.S. Department of Education.

Hannaway, J., & McKay, S. (2001). Taking measure. *Education Next, 1*(3), 9-12.

Kane, T., & Staiger, D. (2002a). Volatility in school test scores: Implications for test-based accountability systems. Brookings Papers on Education Policy. Washington, DC: Brookings Institution.

Kane, T.J., & Staiger, D.O. (forthcoming). The promise and pitfalls of using imprecise school accountability measures. *Journal of Economic Perspectives*.

Koretz, D. (1988). Arriving in Lake Wobegon: Are standardized tests exaggerating achievement and distorting instruction? *American Educator, 12*(2), 8-15, 46.

Koretz, D., Barron, S., Mitchell, K., & Stecher, B. (1996). The perceived effects of the Kentucky Instructional Results Information System. Santa Monica: RAND Corporation, Report Number MR-792-PCT/FF.

Linn, R.L., Baker, E.L., & Betebenner, D.W. (2002). Accountability systems: Implications of requirements of the No Child Left Behind Act of 2001. *Educational Researcher, 31*(6), 3-16.

Linn, R.L., Graue, M.E., & Sanders, N.M. (1990). Comparing state and district results to national norms: The validity of the claims that "everyone is above average." *Educational Measurement: Issues and Practice, 9*(3), 5-14.

Linn, R.L., & Haug, C. (2002). Stability of school building accountability scores and gains. *Educational Evaluation and Policy Analysis, 24*(1), 29-36.

March, J.G., & Olsen, J.P. (1976). *Ambiguity and choice in organizations*. Bergen, Norway: Universitetsforlaget.

Meyer, J.W., & Rowan, B. (1977). Institutionalized organizations: Formal structure as myth and ceremony. *American Journal of Sociology, 83*(2): 340-363.

Milgrom, P., & Roberts, J. (1992). *Economics, organization and management*. New York: Prentice-Hall, 1992.

Olson, K., & Raphael, J. (2001). *Waivers: Flexibility and accountability*. A report to Congress on waivers granted under the Elementary and Secondary Education Act, Goals 2000: Educate America Act, and School-to-Work Opportunities Act. Washington, DC: The Urban Institute.

Quality Counts 2002: Building blocks of success. (2002). *Education Week, 21*(17). Available on the web: http://www.edweek.org/sreports/qc02/

Putterman, L., & Kroszner, R. (Eds.). (1996). *The economic nature of the firm*. New York: Cambridge University Press.

Raphael, J., & McKay, S. (2001). Analysis of the Education Flexibility Partnership Demonstration Program State Reports. Report submitted to the U.S. Department of Education. Washington, DC: The Urban Institute.

Swanson, C. (forthcoming). Organizational coupling, control, and change: The role of higher-order models of control in educational reform. Forthcoming in L. Hedges & B. Schneider (Eds.), *Social organization of schooling*. New York: Russell Sage Foundation.

Weick, K.E. (1976). Educational organizations as loosely coupled systems. *Administrative Science Quarterly, 21,* 1-19.

CHAPTER 3

Liberty, Democracy, and Community: Legitimacy in Public Education

KENNETH A. STRIKE

Education and Legitimacy

In this chapter I follow a path that connects the requirements of a legitimate and stable political order to the notion that schools should be communities. I argue two main claims. First, norms of political legitimacy are more than principles for how schools should be governed. They are inherent in the kinds of communities schools should be. Second, liberal and democratic interpretations of these norms generate different visions of the nature of school communities. That our society is a capitalist one adds additional normative tension. Liberal societies are committed to the idea that individuals have rights that constrain the authority of the state. Democratic societies are committed to the rule of the people. Capitalist societies are committed to free markets and consumer sovereignty. Much about our schools reflects the "dialectical dance" we do to try to be liberal, democratic, and capitalist at once. Our inability to resolve the tension among these "value packages" is a factor in our inability to create schools that are communities and contributes to the legitimacy crisis of education.

Stable governments and their institutions require citizens who respect and can function within the established political order. If government is to be stable without being repressive, it must be legitimate in the eyes of its citizens. If it is to be seen as legitimate without manipulating citizens to accept an unjust regime, citizens must see it as legitimate because it meets appropriate normative criteria of legitimacy.

These comments assume a distinction between subjective legitimacy and objective legitimacy. For an institution to be subjectively legitimate, it must be *seen* as legitimate. To be seen as legitimate, an institution must satisfy such criteria of legitimacy as are held by those it

Kenneth A. Strike is Professor and Chair, Education Policy and Leadership, University of Maryland.

must please. There is no guarantee that these criteria will be reasonable. Schools may be expected to educate well and be just and democratic, but they may also be expected to have winning football teams or to hire from a favored ethnic group. Yet it is subjective legitimacy that counts politically.

Objective legitimacy consists in public institutions meeting reasonable criteria of legitimacy. There may be many such criteria for the legitimization of public institutions, but there are two broad groups. First, institutions should aim to accomplish their legitimate purposes, which, in turn, should aim at the good of those they serve. Second, in our society, institutions must adhere to the fundamental political norms of liberal democracy. (Below, I refer to such norms as "constitutional," meaning not that they are part of the U.S. Constitution but that they are core to the self-understanding of liberal democratic societies.)

Recent public discussion and assessments of public education, including its governance, have tended to emphasize considerations of efficiency to the exclusion of considerations of legitimacy. Such discussions assume efficiency (typically in raising achievement scores) to be central to legitimacy. While efficiency counts, it is not sufficient, and the preoccupation with it can be unfortunate. Useful examples are the familiar debates about choice or decentralization. These policies include proposals to change the governance of schools. They redistribute power among parents, legislatures, and educators. They influence intellectual liberty and religious freedom. Vouchers, for example, are not just a means to introduce competition into the educational system. They institutionalize free association as a significant factor in determining who goes to school with whom, and they substitute commonality of purpose for geographical proximity as the basis for school community. Such changes represent a shift in how core constitutional values are applied to schools. They need to be appraised via a discussion of the relative import of these values.

A deeper reason to be concerned about the ascent of efficiency is that this preoccupation may manifest a failure of memory about the kind of people we wish to be and how we are to become such people. We may be a capitalist society, but the constitutional values of our society do not suggest that we are either a plutocracy or a commercial republic. It is, however, sometimes difficult to notice this from the way in which educational policy is discussed. Business roundtables, groups who may (or may not) be public spirited, but who are certainly not elected, have come to be among the more powerful influences on educational policy. The act of unilateral educational disarmament bemoaned by *A Nation at Risk* (National Commission on Excellence in Education, 1983) was economic treason, not a failure to create good citizens. Indeed, citizenship is often associated with economic contribution. In theory, however, our political norms are internal to our educational aspirations. Not only do we want schools to conduct themselves justly and democratically, we want them to produce just and democratic citizens. We cannot appropriately decide what we are to be efficient at without considering our constitutional norms.

Consider the following argument:

1. Other things being equal, it is desirable that the criteria that must be satisfied for public institutions to be objectively legitimate also form the basis for citizens' judgments of subjective legitimacy.

2. If citizens' judgments of subjective legitimacy are to be made on objective grounds, the institutions of a society must shape the consciousness of citizens so that citizens apply appropriate criteria of legitimacy to their appraisal of public institutions.

3. If institutions are to do this appropriately, they must create discursive forums and practices in which public opinion can be shaped through reasoned discourse rather than manipulation or indoctrination.

4. Schools are among the public institutions that have a responsibility to shape the consciousness of citizens in this way.

This task of creating citizens requires more than the development of the capacity to assess political institutions and practices. It also requires a cultivation of certain views and feelings towards other citizens. To give one's consent to some regime because it is just and democratic is to assent not only because of how one is treated, but also because of how others are treated. Hence, it requires not only a commitment to a set of principles, but some form of appropriate attachment to one's fellow citizens (Strike, 2000a).

If so, schools, whatever else they are expected to do, should have among their public functions two tasks. First, they must shape citizens to accept appropriate criteria of legitimacy for public institutions. Second, they must create the basis of political community and political solidarity by developing the feelings and attachments towards others and the skills and capacities that render public institutions stable and functional.

Some Principles of Legitimacy for Education

Below I enumerate a modest list of some legitimacy principles for education that are rooted in the constitutional self-understandings of liberal democratic societies. It is intended to be more illustrative than exhaustive.

Fair participation: Public schools should be democratically governed. One interpretation of this idea emphasizes the sovereignty of the legislature. Schools would be democratically governed when they are governed by elected bodies that conform to such norms of fair participation as "one person—one vote." This norm, however, gives minimal expression to the idea of participation. Vote is neither voice nor involvement. Fair participation may require institutions that permit students, parents, or citizens to have a more active role in decision making.

Liberty and pluralism: We are a society that claims to value both liberty and diversity. Public schools must respect religious freedom, free association, free speech, and free press. They must respect diversity.

We value these various liberties for diverse reasons. Free speech and a free press are rights that enable participation. They give people voice in the public square. Religious liberty, however, is more a protection of worship and of conscience from the coercive authority of the state. It allows people to associate for purposes they do not share with others. Free association enables both political participation and the pursuit of private purpose in association with the like-minded. Pluralism is a close kin to religious liberty, although it has more to do with the affirmation of diverse identities than with freedom of conscience. It grants those who see themselves as possessing a shared culture the right to pursue a shared life without domination by others, as well as a right to fair consideration in public affairs.

Equal opportunity: Narrowly construed, equal opportunity is an expression of the equal protection of the laws, a doctrine that achieved constitutional standing in the Fourteenth Amendment to the U.S. Constitution but whose pedigree can be found much earlier—for example in Locke's (1960) claim that there may not be one law for the rich and another for the man at plow. Thus understood, equal opportunity provides a formal legal guarantee for nondiscriminatory access to education as well as to other social institutions. This view, however, falls short of the vision of equal opportunity that is, in part, responsible for the creation of public schools. That view holds that in life's competition, while no one can be or should be guaranteed a given outcome, people are entitled to a level playing field. They should not be handicapped or advantaged by the circumstances of their birth. And, as we shall see, the notion can be further expanded.

Political socialization: A legitimate and necessary task of the schools of any society is to produce good citizens. One approach to what this means is the one I have taken above—an inquiry into the conditions of stability and of reasoned, autonomous consent. We might also ask other questions, such as what do students need to know, and what kinds of character do they need to have to function appropriately in a liberal democratic society? And this, of course, raises the question of what appropriate functioning is. Is it sufficient that students aspire to vote? Is it adequate for them to have a sense of justice? Do we wish to prepare them for more demanding forms of participation?

Professionalism: The central norm of professionalism is "Those who know should rule." That is, professionalism can be understood as the idea that decisions that require specialized training or expertise should be made by those who possess such training and expertise. This norm has an undemocratic pedigree. As Plato (1962) understood it in the *Republic*, it affirmed the primacy of reason expressed through the rule of philosopher kings and was juxtaposed to the rule of the passions and of the mob that Plato associated with democracy. In Western liberal democracies, the scope of "Those who know should rule" is generally restricted to professions and guilds, where it is supposed that good decisions rest on expertise that is unlikely to be possessed by citizens or their representatives. Medicine, law, and engineering are typical cases. Few of us would wish to drive over bridges designed by legislative committees or plebiscites. Here it is better to respect the laws of physics than the will of the majority. Yet, in democratic societies, we expect that the authority of such guilds over their domains will be legitimated and monitored by democratically elected bodies.

Legitimacy: Liberal and Democratic Interpretations

Socratic argument ... is essential to a strong democracy and to any lasting pursuit of justice. In order to foster a democracy that is reflective and deliberative, rather than simply a marketplace of competing interest groups, a democracy that takes thought for the common good, we must produce citizens who have the Socratic capacity to reason about their beliefs. ... To unmask prejudice and to secure justice, we need argument, an essential tool of civic freedom. (Nussbaum, 1997, p. 19)

... a continuing, shared understanding on one comprehensive doctrine can be maintained only by the oppressive use of state power. If we think of political society as a community united in affirming one and the same comprehensive doctrine, then the oppressive use of state power is necessary for political community. (Rawls, 1993, p. 37)

These two quotations, both of which express central themes in modern interpretations of liberal democracy, also reveal some of its tensions. To see why and how the issues become educational ones, I want to construct two different interpretations of the legitimacy principles sketched above. Below I contrast participatory democracy with a Rawlsian understanding of liberalism. The primary aim of participatory democracy is to create a democratic community in which the common good is sought in and through democratic deliberations that, ideally, aim at consensus. The primary aim of the liberal interpretation is to enable people to pursue their own conception of the good with like-minded others within the fabric of a just society.

In the Anglo-American liberal tradition, democracy is identified primarily with the sovereignty of an elected legislature. However, some views of democracy see participation as part of the good of democracy and argue that at the heart of democracy are institutions that conduct rational deliberations concerning the common good. (Examples include Guttman & Thompson, 1996; Habermas, 1984; and in education Dewey, 1916 and Gutmann, 1987.) Here I will use the term participatory democracy to refer to a set of (otherwise diverse) views that include two claims. These claims are: (1) democratic participation and democratic deliberation are important both to making legitimate decisions and to constructing the common good, and (2) democratic participation and deliberation are intrinsic goods, a part of any reasonable conception of a good life, and must be provided for by any adequate democratic society.

Consider how such a view would shape the meaning and application of each of the legitimacy principles listed above. First, fair participation means more than "one person—one vote" in electing a legislature. Opportunities for involvement are important. A desire to increase participation may require some form of democratic localism (Bryk, Sebring, Kerbow, Rollow, & Easton, 1998). This kind of decentralization seems at odds with the centralizing tendencies inherent in currently popular standards-driven reform. The maxim "The state decides the 'what' and the district decides the 'how'" (*A New Compact for Learning*, 1994, p. 77) seems perilously close to telling locals that they are free to accomplish the state's directives in any way they wish. A participatory democracy of means, but not ends, may be educationally efficient (or not), but it falls short of a robust view of local control (Strike, 1997).

Second, participatory democracy may color the meaning of liberty and pluralism in several ways. Liberty may be viewed more in terms of equal participation in shared decision making than as an individual's rights vis-à-vis the authority of the state. Rights such as free speech, press, and assembly take on importance more as part of the process of political participation than as means to assert the interests of one's self or one's group. Pluralism will emphasize the equal right of members of each culture to participate in cultural exchange over the right of each group to the autonomy to live a life of its own choosing. The market-place of ideas will be viewed as a means of cultural exchange and as a significant part of multicultural education.

Third, the idea of equal opportunity is likely to expand beyond notions of equal access to education and beyond the economically dominated notion of fair competition to include the ideas of equal par-ticipation, equal voice, and equal inclusion.

Fourth, participatory democracy suggests that citizenship must en-compass more than what would be required to be a competent and will-ing voter and more than the possession of a sense of justice. The capac-ities and the desire to participate are required. People must develop a democratic character (Gutmann, 1987) with an emphasis on the values and capacities required for public deliberations. Attachments and loy-alty are formed through participation and result in civic friendship.

Finally, participatory democracy is likely to be suspicious of profes-sionalism. No doubt few advocates of participatory democracy will find it useful to encourage democratic deliberations about the best forms of brain surgery or quantum mechanics. Nevertheless, participatory democ-racy will wish to see the rule of reason vested in informed public delib-eration among citizens and, where possible, will resist ceding it to ex-perts. In education and other areas that are value laden and where there is little well established esoteric knowledge on which practice depends, professionalism is likely to be especially resisted as undemocratic (Strike, 1993).

Consider two objections to this democratic construction of liberal democracy. Participatory democracy may violate fair participation by giving excessive weight to the voice of the active and the articulate (Young, 1966). Not all have the time. Not all have the ability to articu-late their interests. Not all are equally schooled in the recognized practices of discourse. Norms of discourse may be culturally biased.

Participatory democracy may also erode cultural and religious plu-ralism. As I have characterized it, participatory democracy seeks con-sensus about a substantive vision of the common good. Consider Gut-mann's (1987) view of how educational goals are to be chosen. She argues that in democratic schools the creation of democratic character is the paramount goal. Beyond this, the goals of education may be shaped by democratic deliberation and may be whatever is democratically chosen, so long as two principles—the principle of nonrepression and the principle of nonexclusion—are honored. These principles are viewed as regulatory principles of democratic deliberation. In effect, they assert that the central norms of participatory democracy are equal participation and equal voice. No one can be excluded; no view can be denied expression.

This presents a choice. On the one hand, participatory democrats may claim that collective decisions are constrained by an expectation of consensus. We are to keep talking until we have achieved a decision on which everyone agrees (or, to suggest a weaker form of the claim, a decision to which everyone, in principle, could agree (Habermas, 1990)). That consensus can be achieved on most matters of complexity, however, seems unlikely. Disagreement is a durable feature of liberal democracies (Rawls, 1993). The alternative is to claim that democracy constrains the manner in which decisions can be made but does not constrain the substance of decisions that can be made, unless the effect is to exclude people or deny them voice in further deliberations. This is the force of the principles of nonrepression and nonexclusion. However, once adequate deliberation has occurred, the majority rules. Such regulatory principles may be insufficient to prevent majorities from overriding the cultural or educational interests of minorities. These principles may provide for a continued and respectful hearing. They do not clearly provide for the protection of a private sphere in which different groups have the autonomy required to pursue their distinctive educational interests.

Liberalism, as I shall interpret it here, is distinguished by four characteristics. First, liberalism has a strong commitment to neutrality among different religions, cultures, and views of human flourishing. In its Rawlsian version (Rawls, 1993), the state is to be neutral among reasonable comprehensive doctrines. Comprehensive doctrines are reasonable if they justify reciprocity (a willingness to cooperate with others in just institutions) among citizens. Second, the primary function of rights is to secure a just distribution of those social resources that sustain the pursuit of a self-chosen conception of the good. Third, liberalism has a narrow conception of the common good. For liberals the common good consists in a set of just institutions that provide a fair chance to pursue one's own conception of the good life. It does not consist in a democratically achieved, shared, and substantive conception of the good. Finally, for liberals the state is not a community. The citizens of the liberal state are not bound together by shared ends or a shared identity (for a useful critique see Hollenbach, 1995).

A liberal interpretation of liberal democratic aspirations suggests differing interpretations of the legitimacy principles discussed above. This form of liberalism is fundamentally about equal opportunity, but the kind of equal opportunity it is about is the creation of institutions that permit individuals and groups an equal chance to pursue their own conception of a good life, individually or in association with others. This view does not preclude democratic deliberation or participation, but it views them neither as privileged intrinsic goods nor as a means of constructing a democratically achieved view of the good life. It sees them rather as instruments of equal opportunity. Similarly, as noted above, the basic function of rights and liberties is to facilitate the pursuit of one's own good on equal terms. In such a view, tolerance of diversity and sufficient autonomy to pursue a self-chosen view of the good in association with the like-minded are significant parts of the meaning of freedom and equality.

For liberals, fair participation serves equal opportunity. Such a view is perhaps best expressed through a commitment to such principles as "one person—one vote," along with what Rawls (1971) calls the fair value of equal liberty. Democratic participation is not viewed as an essential component of the good life (although individuals may choose a life in which participation is important). Moreover, because for liberals the scope of democratic decision making is constrained by neutrality, there is less need to emphasize consensus.

Liberalism, like participatory democracy, provides some grounds for decentralized decision making. The Supreme Court has occasionally noted (*Milliken v. Bradley*, 1974; *San Antonio v. Rodriguez*, 1973) that there is a liberty interest in local control, insofar as local control permits the goals that prevail to more adequately reflect local preferences. The Court might also have noted that local school districts themselves are often highly diverse and that some element of free association may also be required if such interests are to be protected (Arons, 1997). For liberals, the purpose of decentralized decision making is not to provide increased opportunity for democratic participation as much as it is to create a better fit between local programs and local values.

For liberals, the chief aim of political socialization is the creation of a sense of justice. Reciprocity, the willingness to live with others on fair bases of cooperation, is what is required, more than the development of democratic character. Liberalism is not, of course, opposed to deliberation, dialogue, or mutual understanding. At the same time it gives them less weight than participatory democracy does.

Liberals, like participatory democrats, are likely to respect professionalism when decisions requiring expertise are required. Also, like democrats, liberals will wish to be careful not to allow professionalism to overstep its proper boundaries. For liberals, this is likely to occur when those claiming professional knowledge also claim expertise regarding the values that define the ends of good living. Are teachers authorities over the ends of education, or the goods that are to be realized through the curriculum? To give an affirmative answer to this question is to suggest that teachers have expertise and authority over the goods that people will pursue through their education. This is a claim of which liberals are likely to be wary, since it may infringe on the right of individuals to choose their own conceptions of the good.

One way to summarize these differences concerns the extent to which the state and its institutions should be viewed as communities. Liberals are inclined to see the state as what Rawls (1971) calls a union of social unions. The state has no ends of its own and has no view of the common good except to create fair institutions in which the members of various communities can pursue their good as they choose to understand it. Participatory democrats are more willing to view the state as a community—and to seek community within the state. The common good is substantive and democratically constructed. Membership in a democratic polity is a good in its own right. These differences translate into different visions of schools as communities.

Schools As Communities

How might we think about schools as communities? Sergiovanni (1993) begins his book on schools as communities by talking about *Gemeinschaft* communities. According to Tonnies (1988), on whom Sergiovanni relies, such communities are constituted by a common life and deep shared understandings. Tribal societies and medieval villages are *Gemeinschaft* communities. Modern liberal democracies have few such communities. Our communities are more like congregations or clubs than tribes or villages. We may be deeply attached to them, but we do not live all of our lives in them. This is true even of those ethnic groups that are central to the identity of their members. Members of such groups are plumbers and lawyers, Catholics and Presbyterians. They live in one place, work in another, and go to school in a third—all with a different cast of characters. There is little common life for school to be a part of. And we would not wish our schools to be more like tribes or medieval villages than congregations. They would be neither liberal nor democratic. They would be characterized by a received religion, inherited status, limited choice, and limited opportunity. And Sergiovanni really does want *Gemeinschaft* communities. By the end of his book he is claiming that schools that are communities are held together by respect, justice, altruistic love, and caring. But this is not right either. Respect and justice are good things, but they are the virtues of *Gesellschaft*, not of community. They are an ethic for strangers (Strike, 2000a). They are crucial for liberal societies where the members of diverse communities must live together, but they are not the stuff of which community is made. Nor are love and caring. These ties are either too exclusive, such as the love we have for our families, or too universal. Consider that the paradigm case of love of neighbor, the Good Samaritan, continued to be a Samaritan and his beneficiary a Jew after their encounter. No community was created by this act of love of neighbor. Neither would have wished for it.

Three conclusions: First, the kinds of school communities that it makes sense to consider in liberal democratic societies such as ours are communities that are united by shared educational aims. The frequently invoked idea of shared values is too vague and too expansive. People in schools may all value functional plumbing, but that will not make them a community. Rugged individualists may agree on certain values with educational relevance, but rugged individualism is unlikely to unite them in common educational pursuits. What is needed is a shared educational project (Strike, 1999, 2000b). Such a project is constituted by shared educational aims that elicit cooperation in their pursuit and establish a shared frame of reference that structures deliberations about how they are to be pursued. Put simply, schools that are communities share basic aims and a common language of deliberation. Such schools are communities because they are coherent. They have a shared sense of what they are about.

There are some values that are praiseworthy and that might appear at the outset to provide the basis for community but, on examination, do not. These values include justice, caring, and love. What makes these inadequate as the basis of an educational community is that they lack educational content and thus do not provide a basis for shared aims. They do not help us to understand why we should care about how math or literature can contribute to human flourishing. What makes these popular candidates for the basis of school communities may be that they seem to provide a kind of social glue that will bind people together in community while permitting a wide diversity of educational projects and aspirations to flourish (see Noddings, 1992). But this diversity is their weakness. These values do not provide a framework for common effort or a shared language of deliberation. If these values are able to establish community, we must believe that they can do so among comparative strangers, where the "natural" bonds of kinship do not hold and where common purpose is lacking. That seems optimistic.

There are certain kinds of educational aspirations that may seem to provide the basis for community but do not. Such aspirations as teaching to high standards, providing a rigorous education, or leaving no child behind, worthy as they may be, are unlikely to create community, because they do not tell us the purposes of a good education. Rather, they tell us that no matter what we do and why we do it, we should do it well. While such things may be worth saying, they are as likely to support competition as they are to support shared educational projects.

The second conclusion is that what one means by schools as communities must be constrained both by the norms of liberal democracy and by the conditions of modernity. In our society we do not have tribes; we have associations. High population mobility and the diversity of many neighborhoods make it difficult to create communities of place. We are unlikely to want to deliberately create schools with educational projects that are expressly at odds with basic liberal democratic norms.

The third conclusion is that much of the "dialectic" about schools as communities concerns the tension between the need for coherence and the need for inclusiveness (Strike, 1999). In liberal democratic societies those who attend a given school often are there because they live in some catchment zone. These individuals may be of diverse religions and ethnic groups and may have quite incompatible educational aspirations. Schools are expected to be decently respectful of this diversity. Even within the school, we may find little coherence concerning basic educational values. Math teachers, physical education teachers, and music teachers notoriously disagree about what is educationally important. We are rarely much bothered by this. Yet it erodes the possibility of community.

The coherence provided by a shared educational project, however, may be troubling. Community not only includes, it excludes. Where there is community there is an US who belong and a THEM who do not. If what creates a school community is a shared educational project, then those who share the educational vision that constitutes the community will be included, and those who do not will be excluded or, if they are present, marginalized. Whether this exclusion is pernicious is another matter. To hold that such exclusion is always objectionable is inconsistent with free association and other values that depend on it. Freedom of worship would be impossible if religious groups were unable to exclude those whom they view as unbelievers.

Yet exclusion may be problematic in schools. A shared view of education may place constraints on what can be thought and debated and who can speak or be heard. Hence there may be "bads" associated with schools that have a shared educational project. Such schools may be parochial or sectarian. They may fail to respect the marketplace of ideas and diminish their students' opportunity for free and autonomous choice. While the degree to which various educational communities produce these various "bads" will depend very much on the character of their shared educational project, it seems difficult to claim that they will not produce at least some of them. If schools are fully inclusive, or if they are equally open to all conceptions of a good education, then they are not communities.

Addressing the Dilemma

I want to consider one democratic and two liberal responses to this dilemma. The most likely democratic response is to propose that schools be democratic polities. In such schools the project is the creation of democratic character through the creation of a democratic culture. Members of the community are bound to the school through a sense of ownership created by participation and to one another by a sense of civic friendship acquired by collaborative engagement in the processes of ruling and being ruled. Other features of the school's program are determined by democratic deliberation. In such schools, to use a Deweyan phrase, democracy is not just a way of decision making, but a way of life (for examples see Dewey, 1916 and Westheimer, 1998).

A crucial assumption of democratic schools is what might be called the correspondence principle (Rosemblum, 1998; Strike, 1998). The basic idea of the correspondence principle is that democratic character is acquired largely by modeling and practice. The requirement of the correspondence principle is that democratic schools must have a democratic culture in which students are participants in the governance of schools.

It is significant that despite much advocacy, there are few schools that seem to express the ideals of democratic community well, and most of these seem to involve some element of free association in their creation. There are a number of reasons why such schools are not immediately seen as the best expression of the educational aspirations of the citizens of liberal democratic societies. One is that parents are often more interested in the economic prospects of their children than they are in creating citizens. Democratic schools may seem to deflect attention from the development of human capital. A second is that such schools require significant decentralization of authority, commanding attention and time that is not always available or freely given. A third is that the authority structure of the intellectual professions is meritocratic and vested in experts. It is difficult to be democratic about the laws of physics. Knowledge is not democratic. Finally, there is a sense in which democratic schools are illiberal. They are likely to contest the values of some members of the community, especially those that flow from traditional religions (Macedo, 1995). They also face significant difficulties being fully multicultural. It may be that no voice will be excluded from democratic deliberation, but at the end of the day, a coherent education program requires agreement on more than democratic character. How these agreements are to be achieved and how they are to do justice to cultural diversity is always something of a mystery in democratic schools.

Liberals may solve the problem of community in two ways. One is to opt for a kind of pluralism. The second is to abandon community as far as schools are concerned.

The pluralistic solution is to permit a diversity of schools, each with its own shared educational project and with sufficient autonomy to be able to pursue it. Examples of such schools might be religious schools, schools that emphasize the intrinsic values of the liberal arts, schools emphasizing one or another subject matter grouping (science and math or the performing arts), or schools emphasizing the culture of one or another ethnic group. Indeed, democratic schools might well be included as one option in a liberal pluralist view.

Arguably, one difficulty with such schools is that they may not always produce good citizens. They run the risk of parochialism and sectarianism. They are unlikely to model democratic practices or provide extensive opportunity for democratic participation. Liberal pluralists, however, may wish to tell a different story about how schools create citizens. Part of their story may emphasize the content of their views. Not all "sects" are sectarian as far as citizenship is concerned. Bryk, Lee, and Holland (1993) argue that Catholic schools are better at creating citizens than public schools, because while the latter emphasize competition for scarce social resources, Catholic schools emphasize justice and caring. "Love your neighbor as yourself" may be the teaching of a sect, but if taken seriously, it seems more likely, rather than less likely, to produce good citizens.

Another part of the story is Rawls's (1971) argument about how a sense of justice is acquired. People come to love the members of their families because they are loved. They develop trust in coherent communities by working together toward common aims. They come to have a sense of justice because they come to value the principles and institutions of a society that views them as free and equal and permits them to seek their own good in their own way. A sense of justice, in this view, depends on being raised in good communities, but not necessarily in democratic ones.

In a liberal pluralistic conception, the scope of permissible pluralism in schooling might be constrained by two criteria. First, the kind of pluralism advanced by liberals such as Rawls is a pluralism of reasonable comprehensive doctrines. Comprehensive doctrines are reasonable when they encourage their adherents to interact with other citizens on the basis of reciprocity. In effect, schools would be expected to promote a sense of justice among their students.

Second, schools might be expected to develop the autonomy of their students. But this is a bone of contention among liberals (see Brighouse, 2000; Callan, 1997). Some liberals have argued that a condition of any life that is genuinely good is that it be autonomously chosen. I argued at the beginning of this chapter that for a political order to be legitimate it must be capable of earning the autonomous consent of its members. Callan argues that any education adequate to develop a sense of justice among its citizens will also promote their autonomy. At the same time, to insist that all schools aim for the autonomy of their students might reduce the scope of pluralism considerably (Galston, 1995).

In liberal pluralist theory, schools would need reasonable autonomy, and membership in school communities would be by free association. Such schools might be created as charter schools or through vouchers. There might be schools within schools. Note that currently only religious schools could not be public schools, and it is at least imaginable that the interpretation of the religion clauses of the First Amendment might evolve to permit religious schools to function as public schools so long as their autonomy is respected. Many liberal democratic societies have such arrangements. Whether this would be a good thing is a harder question. What is clear is that creating schools that are communities on the model of liberal pluralism would require a dramatic change in how we think about the governance of schools.

The second liberal "solution" to the problem of community is to abandon community as an aspiration for schools. Instead, we would think of schools much as we think of banks. Schools would be associations that enabled people who are quite diverse in the values they seek to function together, because the school's aspirations are limited and fundamental ends are kept private. People who use banks need not agree on why they are saving or what they wish to borrow for. Money is a kind of universal instrumentality (in Rawlsian (1971) terms, a primary good). People are likely to need money regardless of their vision of the good. Banks do not care whether we are Jews or Mormons, whether we are saving for our children's college or a boat, or whether we are Philistines or esthetes.

In schools that are like banks we would expect to see an emphasis on a curriculum that serves the diverse aspirations of students, whatever they are. The ends that education serves will be viewed as a private matter. If the larger ends of a good life are discussed at all, it will be most important that they be discussed fairly and open-mindedly and with the primary aim of producing tolerance. Because such attempts are likely to produce more controversy than dialogue, they will largely be avoided. Certainly such discussion will not be undertaken with the expectation that agreement will be sought and that such agreement will inform the programs of the school. Indeed, the perspective that is most likely is that views of good living are merely subjective values, personal preferences, or individual choices, but not objects of collective deliberation. Where schools are like banks, something like values clarification (Raths, Harmin, & Simon, 1966) will be popular.

The main business of such schools will be the development of human capital, or the economic potential of students. This, it is assumed, is neutral among competing visions of a good life. The norms that will dominate schools that are like banks will be justice, equality of opportunity (here understood as fair competition), and tolerance. These are the values that govern the arm's-length transactions of liberal societies. What will be sought is a level playing field, but no one will be expected to sacrifice his or her interests to anyone else, to the common good, or to the community. Such schools are handmaidens to capitalism and have an ethos of the market. The forms of cooperation expected must respect consumer sovereignty and the privacy of individual ends.

The conception of citizenship here will be modest. Students, it is hoped, will be law abiding and tolerant and will vote. More ambitious conceptions of citizenship are likely to invoke larger and more collective ends.

To summarize: Americans often struggle to accommodate different understandings of their central constitutional ideals. We are motivated by ideals of tolerance and pluralism. We claim to respect different religions,

cultures, and visions of human flourishing. At the same time, we wish to
be one society with a big-tent common democratic culture. These ideals
are not so inconsistent that we are unable to muddle through. They are
not so consistent or so sharp as to allow us to be clear about how the
details will be worked out. Education is especially difficult, perhaps because in education our ideals make a difference in what we do to a
greater extent than in other areas of life. We want to create good citizens,
but our differing understanding of our constitutional ideals suggests different pictures of what this means. These different understandings,
along with our diverse cultures and religions, have implications for what
counts as good educating. One can go to work and leave one's religion
at home. Catholics, Protestants, Jews, and Muslims can all be good car-
penters, and they need not disagree about what this means. But these
differences are not neutral when it comes to what counts as good educating. So it is harder to muddle through in schools. We struggle over
the kinds of communities schools should be because our ideals of how
to be *one* and how to be *many* do not offer clear guidance.

Conclusions

I have sketched three pictures of the character of school communities that arise largely from how we interpret and apply the constitutional norms of liberal democratic societies. Participatory democrats
will wish schools to be democratic polities, with the aim of creating
democratic character through a democratic culture. Liberals may opt
for a kind of pluralism characterized by diverse shared educational
projects. In such a view schools are likely to resemble congregations
or guilds. That is, they will be organized around some shared comprehensive doctrine, some shared culture, or an emphasis on some preferred subject matter. The liberal alternative is to see schools as being
like banks. Such schools seek to provide an education that is neutral
regarding different religions, cultures, and conceptions of the good,
viewing these as private matters. They are not communities in that
they do not have a shared educational project. Because they are not
communities, they may exact a cost in alienation and disengagement.

Some schools may find ways to be communities apart from generat-
ing a shared educational project. Size and durable relationships are also
factors in creating community. Some schools may be able to achieve a
caring environment apart from achieving the kind of coherence involved
in a shared education project. But I suspect that in large and diverse
secondary schools—schools where many students enter as strangers to

each other and to the staff, schools where the staff may agree on little of educational substance—a sense of community will be rare and will be made harder by diversity. In such schools those students who do find community are likely to find it in subgroups that may not be uniformly friendly to the mission of the school.

These pictures of school communities are, of course, ideal types. Few schools will reflect any ideal type perfectly. The American educational system includes some of each. Ideal types are useful as analytic tools. They help clarify what is at stake in educational debates. They have some explanatory value. Sometimes the world actually looks and works as such models suggest it should. In these cases, the ideal types explain by showing how reality flows from how we think about certain central issues. If the world does not cooperate, the models may be wrong in their conception, or there may be intervening factors at work.

I think these models have explanatory value in that they explain why it is difficult to have schools that are communities, despite seemingly widespread agreement that community is a good thing. The difficulty derives in part from the fact that the norms of liberal democratic societies do not present a clear picture of the ways in which schools should be communities. Democratic schools reflect one interpretation of American ideals. But they threaten to impose a tyranny of the majority. Liberal pluralism expresses a respect for diversity but may not serve the goals of autonomy or of democratic citizenship well. Our inability to resolve the dialectical dance of liberal and democratic interpretations of our constitutional norms leaves us unable to generate a coherent picture of what it would mean for schools to be communities. So we seek community with ties such as love, caring, and respect that do not depend on coherence, but that are also likely to prove too weak to create community in diversity. The result is that we continue to view schools as though they were like banks. That we are a capitalist society at least as much as we are a liberal democratic one supports this view of schooling, but such schools are also the default resulting from our lack of clarity about our constitutional norms. Alienation, anomie, and disengagement are among the costs. Some difficulties in achieving a sense of the legitimacy of educational institutions flow from the inability to realize constitutional norms that are inconsistently interpreted.

The research reported in this article was made possible, in part, by a grant from the Spencer Foundation. The data presented, the statements made, and the views expressed are solely the responsibility of the author.

REFERENCES

Arons, S. (1997). *Short route to chaos*. Amherst, MA: University of Massachusetts Press.

Brighouse, H. (2000). *School choice and social justice*. Oxford, U.K.: Oxford University Press.

Bryk, A.S., Lee, V.E., & Holland, P.B. (1993). *Catholic schools and the common good*. Cambridge, MA: Harvard University Press.

Bryk, A.S., Sebring, P.B., Kerbow, D., Rollow, S., & Easton, J.Q. (1998). *Charting Chicago school reform*. Boulder, CO: Westview Press.

Callan, E. (1997). *Creating citizens: Political education and liberal democracy*. Oxford, U.K.: Oxford University Press.

Dewey, J. (1916). Democracy and education. New York: The Macmillan Company.

Galston, W. (1995). Two concepts of liberalism. *Ethics, 105*(3), 516-534.

Gutmann, A. (1987). *Democratic education*. Princeton, NJ: Princeton University Press.

Gutmann, A., & Thompson, D. (1996). *Democracy and disagreement*. Cambridge, MA: Harvard University Press.

Habermas, J. (1984). *The theory of communicative action*. Boston: Beacon Press.

Habermas, J. (1990). *Moral consciousness and communicative action*. Cambridge, MA: MIT Press.

Hollenbach, D. (1995). Virtue, the common good, and democracy. In A. Etzioni (Ed.), *New communitarian thinking* (pp. 143-153). Charlottesville, VA: University Press of Virginia.

Locke, J. (1960). *Second treatise: Two treatises of government*. New York: Cambridge University Press.

Macedo, S. (1995). Liberal civic education and religious fundamentalism: The case of God v. John Rawls. *Ethics, 105*(3), 468-497.

Milliken v. Bradley, 418 U.S. 717 (1974).

National Commission on Excellence in Education. (1983). *A nation at risk*. Washington, DC: U.S. Department of Education.

Noddings, N. (1992). *The challenge to care in schools: An alternative approach to education*. New York: Teachers College Press.

Nussbaum, M. (1997). *Cultivating humanity: A classical defense of reform in liberal education*. Cambridge, MA: Harvard University Press.

Plato. (1962). *The Republic of Plato* (F. M. Cornford, Trans.). New York: Oxford University Press.

Raths, L.E., Harmin, M., & Simon, S. (1966). *Values and teaching: Working with values in the classroom*. Columbus, OH: C.E. Merrill Books.

Rawls, J. (1971). *A theory of justice*. Cambridge, MA: Harvard University Press.

Rawls, J. (1993). *Political liberalism*. New York: Columbia University Press.

Rosemblum, N.L. (1998). *Membership and morals*. Princeton, NJ: Princeton University Press.

San Antonio Independent School District v. Rodriguez, 411 U.S. 1 (1973).

Sergiovanni, T.J. (1993). *Building community in schools*. San Francisco: Jossey-Bass.

Strike, K.A. (1997). Centralized goal formation and systemic reform: Reflections on liberty, localism and pluralism. *Educational Policy Analysis, 5*(11), http://olam.ed.asu.edu/epaa/v5n11.html (25/3/98)

Strike, K.A. (1998). Freedom of conscience and illiberal socialization: The congruence argument. *Journal of Philosophy of Education, 32*(3), 345-360.

Strike, K.A. (1999). Can schools be communities? The tension between shared values and inclusion. *Educational Administration Quarterly, 35*(1), 46-70.

Strike, K.A. (2000a). Liberalism, communitarianism and the space between: In praise of kindness. *Journal of Moral Education, 29*(2), 133-147.

Strike, K.A. (2000b). Schools as communities: Four metaphors, three models, and a dilemma or two. *Journal of Philosophy of Education, 34*(4), 617-642.

The State Education Department. (1994). *A new compact for learning*. Albany, NY: The University of the State of New York.

Tonnies, F. (1988). *Community and society*. New Brunswick, NJ: Transaction Books.
Westheimer, J. (1998). *Among schoolteachers: Community, individuality, and ideology in teachers' work*. New York: Teachers College Press.
Young, I.M. (1966). Communication and the other: Beyond deliberative democracy. In S. Benhabib (Ed.), *Democracy and difference*. Princeton, NJ: Princeton University Press.

Section Two
HOW TO FIX THE EDUCATIONAL GOVERNANCE SYSTEM

CHAPTER 4

What's Wrong with Public Education Governance in Big Cities ... And How Should It Be Fixed?

PAUL T. HILL

Does governance matter? This question is sure to spark an argument among education reformers.

On the "nay" side are those who observe that school districts run by mayors or by appointed school boards are not consistently different or better performing than districts run by elected school boards. The American Academy of School Administrators recently reinforced the "nay" side with a report saying that charter districts—districts nominally freed from many state rules—are not able to make all that many significant changes (Lockwood, 2001).

On the "yea" side are those who observe the ways schools are burdened by school board politics, union contracts, and state-imposed rules. They argue that a different sort of public oversight could allow teachers and principals to focus more effectively on instruction. Some point to the relative success of urban Catholic schools as evidence of what could be accomplished if public schools were governed differently (Chubb & Moe, 1990; Hill, Foster, & Gendler, 1990).

This chapter comes down firmly on the "yea" side of the debate. But it further argues that governance of public education, especially in big cities, often matters for the worse. It shows how current governance arrangements burden and disrupt schools, tells how governance

Paul Hill is Acting Dean and Professor in the University of Washington's Daniel J. Evans School of Public Affairs, and director of the Center on Re-Inventing Public Education.

came to have such adverse effects, and suggests how public governance can be made school-friendly.

The dispute over whether governance matters is analogous to an earlier dispute about whether schools themselves matter. Sparked by the original Coleman et al. (1966) report, which found that common-sense measures of school quality do not explain variations in student achievement, some took the position that the influence of students' family backgrounds is so strong that schools do not matter. Others noted that the averages hid important examples of schools that *do* matter—where students achieve far more than could be predicted from their family's income or minority status (Edmonds, 1979). Coleman himself joined those who rejected the proposition "schools don't matter," and led a number of studies that examined the characteristics of schools whose students "beat their demography." These efforts spawned several current-day school reform movements, including programs based on "Effective Schools" research, New American Schools designs and the federal government's Comprehensive School Reform demonstration, and charter schools.

Concerning both governance and schools, the debate over "what matters" becomes confused in two ways. First, there is confusion over the difference between *averages* and specially constructed cases. On average, governance changes don't matter much. Similarly, on average, schools perform about as well as could be predicted from knowledge of their student body composition. But this does not mean that well-designed alternatives, either in governance or school design, can't have strong effects. In the history of the world, on average, items leaving the surface of the earth (animals, insects, and fish jumping; items bouncing after a fall; objects shot out of volcanoes) ascend to a height of only a few feet. Clearly, though, this has not prevented engineers from creating airplanes that ascend to 40,000 feet or spacecraft that travel practically infinite distances.

The second confusion is over the distinction between *necessity* and *sufficiency*. Changes in governance or school design are necessary elements in a change process, but they are not sufficient in themselves. We know that changes in school board roles and missions, or in the design of schools, can remove constraints and encourage certain lines of action. However, everything depends on what happens next. If a mayor-appointed school board leaves all the old rules in place, or if a school that claims to adopt a new design does not work to change teacher behavior, no real changes will ensue. If, however, changes in governance lead to new incentives and capacities at the school level, and if teachers and principals seize the opportunity to change their teaching methods and their use of time, there can be real changes in teaching and learning.

We know that some schools are more effective than others, even in the same district and with similar children. We also know that improved instruction comes from a complex interaction that includes school leadership, better pedagogy, teacher learning, teacher effort, and student work. Each of these factors is necessary, but none alone is sufficient.

With respect to governance, however, we can still fall into the trap of concluding that governance changes make no difference. This is understandable because, as Frederick Hess and others have amply documented, so many governance changes are poorly implemented (Hess, 1999; Hill, Campbell, & Harvey, 2000). But the failure of half-baked or fatally compromised schemes does not prove that governance cannot make a difference.

Members of groups that have the greatest influence under current governance structures (e.g., leaders of school board associations and teachers' unions) hotly attack proposed governance changes as "risky schemes." This is not because they are indifferent about governance. It is because they know that governance can matter a great deal.

Americans' deliberations about education governance would be more productive if we got beyond the "averages" and "sufficiency" fallacies. This chapter therefore focuses on the question, "How can governance strengthen public schools?" It has three main sections. The first provides an expansive definition of governance and shows how current government arrangements, particularly school districts, take care of adult interests and leave the effectiveness of schools to chance. The second discusses how school districts have evolved. The third formulates three alternative ways in which governance can be made school-friendly.

The Meaning (and the Current Harms) of Governance

Most discussions of education governance focus on the hierarchical relationships between the people in schools and central office staff, superintendents, school board members, and state legislators. In this most familiar sense, governance of public education creates links—or should—between the voters who elect governors, state legislators, and school board members and the people who teach children. The links consist of appointed officials like superintendents and the permanent civil servants who staff state and local education agencies, whose job is to make sure the goals and preferences of elected officials are implemented.

"Lingering" Governance

This description of governance is important, but it is incomplete. A broader definition of governance is *the consistent exercise of influence.* Due to the political character of school boards, and to the policies they enact and the agreements they enter into, there are others who influence schools. Elected officials and appointed executives certainly govern schools in the primary sense. But in another sense, public schools are governed by the demands of groups other than schools' hierarchical superiors. Aside from school boards, superintendents, and others of high rank, schools must consider many other groups that have privileges, guarantees, and rights to consult, bargain, or complain. Many times, these groups govern schools through the force of policies that contemporary elected officials did not enact and might even oppose. Old court orders, statutes, policies, and contracts, for example, govern schools in their own ways.

A homely example can illustrate the difference between these two sources of governance. A bus driver steers, sets the throttle, and applies the brakes. But her actions do not always determine where the bus goes, or how fast, or when it stops. Other devices (interestingly, called governors) can determine the bus's maximum speed, limit its turn radius, and even stop it from moving at all under some circumstances. The driver governs the bus, but only within tolerances set by the governors. She might be perfectly happy about the limitations on her control, or she might resent them.

Terry Moe (1989) has explained how groups other than hierarchical superiors come to govern schools in this second sense. Control of legislatures and other decision making bodies shifts from time to time. The groups in control at a particular time perpetuate their advantages by enacting laws and policies that often last indefinitely. As the memberships of decision making bodies change, new groups take charge and enact policies that, in turn, create lasting advantages for themselves. Though old laws and policies are repealed on occasion, it is easier to defend an established policy than to establish a new one. Groups that have fallen into minority status can usually protect the policies that benefit them. Thus, public schools can be governed by at least some laws and policies that present-day elected officials would not enact.

Much the same analysis would apply to court orders, in which settlements among litigants long dead can affect current-day policies, as well as to labor contracts, in which settlements reached years ago serve as baselines for current bargaining. This second source of governance therefore affects schools whether current-day legislatures, school boards, and superintendents like it or not.

None of the people who negotiated these agreements and policies are—or were—indifferent about whether children are taught well. But all of them, deliberately or not, imposed constraints on the ways schools are run and on the way children learn today, and none of them took responsibility for these burdens. How much less will children learn if some portion of already limited funding must be allocated to comply with a court order, or if schools are forced to keep just a few teachers who are not effective, or if principals are required to spend a few hours each week in meetings where district officials explain their initiatives, or if teachers are required to keep just a few disruptive students in their class? None of these constraints does a great deal of harm by itself, but taken together they can divert substantial resources, including the strictly limited time of principals, students, and teachers for instruction. These limitations are most severe in big city public schools, which face more political and contractual constraints than schools in smaller and less complicated systems.

Understood in this way, the governance of public schools is extremely complex. In addition, although state education codes are compendia of laws and regulations, they do not include all the court orders, collective bargaining agreements, federal regulations, or requirements imposed by private donors. Consequently, few people understand all the constraints that affect schools. In Michigan, where charter schools must abide by all the rules and reporting requirements that apply to conventional public schools, an agency that had granted several charters set out to inform school leaders of all their obligations. Agency staff discovered that no one in the state education agency could give them a comprehensive list of all the necessary reports. Many different bureaus simply sent out demands for information on their own schedules, and schools generally found out what they had to do when the demands appeared (Hill, Lake, & Celio, 2001).

The Rules of Governance

How, then, do we understand who now governs public schools? One approach would be to enumerate all the groups, within government and outside, that can make claims or demands on schools. Useful as this might be, it would take far more resources and space than are available for writing this chapter. Perhaps one useful way to characterize a governance system is by distinguishing what higher authorities and their policies control, and what is left to be decided at the school level.

Optimists about governance think rules can control "just enough" to allow professional judgment to be used effectively. Standards-based reform, today's mainstream approach to improvement of public education, takes this "just enough guidance" approach. Its supporters urge states and localities to strip away all requirements that do not promote good instruction, and to make sure that remaining requirements are mutually reinforcing. Supporters argue that all students can learn to high minimum standards if requirements for teaching, testing, and accountability are properly aligned. They criticize the extant governance system for getting in the way of good instruction.

Pessimists about governance doubt that rules can be so perfectly aligned. They think rules are made to control whatever matters to two groups: the people in charge, and the people with the greatest capacity to organize politically. What is not controlled—what is literally left to chance—is whether teachers, principals, and parents retain the capacity, resources, and freedom required to provide and to support good instruction.

Pessimists, including this author, view governance as inevitably a squeaky wheel system. The governors of the system are the factors that attract attention and force the allocation of resources—no matter what the stated goals or the intentions of individual actors might be. The pessimistic approach to governance does not assume that the key actors are malevolent. To the contrary, it assumes that almost everyone in the system is frustrated by its results. All of them think children could be served more effectively if only others controlled fewer resources, intruded less on the agenda, and limited their demands for processing of conflicts. According to this pessimistic view, governance is tragedy, not melodrama; good intentions clash and the results go badly awry.

Under the pessimistic view of governance, the things that are controlled by rules and by higher authorities include:

- The protection of elected officials from any taint of scandal and corruption
- School board members' ability to intervene on behalf of constituents
- District compliance with court orders, labor contracts, and the demands of external funders
- The funding of teacher salaries and other contractual commitments

- The funding of central office units
- The provision of facilities for ongoing district programs
- Job security and placement rights for tenured employees

There is nothing new about this list. Jane Hannaway and Lee Sproull (1978-79) outlined much the same set of ideas in the 1970s, when school districts were first learning to cope with the demands of federal categorical programs. Later work showed how court orders and threats of litigation supersede other demands (Hill & Madey, 1983).

Many of the items lower down on the list take their place as the natural result of public agencies' normal budgeting priorities—filling long-term commitments before funding discretionary items and new commitments. Districts give high priority to fulfilling commitments to incumbent teachers and central office employees and making sure there are facilities to house existing instructional programs. Job placement and tenure rights of incumbent employees also come high on the list of priorities; they, too, are fixed obligations based on regulation and contract.

These concerns can conflict with one another, especially when budgets are tight; however, no other concern supersedes anything already on the list above.

Researchers who study the operation of multiple school districts see these realities at work every day. In this author's recent studies of districts, he encountered several superintendents who echoed former New York City schools Chancellor Rudy Crew's observation: "Any other priorities go out the window if money is missing or an employee is found to have a criminal record." Principals commented that only master manipulators of "the system" are able to fill an open position with a teacher other than the most senior applicant, or to replace a teacher who has a clean record but will not cooperate with the school's instructional improvement strategy. Most complain that their time can be dominated by casework demands from school board members and by meetings called by the central office. In the same vein, a school district financial manager said, "Any other initiatives we take come only after we have settled with the teachers union. That is why we don't publish a budget for building repairs or other flexible items like professional development" (quotations in this paragraph are based on interviews conducted by the author).

Table 1 summarizes the pessimistic view of governance by comparing what the current district governance system controls for, and what it leaves to chance. The table does not purport to characterize the behavior of everyone in the system; some school board members, superintendents, central office administrators, union leaders, principals, and teachers assert their own interests less aggressively than they could and ignore the demands of the other governors of the system. These individuals are loved and lionized, because what they do is so risky and improbable. The fact that educators say it takes moral courage to put teaching and learning first is a powerful criticism of a governance system that puts many other considerations at the head of the line.

TABLE 1

WHAT THE GOVERNANCE SYSTEM TAKES CARE OF AND WHAT IT LEAVES TO CHANCE

Takes Care Of	Leaves to Chance
District's reputation as free of scandal and corruption	School leaders' freedom to focus on instructional improvement
Compliance with federal and state requirements and court orders	
School board members' opportunity to serve constituents	
Compliance with court orders	School-level flexibility in use of funds for innovation and development
Compliance with court orders	Schools' freedom to adapt instruction and staffing to student needs
Compliance with labor contracts	Schools' ability to manage human resources on basis of "fit"
Funding of teacher salaries and other contractual commitments	School-level flexibility in use of funds for student support
Funding of central office units	
Provision of facilities for ongoing instructional programs	Availability of facilities for new and innovative programs

Some might think Table 1 is a lurid exaggeration, but it reflects reality. To elaborate further on the right hand column items:

- School-level administrators consistently report that they are overburdened, forced to attend to the district's crisis of the day, and unable to focus attention on their own school's needs.
- School boards and superintendents are always strapped for new investment funds, including funds for teacher training and for experimentation with new teaching methods and materials.

- Schools can seldom choose or configure their staffs, and their instructional programs reflect what incumbent teachers can and will do, more than they reflect what current students need.
- Teachers are paid at the district level and few schools are able to trade in a teacher for flexible funds, or to replace a highly paid teacher with two less expensive ones. Schools in less desirable neighborhoods often have less experienced and lower paid staffs, but they do not have any more flexible funds than other schools with more experienced and higher paid staffs.
- In most school districts, budgets are not allocated on a per-student basis, but to support adults—to pay for the work of central office bureaus and for teacher salaries. The amount of money available to teach a particular student depends on how much his teacher is paid and how many centrally run programs he is eligible for.
- People with new ideas about school design and instructional programs are seldom able to find space, and charter schools, even those supported by the superintendent (as in Chicago), often have to seek and pay for commercial space. Schools have very little flexible funding, often in the range of $20-60 thousand per year; all the money is spent at the district level.

Table 1 is also consistent with research on urban district reform initiatives. Though there has been a lot of action on big-city reforms, there has not been much progress. This is due in part to the fact that few big cities have been able to sustain any reform effort long enough to make a difference (Hess, 1999; Hill, Campbell, & Harvey, 2000).

Big city districts, and the interest groups that help govern them, continue to resist the kinds of changes that could lead to increased performance. It is difficult to make the kind of hard decisions that are crucial to improvement, since inevitably someone's toes get stepped on. Even officials nominally at the apex of power in a district can lose everything if they offend the wrong people. Everyone knows the stories of superintendents who are fired as soon as they become controversial or run afoul of interest groups (Hess, 1999; Hill, Campbell, & Harvey, 2000). Fewer know about how Roger Erskine of Seattle and Rick Beck of Cincinnati, visionary teacher union leaders who negotiated contracts giving teachers more freedom from regulation in return for greater performance accountability, were later ousted by vote of their members (personal communication, n.d.; *Education Intelligence Agency Report*, April 29, 2001).

For the author, these lessons came together over the course of a 5-year Brookings Institution project on big city school reform. The project was motivated by a simple question: What would we say to a mayor or civic leader who asked how she could turn around a low-performing urban school district? At this point our initiative has produced two books, one that critiques the most popular school reform proposals and suggests how rival approaches might be combined into more potent strategies for system change (Hill & Celio, 1998), and one that draws on the experience of six districts (Boston, Memphis, San Diego, San Francisco, Seattle, and New York City Community District #2) to suggest how communities can build political support and implementation capacity for deep and lasting reform of public education (Hill, Campbell, & Harvey, 2000).

The districts we studied for the latter book were thwarted in their education reform efforts by the *de facto* governance system of organized interest groups, coupled with policies that had outlived their originators. Each district's reform initiative attempted to address one or more negative aspects of its current public education system. Some adopted standards to attack the system's tolerance of mediocrity; others invested in professional development to remedy years of inattention to teacher quality; others introduced new school designs to unify chaotic schools; others decentralized control of funds to correct for micromanagement by school boards and central offices; and a few created charter schools to develop the capacity to hold schools accountable for performance.

However, no district's initiative was strong enough by itself to transform large numbers of schools. As conceded by even their most ardent proponents, none of these initiatives could spark all the changes their supporters hoped to bring about. Each initiative required other changes— over which there was little control—to happen at the same time. For example, reforms based on teacher training did not create incentives to overcome the rules and habits that made it unnecessary for teachers to put in time and effort to improve their knowledge and skills. Reforms based on establishing standards often did not create new investments in teacher learning or free schools from regulations that prevented change. Reforms based on rewards and sanctions for performance often did not provide for capacity building or for support for school staff to pursue promising ideas. With the exception of New York City District #2, each of the reform initiatives had a "zone of wishful thinking": it could work only if educators somehow spontaneously overcame a lack of capacity, or found ways to do things that were contrary to regulations, or took initiative in the absence of incentives to do so.

Not surprisingly, few of the cities' reform strategies had detectable effects on school performance. By early 2000 three of the six reforms had been abandoned, and by mid-2001 the casualty rate was four of six. Only Boston, with a gradual but persistent approach to standards-based reform, and New York City District #2, with its rigorous approach to literacy, persisted.

The next section addresses the question: How did public education governance come to produce such negative effects while proving so difficult to reform?

How Governance Got This Way: The Role of School Boards

Nobody becomes a teacher, school administrator, or school board member unless he or she cares about children. However, good intentions can ultimately clash, especially in big cities, where schools burdened by poverty and social turbulence also experience competing currents of regulation and politically generated policy. Big city school boards do a nice job representing the social, economic, ethnic, and political complexity of their communities; however, as coalitions of board members and key interest groups form and dissolve, the result can be chaotic, inconsistent policy and instability at the top. Big city superintendents are often victims of these shifting coalitions.

The clash of good intentions can also make big city school districts into hostile environments for education. Big city school boards resolve complex situations by bargaining. The result can be policies and rules that are acceptable to powerful contending groups but that impose burdensome constraints on schools. The results, not surprisingly, are not good. School leaders are often so constrained by rules that many come to define their jobs as simply "keeping the lid on." School boards do not bear the sole responsibility for these problems, but they *are* parties to the deals that limit and burden schools. Are these consequences the inevitable results of public oversight? If so, there is little reason to hope that city public schools will improve.

The argument of this chapter is that these unfortunate results are not inevitable, and that public oversight need not create a hostile environment for schools. However, it is necessary to understand how the current situation has come to be, starting with the role of the school board. Big city school boards are composed of people who openly advance the interests of specific organizations, neighborhoods, or "cause" groups, and this is generally the basis of school boards' interventionism and the resulting policy instability. How and why does this happen?

It must be recognized that school boards do not have to be constant sources of instability and disruption. Boards in other kinds of organizations are responsible for preserving broadly defined interests—those of the shareholders or of the public. In business law, a board member who put the interest of a faction over that of the whole organization (e.g., an employees' union or a supplier) could be found to be in violation of the law. For example, Douglas Fraser of the United Auto Workers, upon appointment to the Chrysler board of directors in 1982, announced that he intended to represent the interests of the union. He was told that this would be a violation of federal laws governing the responsibilities of corporate board members. Fraser consequently announced that he would act for the stockholders, and apparently did for the remainder of his tenure. His story provides enough lessons to be included in the case materials used by participants in Harvard Business School training for corporate board members.

History matters. Unlike corporate boards, whose roles were always sharply distinguished from those of management, school boards started out *as* management. In 18th-century New England, legislatures required town councils to provide schools, and the town councils delegated responsibility to school committees. Committee members were appointed and they exercised management responsibility. These school boards were the functional equivalent of today's school district central office. Boards created committees that specialized in areas such as teacher hiring, curriculum oversight, and budgeting. Individual members were responsible for visiting the schools in their areas, for assessing the school facilities, and for testing students annually.

As cities grew, school boards expanded, so that some had as many as 70 members. Growth led to pressure for the election, rather than appointment, of members, because neighborhoods wanted control of their own schools (Cistone, 1975).

During the mid-1800s Horace Mann, the first Secretary of the Massachusetts Board of Education, proposed a dramatic change in board roles and powers. He urged that boards hire an expert educator who would serve as chief administrator of all schools in a community. This administrator, the superintendent, would answer to a small school board that would have the authority to hire and fire the superintendent and to set general administrative and instructional policies. Though most communities hired superintendents, few boards fully accepted the "hands-off" approach Mann had proposed for them. Boards retained the power of final approval over many administrative decisions, even as they shrank to an average of 10 members.

More recent political events have reinforced the tendency of school boards to be overinvolved in the management of schools. Starting with the Supreme Court *Brown v. Board of Education* decision in 1954, public schooling became absorbed into the public policy process. Before 1954, school boards were rarely subject to lawsuits, nor did their state governments closely monitor them. After 1954, however, the actions of school boards came under increased scrutiny; methods of school funding, staffing, and student assignment were increasingly influenced by state laws and court orders; and school boards found themselves subject to lawsuits and civil rights agency enforcement actions. Once the federal government became a funder of public education, via the Elementary and Secondary Education Act of 1964 and subsequent federal statutes, local school systems unambiguously became subordinate elements of a complex intergovernmental regulatory structure.

Starting in the late 1960s, state legislatures started enacting their own categorical programs that gave school districts money tied to specific services or groups of students. Lawsuits charging that reliance on local property taxes had resulted in unequal spending on students also led most states to increase their share of school funding. Legislatures started treating school districts as state agencies, meaning that legislatures could respond to perceived problems by assigning new responsibilities to local school boards. As a result, school boards became more intrusive as their duties became more detailed and explicit over time.

School boards also became much more overtly political. Though politics had always been a consideration, controversies were mostly nonideological, and there were few well-organized interest groups other than the PTA and the business community. After 1964, however, federal programs like ESEA Title I encouraged the formation of parent groups that could advocate for the disadvantaged children meant to benefit from these funds. The federal Office for Civil Rights also reviewed district spending and student assignment policies and investigated citizen complaints. Families that objected to desegregation plans or other district policies organized as well. School employee unions and cause groups, including members of the religious right concerned about reading assignments and members of the right and left disputing teaching methods, learned they could advance their interests by electing their candidates to the school board.

Critics say that school boards meddle in issues that should be left to professionals, treat schooling as a formal government program rather than as a community-based caring function, and provide perches from which ambitious individuals can run for higher office. They are right in all respects. However, as illustrated, these tendencies are deeply rooted in history. Members who micromanage, play politics, or intervene on behalf of individual parents or school employees do not misunderstand traditional school board roles; they understand them all too well.

If these actions weaken schools, as the preceding section suggests, what can be done? Some organizations, including national school board associations and the Institute for Educational Leadership, have suggested that training is the answer (see, for example, Bushweller, 1998). They encourage school board members to restrain themselves enough to focus on the big policy issues. Others, including big city business groups that recruit executives to run for school boards, suggest that school boards can be transformed with the addition of members who have had experience on corporate boards (see Cuban, 2001, for a critique of this belief). Neither of these approaches, though, has made much difference. Board members still encounter pressures—and irresistible opportunities—to intervene in everyday school business when it suits them or their constituents.

Moreover, board members who restrain themselves often find they are less influential, and have fewer useful contacts in the community and school system, than do members who play the casework and patronage games. Based on the author's interviews with business leaders who have joined boards of education, few have proven able to maintain the detachment typical of corporate board members (see McAdams, 2000). School board members' actions are structured more by the demands, opportunities, and incentives implicit in the role than by the particular experience of individual members.

So the question remains: How can school boards be structured to oversee public schools without harming them in the process? The next section will review some options that have been proposed by policymakers and scholars, and suggest which ones are most promising.

Building the Right Governance System

Disentangling the problems discussed above will be a monumental task. However, at least the goals are clear. We need to find a way for school boards, and those whose educational leverage is derived from a relationship with a school board (i.e., superintendents, central offices, and teacher unions), to operate as if they had only one job: to make it possible for schools to be effective.

Governance that Supports Schools

Effective schools need a governance environment that provides:

• *Predictable funding and a stable regulatory environment.* Schools can adapt over time to changes in funding levels, but they cannot be effective if they must re-staff or re-program in the middle of an academic year. Similarly, schools can adapt to a limited number of changes in the rules under which they operate. But schools that must continually adapt to new policies made monthly by school boards or superintendents lose their focus on instruction and become dominated by the imperative to comply.

• *Access to a variety of ideas, assistance, and materials.* Few schools run entirely on the ideas and knowledge of the people they directly employ. Virtually all schools need ideas, advice, and help with solving problems, and sometimes guidance on how best to meet the distinctive needs of current students. Sometimes schools need help using new methods and technology. Schools that are denied access to help or that are constrained to accept help offered by a monopoly supplier, whether or not their needs are met, cannot always solve problems or exploit opportunities.

• *Benign pressure to demonstrate performance.* Like all adult organizations, school personnel need some external demands. Productive collaboration is taxing, and groups that face no such pressures can easily fall into indulging individual tastes and preferences. On the other hand, schools can be hindered by requirements to meet arbitrarily set quotas or to emphasize the most easily measured results. Schools need to be accountable, but no one audience—not government, not parents, not education professionals—has a complete picture of what students need to learn and experience. As I will argue below, schools should not be accountable to just one party on the basis of just one measure. Instead, they should balance accountability to parents, students, teachers, and the broader community.

• *Freedom to choose staff on the basis of fit with a defined approach to instruction.* Schools need to be able to select people who have the skills they need and who endorse the school's mission and its approaches to instruction. Not every highly qualified teacher or administrator is prepared to work as a full partner in every type of school. Schools forced to employ people who do not fit cannot remain focused and coherent.

- *Access to competent teachers and administrators.* Schools need to be able to draw from a pool of well-prepared individuals who can lead and teach. This pool must be broad enough to allow schools to find individuals to fit particular needs. Schools in areas where few good people are available, or where the pool is arbitrarily constrained by unproductive training or certification requirements, have trouble delivering quality instruction.

- *The freedom to reconfigure programs and spending.* Schools need to be able to adapt to changes in student needs and take advantage of learning about alternative approaches to instruction. They also need freedom to reconfigure staffing to minimize unproductive expenditures and to make capital-labor tradeoffs, e.g., in favor of materials and technology that enhance student learning.

Political bodies like school boards have a strong tendency to create bargained-out solutions to complex problems. Bargaining leads to answers that powerful contending groups can live with, but these answers are seldom right for all the situations they cover. In K-12 education, there is rarely one best solution. Diversity of approach and decentralization of decision making is necessary.

So, for example, districts have provided money and recruited teachers, but they have done so in ways that weaken schools as organizations—by assigning these assets without reference to the specific needs of schools. It is easy to see the results of schools' dependency on a governance system that prioritizes everything but the schools themselves (Darling-Hammond, Ancess, MacGregor, & Zuckerman, 1994). Teacher candidate pools are weak, and the schools that enroll the most challenging students get the newest and least prepared teachers. Schools have limited choices for assistance and advice, and districts seldom have the internal capacity to provide the service schools need most: organizing a turnaround effort for a low-performing organization. Many families are unable to escape schools they are unhappy with, so they either give up or become constant sources of opposition and disruption (see Bryk and Schneider, 2002, on the consequences of conflict within a school).

Yet communities need some sort of governing body that will ensure equitable access to education and that will guarantee that children learn what they need to learn in order to function as adults. The fact that government agencies have largely failed to discharge these responsibilities, especially in big cities where most children are racially isolated and many do not learn to read, does not erase these needs.

However, accomplishing these goals actually means school districts doing less, encouraging diverse providers and broader sources of expertise to become involved, while focusing their own oversight capabilities on standard-setting equitable access.

Hill, Campbell, and Harvey (2000) formulated some new governance options that would include powerful performance incentives, considerable investments in school capacity, and provisions giving schools significant opportunities to change. We built these governance approaches from the ground up, by identifying the most promising incentives, approaches to capacity investment, and arrangements for freedom of action. The next three subsections summarize the results.

School Performance Incentives

Incentives for school performance can be negative, creating powerful consequences for schools that will not or cannot improve, *and* positive, creating opportunities for recognition and professional advancement for teachers and principals who succeed in challenging situations. They might include:

Giving families open choice among public schools. The need to attract families and build loyalties gives teachers and principals strong incentives to clarify the school's goals and methods. This gives parents a basis for choice and motivates teachers to work closely with individual children, collaborate with one another, and demonstrate performance.

Promoting competition among schools. A city policy of creating new schools or encouraging charter schools in neighborhoods with poorly performing schools makes it clear that teachers and principals must make the best possible use of their pooled time and talent. Permitting low-income students from failing schools to transfer to private schools also creates performance incentives for public school staff.

Creating professional and earning opportunities for high-performing professionals. Initiatives allowing teachers and principals in high-performing schools to expand their schools or to open branches in new neighborhoods, or permitting staff members from successful schools to charge for help and advice given to other schools, create both group and individual performance incentives.

Allowing individual teachers and principals to negotiate salary and work assignments with schools. A teacher labor market gives every teacher a strong reason to build her reputation by making valuable contributions to her school. It also allows professionals with excellent reputations to negotiate higher pay and interesting assignments, regardless of years of experience or how many degrees they hold. This arrangement also creates opportunities for schools to change, as discussed below.

All of these proposals are, to say the least, controversial. They are also more promising and less dangerous proposals than stakeholders in the existing public education system would allege.

Investments in School Capacity

Investments in school capacity can also be promoted in numerous ways. Some of them involve segmenting existing funds so that investments are made, and others involve creating new sources of assistance for schools. Together they include:

Guaranteeing every school a minimum set-aside for purchasing materials, advice, and assistance. This guarantees that no school will be unable to work on improving its instructional program. It also prevents school staff from having to "eat their seed corn" (because of spending every cent on current services) and being unable to invest in new capabilities.

Creating independent new institutions to provide assistance, advice, and teacher training. This can increase the options available to schools and make them less dependent on whatever the central office bureaucracy offers, and may also encourage central office professional development providers to be more "customer friendly."

Setting up "venture capital" funds to encourage formation of new nonprofit and university-based assistance organizations. This can create an entrepreneurial sector that constantly searches for ways to help individual schools; coupled with a good privately funded "user's guide" to sources of assistance, it can also increase the options available to schools.

These options are less controversial than the ones listed under "incentives." They are, however, expensive. All of them imply changes in public spending and in long-term business and foundation investment.

Arrangements That Give Schools Opportunities to Change

Guaranteeing that school communities—administrators, teachers, staff, and parents—have the freedom to change their schools in ways that could work better for students may not be as difficult as many like to imagine. Possible changes for schools include:

Supervising schools via performance agreements, not codes of rules. This allows school personnel to focus on one issue only, improving instruction and student learning, and can at least in theory eliminate public schools' unproductive preoccupation with compliance.

Giving schools real-dollar budgets and the discretion to spend money. This, more than anything else, makes it clear that schools are in control of their instructional programs and are responsible for choices about materials, assistance, and teacher training.

Ensuring schools that they can reallocate and spend the money they save by reducing expenditures. This ensures that schools benefit by eliminating what is no longer useful or necessary, and increases the likelihood that school leaders will carefully review expenditures in light of real needs. In the past, many schools have been reluctant to cut unnecessary expenditures because they expected that someone else—the school board, central office, or state treasurer—would capture the benefits.

Allowing schools to decide how they will organize and staff themselves. This ensures that schools can optimize their staffing for instructional purposes. Judging from the experience of independent and charter schools, administrative structures are likely to flatten, and the amount of time adults spend in contact with students increases (see Nelson et al., 2000).

Allowing schools to choose whom to hire and, within wide boundaries, what to pay them. This allows schools to choose and reward adults according to their "fit" with the school's program, and to seek a productive mix of highly paid senior and less expensive junior teachers. It also allows schools to pay high salaries to individuals they consider indispensable and to keep good teachers and principals who might, under a district-controlled personnel system, be transferred involuntarily or "bumped" by those with seniority. This arrangement also enhances performance incentives by allowing schools to define and sustain coherent instructional programs in order to compete for students, while encouraging teachers to build reputations as productive team members.

These are the building blocks of a new governance system for public education. They imply sharp and inevitably wrenching changes in the ways school boards, superintendents, and school district central offices do business. They do not, however, require competencies beyond the reach of intelligent and well-educated people; small businesses, nonprofit organizations, and private and independent schools cope effectively under similar circumstances.

Combining the Building Blocks into New Governance Models

Every one of the building blocks described above is guaranteed to perturb someone—school board members, central office administrators, lay people who fear market-like mechanisms, or teachers who value civil service protection over opportunities for innovation and advancement. None of these building blocks is magic in itself, and every one of them can be implemented badly. However, if assembled into a well-balanced approach to governance, performance incentives, capacity investment, and school opportunities to change can compensate for one another's weaknesses as well as create new hopes for urban school performance. This section formulates some potential governance systems that combine the building blocks in different ways.

Table 2 summarizes three alternative governance systems. In the first, a CEO-style superintendent manages a portfolio of strong, distinctive schools. In the second, a superintendent and school board create a diverse system of public schools by entering into performance contracts with independent organizations—groups of teachers and parents, teacher cooperatives and unions, nonprofit human service organizations, colleges and universities, civic groups, and for-profit contractors. The third option attempts to make the educational resources of an entire urban community available for the education of the city's children. Each of these governance systems creates new combinations of strong incentives, serious investments in school capabilities, and real opportunities for change to allow schools to solve problems.

CEO-Strong Schools Governance

Under this approach to governance, the local superintendent would operate as the head of a decentralized enterprise. As the chief executive officer (CEO), the superintendent would recognize that the critical work of teaching is done at the school level, not in the central office or boardroom. His or her job would be to ensure that teachers and principals have every possible performance incentive, every resource, and every opportunity for flexibility that they need in order to serve students well. The superintendent's job, in short, is to make sure nothing inhibits school productivity. Though the superintendent has the authority to issue rules, or to require schools to hire particular people or use the services of the school system central office, the improvement of school productivity would be the only reason to impose these constraints.

The most important transactions between a CEO-superintendent and an individual school would occur around the school's annual performance agreement. This agreement, negotiated between school leadership and the CEO, would identify each school's instructional deficiencies and define concrete plans to improve instruction. It would also provide grants of authority to the school to spend money, and to train, hire, and fire adults in fulfillment of its instructional improvement plan. The CEO could also require, as a condition of approval of a school's plan, replacement of teachers and principals who had not acted as promised under previous school plans.

TABLE 2

ALTERNATIVE GOVERNANCE SYSTEMS

	Incentives	Investments in Capabilities	Opportunities for Schools to Change
CEO-Strong Schools	Superintendent uses state standards as the basis of yearly agreements regarding each school's strategy and performance; can reassign staff, open and close	Funds are set aside for investment in new methods, materials, and teacher training. Superintendent helps schools find the best providers of help.	Schools control improvement funds as long as they fulfill agreements with superintendent. School staffs can initiate staff transfers and choose new hires.
Diverse Providers	Every school works under a contract that specifies instructional approach and goals for students. Parents can choose schools. New contracts are established to replace failing schools.	District recruits and stimulates many independent sources of curricular advice, instructional materials, and teacher training. Schools choose the ones that meet their needs.	Schools control all funds, hire staff, and purchase their own advisors and providers of assistance. Teachers may unionize at the school level.
Community-Wide Options Strategy	One public coordinating board stimulates supply of schools, allocates funds on a per-pupil basis to any school a child attends, licenses public and private groups to operate and charter schools. Parents choose schools.	State and local public coordinating board invests in creation of diverse school providers; makes sure there are many independent sources of curricular advice, instructional materials, and teacher training. Schools choose the ones that meet their needs.	Money comes to schools on a per-pupil basis. Schools control all funds, hire staff, and purchase their own advisors and providers of assistance. Teachers may unionize at the school level.

Diverse Providers Governance

Diverse Providers Governance is a widely recognized option that has not been seriously implemented by any American city. It is briefly sketched here; many more thorough analyses of this proposal are available (see, for example, Brandl, 1998; Finn, Manno, & Vanourek, 1999; Hill, Pierce, & Guthrie, 1997).

Under this approach to governance, the local school board has but one job: to aggressively use its state-delegated power to provide public schools. While it could maintain some publicly managed schools, a local school board could also use contracts to support public schools run by independent providers. All schools, whether managed by the traditional school system or by independent contractors, would have similar performance agreements and freedom of action. The school board could not treat schools run by the traditional public school system any differently than it would treat schools administered by independent contractors. Schools would receive real-dollar funding on a per-pupil basis and could spend money at their own discretion, bounded only by their contractual commitments. School boards could hold back only small amounts of funds to support their oversight of individual schools. Thus, schools would control almost all public funds and would make their own capabilities investments and purchase their own advice and assistance. To prevent unwarranted subsidies to wealthy families, schools that accepted public funds would not be allowed to charge extra tuition.

Parents would choose schools, and schools would admit students via a publicly managed lottery in which every student who applied had an equal chance of acceptance. No student could be excluded, although schools could tell parents in advance what levels of student attendance, effort, and deportment were required. Schools would choose and pay for their own instructional methods, staffing patterns, and sources of help. They would also directly employ teachers, negotiating pay, benefits, and responsibilities.

The school board would be able—even obligated—to shift contracts from low-performing school providers to more promising ones, thereby providing strong incentives to promising new providers.

There are few, if any, real-world matches to the Diverse Providers Strategy. Small districts in Colorado, California, and Georgia are attempting to establish charters for all their schools. Chicago is experimenting with forms of contracting, as are Portland, Oregon and Wichita, Kansas. A new Pennsylvania law would permit contracting for many Philadelphia schools under some circumstances. However, it is not clear whether these districts will allow anyone other than their own employees to propose and operate charters, nor whether these charters will be real contracts between independent parties or simply agreements that the school board can amend unilaterally at any time. The Diverse Providers Strategy implies that individual schools will be regulated only through their contracts and will operate as independent entities. As Katrina Bulkley (2001) shows, few agreements between charter operators and their government sponsors are so clear, or give schools such freedom of action. Thus, despite the fact that the Diverse Providers Strategy is based on now-familiar ideas, it probably is not in operation anywhere.

Governance Via Open Community Partnerships

Governance via open community partnerships is based on a radical approach to improving the educational opportunities available in a community. It does not give any school board the exclusive right to provide schools in one geographic area, not does it respect the traditional boundaries between assets owned by the public school bureaucracy and those owned by other institutions, whether public or private. To the contrary, as the idea's originator, Lawrence Pierce, has argued to the author, the open partnerships governance approach implies a no-holds-barred attitude toward the question, "How can this community use all its assets to provide the best education for all our children?"

A new community authority—one with jurisdiction over an entire metropolitan area encompassing several school districts—would oversee the supply of educational opportunities for all children. This authority would license multiple entities to provide K-12 instruction anywhere in the metropolitan area. Providers could include existing public school systems, contractors of the kind described under Diverse Providers Governance, and unconventional providers such as colleges, universities, libraries, church-supported systems willing to operate under First Amendment constraints, and dispersed "cyber schools." The only schools excluded would be those that could not be licensed (due to unsafe conditions, neglect of basic skills instruction, or lack of capacity to manage money), that did not want to be considered part of a public system, or that would not accept the public per-pupil expenditure as full payment of tuition. Parents would have choices among all these opportunities.

The new community authority would control all funds for public education, social services, and recreation for children. It would write checks to schools based on their enrollments, weighted by the numbers of children from poor and minority families. It could enter master contracts with local public systems, but it would also be free to license other providers to serve children in the same areas. Public school boards would receive per-pupil amounts for all children served by their schools, possibly weighted for the added cost of serving low-income, non-English-speaking, or handicapped students. Public school boards could then run their own schools, or they could contract with independent providers to run them. Because their schools would compete with other schools run under very different auspices, public school boards would have strong incentives to eliminate unnecessary overhead costs and put as much money into the schools, and into instruction, as possible.

The new authority could retain a small amount of money to incubate new schools and to encourage development of new options for poorly served groups or neighborhoods. Public school boards would have to compete with one another and with other providers. With their broad portfolios of schools and economies of scale, they would presumably have an advantage over private providers when it came to meeting new needs.

Conclusion

How a community governs its schools is very important. Shifting oversight responsibility from one entity to another—for example, from elected school boards to mayors—shakes things up and offers the possibility that things will be done differently. But no entity is likely to run schools well unless its role is clearly defined and it has incentives to *support* schools, not control them.

These reform combinations are theoretical, but there are some real-world initiatives that incorporate some of their key features. All-charter school districts, which are beginning to emerge in the states of Pennsylvania, California, and Florida, have many of the features of the "diverse providers" model. Social welfare and health care systems across the country work in these ways, with public and private agencies offering government-funded services.

Today, the arrangements by which schools are governed cost too much, both financially and in terms of lost opportunities for effective schooling. Governance that diverts money and energy away from instruction also wastes the most important resource in public education: children's precious time. There is never a good reason to squander public money. But the stakes in education are far higher than mere money, and efforts to ensure detailed government control over the use of school money are, in the end, tragically wasteful. In big cities, the waste will continue as long as schools are dominated by politically-oriented decision making bodies, central management systems, and labor contracts, and as long as nontraditional but effective approaches to governance do not receive the attention they deserve.

References

Brandl, J. (1998). *Money and good intentions are not enough.* Washington, DC: Brookings Institution.

Bryk, A.S., & Schneider, B. (2002) *Trust in schools: A core resource for improvement.* New York: Russell Sage.

Bulkley, K. (2001, October 1). Educational performance and charter school authorizers: The accountability bind. *Education Policy Analysis Archives, 9*(37). Retrieved December 14, 2001 from http://epaa.asu.edu/epaa/v9n37.html

Bushweller, K. (1998). Under the shadow of the state: Do state takeovers work? *American School Board Journal, 185*(8), 16-19.

Chubb, J.E., & Moe, T.E. (1990). *Politics, markets, and America's schools.* Washington, DC: Brookings Institution.

Cistone, P.J. (1975). *Understanding school boards: Problems and prospects.* Lexington, MA: Lexington Books.

Coleman, J.S., Campbell, E.Q., Hobson, C.J., McPartland, J., Mood, A.M., Weinfeld, F.D., & York, R.L. (1966). *Equality of educational opportunity.* Washington, DC: National Center for Educational Statistics (DHEW).

Cuban, L. (2001). *Leadership for student learning: Urban school leadership—different in kind and degree.* Washington, DC: Institute for Educational Leadership.

Darling-Hammond, L., Ancess, J., MacGregor, K., & Zuckerman, D. (1994).*The Coalition Campus Project: Inching toward systemic reform in New York City.* Unpublished manuscript. Teachers College Columbia University.

Edmonds, R. (1979). Effective schools for the urban poor. *Educational Leadership, 37,* 15-18.

Education Intelligence Agency Report. (April 29, 2001).

Finn, C.E., Manno, B.V., & Vanourek, G. (1999). *Charter schools in action: Renewing public education.* Princeton, NJ: Princeton University Press.

Hannaway, J., & Sproull, J.S. (1978-79). Who's running the show? Coordination and control in educational organizations. *Administrators Notebook, 27*(9).

Hess, F. (1999). *Spinning wheels.* Washington, DC: Brookings Institution.

Hill, P.T., Campbell, C., & Harvey, J. (2000). *It takes a city: Getting serious about urban school reform.* Washington, DC: Brookings Institution.

Hill, P.T., & Celio, M.B. (1998). *Fixing urban schools.* Washington, DC: Brookings Institution.

Hill, P.T., Foster, G.E., & Gendler, T. (1990). *High schools with character.* Santa Monica, CA: Rand Corporation.

Hill, P.T., Lake, R., & Celio, M.B. (2001). *A study of charter school accountability.* Washington, DC: US Department of Education.

Hill, P.T., & Madey, D. (1983). *Education policymaking through the civil justice system.* Santa Monica, CA: Rand Corporation.

Hill, P.T., Pierce, L.C., & Guthrie, J.W. (1997). *Reinventing public education.* Chicago: University of Chicago Press.

Lockwood, A.T. (2001). *Charter districts—Much fuss, little gain.* Washington, DC: American Association of School Administrators.

McAdams, D. (2000). *Fighting to save our urban schools...and winning!* New York: Teachers College Press.

Moe, T.E. (1989). The politics of bureaucratic structure. In J.E. Chubb and P.E. Peterson (Eds.), *Can the government govern?* (pp. 267-329). Washington, DC: Brookings Institution.

Nelson, B., Berman, P., Ericson, J., Kamprath, N., Perry, R., Silverman, D., & Solomon, D. (2000). The state of charter schools, 2000. National Study of Charter Schools, Fourth-Year Report. Washington, DC: Office of Educational Research and Improvement.

CHAPTER 5

Rethinking the Finance System for Improved Student Achievement[1]

ALLAN ODDEN, SARAH ARCHIBALD AND MARK FERMANICH

Some version of standards-based education reform is likely to remain the focus of education policy for several more years, if not decades. By standards-based education reform, we mean a more general goal to have the education system—however financed and governed—educate more students to high achievement levels. This goal has equity and excellence elements, and is generally supported by education, political, civic, and business leaders around the country, if not the globe. Since the 1990s, standards-based education reform has been associated with a specific set of initiatives that include curriculum content and student performance standards, tests that measure how well students are learning that curriculum, and restructured finance and governance systems that make it more likely that the goal underlying these standards—teaching all students to high standards—is accomplished, or significant progress toward that goal is made. To be sure, the specific incarnations of these general postulates vary across the country, rhetoric often exceeds actual policy within and across states, and the education system is closer to what it has been in the past than to what a complete restructuring would look like.

Nevertheless, the education policy directions that originated in the mid-1980s seem to be gaining strength—witness the 2002 federal No Child Left Behind initiative. Most observers anticipate continued movement forward on these general education goals for many years to come. These policies have already begun changing the structure of educational finance and could well change educational governance.

Allan Odden is Professor of Educational Administration and Co-Director of the Consortium for Policy Research in Education at the University of Wisconsin–Madison. Sarah Archibald is an associate researcher of school finance for the Consortium for Policy Research in Education at the University of Wisconsin–Madison. Mark Fermanich is a doctoral student of Educational Administration at the University of Wisconsin–Madison.

Long focused on fiscal *equity*, school finance is shifting towards fiscal *adequacy*. This shift represents a fundamental change: it means that school finance, including teacher compensation, encompasses not only inputs but also education processes and results.

The shift of school finance from equity to adequacy is caused by both the substantive demands of standards-based education reform and changes in school finance litigation that rely more heavily on imputing substantive meaning to state education clauses. Under standards-based education reform, the benchmark test of school finance policy is whether it provides *adequate* revenues per pupil for districts and schools to employ strategies proven successful in educating students to high performance standards. Determining adequate revenue levels entails first identifying effective programs and then identifying the costs of those programs; translating those costs into appropriate school finance structures; and then ensuring that resources are used in districts and schools to produce the desired results. Implementing this school finance approach should also produce gains in fiscal equity, because in most states it requires a "leveling up" of low-spending districts. This new school finance focus was recommended by the recent report of the National Research Council's Committee on Education Finance Equity, Adequacy, and Productivity (Ladd & Hansen, 1999).

School finance litigation, which began with an equity focus, has also shifted from equity to adequacy (Minorini & Sugarman, 1999a, 1999b; Odden & Picus, 2000). Using an adequacy argument, the legal test, usually originating in the state education clause, begins with the question of whether a state's school finance system provides adequate revenues for the average school to teach the average student to state-determined performance standards. It goes on to ask whether adequate revenues are available for extra help to raise the performance of struggling and special needs students to the same standards. The legal problem is not whether district A has less or more than district B. Rather, the question is whether both districts—indeed all districts in the state—have adequate revenues for the programs and strategies needed to educate students to high achievement levels.

Drawing from how adequacy was being defined in school finance litigation (Clune, 1994, 1995a, 1995b, 1997; Minorini & Sugarman, 1999a, 1999b; Underwood, 1995a, 1995b) as well as from the finance implications of standards-based education reform (Odden, 1998a, 1998b, 1999a, 2000b; Odden & Picus, 2000), the shape of the new school finance seems to be as follows. First, allowing districts to select their own spending levels is no longer sufficient, because all districts and schools must spend at least at an adequate level. Thus, one structural implication of the new school finance is a foundation type of school finance funding formula. But the foundation expenditure level can no longer be minimal, as it has been in many states in the past. Rather, it must be "adequate," i.e., high enough to enable each district and each school to deploy a set of educational programs that are successful in educating students to the district's and state's student performance standards.

Once an adequate expenditure level has been determined and funded, the resources must then be managed at the district and school levels to produce expected results. Drawing on the experience of the private sector (Lawler, 1986; Lawler, Mohrman, & Benson, 2001), which beginning in the 1980s was under pressure to dramatically improve results, one management option to improve both program effectiveness and efficiency is decentralized or school-based management. Several studies in the early 1990s focused on how to design school-based management that would potentially support changes in curriculum and instruction to improve student learning (Beck & Murphy, 1996; Odden & Wohlstetter, 1995; Odden, Wohlstetter, & Odden, 1995; Wohlstetter, 1995; Wohlstetter, Mohrman, & Robertson, 1997; Wohlstetter, Van Kirk, Robertson, & Mohrman, 1997). But improving school effects can also be accomplished through improved centralized management (e.g., McAdams, 2000). Other governance and management strategies addressed in this volume might also be possible, including charter schools, vouchers, and related choice strategies (see Chubb & Moe, 1990 for an early explication of this argument). But whatever governance or management strategy is chosen, each requires that schools be resourced at an adequate level.

Thus, section one of this chapter describes four approaches to determining an adequate level of funding. It also addresses an important aspect of an adequately financed system: setting teacher salaries at a level where high-quality teachers can be recruited and retained. This is included to serve as an example of how the cost of one of the ingredients in a school, teacher salaries, should be considered in this new era of adequacy-based school finance. Section two addresses how districts (or states) could design needs-based, per-pupil funding formulas in order to provide each school building with a fair budget that is adequate for its students' needs (see, for example, Ross & Levacic, 1999).

Section three addresses effective resource use in an adequacy-based system of school finance. Once schools have adequate revenues, their challenge is to improve student achievement. Since many schools are not yet funded using an adequacy-based formula, accomplishing the goals of standards-based education reform is an even greater challenge. Even with adequate funding, these standards require schools to use resources more productively by reallocating resources to more effective education strategies. This section gives some examples of how schools have reallocated resources to improve student achievement (for an overview, see Odden & Archibald, 2001). It also introduces an expenditure structure that could be used by both researchers and practitioners to display school spending in a manner that represents the strategic allocation of resources to specific programs (Odden, Archibald, Fermanich, & Gross, 2002). If school finance systems are to change in ways that improve student achievement, thinking about resources as they relate to specific educational strategies is the next logical step in a progression that leads to schools where all students achieve at adequate levels.

In sum, whether managed within the current centralized or decentralized governance systems, or set free in a charter or voucher structure, schools must receive an adequate level of revenue. In addition, schools must select a cohesive school strategy powerful enough to educate students to high achievement standards. This educational strategy will need to be implemented by high-quality teachers who are paid sufficiently to enter and remain in education, and who receive appropriate ongoing training and professional development. The remainder of this chapter focuses on these finance topics that are endemic to all possible governance and management strategies.

Determining Adequacy

Designing an adequate school finance system requires three interrelated decisions: identifying an adequate expenditure level for the typical student in the typical district; ensuring that the foundation base has sufficient adjustments for student needs and price differentials; and making sure that the overall system supports teacher salary levels that are sufficient to recruit and retain the caliber of teacher needed to implement standards-based educational strategies in school sites.

Four methodologies are being developed and used to determine an adequate foundation expenditure level: (1) the successful district approach, (2) the cost function approach, (3) the professional consensus approach (initially called the resource cost model approach), and (4) the state-of-the-art approach (for longer discussions, see Guthrie & Rothstein, 1999; Odden & Picus, 2000).

Successful District Approach

The successful district approach, used in Ohio (Alexander, Augenblick, Driscoll, Guthrie, & Levin, 1995; Augenblick, 1997), Illinois (Augenblick, 2001; Hinrichs & Laine, 1996), and Maryland (Augenblick, 2001), identifies districts that have successfully taught their students to proficiency standards and sets the adequacy level at the weighted average of the expenditures of such districts. Usually, atypical districts—often the highest and lowest spending and highest and lowest income districts—are eliminated from the analysis. Atypical districts also frequently include big city districts. Consequently, the typical sample of districts in this analysis includes nonmetropolitan districts of average size and relatively homogeneous demographic characteristics, which generally spend below the state average. Critics of this approach argue that the adequate expenditure level typically identified is difficult to align with the fiscal adequacy needs of big city districts, even with adjustments for pupil needs and geographic price differentials. Nevertheless, it is one method being tried around the country.

Cost Function Approach

The second approach uses economic cost function analysis. This approach employs regression analysis with expenditure per pupil as the dependent variable, and student and district characteristics, along with performance levels desired, as the independent variables. The result produces an adequate expenditure per pupil for the average district, and then, for all other districts, adjusts that figure to account for differences in pupil need and education prices as well as diseconomies of both large and small size. The expenditure level is higher (lower) as the performance level is higher (lower). This analysis usually produces an adjustment for city districts of two to three times the average expenditure level; combined with the complex statistical analysis, this makes its use problematic in the real political context.

No state currently uses this approach to determine adequacy, though cost function research has been conducted for New York (Duncombe, Ruggiero, & Yinger, 1996), Wisconsin (Reschovsky & Imazeki, 1999), Texas (Imazeki & Reschovsky, 1999), and Illinois (Reschovsky & Imazeki, 2000). The Reschovsky and Imazeki cost function research found that the adequate expenditure levels in Wisconsin and Texas were close to the median spending levels in those states. The studies also indicated that there was substantial variation in the average adequacy level due to student and district needs, ranging from a low of 49% to a high of 460% of the average in Wisconsin, and a low of 75% to a high of 158%

of the average in Texas. In both states, the large urban districts had adequate expenditure figures at the highest levels.

Reschovsky and Imazeki (2001) produced an overall assessment of the utility of the cost function approach, arguing that it is the only approach, using data from all districts, that links a specific spending level to a specific performance level, and thus is the preferred approach in a standards-based environment. However, they did not note that the approach is limited by the strategies being used in extant management and governance systems, and does not capture efficiencies that could be produced by more dramatic reengineering or restructuring. Further, this system is so complicated that state policymakers avoid using it; too few legislators understand how it works. Last, the procedure produces cost figures at just the *district* level and has not been used to determine an adequate expenditure figure at the *school* level, which is what ultimately is needed.

These two different systems—the successful district approach and the cost function approach—produce widely varying estimates of an adequate expenditure level, suggesting that more research is needed to determine why these large differences emerge. Moreover, while both the successful district and the cost function approaches link spending levels to performance levels, which is what many policymakers want, neither indicates what educational strategies produce those performance levels. So at best, the approaches indicate what an adequate spending level might be at the district level, but not how those resources can be used at the school level to produce the desired results. The next two approaches address these issues.

Professional Consensus Approach

This approach, initially developed in the 1980s as the resource cost model (Chambers & Parrish, 1994), has been used most recently in Wyoming (Guthrie, et al., 1997). This approach assembles a group of educational experts and asks them to identify effective educational strategies for elementary, middle, and high schools and for special needs students, and then to specify the necessary ingredients for each, attach a price to each ingredient, and sum these up to obtain a total expenditure per pupil. The strategy can incorporate adjustments for both small and large schools, for a variety of special needs students, and for geographic price indices, to ensure that the adequate expenditure level is sufficient for each region and type of school in a state.

A major advantage of this approach is that it identifies in some detail what is required to produce student performance results. The disadvantage is that, other than the expert educational judgments offered, the strategies and ingredients have no clear link to actual performance levels. It is also the case that expert judgments vary both across states (compare, for example, Guthrie, et al., 1997 with Augenblick, 2001) and within states (compare Augenblick, 2001 with Management Analysis & Planning, 2001). This could confuse state policymakers rather than bolster their confidence in the adequate expenditure levels produced.

State-Of-The-Art Approach

The fourth major approach to determining an adequate expenditure level is to identify research-based state-of-the-art educational strategies, cost them out, and then aggregate them to identify adequate site, district, and state expenditure levels. This approach is more likely to identify educational strategies that produce desired results, so it also helps guide school sites in how to use dollars in the most effective ways. Initially, this strategy used the ingredients of a "high performance" school model (Stringfield, Ross, & Smith, 1996)—a schoolwide design crafted specifically to produce desired levels of student academic achievement—to determine an overall cost level; for example, "whole school" designs created by the New American Schools models (see Odden, 1997, and www.naschools.org). The costs of these models generally fell within the revenues available to the average elementary, middle, and high school in the country (Odden & Busch, 1998; Odden & Picus, 2000).

More recently, the state-of-the-art approach has merged research findings on effective educational practices with common features across several "comprehensive school designs," which themselves are compilations of research and best practice knowledge. This approach identifies a set of ingredients that are required to deliver a high-quality instructional program and determines an adequate expenditure level by placing a price on each ingredient and aggregating to a total cost (e.g., Odden, 2000a, 2001a, 2001d). It proceeds in the following way:

Research shows that high-quality preschool, particularly for students from lower income backgrounds, significantly affects future student academic achievement, as well as other desired social and community outcomes (Barnett, 1995, 1996, 2000; Karoly et al., 1998; Slavin, Karweit, & Wasik, 1994). Thus, the state school finance system should allow each district to provide preschool for at least every child aged 3-4 from a family with an income below something like 1.5 times the poverty level.

Research further shows that full-day kindergarten, particularly for students from low-income backgrounds, has significant positive effects on student learning in the early elementary grades (Slavin, Karweit, &

Wasik, 1994). Thus, the state school finance system should allow each district to count each kindergarten student as a full 1.0 student in the formula in order to provide a full-day kindergarten program.

Research on school size is clearer than research on class size, indicating that the optimum size for elementary schools is 300-600 students and the optimum size for secondary schools is 600-900 students (Lee & Smith, 1997; Raywid, 1997/1998). Thus, no elementary school unit should be larger than 500 students, and no secondary school unit should be larger than 1,000 students. Given the current stock of large school buildings, this means creating several independent "schools" within these larger buildings, each with a separate student body, separate principal, and separate entrance if possible (see also Murphy, Beck, Crawford, Hodges, & McGaughy, 2001). It also means an end to future construction of large school buildings. All subsequent cost figures are for a school unit of 500 students.

Research on class size shows that small classes of *15* (not 18, not 20, and not a class of 30 with an instructional aide or two teachers) in kindergarten through grade 3 have significant positive effects on student achievement in mathematics and reading (Achilles, 1999; Grissmer, 1999). The impact is larger for students from low-income and minority backgrounds. Thus, class sizes should be 15 in kindergarten through grade 3. This policy might arguably be limited to schools serving primarily lower income and minority students, but politically such a policy would be problematic. Class sizes in other grades should be no larger than an average of 25, which is about the national average and the size on which most comprehensive school reform models are based.

Teachers need some time during the regular school day for collaborative planning and ongoing curriculum development and review. Schools also need to teach art, music, library, and physical education. Providing each teacher one period a day for collaborative planning and curriculum development requires an additional 20% allocation of teachers necessary to maintain the above class sizes.

Every school should have a powerful and effective strategy for struggling students, i.e., students who must work harder and who need more time to achieve to proficiency levels. Such students generally include those from lower income backgrounds, those struggling to learn English, and those with learning and other mild disabilities. The most powerful and effective strategy is individual one-to-one tutoring provided by licensed teachers (Shanahan, 1998; Wasik & Slavin, 1993). The standard of many comprehensive school designs is a ratio of one fully licensed teacher-tutor for every 20% of students in poverty, with a minimum of one for every school. Thus, school units of 500 students should have from one to five teacher-tutors.

This allocation would cover the needs of students from low-income backgrounds, students whose native language is not English and are learning English, and students who are learning disabled. Schools should be free to use the resources for whatever strategy they select, but should be held accountable for having these students learn to proficiency levels. Students with more severe disabilities would need to be funded on a program and service basis. It might be most equitable for the extra costs of all low-incidence, high-cost, severely disabled students to be fully borne by the state.

Schools also need a student support and family outreach strategy. Various comprehensive school designs have suggested different ways to provide such a program strategy (for further discussion, see Brabeck, Walsh, & Latta, 2003). In terms of ingredients, the more disadvantaged the student body, the more comprehensive the strategy should be. The general standard is one licensed professional for every 20-25% of students from a low-income background, with a minimum of one for each school.

All school faculties need ongoing professional development. Research on the costs of effective professional development—professional development that produces change in classroom practice that leads to improved student achievement—and research on the costs of professional development to implement comprehensive school designs suggest that schools need at least $4,000 per teacher for ongoing professional development (Elmore, 2002; Miles, Odden, Archibald, Fermanich, & Gallagher, 2002; Odden, Archibald, Fermanich, & Gallagher, 2002). This would allow each school unit to have one full-time professional development coach/instructional facilitator on site and to provide for 100-200 hours of professional development per teacher each year.

Finally, over time, schools need to embed technology in their instructional program and school management strategies. Based on school designs that include such technology, the costs are about $125,000 for purchasing, updating, and maintaining hardware and software, which for at least the next decade should be viewed as an annual operating cost (Odden, 1997).

In sum, school units of 500 students would need the resources indicated in Table 1. The numbers need to be doubled for a secondary school with 1,000 students and prorated for schools with fewer students. Schools should not have fewer than 300 students, except in sparsely populated rural areas. The figures include full-day kindergarten. The resources shown below enable schools to deploy any of

TABLE 1

SCHOOL INGREDIENTS FOR THE STATE-OF-THE-ART APPROACH TO ADEQUACY

Elementary School Unit of 500 Students	Secondary School Unit of 500 Students
1 principal	1 principal
1 full-time instructional facilitator, coach	1 full-time instructional facilitator, coach
29 teachers; class size of 15 in K-3, otherwise 25	20 teachers; class sizes of 25
6 art, music, physical education, library, etc. teachers	4 art, music, physical education, library, etc. teachers
1-5 teacher-tutors; 1 for each 20% students from low-income background, with a minimum of 1	1-5 teacher-tutors; 1 for each 20% students from low-income background, with a minimum of 1
1-5 positions for student/family support; 1 for each 20-25% students from low-income background, with a minimum of 1	1-5 positions for student/family support; 1 for each 20-25% students from low-income background, with a minimum of 1
$70,000 for professional development	$70,000 for professional development
$125,000 for computer technologies	$125,000 for computer technologies
Secretarial support, lunch and food service support, and operations and maintenance	Secretarial support, lunch and food service support, and operations and maintenance

the more than a dozen comprehensive school reform strategies currently in use (Erlichson, Goertz, & Turnbull, 1999; Odden, 2000a).

Only preschool for children aged 3 and 4 from lower income backgrounds is missing in the resource structure shown above. The easiest way to add preschool would be to allow each district to count each 3- and 4-year-old in determining the number of students in the district for state aid purposes. Preschool teachers would then need to be paid according to the district's salary structure. It would be wise, however, to encourage neighborhood institutions to provide preschool programs, including not only the public schools (if there is space), but also other community institutions, such as churches, where many Head Start programs are already housed.

Note that there are no instructional aides in the above model, mainly because comprehensive school designs do not include instructional aides and also because research generally shows that they do not add value (Achilles, 1999; Gerber, Finn, Achilles, & Boyd-Zaharias, 2001).

It would be fairly easy to compare the staffing in any district's schools with the above numbers. Differences would indicate whether the state and district systems were adequate, at least in terms of numbers (see also Odden & Picus, 2001).

New Jersey has attempted to settle its 25-year-old school finance case, *Abbott v. Burke,* by using this state-of-the-art approach to determine fiscal adequacy, or in the New Jersey context, a "thorough and efficient" funding level. After a series of hearings in 1997, a remand court concluded that the schools covered under the New Jersey Supreme Court mandate overturning the finance system had, by 1998, been given sufficient resources to finance the most expensive school design, Roots and Wings (Odden, 1998c). Moreover, the level of funds provided—approximately $9,000 per child, plus state and federal categorical program dollars—was sufficient to fund an enhanced version of that school design, which included smaller class sizes, more professional development, more tutors, a full family-social services support team, and ample computer technologies. The court required the state to continue providing that level of funding and mandated that schools adopt and implement a research-based design and fund it through resource reallocation (see section below on reallocation). It is likely that such an approach will be part of North Carolina's *Leandro* adequacy case (*Leandro v. State*, 1997) and will emerge in other school finance cases as well.

Research on the implementation of the most recent New Jersey court decree (Erlichson & Goertz, 2001; Erlichson, Goertz, & Turnbull, 1999) shows that such implementation is difficult. Many schools expected more dollars as a result of the court case and were reluctant to sunset old education strategies and adopt new ones through substantial resource reallocation. Researchers also documented insufficient training and the need for more management expertise to help orchestrate the process at both the district and state level.

The move from fiscal equity to adequacy in school finance is a momentous one. It has numerous facets and affects various aspects of school finance; many of these are being researched as this chapter is being written. At this point, researchers know a fair amount about how teachers should be paid in this era of adequacy-based school finance. The next section explains how compensation can be handled in a manner that satisfies the demands of an adequacy-based system.

Paying Teachers Fairly Within the Context
of an Adequate School Finance System

The last step in both the professional consensus and the state-of-the-art approaches to determining adequacy is appropriately pricing all ingredients. This includes setting teacher salaries. At this step, both procedures often use a statewide average teacher salary, which significantly mis-specifies what districts need to pay for quality teacher talent. Adjusting the statewide average by the geographic cost of education index developed by the National Center for Education Statistics (Fowler &

Monk, 2001), which generally shows, for a given set of teacher qualities, the variation districts need to pay for teacher quality, is an improvement over using just the statewide average. These cost indices usually show that big city districts need to spend 20-30% more than other districts to recruit a comparable level of teacher quality. Imazeki (2000) also found this wage premium in a recent study of Wisconsin districts, concluding that Milwaukee would need to pay teachers 30% more than its surrounding suburbs in order to recruit and retain the same level of teacher talent.

A second and more comprehensive strategy would be to determine salary benchmarks by labor market regions in a state. This approach would identify not only the salary benchmark for beginning teachers, but also benchmarks for mid-career and top-career teacher salaries. Benchmarks should be developed through comparisons with both the education and the non-education private sector labor market, which increasingly is recruiting education talent. At some point the education system will need to recognize that all teachers do not compete in the same labor markets, and that schools may have to pay higher salaries for mathematics, science, and other teachers with sought-after specialties or lose their ability to retain high-quality individuals in these subject-matter areas (Goldhaber, 2001; Milanowski, 2002; Murnane, 1996).

In addition, the current teacher salary structure, which provides salary increases on the basis of years of experience (steps) and education units/degrees (columns), is ineffective in recruiting and paying high-quality teachers (Ballou & Podgursky, 1997; Odden & Kelley, 2002). Several researchers (Goldhaber, 2001; Kelley, 1997; Mohrman, Mohrman, & Odden, 1996; Murnane, 1996; Odden & Kelly, 1997) argue that the single salary schedule is no longer aligned with the goals and strategies of standards-based education reform and does not pay for teacher qualities that are linked to teacher effectiveness. By contrast, knowledge and skills-based pay (KSBP) programs can reward teachers for acquiring and deploying the knowledge and the skills needed to successfully teach a standards-based curriculum (Odden, 2000c, 2001c).[2]

Knowledge and skills-based salary schedules would link teacher pay levels to teacher knowledge, skills, classroom performance, and effectiveness in the classroom. If instructional practice—teacher clinical expertise—were the basis of key salary increases, instead of years of experience and education units, the salary structure would link salary hikes to enhanced classroom effectiveness. Indeed, preliminary evidence of the knowledge and skills-based teacher salary schedules in Cincinnati and the Vaughn Charter school indicate that the higher the teacher evaluation score, which indicates instructional expertise, the greater value-added student learning produced in the individual teacher's classroom (Gallagher, 2002b; Holtzapple, 2002). In addition, Wayne and Youngs (under review), Goldhaber (2001) and Murnane (1996) conclude that additional salary differentials should be provided for teachers with majors or master's degrees in mathematics or science, with higher SAT scores and grade point averages, and with degrees from higher quality colleges and universities, as these qualities are linked to improved student learning.

Linking teacher compensation levels to school finance formulas. There are several recent examples of states specifically linking teacher pay to state school finance policies. In 2001, Iowa enacted legislation to create a statewide approach to knowledge and skills-based pay for teachers. The goal of this legislation was to use the structure to raise teacher salaries by $5,000-$6,000. Arizona approved a tax increase referendum in November 2000 that dedicated a portion of a sales tax increase to districts implementing pay-for-performance salary structures (Heneman & White, 2002). Florida districts are under a legislative mandate to allocate some portion of pay on a performance basis. Finally, Minnesota is piloting several models across the state, and several other states have considered proposals to adopt similar approaches to the structure of teacher pay.

One major question is how a state would finance such a statewide approach to teacher salaries. One option would be to have minimum salary figures attached to each level of teacher performance, as well as minimum differentials for mathematics and science degrees and college quality. All salary figures should be benchmarked to a level that allows districts, regions, and the state to compete in the education and broader labor market for necessary teacher talent. The foundation expenditure level in the school finance formula, then, needs to be calibrated so that the average district, with the average staffing level, would be able to pay those minimum but benchmarked salary levels. This would make both the structure of teacher pay more appropriate and the level of teacher pay adequate. In this way, the finance structure promotes adequacy as well as an element of equity: teacher salary levels high enough to allow all districts and schools to recruit and retain the quality of teachers they need.

Summary

School finance system designers need additional research to identify adequate expenditure levels that include adequate teacher salary levels. Each methodology discussed above illustrates the strengths and weaknesses of determining levels of adequate funding, and none has been perfected. But at their core, these new approaches to school finance seek to link spending levels with student achievement results, a necessary objective for a school finance system that would be adequate for standards-based education reform. Further, they all could be used to identify an adequate expenditure level regardless of how the education system is governed and managed. Under all governance systems, schools need an adequate level of resources in order to accomplish their primary task—educating their students to appropriate performance standards.

Needs-Based Formula Funding of Schools

If we assume that an adequate expenditure level is determined at the district level, the next step in designing the new school finance system is allocating to each school site an adequate level of funding. This level must cover the costs of effective programs and the various special needs of its student body.

Why school-level formula funding? There are several important policy reasons. First, the underlying principle of standards-based reform involves establishing academic performance standards at the state or district level and then holding *schools* accountable for achieving them (Fuhrman, 1999; Fuhrman & Elmore, in press). However, if schools are to be held accountable, they must also be given the tools to accomplish their task. Research in both the business and education sectors has shown that one critical tool is decision making power over the budget (Lawler, 1986; Wohlstetter, Van Kirk, Robertson, & Mohrman, 1997). In other words, without authority over how to deploy their own resources, schools cannot make the necessary changes in curriculum, instruction, and school organization that lead to significant gains in student achievement. Schools that receive *dollars* rather than objects (e.g., staff, computers, or textbooks) gain much of the flexibility necessary to reallocate resources according to their needs and priorities.

This thinking is reflected in the increasing number of large urban districts in the U.S. and Canada that have adopted needs-based school funding formulas (for examples, see Odden, 1999b). As state and local accountability systems exerted increasing pressure on urban schools to radically improve student outcomes, these districts abandoned incremental strategies in favor of large-scale reform efforts that included the restructuring of their management and finance systems. Districts also implemented formula funding of their schools in an attempt to increase operational efficiencies (for a description of the school funding formulas in five North American urban districts, see Odden, 1999b and Ross & Levacic, 1999). Even districts like Houston, which began reform efforts with a more district-directed approach, eventually provided schools with budget authority via a needs-based funding formula.

Second, although school finance equity and adequacy are commonly the subject of state policy debates and court actions at the district level, researchers and policymakers are just beginning to address these issues from an intradistrict perspective (Busch & Odden, 1997; Goertz & Stiefel, 1998; Hertert, 1995; Odden & Picus, 2000). The funding of schools within districts may vary significantly, particularly when the value of teachers' salaries is taken into consideration. Often these differences among schools may not be obvious, having been established by historical precedent, cronyism, or the preferences of district administrators (Ross & Levacic, 1999). A well-designed needs-based formula can make school funding much more transparent. Formula funding establishes a clear link between a school's student characteristics and the amount of funding the school receives. Both school staffs and the public can better understand the rationale for funding decisions and even participate in the formula design process through school formula review committees.

Finally, a needs-based school funding formula, particularly one that is student-based, facilitates the operation of school choice programs (Odden, 1999b; Odden & Busch, 1998). Whether a school choice program takes the form of public school choice, charter schools, or vouchers, needs-based formula funding provides a straightforward method for financing individual schools as students move from one school to another; the amount of revenue generated by a particular student under a school funding formula follows that student to whichever school he or she attends. Houston's per-pupil school-site funding formula is used for its district-operated schools as well as its charter schools. The funding system in the two types of schools is the same, even though operating responsibility differs.

The following section provides an overview of how a district may go about designing a needs-based funding formula for its schools.

Designing a Needs-Based School Funding Formula

The first step a district must undertake when developing a needs-based school funding formula is to determine which functions should be provided by the district, which by the site, and which by either level, depending on the context. This analytic procedure identifies the "pot" of dollars a district can budget to its schools through a needs-based formula. Odden and Busch (1998) conducted this functional analysis for a typical state, and suggest quite strongly that each state, as England has done, should create an overall school-based budgeting framework that includes a functional allocation to guide districts in the processes of decentralizing their finances to school sites. Odden and Picus (2000) make the same suggestion but propose a simplified framework.

Drawing on the site-based funding formulas being used in several districts, Odden (1999b; see also Ross & Levacic, 1999) and Odden and Goertz (1999) show that once the amount or "pot" of dollars budgeted to school sites has been determined, the formulas for allocating funds have five general elements: (1) a base allocation for the "norm" student; (2) adjustments for grade-level differences; (3) enhancements for curriculum purposes; (4) adjustments for different student needs, and (5) adjustments for different and unique school needs.

Overall, these elements mirror the general categories of state-to-district funding formulas. Districts using such systems in the United States, as well as most systems in other countries, used all of these elements (Ross & Levacic, 1999). Such formulas address not only core educational needs but also additional educational needs related to curriculum, students, and the particular site.

Odden (2000a) identified another approach that represents a hybrid between current strategies and the above school-based funding method and draws from the ingredients in Table 1. Such an approach provides schools with the following for each group of 500 students:

- 1 principal
- 1-2 instructional facilitators, plus $50,000 for professional development
- 20 regular classroom teachers for a class size of 25, or in elementary schools, 29 teacher positions so that the maximum kindergarten through grade 3 class size is 15
- 4 more teachers for planning and preparation time
- a strategy for struggling students, such as a base of one reading tutor plus $1,000 for each child from a low-income family to hire additional tutors (from a combination of any state compensatory education money and federal Title I dollars)
- 1-4 positions for parent outreach/student support
- $125,000 for computer technologies
- an appropriate amount for supplies, materials, etc.

• funding for the school's mildly disabled and English-language learning students.

This represents a budget level that falls within the current resources now provided to the national average elementary, middle, and high school, and it provides resources sufficient to fund the most expensive comprehensive school strategies (Odden, 2000a; Odden & Picus, 2000).

Summary

Needs-based formula funding of schools is a valuable strategy for addressing the important educational policy goals of ensuring intradistrict and cross-school fiscal equity and adequacy, radically increasing school productivity, and facilitating school choice options, whether they take the form of intra- or extra-district choice, broader public school choice, or vouchers. Although a number of districts throughout the U.S. and Canada, particularly large urban districts (e.g., Cincinnati, Houston, San Francisco, Seattle, and Washington, D.C.), have implemented formula funding of their schools following the general outline above, the strategy has yet to be implemented more broadly on a statewide basis.

Once provided adequate funding, the financial task for school buildings is to use these dollars in the most effective ways to educate their students to rigorous performance standards. The next section addresses critical issues of resource use—how resources have been used in the past, and how some schools, using the funds generated by lump-sum financing via a needs-based formula, have reallocated resources to boost student performance. The next section also introduces the expenditure structure mentioned in the introduction, a useful tool for arraying school budget data that more clearly illustrates how resources are tied to specific educational strategies.

Effective Resource Use

A series of empirical studies conducted with national, state, district, and school databases in the first part of the 1990s found that across states and districts with widely varying characteristics and spending levels, functional resource use patterns were quite consistent (Monk, Roelke, & Brent, 1996; Odden, Monk, Nakib, & Picus, 1995; Picus & Fizal, 1995; Picus, Tetrealt, & Murphy, 1996; Picus & Wattenberger, 1995). Though there was some variation, in general 60% was spent on instruction, about 10% on instructional and student support, about 8-10% on administration (with the bulk of administrative costs at the site and not central office level), about 10% on operation and maintenance, about 5% on transportation, and about 5-7% on debt service, food and miscellaneous.

The studies seemed to show that expenditure patterns—the uses of the education dollar—had not changed much over time. The functional uses of education dollars at the end of the century were quite close to what they were at the middle of the century. Remarkably, spending functions remained relatively consistent despite large real (inflation adjusted) increases in education dollars per pupil, dramatic changes in student sociodemographic characteristics, and the proliferation of categorical programs focused on a variety of special needs students (Odden & Picus, 2000).

However, changes did occur over several decades within the category of instruction. With the passage of legislation in the 1960s and 1970s targeted to special needs students, many schools accumulated additional funds from federal and state categorical programs. Because federal and state agencies intended these funds to supplement rather than supplant regular education dollars, most schools used these resources to hire specialists to work with special needs students outside the regular classroom. Because these funds came from different sources and at different times, schools often added on programs over the years without conducting a thorough assessment of how those programs fit into the school's overall educational strategy.

As a result, schools spent a growing proportion of education dollars outside of the regular education classroom—ostensibly to help students with special needs—but with little evidence that this goal was actually being accomplished (Borman & D'Agostino, 2001; Odden, 1991). As it became clearer that these strategies were not working, many schools began to think about how resources could be better used and engaged in a resource reallocation process, thus foreshadowing the key site role in the new school finance—using adequate resources to meet rigorous district and state student performance goals.

Reallocating School Resources

Once a school receives adequate resources by one of the methods described above in the needs-based formula funding section, part of the process of rethinking school finance to improve student achievement—how to use resources in the most effective manner—must occur at the school site. Whether the impetus to improve student performance emanates from the state, district, or site, having control over a substantial part of their budget enables sites to match resources with new strategies designed to bolster performance. Odden and Archibald (2001) studied several schools that engaged in restructuring and resource real-location processes and found that most went through some version of the following four steps:

First, school leaders (sometimes at the urging of district officials, sometimes on their own) reached the conclusion that their current strategies were not only insufficient for accomplishing earlier goals but also inadequate to accomplish new goals, particularly the goal of educating students with special needs to high standards.

Next, school leaders engaged in an analysis of their actual student achievement data, demographic data, and educational situation. Often, data were collected from teacher, student, and parent surveys and from weekend retreats with parents. The combination of the analysis of test score data, student characteristics, and the surveys and retreats tended to result in joint faculty and parent understanding of the condition of the school. It also helped achieve teacher "ownership" of the identified problems, along with agreement regarding the key needs of the school.

Once key school needs were identified, the next step was to locate new strategies that fit the school's needs, whether through an examination of the research literature or through exploration of other mechanisms for identifying best practices (e.g., a comprehensive school design marketing fair). In some cases this meant adopting a class size policy of 15 or lower in grades K-3 (Grissmer, 1999); in some cases it meant adopting a comprehensive school design like Success For All (Slavin & Madden, 2001); and in some cases it meant designing an original "homegrown" educational strategy. In almost all cases, the new educational strategy was significantly different from the school's previous strategy (which often predated many of the current staff). Because faculty conducted the search and adoption process, strong faculty commitment was engendered; school leaders believed that the new strategy would allow them to boost student performance, including the performance of special needs students.

School staff then began the program restructuring and resource reallocation processes, which often took 2-3 years to complete. First, school leaders identified what resources the new strategy required, as well as which existing resources could be reallocated. Since reallocation often entailed eliminating certain staff positions and creating others, sometimes "cashing out" staff positions for professional development contracts, schools had to phase in the new program and reallocate resources as personnel changes could be made. In some cases, administrators shifted staff to new roles, but in many cases they released staff and replaced them. The new educational strategy "drove" the resource reallocation process, by identifying new types of staff who were needed and, by implication, identifying obsolete positions in the school.

During the process of resource reallocation, moreover, each school encountered various problems—regulatory constraints, personal connections to individuals whose jobs were eliminated, appeals to local teacher unions to block the changes, etc. In each instance, faculties overcame the problems because of the ownership of the schools' performance problems that emerged from the needs assessments and because of faculty commitment to the new educational strategies. Rather than barriers to progress, glitches became something that joint faculty action overcame in order for the faculty as a whole to realize the new educational vision for the school.

Schools most often reallocated categorical dollars from state and federal programs for students from low-income backgrounds, students with mild disabilities, and students whose native language is not English. But they also reallocated many other staff resources. Schools replaced many instructional aides with licensed teachers who either taught a smaller class of students or provided tutoring for struggling students. In the process, Special Education teachers and administrators revised Individual Education Programs (IEPs) for disabled students to reflect the new service strategy.

After the reallocation process, schools in the study maintained or increased the number of regular teachers; the latter occurred when the schools chose lower class size all day as their primary new educational strategy. Art, music, and physical education teachers remained, thus retaining planning and preparation time. Specialist teachers and instructional aides working in resource rooms were usually eliminated or dramatically reduced, and the funds were used for training the entire faculty in better instructional skills and for more powerful interventions, such as individual tutoring, to help students master the regular curriculum. Assistant principals, usually found only in larger schools, were often eliminated as schools divided themselves into smaller, relatively independent units of no more than 500 students, each headed by 1-2 instructional facilitators who provided ongoing training and coaching for these schools within schools. Finally, the professional development pot was enlarged to engage outside expert trainers, often individuals associated with the comprehensive school design adopted. In general, schools made only small changes with classified staff, and similar numbers of student support staff usually remained, though they were reorganized into more cohesive teams.

These changes represented a shift from specialist to generalist teachers and increased resources spent on professional development and training. This shift was the strongest for schools that reduced class sizes to 15 for the entire day (see, for example, Odden & Archibald, 2001).

When this resource reallocation research was conducted, no single report or framework was available that could be used to array the schools' expenditure data in a way that also provided some insight into the allocation of resources to specific strategies. Because characterizing resource reallocation entails tracking the changes in spending that are linked to changes in the instructional program and organization of the school, such a structure would facilitate before and after comparisons of resource use. The next section introduces just such a structure.

School Expenditure Structure

Odden, Archibald, Fermanich, and Gross (2002) developed a school expenditure structure that provides a comprehensive list of resources in a school and reflects the major features of the school's educational strategy. This expenditure structure is specifically designed to report school-level expenditures. It is useful for arraying school expenditures for a single school for a single year, for comparing two schools in the same year, and for arraying before and after comparisons of resource use in the same school. It is also useful for arraying the expenditures of multiple educational units within a single school building to reflect "schools within schools" organizational structures. Finally, it categorizes expenditures by expenditure elements that reflect current thinking about effective instructional strategies and resource deployment.

The expenditure structure provides two distinct yet related sets of information about school resources and strategies. The combined reporting format is summarized in Table 2. The first part is a set of resource indicators that provide context and insight into school instructional priorities and strategies, such as use of time in the school day. The second, the expenditure structure itself, classifies school expenditure data according to nine expenditure elements, which are described in more detail below.

The nine expenditure elements are broadly categorized as either instructional or non-instructional in nature. The seven instructional elements are:

1. *Core academic teachers.* The licensed classroom teachers primarily responsible for teaching a school's core academic subjects of reading/English/language arts, mathematics, science, and history/social

TABLE 2

SCHOOL EXPENDITURE STRUCTURE AND RESOURCE INDICATORS

School Resource Indicators	
School building size School unit size Low-income concentration Percent ESL/LEP Percent special education Expenditures per pupil Professional development expenditures per teacher Special academic focus of school/unit Length of instructional day	Length of class periods Length of reading class (elementary) Length of mathematics class (elementary) Reading class size (elementary) Mathematics class size (elementary) Regular class size (elementary) Length of core* class periods (secondary) Core class size (secondary) Non-core class size (secondary) Percent core teachers
	*Math, English/LA, science, & social studies

School Expenditure Structure	

Instructional	1. Core academic teachers
	  -English/ reading/ language arts
	  -History/ social studies
	  -Math
	  -Science
	2. Specialist and elective teachers/Planning and preparation
	  -Art, music, physical education, etc.
	  -Academic focus with or without special funding
	  -Vocational
	  -Drivers education
	  -Librarians
	3. Extra help
	  -Tutors
	  -Extra help laboratories
	  -Resource rooms (Title I, special education or other part-day pull-out
	    programs)
	  -Inclusion teachers
	  -English as a second language classes
	  -Special education self-contained classes for severely disabled students
	    (including aides)
	  -Extended day and summer school
	  -District-initiated alternative programs
	4. Professional development
	  -Teacher time—Substitutes and stipends
	  -Trainers and coaches
	  -Administration
	  -Materials, equipment and facilities
	  -Travel & transportation
	  -Tuition and conference fees
	5. Other non-classroom instructional staff
	  -Coordinators and teachers on special assignment
	  -Building substitutes and other substitutes
	  -Instructional aides
	6. Instructional materials and equipment
	  -Supplies, materials and equipment
	  -Computers (hardware, software, peripherals)
	7. Student support
	  -Counselors
	  -Nurses
	  -Psychologists
	  -Social workers
	  -Extra-curricular and athletics

Non-Instructional	8. Administration
	
	9. Operations and maintenance
	  -Custodial
	  -Utilities
	  -Security
	  -Food Service

Reprinted with permission from the *Journal of Education Finance.*

studies. In elementary schools, core academic teachers would consist of the teachers in the self-contained regular education classrooms.

2. *Specialist and elective teachers.* This element consists of licensed teachers who teach non-core academic classes and usually provide planning and preparation time for core academic teachers. It includes art, music, and physical education teachers as well as teachers of other subjects outside the core defined above (e.g., foreign language, vocational education, etc.).

3. *Extra help.* This category consists mainly of licensed teachers representing a wide variety of strategies designed to assist struggling students, or students with special needs, to learn a school's regular curriculum. They include tutors and other teachers who work in extra help labs and resource rooms, some of whom serve Title I, ESL, and special education students (except the severely disabled).

4. *Professional development.* This element includes spending on the professional development of a school's staff. The expenditures included are the same ones collected in the professional development cost structure proposed by Odden, Archibald, Fermanich, and Gallagher (2002): the costs of teacher time for professional development; trainers and coaches; professional development administration; materials, equipment, and facilities; travel and transportation; and tuition and conference fees. Research using this cost structure identified levels of professional development spending that exceeded even the most optimistic assumptions, and suggested that in many places, it was not the level of professional development dollars that was the problem, but the use of those substantial dollars (for more detail, see Archibald & Gallagher, 2002; Fermanich, 2002; Gallagher, 2002a).

5. *Other non-classroom instructional staff.* Included here are licensed and non-licensed instructional staff who support a school's instructional program, such as curriculum and technology coordinators, substitutes, and instructional aides other than those working in self-contained special education classrooms.

6. *Instructional materials and equipment.* This category includes books, instructional supplies, materials, equipment, and computer hardware and software for all instructional programs.

7. *Student support.* This element consists of school-based student support staff such as counselors, nurses, social workers, psychologists, and parent liaisons, as well as school expenditures for extracurricular activities and athletic programs.

The final two non-instructional expenditure elements are:

8. *Administration.* This element consists of all expenditures pertaining to the administration of a school, including the principal, assistant principal(s), clerical staff, administrative office supplies, equipment and technology, and school reserve funds.

9. *Operations and maintenance.* This expenditure element includes the costs of staff, supplies, and equipment for custodial services, food services, and security, as well as utilities and building and grounds maintenance charged to a school.

As previously mentioned, the expenditure structure presented here can be determined for each unit of a school where a schools-within-schools strategy is employed, as well as for schoolwide programs or for a school in its entirety. To see an illustration of how the expenditure structure arrays data from different schools, one a traditional high school and the other a high school with a schools-within-schools organizational structure, see Tables 3 and 4 below.

TABLE 3

EXPENDITURE STRUCTURE OF A TRADITIONAL COMPREHENSIVE HIGH SCHOOL

Components	FTE	Dollars
Core academic teachers	66.4	$1,280,007
Specialists and electives	38.2	$2,417,895
Extra help total	29.0	$1,650,751
Tutoring	0	0
Extra help labs	0	0
Resource room	10.2	$639,275
Extended day/Summer school	0	0
ESL/Bilingual	4.8	$300,835
Special ed inclusion	1.4	$87,744
Special education self-contained classes	9.0	$397,271
District alternative program	3.6	$225,626
Professional development	0	$14,684
Other non-classroom instructional staff	25.2	$822,251
Instructional materials and equipment	–	$173,322
Student support	12.5	$1,028,620
Administration staff and supplies	18.5	$1,280,008
Operations and maintenance	20.7	$1,221,670

The instructionally relevant categories of this expenditure structure make it useful for analyzing the distribution of spending within the school. Furthermore, when the expenditure structure is used to represent subunits, as in Table 4, the expenditure structure indicates the extent to which these schools operate as separate units.

TABLE 4
Expenditure Structure for a Schools-Within-Schools Design

Components	Math and Science 372 students		Communications 240 students		Health Fields 216 students		Humanities 392 students		Technology 232 students		Schoolwide		Total
	FTE	Dollars	FTE	Dollars	FTE	Dollars	FTE	Dollars	FTE	Dollars	FTE	Dollars	
Core academic teachers	24.6	$1,721,557	12	$839,784	12	$839,784	23	$1,609,586	12	$839,784			$5,850,495
Specialists and electives	0	0	2	$139,964	2	$139,964	0	0	2	$139,964	18.3	$1,282,770	$1,702,662
Extra help total	0	0	0	0	0	0	0	0	0	0	29	$1,410,362	$1,410,362
Tutoring											0	0	
Extra help labs											0	0	
Resource room											6	$419,892	
Extended day/Summer school											0	0	
ESL/Bilingual											0	0	
Special ed, inclusion											6	$419,892	
Special ed, self contained											17	$570,578	
District alternative program											0	0	
Professional development	1	$74,982	1	$74,982	1	$74,982	1	$74,982	1	$74,982	0	$236,996	$611,906
Other non-classroom instructional staff	0	$8,000	0	$3,500	0	$3,500	0	$8,000	0	$3,500	5	$91,945	$118,445
Instructional materials and equipment	–	$27,500	–	$21,141	–	$21,000	–	$31,000	–	$25,000	–	$171,270	$296,912
Student support	0	0	0	0	0	0	0	0	0	0	3.2	$241,146	$241,146
Administration staff and supplies	0	$2,500	0	$1,000	0	$1,485	0	$3,000	0	$1,000	10.3	$446,210	$455,194
Operations and maintenance	0	0	0	0	0	0	0	0	0	0	16.7	$847,979	$847,978

SUMMARY

Although resources spent on instruction have remained the same proportion of school budgets—about 60%—for years, changes within the instructional budget of schools reflect important changes in instructional strategies and resource use over the past several decades. The trend for many years was to hire specialist teachers to work outside the regular education classroom, often funded by categorical programs such as Title I, ESL, and special education programs.

More recently, schools and districts disappointed with low levels of student achievement and spurred by the demands of standards-based education reform have begun to engage in a resource reallocation process. This process is characterized by the adoption of more powerful educational strategies, the elimination of remedial positions outside regular education classrooms, and the use of these newly available resources to hire more regular classroom teachers, provide individual tutoring for struggling students, and strengthen systemic professional development.

These program restructuring and resource reallocation initiatives reflect key new site roles under an adequacy-calculated, school-based financing system designed to provide a stronger fiscal foundation for the education system. Further, tracking such strategic changes in the allocation of resources is facilitated by a new school expenditure structure presented in this section, which suggests the type of modifications needed in fiscal reporting structures so that school-based resource use patterns can be identified and analyzed for effectiveness.

In particular, the addition of the professional development expenditure category reflects the critical importance of teacher capacity development to standards-based education reform (see, for example, Elmore, 2002). In order to teach students to higher standards, teachers need more expertise, and high-quality professional development experiences are the best way for practicing teachers to obtain the necessary knowledge and skills. But current fiscal reporting systems ignore this important need. By adding this expenditure element to new fiscal reporting systems and by specifying how such expenditures are to be identified, the current substantial but ineffective professional development expenditures will be highlighted, and more effective professional resource uses can be identified.

Conclusion

School finance issues and structures are changing, largely in response to the more rigorous demands of state education systems. Today, school finance must provide districts and sites with adequate education dollars so that education leaders can dedicate resources to more powerful education strategies that produce higher levels of student academic performance. In general terms, the key role for the state is to determine an adequate level of education spending for each of its school districts. Districts must then allocate these dollars to schools via a needs-based per-pupil formula that ensures that each school has adequate dollars for meeting the needs of each of its students. This system should be used for schools operating in all forms of governance systems, including district-operated schools, charter schools, and even voucher schools. Furthermore, each school supported by public funds should be held to the same student performance standards, and will thus need a level of resources that is adequate for it to produce those results.

Once adequately funded, school sites need to deploy their dollars to educational strategies that produce the educational results that are expected. The expenditure structure presented in this chapter is an effort to facilitate progress toward that goal. Arraying school-level resources in a manner that represents their strategic allocation to various programs will help both practitioners and researchers learn about and focus on those strategies that yield the highest levels of student performance. Similarly, taking a comprehensive look at what is spent on professional development at the school level will help researchers and practitioners learn which professional development programs are most effective when the expenditure data are compared with data on student outcomes.

There has been some progress made in identifying the shape of the new school finance and finding some answers to many of the hard questions entailed in designing and implementing such new systems—how to determine an adequate spending level, including adequate teacher pay; how to get adequate dollars to school sites; how to use those dollars more effectively; and how to display those expenditures so that they represent the strategic allocation of resources. Still, much additional research is needed to flesh out these broad dimensions of the new school finance, so that the best policies and implementation strategies at the state, district, and site levels can be identified.

NOTES

1. Portions of this chapter draw heavily from Odden (2000a, 2001a, 2001b, 2001d).

2. In addition, school-based performance award programs can provide salary bonuses for all teachers in a school when the school as a whole meets pre-set targets for improved student performance (for a review of the operation and effects of such programs, see Kelley, Heneman, & Milanowski, 2002; Milanowski, 2000).

REFERENCES

Achilles, C. (1999). *Let's put kids first, finally: Getting class size right*. Thousand Oaks, CA: Corwin Press.

Alexander, K., Augenblick, J., Driscoll, W., Guthrie, J., & Levin, R. (1995). *Proposals for the elimination of wealth-based disparities in public education*. Columbus, OH: Department of Public Instruction.

Archibald, S., & Gallagher, H.A. (2002). A case study of professional development expenditures at a restructured high school. *Education Policy Analysis Archives*, *10*(29), 1-24.

Augenblick, J. (1997). *Recommendations for a base figure and pupil-weighted adjustments to the base figure for use in a new school finance system in Ohio*. Columbus, OH: Ohio Department of Education.

Augenblick, J. (2001). *Calculation of the cost of an adequate education in Maryland in 1999-2000 using two different analytic approaches*. Denver, CO: Augenblick and Meyers.

Ballou, D., & Podgursky, M. (1997). *Teacher pay and teacher quality*. Kalamazoo, MI: W.E. Upjohn Institute for Employment Research.

Barnett, W.S. (1995). Long-term effects of early childhood programs on cognitive and school outcomes. *The Future of Children: Long-Term Outcomes of Early Childhood Programs*, *5*(3), 25-50.

Barnett, W.S. (1996). *Lives in the balance: Age-27 benefit-cost analysis of the High/Scope Perry Preschool program*. Ypsilanti, MI: High/Scope Press.

Barnett, W.S. (2000). Economics of early childhood intervention. In J. Shonkoff & S. Meisels (Eds.), *Handbook of early childhood intervention* (2nd ed., pp. 589-612). New York: Cambridge University Press.

Beck, L., & Murphy, J. (1996). *The four imperatives of a successful school*. Thousand Oaks, CA: Corwin Press.

Borman, G.D., & D'Agostino, J. (2001). Title I and student achievement: A quantitative synthesis. In G.D. Borman, S.C. Stringfield, & R.E. Slavin (Eds.), *Title I: Compensatory education at the crossroads* (pp. 25-57). Mahwah, NJ: Lawrence Erlbaum Associates.

Brabeck, M.M., Walsh, M.E., & Latta, R. (2003). *Meeting at the hyphen: Schools-universities-communities-professions in collaboration for student achievement and well being. The 102nd yearbook of the National Society for the Study of Education*, Part II. Chicago: National Society for the Study of Education.

Busch, C., & Odden, A. (1997). Collection of school-level finance data. [Entire Issue.] *Journal of Education Finance*, 22(3).

Chambers, J., & Parrish, T. (1994). State-level education finance. In H.J. Walberg (Ed.), *Advances in educational productivity* (pp. 45-74). Greenwich, CT: JAI Press.

Chubb, J., & Moe, T. (1990). *Politics, markets, & America's schools*. Washington, DC: Brookings Institution.

Clune, W.H. (1994). The shift from equity to adequacy in school finance. *Educational Policy*, *8*(4), 376-394.

Clune, W.H. (1995a). Adequacy litigation in school finance symposium. [Entire Issue.] *University of Michigan Journal of Law Reform*, *28*(3).

Clune, W.H. (1995b). Introduction: Educational adequacy: A theory and its remedies. *University of Michigan Journal of Law Reform*: Adequacy Litigation in School Finance Symposium, *28* (No. 3, Spring), 481-491.

Clune, W.H. (1997). The empirical argument for educational adequacy, the critical gaps in the knowledge base, and a suggested research agenda. In W.J. Fowler (Ed.), *Selected papers in school finance 1995* (NCES 97-536, 101-124). Washington, DC: National Center for Education Statistics.

Duncombe, W., Ruggiero, J., & Yinger, J. (1996). Alternative approaches to measuring the cost of education. In H.F. Ladd (Ed.), *Holding schools accountable: Performance-based reform in education* (pp. 327-356). Washington, DC: The Brookings Institution.

Elmore, R.F. (2002). *Bridging the gap between standards and achievement: The imperative for professional development in education.* Washington, DC: Albert Shanker Institute.

Erlichson, B.A., & Goertz, M. (2001). *Implementing whole school reform in New Jersey: Year two.* New Brunswick, NJ: Rutgers, The State University of New Jersey, Edward J. Bloustein School of Planning and Public Policy.

Erlichson, B.A., Goertz, M., & Turnbull, B. (1999). *Implementing whole school reform in New Jersey: Year one in the first cohort schools.* New Brunswick, NJ: Rutgers, The State University of New Jersey, Edward J. Bloustein School of Planning and Public Policy.

Fermanich, M. (2002). School spending on professional development: A cross-case analysis of seven schools in one urban district. *The Elementary School Journal, 103*(1), 27-50.

Fowler, W. Jr., & Monk, D.M. (2001). *A primer for making cost adjustments in education.* Washington, DC: U.S. Department of Education, National Center for Education Statistics.

Fuhrman, S.H. (1999). *The new accountability.* (CPRE Policy Brief No. RB-27). Philadelphia: University of Pennsylvania, Consortium for Policy Research in Education.

Fuhrman, S.H., & Elmore, R.F. (Eds.). (In press). *Redesigning accountability systems.* New York: Teachers College Press.

Gallagher, H.A. (2002a). Elm Street School: A case study of professional development expenditures. *Education Policy Analysis Archives, 10*(28), 1-32.

Gallagher, H.A. (2002b). The relationship between measures of teacher quality and student achievement: The case of Esperanza Academy. Paper presented at the Annual Conference of the American Educational Research Association. New Orleans, LA.

Gerber, S., Finn, J., Achilles, C., & Boyd-Zaharias, J. (2001). Teacher aides and students' academic achievement. *Educational Evaluation and Policy Analysis, 23*(2), 123-143.

Goertz, M.E., & Stiefel, L. (1998). Introduction to the special issue. *Journal of Education Finance, 23*(4), 435-446.

Goldhaber, D. (2001). How has teacher compensation changed? In *Selected papers in school finance: 2000-2001* (pp. 15-40). Washington, DC: National Center for Education Statistics.

Grissmer, D. (1999). Class size: Issues and new findings. [Entire Issue]. *Educational Evaluation and Policy Analysis, 21*(2).

Guthrie, J., Hayward, G., Smith, J., Rothstein, R., Bennet, R., Koppich, J., Bowman, E., DeLapp, L., Brandes, B., & Clark, S. (1997). *A proposed cost-based block grant model for Wyoming school finance.* Davis, CA: Management Analysis and Planning Associates, LLC.

Guthrie, J.W., & Rothstein, R. (1999). Enabling "adequacy" to achieve reality: Translating adequacy into state school finance distribution arrangements. In H.F. Ladd, R. Chalk, & J. Hansen (Eds.), *Equity and adequacy in education finance: Issues and perspectives* (pp. 209-259). Washington, DC: National Academy Press.

Heneman, H.G., III, & White, B. (2002). *A case study of Proposition 301 and performance-based pay in Arizona.* Madison: University of Wisconsin, Wisconsin Center for Education Research, Consortium for Policy Research in Education.

Hertert, L. (1995). Does equal funding for districts mean equal funding for classroom students? Evidence from California. In L.O. Picus & J.L. Wattenbarger (Eds.), *Where does the money go? Resource allocation in elementary and secondary schools* (pp. 71-84). Thousand Oaks, CA: Corwin Press.

Hinrichs, W.L., & Laine, R.D. (1996). *Adequacy: Building quality and efficiency into the cost of education.* Springfield, IL: Illinois Board of Education.

Holtzapple, E. (2002). *Report on validation of teacher evaluation system instructional domain ratings.* Cincinnati, OH: Cincinnati Public Schools.

Imazeki, J. (2000). *School finance reform and the market for teachers.* Unpublished Ph.D. dissertation. University of Wisconsin-Madison.

Imazeki, J., & Reschovsky, A. (1999). Measuring the costs of providing an adequate public education in Texas. In H. Chernick (Ed.), *Proceedings of the 91st Annual Conference on Taxation* (pp. 275-290). Washington, DC: National Tax Association.

Karoly, L., Greenwood, P., Everingham, S., Hoube, J., Kilburn, M.R., Rydell, C.P., Sanders, M., & Chiesa, J. (1998). *Investing in our children: What we know and don't know about the costs and benefits of early childhood interventions*. Santa Monica, CA: The RAND Corporation.

Kelley, C. (1997). Teacher compensation and organization. *Educational Evaluation and Policy Analysis, 19*(1), 15-28.

Kelley, C., Heneman, H.G., III, & Milanowski, A.T. (2002). Teacher motivation and school-based performance awards. *Educational Administration Quarterly, 38*(3), 372-401.

Ladd, H.F., & Hansen, J. (1999). *Making money matter*. Washington, DC: National Academy Press.

Lawler, E.E. (1986). *High involvement management*. San Francisco: Jossey-Bass.

Lawler, E.E., Mohrman, S.A., & Benson, G. (2001). *Organizing for high performance*. San Francisco: Jossey-Bass.

Leandro v. State, 346 N.C. 336, 488 S.E.2d 249 (1997); Hoke County v. State (Case # 95CVS1158).

Lee, V., & Smith, J. (1997). High school size: Which works best, and for whom? *Educational Evaluation and Policy Analysis, 19*(3), 205-228.

Management Analysis and Planning. (2001). A professional judgment approach to determining adequate education funding in Maryland. Davis, CA: Management Analysis and Planning, Inc.

McAdams, D.R. (2000). *Fighting to save our urban schools—and winning! Lessons from Houston*. New York: Teachers College Press.

Milanowski, A. (2000). School-based performance award programs and teacher motivation. *Journal of Education Finance, 25*(4), 517-544.

Milanowski, A. (2002). *The varieties of knowledge and skill-based pay design: A comparison of seven new pay systems for K-12 teachers*. Philadelphia: University of Pennsylvania, Graduate School of Education.

Miles, K.H., Odden, A., Archibald, S., Fermanich, M., & Gallagher, H.A. (2002). *A cross-district analysis of professional development expenditures in four urban districts*. Madison, WI: University of Wisconsin-Madison, Wisconsin Center for Education Research, Consortium for Policy Research in Education.

Minorini, P., & Sugarman, S. (1999a). School finance litigation in the name of educational equity: Its evolution, impact and future. In H.F. Ladd, R. Chalk, & J. Hansen (Eds.), *Equity and adequacy in education finance: Issues and perspectives* (pp. 34-71). Washington, DC: National Academy Press.

Minorini, P., & Sugarman, S. (1999b). Educational adequacy and the courts: The promise and problems of moving to a new paradigm. In H.F. Ladd, R. Chalk, & J. Hansen (Eds.), *Equity and adequacy in education finance: Issues and perspectives* (pp. 175-208). Washington, DC: National Academy Press.

Mohrman, A., Mohrman, S.A., & Odden, A. (1996). Aligning teacher compensation with systemic school reform: Skill-based pay and group-based performance rewards. *Educational Evaluation and Policy Analysis, 18*(1), 51-71.

Monk, D.H., Roellke, C.F., & Brent, B.O. (1996). *What education dollars buy: An examination of resource allocation patterns in New York State public school systems*. Madison, WI: University of Wisconsin, Wisconsin.

Murnane, R. (1996). Staffing the nation's schools with skilled teachers. In E. Hanushek & D. Jorgenson (Eds.), *Improving America's schools: The role of incentives* (pp. 241-258). Washington DC: National Academy Press.

Murphy, J., Beck, L., Crawford, M., Hodges, A., & McGaughy, C. (2001). *The productive high school: Creating personalized academic communities*. Thousand Oaks, CA: Corwin Press.

Odden, A. (1991). *Educational policy implementation.* Albany, NY: SUNY Press.

Odden, A. (1997). How to rethink school budgets to support school transformation. *Getting better by design series,* Volume 3. Arlington, VA: New American Schools.

Odden, A. (1998a). *Improving state school finance systems: New realities create need to re-engineer school finance structures* (CPRE Occasional Paper Series OP-04). Philadelphia: University of Pennsylvania, Graduate School of Education, Consortium for Policy Research in Education.

Odden, A. (1998b). Making better use of resources for educational reform? In D. Marsh (Ed.), *Preparing our schools for the 21st century* (pp. 143-164). Alexandria, VA: Association for Supervision and Curriculum Development.

Odden, A. (1998c). Recommendations for resolving New Jersey Abbott v. Burke IV, after the November and December 1997 hearings. Report to the Honorable Judge Patrick Michael King.

Odden, A. (1999a). Repositioning school finance: Providing adequacy and improving equity. In B.A. Nye and G.L. Peeveley (Eds.), *Education funding adequacy and equity in the next millennium: Conference proceedings* (pp. 1-34). Nashville, TN: Tennessee State University.

Odden, A. (1999b). School-based financing in North America. In M.E. Goertz & A. Odden (Eds.), *School-based financing* (pp. 155-187). Thousand Oaks, CA: Corwin Press.

Odden, A. (2000a). Costs of sustaining educational change via comprehensive school reform. *Phi Delta Kappan, 81*(6), 433-438.

Odden, A. (2000b). The new school finance: Providing adequacy and improving equity. *Journal of Education Finance, 25*(4), 467-487.

Odden, A. (2000c). New and better forms of teacher compensation are possible. *Phi Delta Kappan, 81*(5), 361-366.

Odden, A. (2001a). Chicago education reform and Illinois school finance. In J. Simmons (Ed.), *School reform in Chicago: Lessons and opportunities* (pp. 205-214). Chicago: Chicago Community Trust.

Odden, A. (2001b). The new school finance. *Phi Delta Kappan, 83*(1), 85-91.

Odden, A. (2001c). Rewarding expertise. *Education Matters, 1*(1), 16-24.

Odden, A. (2001d). On school productivity from a resource allocation perspective. In J. Adams, Jr. (Ed.), *Investing in adequacy: Critiquing the challenges* (pp. 23-26). Washington, DC: National Research Council.

Odden, A., & Archibald, S. (2001). *Reallocating resources: How schools can boost student achievement without spending more.* Thousand Oaks, CA: Corwin Press.

Odden, A., Archibald, S., Fermanich, M., & Gallagher, H.A. (2002). A cost framework for professional development. *Journal of Education Finance, 28*(1), 51-74.

Odden, A., Archibald, S., Fermanich, M., & Gross, B. (2002). *Defining school-level expenditure structures that reflect educational strategies.* Madison: University of Wisconsin, Wisconsin Center for Education Research, Consortium for Policy Research in Education.

Odden, A., & Busch, C. (1998). *Financing schools for high performance: Strategies for improving the use of educational resources.* San Francisco: Jossey-Bass.

Odden, A., & Goertz, M. (Eds.). (1999). *School-based financing.* Thousand Oaks, CA: Corwin Press.

Odden, A., & Kelley, C. (1997). *Paying teachers for what they know and do: New and smarter compensation strategies to improve schools.* Thousand Oaks, CA: Corwin Press.

Odden, A., & Kelley, C. (2002). *Paying teachers for what they know and do: New and smarter compensation strategies to improve schools* (2nd ed.). Thousand Oaks, CA: Corwin Press.

Odden, A., Monk, D., Nakib, N., & Picus, L. (1995). The story of the education dollar: No Academy Awards and no fiscal smoking guns. *Phi Delta Kappan, 77*(2), 161-168.

Odden, A., & Picus, L.O. (2000). *School finance: A policy perspective* (2nd ed.). New York: McGraw Hill.

Odden, A., & Picus, L.O. (2001). *Assessing SEEK from an adequacy perspective.* Report prepared for the Kentucky State Department of Education.

Odden, A., Wohlstetter, P., & Odden, E. (1995). Key issues in effective school-based management. *School Business Affairs, 61*(5), 4-16.

Odden, E., & Wohlstetter, P. (1995). Strategies for making school-based management work. *Educational Leadership, 52*(5), 32-36.

Picus, L. O., & Fazal, M. (1995). Why do we need to know what money buys? Research on resource allocation patterns in elementary and secondary schools. In L. O. Picus and J. L. Wattenbarger (Eds.), *Where does the money go? Resource allocation in elementary and secondary schools* (pp. 1-19). Newbury Park, CA: Corwin Press.

Picus, L.O., Tetreault, D.R., & Murphy, J. (1996). *What money buys: Understanding the allocation and use of educational resources in California.* Madison, WI: University of Wisconsin, Wisconsin Center for Education Research, Consortium for Policy Research in Education.

Picus, L.O., & Wattenbarger, J.L. (Eds.). (1995). *Where does the money go? Resource allocation in elementary and secondary schools.* Newbury Park, CA: Corwin Press.

Raywid, M.A. (1997/1998). Synthesis of research: Small schools: A reform that works. *Educational Leadership, 55*(4), 34-39.

Reschovsky, A., & Imazeki, J. (1999). Reforming state aid to achieve educational adequacy: Lessons from Texas and Wisconsin. In B.A. Nye and G.L. Peeveley (Eds.), *Education funding adequacy and equity in the next millennium: Conference proceedings* (pp. 1-30). Nashville, TN: Tennessee State University.

Reschovsky, A., & Imazeki, J. (2000). *Developing a cost index for school districts in Illinois.* Paper submitted to the Illinois State Board of Education.

Reschovsky, A., & Imazeki, J. (2001). Achieving educational adequacy through school finance reform. *Journal of Education Finance, 26*(4), 373-396.

Ross, K.N., & Levacic, R. (Eds.). (1999). *Needs-based resource allocation in schools via formula-based funding.* Paris: UNESCO, International Institute for Educational Planning.

Shanahan, T. (1998). On the effectiveness and limitations of tutoring in reading. *Review of Research in Education, 23,* 217-234. Washington, DC: American Educational Research Association.

Slavin, R.E., Karweit, N., & Wasik, B. (1994). *Preventing early school failure: Research policy and practice.* Boston: Allyn & Bacon.

Slavin, R.E., & Madden, N.A. (2001). (Eds.). *Success for All: Research and reform in elementary education.* Mahwah, NJ: Lawrence Erlbaum.

Stringfield, S., Ross, S., & Smith, L. (1996). *Bold plans for school restructuring: The New American Schools designs.* Mahwah, NJ: Lawrence Erlbaum.

Underwood, J. (1995a). School finance litigation: Legal theories, judicial activism, and social neglect. *Journal of Education Finance, 20*(2), 143-162.

Underwood, J. (1995b). School finance as vertical equity. *University of Michigan Journal of Law Reform, 28*(3), 493-520.

Wasik, B., & Slavin, R.E. (1993). Preventing early reading failure with one-to-one tutoring: A review of five programs. *Reading Research Quarterly, 28,* 178-200.

Wayne, A., & Youngs, P. (Under review). Teacher characteristics and student achievement gains: A review. *Review of Educational Research.*

Wohlstetter, P. (1995). Getting school-based management right: What works and what doesn't. *Phi Delta Kappan, 77*(1), 22-26.

Wohlstetter, P., Mohrman, S., & Robertson, P. (1997). Successful school-based management: Lessons for restructuring urban schools. In D. Ravitch and J. Viteritti (Eds.), *New schools for a new century: The redesign of urban education* (pp. 201-225). New Haven, CT: Yale University Press.

Wohlstetter, P., Van Kirk, A., Robertson, P., & Mohrman, S. (1997). *Organizing for successful school-based management.* Alexandria, VA: Association for Supervision and Curriculum Development.

CHAPTER 6

Breaking the Mold: Charter Schools, Contract Schools, and Voucher Plans

FREDERICK M. HESS

Choice-based and contractual reforms offer a radical approach to addressing the problems that plague school governance. Proponents of choice argue that the traditional design of state-controlled public education tends to produce ineffective, unresponsive, and inequitable schools, and that democratic control and public bureaucracy have given rise to interest group dominance, institutional rigidity, insensitivity to the preferences of families, and weak systems of managerial control (Chubb and Moe, 1990). By introducing market mechanisms into education, choice-based reforms are designed to strike at the root of the problem by enhancing the power of individual consumers (families) at the expense of organized interests and public employees.

Advocates argue that choice- and market-based reforms will permit new, more effective schools to flourish and enable families to enroll their children in schools that match their needs, and that the resulting competition among schools will drive systemic improvement in education. Proponents of educational contracting, in particular, believe such a system will force providers to compete, will permit districts to provide more educational alternatives, and will bring effective management principles to public school systems (Hill, Pierce, & Guthrie, 1997; Vedder, 2000). Critics fear that choice-based reforms may sacrifice notions of the common good, lead to segregation by religion, race, or class, or fail to protect children whose parents are unable or unwilling to make good educational decisions (Brighouse, 2000).

While they agree that education plays an important role in advancing democratic values and helping children grow to become productive and responsible citizens, proponents and critics of school choice disagree both about the extent to which K-12 schooling ought to be shaped by such concerns and about whether schools have to be publicly

Frederick M. Hess is a Resident Scholar at the American Enterprise Institute and author, most recently, of *Revolution at the Margins: The Impact of Competition on Urban School Systems.*

governed in order to produce public benefits (Levin, 1987). Choice proponents argue that most education generates significant private benefits and, within some strictures, ought to be procured privately. Moreover, even where the community wants to ensure that certain public goods are produced, choice proponents believe that the most sensible course is for the state to allow private providers to produce the goods and to use regulation or monitoring to ensure that they do so (Friedman, 1962).

In practice, the central question is the degree to which education should be governed by market mechanisms that allow families to express particular preferences, versus the degree to which everyone's preferences should be aggregated through the political process and then enacted as public policies. Social scientists refer to this tension as that between "exit" and "voice" (Hirschman, 1970). Decisions regarding the structure, practice, and provision of schooling have traditionally been made via "voice"—through shared democratic processes.

In the absence of exit, families dissatisfied with specific policies seek redress primarily by complaining to public officials, mobilizing politically, voting for new officials, or availing themselves of traditional choice mechanisms like petitioning to have their child assigned to another class or school, moving to another school district, or using private schools. Proponents of choice-based reform argue that under this system the exit option has been reserved for wealthy or politically savvy families. They argue that the political process is an ineffective way to redress concerns and one that is too often ineffective.

Historical Context

American education has been marked by tension when the larger community's judgment about what best serves children conflicts with the views of individual families (Macedo, 2000). This conflict became heated in the 1830s and 1840s, when waves of new immigrants—particularly Irish Catholics—settled in eastern cities like Boston and New York. Nativist distrust of these new immigrants, their work ethic, their understanding of democracy, and their "papist" leanings gave rise to an effort to use the public schools as a way to "Americanize" immigrant children and inoculate them against the suspect beliefs and behaviors of their parents. Such concerns helped spur the formation of the American parochial school system, as Catholic authorities set out to create schools in which their religion and their children were not demeaned (Coulson, 1999; Peterson, 1995).

Once Catholics erected this parallel system of schooling, they wanted some of the tax dollars they paid to support education directed to these schools. Such proposals sparked nativist opposition, eventually prompting the majority of states to adopt Constitutional language during the late 19th century that prohibited public money from going to support religiously affiliated schools (Viteritti, 1999). Similar tensions between the majority's conceptions of "good" schooling and family preferences attended efforts to demand English language instruction for immigrant children and to establish standardized state curricula.

Conflicts between familial preferences and community desires have given rise to a variety of arrangements—including the creation of private schools, families' expression of preferences by moving from one community to another, and the provision of an array of programs and options within the traditional public schools—that alleviate conflicts by providing families with exit-based alternatives. Such alternatives allow families to escape schools they deem particularly ineffective or objectionable, giving the most irate some redress.

While exit-based alternatives have historically been available, they became increasingly explicit and transparent after 1960. Efforts to bring together racially diverse populations in the schools and the growing importance of schooling increased conflict and the resulting demand for exit options. From the "white flight" that met forced busing in northern cities to the "home schooling" and "deschooling" movements that rose in answer to the perceived intrusiveness or inadequacy of state curricula, public schools were buffeted by demands for particular services or learning environments. The initial response in the 1960s and 1970s was to provide an array of programs such as alternative schools, magnet schools, and gifted and talented classes. When these programs failed to satisfy all claimants, failed to significantly improve schools in the worst served communities, or failed to respond to ideological complaints about public schooling, pressure built for more radical accommodations. While proposals for more radical choice reforms encountered stiff opposition and were branded by opponents as racist, unconstitutional, elitist, and ideological, more moderate choice-based reforms enjoyed significant success in the 1980s and 1990s (Bulman & Kirp, 1999).

In the 1980s, open enrollment and "controlled choice" plans (both of which permit families to choose among traditional public schools) made steady headway. Building upon that success, charter school programs overcame early opposition to rapidly win widespread acceptance during the 1990s. Choice-based reforms proliferated during the 1990s, as the first charter school laws were adopted and the first public voucher experiments launched.

During the early 1990s, educational contracting had its first significant trial when the private company Educational Alternatives, Inc. (EAI) won and then lost contracts with school boards in Baltimore and Hartford. Hired to manage 12 elementary schools in Baltimore and the entire school system in Hartford, EAI struggled with highly restrictive contracts and fierce union opposition before being terminated by Baltimore in 1995 and Hartford in 1996. Despite EAI's difficulties, for-profit contractors continued to emerge and were managing dozens of schools across the nation by 2001.

By the late 1990s, public opinion surveys indicated that while the public had mixed feelings about school vouchers, it expressed strong support for the broader notion of increasing parental choices. This support showed up most notably in urban and minority communities where families had long been frustrated by the lack of adequate schools. At the same time, however, adults expressed an emotional attachment to public schools and a desire for the government to ensure that schools were effective, congruent with shared national values, and serving common purposes (Moe, 2001).

From Inputs to Outcomes

Choice-based reform seeks to shift education from a compliance-based model controlled by public officials to an outcomes-based system monitored by individual families. Traditionally, public schools were required to abide by mandated procedures and policies, and public officials held them accountable for honoring these strictures. The assumption has been that compliance ensures that educators will do what they are supposed to do and fulfill the public purpose of schooling. In the last 5 or 10 years this view has gradually started to shift towards an approach that puts more emphasis on monitoring public outcomes than on compliance, but the compliance mindset is still central to public school governance.

A choice-based approach rejects the compliance model as bureaucratic and stifling. Rather than having public officials create policies to govern all schools, schools are left largely free to provide services as they see fit. Within certain parameters, educators are free to operate in any way they deem appropriate. Proponents argue that this approach permits a wide variety of schools and approaches to emerge, and that parents searching for quality options will ensure that effective schools flourish and will force ineffective schools to improve or eventually shut their doors. However, critics worry that a choice-based model may have too few safeguards or will fail to regulate schools in important ways.

These two models—the regulatory and the market-based—represent the ends of a continuum. There is no clear point at which a market regime "becomes" a regulatory regime. Rather, every additional regulation shifts choice-based programs away from the market-based end of the continuum. Outcome-based accountability provides something of a common ground in terms of governance, by loosening the strictures on schools so long as they produce adequate results. However, even with outcome accountability, there is still a need to determine how detailed the outcome regime should be and what to do with schools that do not perform adequately. On both counts, the tensions reemerge between the regulatory impulse, which implies rather specific performance expectations and centrally administered remedies, and the market impulse, which leaves these responsibilities largely in the hands of individual families.

In practice, even radical proponents of market-based reforms concede some need for centralized regulation or oversight, recognizing the "spillover" effects schooling has on the larger community as well as the practical and political need to protect both the community and individual children from irresponsible parental choices. Whereas the pure market model assumes that families will hold schools accountable by choosing good schools and fleeing bad schools, while remaining agnostic about what constitutes a "good" or a "bad" school, most school choice proponents expect the state to play a role in monitoring choice schools.

Regulation helps families make "appropriate" choices by shutting down schools that the larger community deems unacceptable. Regulation requires the broader community to do two things that can undermine the market model. First, it requires that communities establish standards against which schools will be judged. This can lead to an emphasis on inputs, undermining the market premise, or on outputs, potentially marginalizing some effective schools that are seeking to pursue nonstandard outcomes. Second, regulatory accountability requires that schools failing to meet these standards be closed—even if families choose to continue using them—forcing regulators to prohibit some families from making free choices (Hess, 2001).

Because charter, voucher, and contract school proposals all rely upon public revenue, such reforms do not remove education from public control so much as they alter the nature of the relationship (Henig, 1994). In a choice-based system, rather than provide schooling or prescribe the particulars of educational provision, public officials set the parameters of the educational market and create monitoring mechanisms. The degree to which these officials choose to deregulate inputs, monitor schools, and empower consumers will have significant implications for the impact of market-based reform efforts.

Voucher Plans, Charter Schools, and School Contracting

Vouchers. University of Chicago economist Milton Friedman first proposed a school voucher system for American K-12 education in 1955. He elaborated on such a system in his 1962 book *Capitalism and Freedom.* Friedman suggested that, rather than simply assigning children to state-run public schools, the state should give each family the money to fund its child's education. The state would ensure that the family spent this money on education by issuing a voucher redeemable at any school. Friedman pointed out that these voucher amounts could be modified in various ways, to account for student needs or otherwise ensure equity.

While Friedman's argument initially attracted little notice, the idea would draw much attention in the late 1960s, as school reformers sought ways to promote desegregation without engendering a backlash against forced busing and related efforts to compel desegregation of schools. In the end, a single, modest voucher experiment was launched in Alum Rock, California in 1972. That program soon petered out due to poor design and lack of serious support, and such reforms came to a halt for a time, but incremental efforts at choice-based reform continued. During the 1980s and 1990s, with Minnesota taking the lead, states gradually adopted and expanded open enrollment and intradistrict choice programs—reforms that allowed students to transfer to other public schools in their state or in their district. Well-known examples of such programs included those operating in two New York City districts (Districts 2 and 4); Minnesota; Montgomery County, Maryland; and Cambridge, Massachusetts.

The 1990s marked a dramatic expansion of choice-based education across the nation. In 1990, an experimental voucher program was launched in Milwaukee. The program provided public funding for approximately 1,000 low-income children to attend private nonsectarian schools. The next year, Minnesota enacted the nation's first charter school law. Although Milwaukee's voucher program preceded Minnesota's charter legislation, vouchers would enjoy little political success, while charter schooling would soon spread across the nation. Charter schooling fared better than voucher programs because it was seen as more "public," less risky, and more in line with traditional school provision (Cookson, 1994; Good & Braden, 2000).

In theory, in an unregulated voucher system the state simply provides some amount of funding for every child that each family is then free to spend on the school of its choice. In practice, as enacted in Milwaukee and later in Cleveland and Florida, publicly funded voucher programs include many additional restrictions. Programs have restricted the availability of vouchers to low-income children or students who attend low-performing schools; have made vouchers worth only a portion of the total amount spent on each pupil in the public school system; have limited the kinds of private schools permitted to accept vouchers; have required that schools accepting voucher students nonselectively admit applicants; and so on. Given that the vast majority of private schools in the United States are sectarian, a key dispute was whether students should be allowed to use publicly funded vouchers to attend religious schools or whether this would violate the Establishment Clause of the U.S. Constitution. That issue was finally resolved in 2002, when the U.S. Supreme Court ruled, in *Zelman v. Harris*, that public choice programs that permitted families to use vouchers at religious schools did not violate the Establishment Clause.

During the 1990s, dozens of private voucher or "tuition scholarship" programs also took root across the nation. The largest of these private programs was The Children's Scholarship Fund, based in Arkansas, which provided partial vouchers to approximately 40,000 students a year starting in 1999. Through these programs, benefactors provide students with a voucher that helps them attend the school of their choice. Since such funds do not involve public money, they are not subject to government regulation. Of course, the reliance on private funding means that private scholarship programs tend to be small and to provide vouchers that cover only a portion of the cost of private schooling. During the last 10 years, Arizona, Florida, and Pennsylvania began to enact tax credit programs that would help support and encourage contributions to tuition scholarship funds.

Outside of such private efforts, school vouchers expanded rather slowly during the 1990s. Public voucher programs operated in Milwaukee, Cleveland, and the state of Florida, and longstanding plans that provided vouchers to students in sparsely populated communities of Maine and Vermont continued to operate, but only the Milwaukee program had grown significantly in size or scope. All told, these programs enrolled fewer than 25,000 students as of 2001.

Charter schools. Whereas voucher programs theoretically reduce the state to nothing more than a funder of education, the aims of charter schooling are less revolutionary. Charter schooling challenges the traditional practice of having school boards oversee all public schools in a geographic district. Instead, the state legislature designates a body (or bodies) that can grant school operators a "charter" to run a particular school. Because their existence depends on this authorization by the state, charter schools are regarded as "public" schools subject to conventional regulations and constraints. Therefore, unlike private schools, charter schools must abide by the same restrictions on religion as public schools, cannot charge tuition, cannot selectively admit students, and are potentially subject to a host of regulations on matters ranging from curriculum to teacher salaries.

Charter schools are issued a charter for a limited period of time—typically about 5 years, although the length of time varies by state—and are accountable to their chartering authority for meeting certain objectives during that time period. The promise that regulators will shut down ineffective charter schools if they do not meet their goals is part of the input-output tradeoff promoted by advocates of charter schooling, and is hailed as providing more protection than less regulated voucher systems. Provisions regarding who can issue a charter, the length of the charter, how heavily charters will be regulated, how charter schools can be staffed and operated, and how charters will be monitored vary widely across states (Finn, Manno, & Vanourek, 2000; Hassel, 1999).

Charter schooling expanded by leaps and bounds during the 1990s. By 2002, more than 2,700 charter schools were in operation, enrolling more than 700,000 students in more than 35 states. States with charter legislation varied dramatically in activity, from Arizona with more than 400 charter schools to states with just a handful. Moreover, charter schooling was expanding at a dramatic rate, with the number of charter schools having increased more than fivefold since 1996-97.

School contracting. School contracting is fundamentally different from either the school voucher or the charter schooling model. Contracting involves hiring a private vendor to manage particular schools or entire school systems. Contractors can be hired by public entities to operate charter schools, traditional public schools, or school systems. The risk of losing a contract creates a powerful incentive for educational providers to ensure that their schools are effective, as measured by whatever criteria families or monitors use to gauge success (typically test scores, graduation rates, college matriculation, etc.).

Contractual language and the ability to readily replace providers make it easier for school boards to clarify goals and to hold contractors responsible for meeting them. In thousands of communities vendors already provide an array of public services, and proponents argue that the research has generally shown these efforts to enhance both the efficiency and quality of service. Moreover, advocates note that vendors already provide a variety of K-12 services, ranging from food services to tutoring to clerical assistance to school maintenance, in some locales (Hill, Pierce et al., 1997). Critics counter with concerns that contractors may fail to protect the public weal, may cut corners on services not explicitly mentioned in the contract, may prey on weak or vulnerable communities, or may pose other logistical or ethical problems.

While choice programs expanded during the 1980s and 1990s, there was far less experimentation with contracting. In general, the claims made for and against contracting have not yet been put to the test in K-12 schooling. Besides the limited experiences of EAI in Hartford and Baltimore during the early 1990s, both of which were terminated within a few years, little educational contracting existed before 1999. By 1999, however, several for-profit management firms had started to operate in the K-12 arena, including Edison Schools, Nobel Learning, the Tesseract Group, the Leona Group, and the National Heritage Academies. By 2002, Edison Schools, the most prominent of these firms, was managing traditional public schools or charter schools in a growing number of cities, including Baltimore, Chicago, Kansas City, Milwaukee, Philadelphia, and Washington, D.C. The steady growth of contracting will increasingly provide opportunities to assess its promise and to understand how it works in practice.

Educational contracting does not fit neatly into the choice debate. Since contracting is primarily concerned with altering who runs schools, rather than with how schools are selected, its fundamental changes are more managerial and less visible. Contracting does not change whether (or how) families choose schools or the role that schools are expected to play in society. It changes who is responsible for providing services and introduces competition among firms vying for that responsibility. It does so by introducing the profit motive into educational governance, summoning both the promise of market discipline and concerns about the perils of commodification or unscrupulous operators. However, the dearth of experiments with contractors running traditional public schools means that most discussion of contracting has thus far been subsumed into the conversation over school choice.

Choice-based reforms vary widely in the degree to which they will alter the governance of education. "Controlled choice" programs, in which families are permitted to choose among traditional public schools, generally do little or nothing to reform public governance, while school voucher plans that include private schools may radically alter the way schools are governed and held accountable, given the implicit need for schools to compete for education dollars. In practice, actual programs do not fit neatly into an abstract continuum. Charter schooling is theoretically a less radical reform than voucher-based reform, but as of 2002, Arizona and Michigan operated charter programs that were more radical in their design (e.g., less demanding screening and regulations; fewer limits on operators) than the circumscribed voucher programs operating in Florida and Cleveland. It is important to differentiate between the abstract version of a particular type of choice-based reform and the actual programs enacted and implemented with that label.

The Case for School Choice

Proponents of school choice make three key claims on behalf of choice-based reforms. Perhaps the best-known argument for school vouchers and charter schooling is that students will have more successful educational experiences in schools of choice. There are a number of hypotheses as to why this would be so. In the most sophisticated case advanced by proponents of choice-based reform, John Chubb and Terry Moe argued in 1990 that more autonomous schools are generally more effective. Chubb and Moe found that principals and teachers in such schools are better able to foster discipline, maintain a sense of their mission, and tend to the needs of their students. Unfortunately, they argued, democratic governance reduces school autonomy by subjecting school personnel to the crosscutting directives, red tape, and bureaucratic constraints produced by competing interests seeking to advance particular agendas. According to Chubb and Moe, reforms freeing schools from democratic control are the answer.

Advocates also expect that choice will permit like-minded families, teachers, and administrators to come together and focus upon a common mission with the support of shared goals (Finn, 1990). Such a development also allows schools to specialize in serving students with particular needs, alleviating the pressure to provide a laundry list of services. Similarly, when students and families select a school, they are more invested in that school and are therefore more likely to take its demands seriously and to contribute to its success.

Second, proponents argue that competition has improved quality and efficiency in a vast array of industries. If competition from Japanese automakers made American auto manufacturers leaner and better, they ask, shouldn't competition from new schools do the same for existing schools (Osborne, 1999)? The need to compete for students and the funding they represent will force schools to attend to the demands of families, making schools more responsive and effective. However, others have noted that competition is influenced by context and available incentives, and that educators will compete for students only if they have the incentives and ability to do so (Hess, 2002).

Third, choice proponents argue that in a democratic society families have the right to control the manner of their children's education. While acknowledging the state's right to ensure that a child receives an education of some designated quality, they argue that permitting the state to dictate the content or nature of instruction constitutes an unnecessary and inappropriate expansion of state authority (Gilles, 1998; Holmes, 2001). Proponents argue that it is not necessary that schools be state-run in order to serve public interests, and that charter schools, contract schools, or private schools might actually serve the "public" interest more effectively than traditional public schools (Hill, 2001).

The Case Against School Choice

Choice critics have answered these assertions with three claims of their own. First, they voice concerns that financially advantaged families will seek out schools where the students are predominantly white and wealthy, segregating poor and minority students into schools that have been drained of motivated students and educationally active families. They fear that choice is primarily a mechanism for allowing the privileged to procure an insular educational setting at public expense, undermining the "melting pot" ideal (Engel, 2000).

Second, critics assert that the nature of education and the uneven capabilities of parents create the risk that an educational "market" will result in problematic and inequitable choices (Elmore & Fuller, 1996; Wells, 1993). Critics fear that less educated, less informed, and impoverished parents will be unlikely to make good choices, compounding the disadvantages with which their children must cope. It is not clear that parents will seek schools that are academically proficient—as opposed to, say, convenient—or that they know how to identify quality schools, and some parents may prefer instruction or pedagogy that the community deems undesirable. Meanwhile, students may prefer to attend school with their friends or with students who look like them, encouraging self-segregation by neighborhood and race. Choice proponents, however, dispute the assumption that markets are likely to increase stratification, arguing that the actual impact of choice on stratification is not well understood, that satisfied families are the least likely to utilize new alternatives, and that choice will help reduce segregation produced by residential housing patterns (Archbald, 2000).

Finally, critics maintain that publicly governed schools are an integral part of democratic society and that they pass on a common set of shared values, foster a sense of national community, provide opportunity to all children, and permit adults to interact as they go about setting policy that speaks to the upbringing of all children. Such analyses suggest that the consumerist impulses of choice-based reform would erode the sense of common purpose and shared values provided by public schools and would undermine democracy (Gutmann, 1987; Henig, 1994).

What Does the Evidence Say?

During the 1990s, social scientists began in earnest to pursue research that could address the validity of these various claims. The recent lineage, tenuous circumstances, and evolving condition of choice programs mean that, so far, most results are less than conclusive. However, thanks to burgeoning research efforts and a series of innovative analyses, we know far more than we did a decade ago.

Do Choice Students Benefit?

Do schools of choice outperform traditional public schools? Do students who enroll in charter schools or voucher schools benefit academically? Research into this issue has dominated the choice debate, with much of the work seeking to compare the performance of children in choice schools or private schools with the performance of students enrolled in traditional public schools.

This work has proceeded in three general waves. During the 1980s, innovative research using data available for the first time through the national High School and Beyond data set suggested that, other things being equal, students in private schools were learning more than their public school peers (Coleman, Hoffer, & Kilgore, 1982). Such work led to the famed Chubb and Moe (1990) analysis arguing that autonomous schools—like private schools—were significantly more effective than democratically controlled schools. Skeptics voiced concerns that private school students are atypical in ways that analyses could not readily account for and noted that findings derived from established private schools cannot be readily generalized to charter schools or new private schools. However, by the end of the 1990s a preponderance of evidence suggested that private schools were educating students, especially urban and minority students, more effectively than similarly situated public schools (Neal, 1998).

The question, though, is not the relative performance of the universe of private school students, but that of students who participate in choice programs. After all, even if existing private schools fare exceptionally well with their conventional student population, it is not at all clear that those benefits would be replicated in new choice schools or would accrue to students who had not previously been in private schools.

The launch of voucher and charter programs in the 1990s permitted questions about the effects of choice to be addressed directly, although program regulations, data collection difficulties, and the fact that families had to volunteer for the choice program limited what could be learned from these experiments. As the first and the most ambitious of the public voucher programs, Milwaukee was studied intensively and became a source of heated conflict. Competing analyses, employing a variety of analytic approaches, differed on the apparent student effects (Greene, Peterson, & Du, 1999; Rouse, 1998; Witte, 2000). Overall, there was a rough consensus that most voucher students did not fare significantly better or worse academically than similar public school students. The handful of students who remained in the voucher program for an extended period did appear to benefit, but the results were tenuous and no analyst could provide a clear causal explanation for the effect.

Seeking more reliable data, scholars pursued a third line of research in the late 1990s. Concerned that the design challenges inherent in public choice programs impeded research efforts, scholars studied the effects of participating in privately funded voucher programs. This approach permitted research to utilize randomized assignment and require that voucher applicants commit to participating in the data collection. The results suggested that participating African American students in urban communities generally appeared to benefit significantly from receiving a voucher, while the other participants showed no clear benefits (Peterson & Howell, 2002). The researchers hypothesized that this might be because poor African American children have traditionally enjoyed fewer educational options than similarly situated students of other races, but this perplexing finding remains largely unexplained.

Moreover, while this research marks a significant improvement over earlier efforts, there are still concerns about the research methodology, analysis, and data (Goldhaber, 2001; McEwan, 2000).

In the case of charter schooling, new programs, atypical and self-selected student populations, and the lack of any standardized outcome assessment make program assessment an extremely challenging proposition. So far there is no reliable data comparing the performance of charter school students to that of their public school peers. There is, however, solid evidence that students and families who utilize charter schools report that they are significantly happier with their new school than they were with their previous school (Finn, Manno, & Vanourek, 2000). The same finding holds for students and families using school vouchers, although it is worth remembering that such expressions of satisfaction do not necessarily reflect school quality or performance.

Who Chooses and Why?

Some critics of choice-based reform fear that such systems may undermine equity and that families who utilize choice will be those most engaged with education, thus draining public schools of their most involved parents. The issue attracts concern both because racial and social heterogeneity are seen as desirable and because the presence of high achievers tends to benefit their classmates. Two questions are particularly relevant in this area. One is whether some parents are especially likely to take advantage of choices by making informed decisions. The second is what qualities parents look for when choosing a school.

Not surprisingly, the research suggests that the parents most dissatisfied with their child's current school are also the ones most likely to seek to change schools. These parents tend to be disadvantaged, to be African American or Latino, and to live in urban areas, meaning that targeted urban choice plans tend to promote desegregation. However, the preponderance of evidence suggests that more educated and wealthier families have more information and knowledge when it comes to choosing schools. Similarly, the first parents to take advantage of choice-based exit tend to be the more educated and more involved (McEwan, 2000; Smrekar & Goldring, 1999). Some research has suggested that minority students tend to self-segregate, preferring to attend schools in their own neighborhood and with students of the same race (Wells, 1996).

Because voucher programs are restricted to disadvantaged, urban populations, participating families tend to be African American and low-income. Relative to their peers in the public schools, participating students do tend to have slightly more educated and more informed parents (Witte, 2000). However, given that participants generally come from one-parent families living near or below the poverty line, it is important not to overstate this difference. In general, charter school students are about as likely to be poor, to have limited English proficiency, and to be labeled special needs as public school students, and are somewhat more likely to be African American or Latino (Finn, Manno, & Vanourek, 2000). Of course, some individual charter schools are more segregated by race or class than is the surrounding community. While neither voucher nor charter programs currently appear to promote stratification, programs designed in other ways might produce different outcomes.

Alleviating concerns that parents may disregard school quality and select schools on the basis of attributes like location or the quality of its athletic teams, the evidence suggests that parents generally focus on teacher quality, school safety, and school test scores when choosing a school (Schneider, Teske, & Marschall, 2000). The same research suggests that urban, minority, and low-income families are particularly likely to view school safety and school test performance as important. However, evidence from New Zealand, the site of a long-running national school choice program, indicates that parents prefer schools where most children come from better-off families, creating a dynamic that can isolate low-SES children in less desirable schools (Fiske & Ladd, 2000).

In sum, advantaged and informed parents are more likely to choose schools than are other parents, and race and income do influence the kinds of choices that families make. Scholars generally agree that the extent to which this occurs appears to be largely a product of how choice mechanisms are constructed (Henig, 1994; Schneider, Teske, & Marschall, 2000). There is no evidence that parents make choices on the basis of criteria *unrelated* to educational quality. In general, it is not yet clear whether, or when, choice processes lead to more or less racially or socioeconomically segregated schools. Finally, it is possible that choice systems might yield mixed results, such as increasing segregation at some schools, while promoting community integration at others by stemming the residential stratification produced by mandatory school assignment (Archbald, 2000).

Do Traditional Schools Benefit from Competition?

Research into how choice-induced competition affects school systems has tended to explore the question in two distinct ways. One line of work has attempted to examine how competition affects educational efficiency and productivity by focusing on outcomes like student test performance, graduation rates, or future student earnings. The second has sought to understand how competition plays out in education, through surveys and case studies that examine how schools or school systems respond when competition is introduced.

Until the late 1990s, a dearth of choice-induced competition in the U.S. forced scholars examining outcome effects to focus on teasing out such findings from existing arrangements. Researchers studied the effects of competition produced by the incidence of local private schools or the concentration of rival public districts. While this work varies in method and includes some research that finds no positive relationship (Smith & Meier, 1995), there is substantial evidence that "natural" competition is associated with better school district performance (Hoxby, 2000). However, even if one accepts the cross-sectional link between competition and system performance and sets aside concerns about possible sources of bias, the limitation of this work is that it is not clear how the association came to exist, how rapidly it emerged, or whether choice-based reforms would produce similar results. Aided by the expansion of large-scale choice experiments, researchers have begun to tackle the problem more directly by examining the impact of charter and voucher competition on nearby public schools. The first such effort found evidence that competition produced significant improvement in student test scores at public schools faced with competition (Hoxby, 2001), but such preliminary findings ought to be interpreted cautiously for the time being.

The second line of research has sought to examine more directly how public schools and school systems answer the competitive challenge. This line of work began to unfold during the late 1990s, as the growing size and scope of charter and voucher programs made such research feasible. Early work in this area found that public schools often responded to charter schools by seeking to undermine these schools or otherwise engaging in unproductive behaviors (Loveless & Jasin, 1998). More systematic work also found evidence that public schools with healthy organizational cultures made some modest efforts to increase outreach and to alter some school practices when faced with high levels of competition (Maranto, Milliman, Hess, & Gresham, 1999). Examining the reaction of school systems to competition found even more muted and uncertain effects, with reactions colored by political pressures and the influence of political and organizational context, and an emphasis on the addition of new programs rather than fundamental change (Hess, 2002; Hess, Maranto, & Milliman, 2001).

While there is substantial agreement that "natural" competition appears to have produced some positive effects, it is not yet clear whether or how choice-based competition will drive a systematic response on the part of the public schools. Especially given the cultural, organizational, and statutory constraints under which school systems operate, and the dearth of incentives rewarding positive performance, it is not clear whether educational competition will produce the desired results short of other, complementary reforms.

The Values Question

The philosophical debate over whether market mechanisms are consistent with or in violation of our nation's educational values cannot be settled empirically. There is no evidence that can "answer" this question. In the end, this strand of the debate must turn on questions of interpretation and belief. However, it is possible to empirically address the narrower question: How effective are choice schools in promoting the kinds of civic values we claim to support? Until very recently, it was taken as a given that public schools would promote "public values" like tolerance, civic participation, or knowledge about public affairs far more effectively than private schools, so little research sought to examine this assumption.

However, beginning in the late 1990s, some research began to argue that private schools are actually better at teaching public virtues than are public schools. Scholars argued that private schools may actually be more effective than their public counterparts at promoting interracial interaction, volunteerism, tolerance of people with different values or beliefs, and knowledge of and participation in public affairs (Campbell, 2001; Wolf, Greene, Kleitz, & Thalhammer, 2001).

Researchers have credited these effects to the strong sense of mission, stringent discipline, concern for service, and lack of tracking and educational fragmentation that tend to characterize private schools (Greene, 1998). Of course, such findings are still tenuous, may be biased by unobserved student characteristics, and cannot necessarily be generalized to charter schools or to newly emerging private schools. Nonetheless, this work provides substantial evidence that privately operated schools may be able to instruct students in civic values at least as effectively as publicly managed schools.

School Choice, School Improvement, and School Governance

Choice-based reform is still in its infancy in the U.S. As of 2002, less than 2% of the nation's K-12 students were enrolled in charter schools, public voucher programs, or traditional public schools operated by private contractors. Accordingly, observers ought to be appropriately cautious about reaching firm conclusions regarding the promise or peril of choice-based reform and its effects on school improvement and governance.

Broadly speaking, the notion of choice- or market-based reform can imply two very different kinds of educational change. A radical vision of parental choice and contracting can call for a fundamental rethinking of the nature and purpose of education and the structure of schooling. A more modest approach to reform focuses on contracting and parental choice as more efficient ways to deliver services as conventionally understood—an approach that views choice as a tool.

Choice-based reform will not necessarily alter school governance in a significant way. Many existing choice plans (public school choice, weak charter laws, small voucher programs) leave governance arrangements largely undisturbed. Public schools are run as they have always been; charter schools operate with those freedoms granted by legislative statute and in the manner in which executive agencies implement the statute; and private schools attract some additional students but otherwise operate as they have operated in the past. Choice does not necessarily alter in any fundamental way how decisions are made, nor does it change who shapes educational policy. Such choice programs may still show significant benefits, but the nature of limited reform ought not be overstated.

Choice-based reforms do have the *potential* to radically alter governance, and some proposed arrangements promise to do just that. If schools or providers are forced to meaningfully compete for student-attached dollars, and if this is permitted to help shape school missions and operations, then the incentives and structure of governance will change in fundamental ways with far-reaching results. However, even an aggressive choice regime will run into real limitations imposed by the statutes and practices governing the administrative and teacher labor markets, compensation, the job security of educators, and so on. In and of themselves, charter schooling, school vouchers, and contracting do not *inevitably* alter these arrangements. Rather, legislators and administrators can choose whether to draft and enact policies that revolutionize schooling or leave current arrangements largely intact.

It is not merely a question of whether market-based reform is a good idea, but how market-based reform ought to be used.

We can use markets to revisit either the means and ends—or just the means—of education. However, we ought to recognize that the changes wrought by choice and contracting may very well slip the bonds we place upon them if we hope to use them merely to tweak American education. In the end, evaluating the promise of markets is far more than simply a technical calculation; it is also a statement about what we value in education and about how we weigh the claims of the individual and the community in a democratic society.

REFERENCES

Archbald, D.A. (2000). School choice and school stratification: Shortcomings of the stratification critique and recommendations for theory and research. *Educational Policy, 14*(2), 214-240.

Brighouse, H. (2000). *School choice and school justice.* Oxford, U.K.: Oxford University.

Bulman, R.C., & Kirp, D.L. (1999). The shifting politics of school choice. In S.D. Sugarman & F.R. Kemerer (Eds.), *School choice and social controversy: Politics, policy, and law* (pp. 36-67). Washington, DC: Brookings Institution.

Campbell, D.E. (2001). Making democratic education work. In P.E. Peterson & D.E. Campbell (Eds.), *Charters, vouchers, & public education* (pp. 241-267). Washington, DC: Brookings Institution.

Chubb, J., & Moe, T. (1990). *Politics, markets, & America's schools.* Washington, DC: Brookings Institution.

Coleman, J.S., Hoffer, T., & Kilgore, S. (1982). *High school achievement: Public, Catholic, and private schools compared.* New York: Basic Books.

Cookson, P.W. (1994). *School choice: The struggle for the soul of American education.* New Haven, CT: Yale University.

Coulson, A. (1999). *Market education, the unknown history.* New Brunswick, NJ: Transaction Publishers.

Elmore, R.F., & Fuller, B. (1996). Empirical research on educational choice: What are the implications for policy-makers? In R.F. Elmore & B. Fuller (Eds.), *Who chooses? Who loses? Culture, institutions, and the unequal effects of school choice* (pp. 187-201). New York: Teachers College Press.

Engel, M. (2000). *The struggle for control of public education: Market ideology vs. democratic values.* Philadelphia: Temple University.

Finn, C.E. (1990). Why we need choice. In W.L. Boyd & H.J. Walberg (Eds.), *Choice in education: Potential and problems* (pp. 3-19). Richmond, CA: McCutchan.

Finn, C.E., Manno, B.V., & Vanourek, G. (2000). *Charter schools in action: Renewing public education.* Princeton, NJ: Princeton University.

Fiske, E.B., & Ladd, H.F. (2000). *When schools compete: A cautionary tale.* Washington DC: Brookings Institution.

Friedman, M. (1962). *Capitalism and freedom.* Chicago: University of Chicago.

Gilles, S.G. (1998). Why parents should choose. In P.E. Peterson & B.C. Hassel (Eds.), *Learning from school choice* (pp. 395-407). Washington, DC: Brookings Institution.

Goldhaber, D. (2001). Significant, but not decisive. *Education Matters, 1*(2), 61-65.

Good, T.L., & Braden, J.S. (2000). *The great school debate: Choice, vouchers, and charters.* Mahwah, NJ: Lawrence Erlbaum.

Greene, J.P. (1998). Civic values in public and private schools. In P.E. Peterson & B.C. Hassel (Eds.), *Learning from school choice* (pp. 83-106). Washington, DC: Brookings Institution.

Greene, J.P., Peterson, P.E., & Du, J. (1999). Effectiveness of school choice: The Milwaukee experiment. *Education and Urban Society, 31*(2), 190-213.

Gutmann, A. (1987). *Democratic education.* Princeton, NJ: Princeton University.

Hassel, B.C. (1999). *The charter school challenge: Avoiding the pitfalls, fulfilling the promise.* Washington, DC: Brookings Institution.

Henig, J.R. (1994). *Rethinking school choice: Limits of the market metaphor.* Princeton, NJ: Princeton University.

Hess, F., Maranto, F., & Milliman, S. (2001). Little districts in big trouble: How four Arizona school systems responded to charter competition. *Teachers College Record, 103*(6), 1102-1124.

Hess, F.M. (2001). 'Whaddya mean you want to close my school?' The politics of regulatory accountability in charter schooling. *Education and Urban Society, 33*(2), 141-156.

Hess, F.M. (2002). *Revolution at the margins: The impact of competition on urban school systems*. Washington, DC: Brookings Institution.

Hill, P., Pierce, L.C., & Guthrie, P. (1997). *Reinventing public education*. Chicago: University of Chicago.

Hill, P.T. (2001). What is public about public education? In T.M. Moe (Ed.), *A primer on America's schools* (pp. 285-316). Stanford, CA: Hoover Institution.

Hirschman, A.O. (1970). *Exit, voice, and loyalty*. Cambridge, MA: Harvard University Press.

Holmes, M. (2001). Education and citizenship in an age of pluralism. In D. Ravitch & J.P. Viteritti (Eds.), *Making good citizens: Education and civil society*. New Haven, CT: Yale University.

Hoxby, C.M. (2000). Does competition among public schools benefit students and taxpayers? *American Economic Review, 90,* 1209-1238.

Hoxby, C.M. (2001). Rising tide: New evidence on competition and the public schools. *Education Next, 1*(4), 69-74.

Levin, H.M. (1987). Education as a public and private good. *Journal of Policy Analysis and Management, 6*(4), 628-641.

Loveless, T., & Jasin, C. (1998). Starting from scratch: Political and organizational challenges facing charter schools. *Educational Administration Quarterly, 34*(1), 9-30.

Macedo, S. (2000). *Democracy and distrust: Civic education in a multicultural democracy*. Cambridge, MA: Harvard University.

Maranto, R., Milliman, S., Hess, F., & Gresham, A. (1999). Do charter schools improve district schools? Three approaches to the question. In R. Maranto, S. Milliman, F. Hess, & A. Gresham (Eds.), *School choice in the real world: Lessons from Arizona charter schools* (pp. 129-141). Boulder, CO: Westview.

McEwan, P.J. (2000). The potential impact of large-scale voucher programs. *Review of Educational Research, 70*(2), 103-150.

Moe, T. (2001). *Vouchers, schools, and the American public*. Washington, DC: Brookings Institution.

Neal, D. (1998). What have we learned about the benefits of private schooling? *Economic Policy Review, 4*(1), 79-86.

Osborne, D. (1999). Healthy competition. *New Republic*, 31-33.

Peterson, P.E. (1995). The new politics of choice. In D. Ravitch & M.A. Vinovskis (Eds.), *Learning from the past: What history teaches us about school reform* (pp. 217-240). Baltimore: Johns Hopkins University.

Peterson, P.E., & Howell, W.G. (2002). *The education gap: Vouchers and urban schools*. Washington, DC: Brookings Institution.

Rouse, C.E. (1998). Private school vouchers and student achievement: An evaluation of the Milwaukee parental choice program. *Quarterly Journal of Economics, 113*(2), 553-602.

Schneider, M., Teske, P., & Marschall, M. (2000). *Choosing schools: Consumer choice and the quality of American schools*. Princeton, NJ: Princeton University.

Smith, K.B., & Meier, K.J. (1995). *The case against school choice: Politics, markets, and fools*. Armonk, NY: M.E. Sharpe.

Smrekar, C., & Goldring, E. (1999). *School choice in urban America: Magnet schools and the pursuit of equity*. New York: Teachers College Press.

Vedder, R.K. (2000). *Can teachers own their own schools? New strategies for educational excellence*. Oakland, CA: Independent Institute.

Viteritti, J.P. (1999). *Choosing equality: School choice, the Constitution, and civil society*. Washington, DC: Brookings Institution.

Wells, A.S. (1993). The sociology of school choice: Why some win and others lose in the educational marketplace. In E. Rasell & R. Rothstein (Eds.), *School choice: Examining the evidence* (pp. 29-48). Washington, DC: Economic Policy Institute.

Wells, A.S. (1996). African-American students' view of school choice. In B. Fuller, R.F. Elmore, & G. Orfield (Eds.), *Who chooses? Who loses? Culture, institutions, and the unequal effects of school choice* (pp. 25-49). New York: Teachers College Press.

Witte, J.F. (2000). *The market approach to education: An analysis of America's first voucher program*. Princeton, NJ: Princeton University.

Wolf, P.J., Greene, J.P., Kleitz, B., & Thalhammer, K. (2001). Private schooling and political tolerance. In P.E. Peterson & D.E. Campbell (Eds.), *Charters, vouchers, & public education* (pp. 268-290). Washington, DC: Brookings Institution.

CHAPTER 7

Vouchers, the Supreme Court, and the Next Political Rounds

TYLL VAN GEEL

On June 27, 2002 the United States Supreme Court in *Zelman v. Simmons-Harris* cleared away a significant constitutional obstacle to the adoption of voucher plans that include the participation of private religious schools. Specifically, the Court in *Zelman* concluded that a voucher program that involved the participation of private religious schools did not violate the Establishment Clause. Thus today the Establishment Clause—which prohibits government from passing laws respecting the establishment of religion (e.g., by providing financial aid to private religious schools)—will no longer be available as a basis for challenging a broad range of voucher plans that permit parents to choose private religious schools for their children. Although the *Zelman* decision is undoubtedly significant, it does not resolve a large number of political and policy issues entailed in any voucher plan, nor does it resolve a number of other important constitutional issues. Following a summary of the majority and dissenting opinions in *Zelman*, this chapter explores those constitutional issues that as a practical political matter may diminish the enthusiasm for and the likelihood of any widespread adoption of vouchers, regardless of the arguably beneficial effects vouchers might have on student achievement and the general improvement of our educational system.

The Opinions

When summarizing and seeking to specify the basic principle that arises out of a judicial opinion, it is important to try to identify those facts that were truly material to the court's decision, i.e., those facts that we can say with some certainty influenced the court, as opposed

Tyll van Geel is the Taylor Professor of Education and the Chair of the Educational Leadership Program, Margaret Warner Graduate School of Education and Human Development, University of Rochester.

to facts that were irrelevant to the outcome of the decision. In *Zelman* we note that the majority opinion opened with the observation that the "Cleveland public schools have been among the worst performing public schools in the Nation." It was against this background that the challenged voucher plan was adopted by the State of Ohio in 1996 as "part of a broader undertaking by the State to enhance the educational options of Cleveland's schoolchildren. ..."[1] The plan was ostensibly available to any family in Ohio who resided in a district under a court order requiring the state to supervise and manage the district, but since Cleveland was the only district actually under direct state control, only Cleveland parents were eligible for the voucher.

Under the voucher plan Cleveland families could choose to obtain either tuition aid to use at participating public and private K-8 schools, or tutorial aid for students who remained in the Cleveland schools. Families could use their tuition aid at any participating private religious or nonreligious school located within the Cleveland school district. The participating schools were required to agree not to discriminate on the basis of race, religion, or ethnic background, or to "advocate or foster unlawful behavior or teach hatred of any person or group on the basis of race, ethnicity, national origin, or religion" (*Zelman v. Simmons-Harris*, 2002, p. 2463).

Tuition aid for use at private schools varied according to the financial need of the family. Families with incomes 200% below the poverty line were eligible to receive 90% of a private school's tuition up to a cap of $2,250, and these lowest income families could not be charged a copay greater than $250. All other families received a voucher worth 75% of tuition costs up to $1,875 with no copayment cap. But these latter families could receive aid only if money was available after the poorest of the poor had made their decision to participate. Once parents received aid, they simply endorsed their state check over to their chosen school.

Parents could also choose to enroll their child in a participating public school adjacent to Cleveland; these parents were eligible for a $2,250 tuition grant that was paid to the participating district above and beyond the full amount of per-pupil state funding it received for each additional pupil. Both public and private participating schools were required to accept students in accordance with rules and procedures established by the Ohio state superintendent of education.

Tutorial aid for students who remained in the Cleveland schools was also graduated, depending on the parents' income; the poorest families were paid 90% of the cost of tutorial assistance up to $360.

In addition, the reform plan included the establishment and funding of community (charter) schools and magnet schools which students could choose to attend. Students who attended a community school brought with them $4,518, and those attending magnet schools brought with them $7,746, on top of the regular state per-pupil assistance of $4,167.

In the 1999-2000 school year more than 3,700 students received the voucher, and most of them (96%) enrolled in 46 religiously affiliated schools, with the remaining 4% scattered among 10 nonreligious private schools.[2] None of the public schools adjacent to Cleveland participated. Sixty percent of the participating students were at or below the poverty line. Roughly 1,400 students received tutorial aid.

In July 1999 Simmons-Harris filed suit in federal court challenging the voucher plan on the grounds that it violated the Establishment Clause of the First Amendment. Two lower federal courts found the plan to be in violation of the clause, but the Supreme Court in a 5-4 decision reversed their rulings.[3] Still working with the traditional tests that a law must not have the purpose or primary effect of advancing or inhibiting religion, the majority concluded that the Cleveland program was constitutionally permissible. The matter of the legitimacy of the purpose of the program was dispatched in one sentence, "There is no dispute that the program challenged here was enacted for the valid secular purpose of providing educational assistance to poor children in a demonstrably failing public school system" (*Zelman v. Simmons-Harris*, p. 2465).

The question of the possibly forbidden effect of the program took the majority several more pages to deal with, beginning with an analysis of precedent. That analysis led the majority to conclude:

> [W]here a government aid program is neutral with respect to religion, and provides assistance directly to a broad class of citizens who, in turn, direct government aid to religious schools wholly as a result of their own genuine and independent private choice, the program is not readily subject to challenge under the Establishment Clause. A program that shares these features permits government aid to reach religious institutions only by way of deliberate choices of individual recipients. The incidental advancement of a religious mission, or the perceived endorsement of a religious message, is reasonably attributable to the individual recipient, not to the government, whose role ends with the disbursement of benefits. (*Zelman v. Simmons-Harris*, 2002, p. 2467)

(Given space limitations, I will not address whether this is a legitimate reading of precedent and comports with a proper interpretation of the Establishment Clause.)

The majority then turned to the facts of the case to determine whether or not the Cleveland plan comported with their announced basic principle. The Court concluded that Cleveland's program was indeed neutral:

- The aid flowed to a broad class of individuals defined without reference to religion.
- The program permitted the participation of religious and non-religious schools.

Furthermore, the program was considered neutral by the Court in the sense that it was a program of "true private choice," and not one that coerced parents into sending their children to private religious schools.

- The program offered parents a wide range of both public and private options.
- Private schools received half the funds community and magnet schools received.
- Adjacent public schools were eligible to receive two to three times the money available to private schools.
- Parents in private schools faced a copayment, creating a disincentive to enroll their children.

Finally, the Court considered the program neutral in the sense that it did not discourage the participation of private nonreligious schools. It was true that 46 of the private schools (82% of the participating schools) were religious schools, but the reality was that 81% of the private schools in Ohio were religious schools. The program thus "captured a remarkable cross-section of private schools, religious and non-religious" (*Zelman v. Simmons-Harris*, 2002, p. 2470). With this statement the Court rejected the argument of Justice Souter and the plaintiffs that capping the amount of tuition favored participation by the religious schools. The majority noted that there were 10 secular private schools within the Cleveland school district and all 10 chose to participate, and "while no religious schools have been created in response to the program, several *nonreligious* schools have been created" (*Zelman v. Simmons-Harris*, 2002, p. 2470, n. 4).

Justices O'Connor and Thomas offered several interesting observations. Justice O'Connor, after reviewing various forms of aid already provided to religious schools, e.g., property tax exemptions, concluded that the aid involved in the Cleveland voucher program was "neither substantial nor atypical of existing government programs" (*Zelman v.*

Simmons-Harris, 2002, p. 2475). Justice Thomas took the audacious position that the Establishment Clause should not be available to oppose neutral programs of school choice. He would interpret the Constitution so that states would be freer than Congress to experiment with involvement in religion on a neutral basis and to pass laws "that include or touch on religious matters so long as these laws do not impede free exercise rights or any other individual religious liberty interest" (*Zelman v. Simmons-Harris*, 2002, p. 2481).

Although the dissenters, especially Justice Souter, raised important technical legal arguments, their central concerns can be captured in five propositions. First, the Cleveland program was in fact not neutral in its effects. Second, the doctrine of the majority will permit a substantial increase in the flow of aid to religious schools, and, third, this public money now and in the future will pay for religious indoctrination. Fourth, expansion of substantial aid to religious schools will in turn lead to a rise of religious strife in our increasingly religiously pluralistic society. Finally, the dissenters claimed that the majority's position was inconsistent with the principles behind the Establishment Clause. Justice Stevens made the point this way: "Whenever we remove a brick from the wall that was designed to separate religion and government, we increase the risk of religious strife and weaken the foundation of our democracy" (*Zelman v. Simmons-Harris*, 2002, p. 2485).

The Interpretations

Zelman and *Brown v. Board of Education*

Supporters of vouchers claim that *Zelman* is of comparable historical significance to the decision in *Brown v. Board of Education* (1954). This claim is not supportable. The decision in *Brown* represented a sweeping prohibition of a widely adopted policy—the policy of segregating pupils in public schools on the basis of race. *Brown* mandated that educational policy must change, whereas *Zelman* imposed no such requirement. *Brown* struck down a deeply rooted educational policy, whereas *Zelman* merely provided a sketch of what policy might be permissible but was not required. That is to say, *Zelman* merely stated that as far as the First Amendment of the U.S. Constitution was concerned, certain forms of voucher plans were permissible options that the state might (but need not) pursue. Furthermore, in some states any legislative effort to adopt a voucher plan may still, as a legal matter, be foreclosed by *state* constitutional provisions (as discussed later). *Brown* was a case in which the Supreme Court required educational policy change; *Zelman* was not.

The proponents of "*Zelman* equals *Brown*"—besides merely deploying this rhetoric as a dramatic way to assert *Zelman's* importance—were seeking to assimilate *Zelman* into the egalitarian message of *Brown*.[4] But *Zelman*, unlike *Brown*, did not lay down a constitutionally based principle of educational equity. At most, *Zelman* cleared away a constitutional hurdle to the adoption of a policy that, if adopted and permitted by state constitutional provisions, might or might not advance educational equity. The effect of *Zelman* on educational equity must stand the test of time. We do not yet know whether *Zelman* will in fact lead to more states embracing voucher plans, and, of course, we cannot yet know whether those plans will have the same, greater, or lesser educational effects on student achievement in comparison with the smaller, scattered plans that have been in operation in Cleveland and Milwaukee.[5]

Interpreting Zelman

The question I want to address here can be asked in several ways. First, must all future voucher plans be identical to the plan adopted in Ohio in order to be constitutionally permissible under the Establishment Clause? Put differently, what is the principle established by the majority opinion in *Zelman*? What is the scope of *Zelman*? How should *Zelman* be interpreted?

If the past history of political conflict over the meaning of Supreme Court precedent is any indication of the future of *Zelman*, the interpretation of *Zelman* will remain a vexing question for some time to come. There is no definitive or authoritative way to answer the questions in advance of an interpretation of *Zelman* by the Supreme Court itself, but I will try to forecast the nature of the debate over the interpretation of *Zelman*.

Opponents of voucher plans and advocates of a strict separation of church and state (regardless of whether they favor or oppose vouchers that involve only nonreligious private schools) will argue for as narrow an interpretation of *Zelman* as possible.[6] They will claim that only voucher plans that resemble the Ohio plan in all significant respects should be accepted as constitutionally permissible. Thus, all future voucher plans would have to be conjoined with a more general public school reform effort in the face of a proven record that the schools in the relevant district were educationally bankrupt. They would have to serve the significant public interest of improving the educational opportunities of the poor; provide students with a range of options that included improved new educational programs in the public schools; offer a voucher that did not create a larger economic incentive than the incentive in *Zelman* to attend religious schools; and include all the regulations imposed on the private schools by Ohio. Advocates of this view would also argue that the small numbers of pupils involved in the Cleveland program (3,700) and the fact that private schools received "only half the government assistance given to community schools and one-third the assistance given to magnet schools" (*Zelman v. Simmons-Harris*, 2002, p. 2468) were other important factors that made this program tolerable under the Establishment Clause. Any acceptable future voucher plan must therefore be targeted to a select number of the poorest of the poor and provide attractive and better funded options in the public schools. Clearly, in any voucher plan the money must be paid directly to the parent and offered to eligible poor parents without reference to their religion. Any plan that involved only religious schools would be constitutionally impermissible. In sum, plans that did not have these features, the advocates of a narrow reading of *Zelman* would assert, would violate the majority's own principle that a voucher plan must have neither the purpose nor effect of advancing or inhibiting religion.

Advocates for vouchers and people who take a different view of the demands of the Establishment Clause will argue that *Zelman* should be interpreted to permit a wide variety of voucher plans. They would argue that any voucher plan designed to serve a secular purpose, such as increasing parental choice, is permissible if it assures "true private choice" and is made available to all parents without regard to their religion.[7] In this view, the size of the voucher, the total amount of money involved, the wealth (or lack thereof) of the participating parents, and the percentage of participating schools that are religious would all be immaterial. Similarly, it would be unimportant whether the voucher plan was accompanied by the creation of community, charter, or magnet schools or the provision of a tutoring program. Advocates of this view of *Zelman* need only repeat the Supreme Court majority opinion cited above on page 138.

Dissenting Justice Souter was aware of the possibility of "the incidental advancement of a religious mission" when he wrote:

> If 'choice' is present whenever there is any educational alternative to the religious school to which vouchers can be endorsed, then there will always be a choice and the voucher can always be constitutional even in a system in which there is not a single private secular school as an alternative to the religious school. (*Zelman v. Simmons-Harris*, 2002, p. 2492)

I will not summarize the various interpretations of *Zelman* that fall between these two extremes. But one can reasonably predict that the majority of the current Supreme Court would be inclined to interpret its own precedent in *Zelman* as permitting a wide range of voucher plans. As discussed more fully later, the Court has been steadily moving toward a view of the Establishment Clause that has been dubbed "non-preferentialism." Under this view government may support religion so long as the aid is distributed without preference of one religion over another (*Wallace v. Jaffree*, 1985, Chief Justice Rehnquist dissenting in a decision striking down a law that would permit public schools to incorporate a period of silence for "meditation or voluntary prayer"). The core idea behind nonpreferentialism is that the Establishment Clause was intended merely to prevent the establishment of a national church or an official national religion, and evenhanded aid programs do not run this danger (Cord, 1982). The second broad interpretation noted above is certainly more consistent with the doctrine of nonpreferentialism than the more restrictive interpretation, with its greater focus on maintaining a wall of separation between church and state.

How *Zelman* may be interpreted is of course important for policy-makers. If Congress were to resurrect President Bush's educational voucher plan (discussed more fully below), it certainly would face constitutional challenges based on *Zelman*. Whether that plan as originally proposed would survive in the Court is, as we shall see, not an open and shut case.

State Constitutional Obstacles

Regardless of how *Zelman* may be interpreted, future voucher plans undoubtedly will face constitutional challenges based on state constitutions. What is constitutionally permissible under the U.S. Constitution may not be constitutionally permissible under a state constitution.[8] Undoubtedly the decision in *Zelman* will influence how state courts interpret their own constitutional provisions—it is not uncommon for state courts to follow the lead of the U.S. Supreme Court in interpreting their own state constitutions (*Campbell v. Manchester Bd. of School Dir.*, 1994). But it is not necessary that they do so. By one estimate, there are 19 states in which the judiciary could read their state constitutions as prohibiting vouchers as a violation of their state's constitutional provisions dealing with the separation of church and state (Kemerer, 1997).

A recent decision of a federal Court of Appeals, however, suggests that any effort to design a voucher program so that it served students undertaking exclusively secular studies may violate the U.S. First Amendment's Free Exercise of Religion clause (*Davey v. Locke*, 2002).

In that case, Washington State made a scholarship to pursue postsecondary education available to high-achieving low- and middle-income high school students. In the case before the Ninth Circuit, the plaintiff was eligible for the scholarship but was denied it when it became known that he wanted to study theology. (He would have been eligible for the scholarship if he had undertaken a different major even at a religious institution.) The state based its denial on the state's constitutional provision (a so-called Blaine amendment) that prohibited any public money from being "appropriated for or applied to any religious worship, exercise or instruction, or the support of any religious establishment" (*Davey v. Locke*, 2002, p. 750). But the Ninth Circuit concluded that denial of the scholarship infringed the federal Free Exercise clause; the denial was a form of viewpoint discrimination, and the state's interest in enforcing its own constitutional provision was not a sufficiently compelling interest to justify the infringement. Relying on an analogy to the abortion funding decisions that *permitted* the government to fund births but not abortions, the dissent said that denial of funding to *study* theology was permissible, especially given the fact that the plaintiff was still permitted to attend a religious school.

The Implications for States

A Federal Mandate of Vouchers and State Sovereignty

Even if state constitutional provisions were to stand in the way of the enactment of a state educational voucher system, those same state constitutional provisions could not serve to block the establishment of a federally funded educational voucher plan.[9] For example, President George W. Bush proposed in January 2001 a comprehensive educational reform package that included a voucher component as one of the tools to be used to motivate a failing public school to take steps to improve itself. Under the plan public schools would be required annually to assess their pupils in reading and math. Schools that failed to make adequate yearly progress with their disadvantaged pupils would first receive federal assistance; if after 3 years such a school did not make adequate yearly progress as measured against the applicable state standards, the disadvantaged students in that school could use federal Title I funds to transfer to a higher performing public or private school or receive supplemental educational services from a provider of their choice. This aspect of President Bush's educational reform plan was ultimately not included in the final legislation, but it represents an example of the kind of federal legislation that could survive challenges based on state Establishment Clause provisions, as well as challenges based on the federal Constitution's Establishment Clause.

It is interesting to note that President Bush's plan arguably could be found to be consistent with *Zelman,* even if *Zelman* were given the narrow interpretation outlined earlier. Like the plan approved in *Zelman,* the Bush plan is a limited voucher scheme targeted at a comparatively small group of students and contained within a larger educational reform effort. The Bush plan does not, however, encompass and financially support the same range of options and educational choices found in the Ohio plan. Because the Bush plan is less aggressive in fostering a range of parental options, it might be vulnerable to the charge that it does not promote "true private choice." However, if *Zelman* were given the broad interpretation described earlier, there is little doubt that the Bush plan would be found to be constitutionally permissible.

President Bush's voucher plan was part and parcel of a system of federal financial assistance to schools and disadvantaged pupils. As such, it was designed to try to avoid not just a constitutional challenge based on the Establishment Clause, but also another potentially formidable constitutional challenge. To explore this point, let us first look at a proposal that the President did not make. If Congress and the President were to adopt legislation that directly commanded the states to establish a voucher program, such legislation could be challenged on the grounds that it violates state sovereignty, a doctrine that in recent years has taken on new potency in limiting Congress (*New York v. United States,* 1992; *Printz v. United States,* 1997; *Reno v. Condon,* 2000). The precedent regarding when and to what degree the doctrine of state sovereignty does limit Congressional power offers no clear guidelines. Nevertheless, this body of cases represents a potential threat to direct federal control over the structure and processes of the states' public school systems.

By tying itself to federal aid, the Bush plan reduces the likelihood of success for such a challenge. Still, even the Bush plan is vulnerable to the state sovereignty claim, to the extent that it would require a state to make its own public schools part of the voucher system and to ignore its own laws allowing local school districts to exclude nonresident pupils. Assuming that this "state sovereignty" argument were successful, the Bush plan could then promote vouchers only for use at private schools; as soon as the plan was limited in this way, it would become more vulnerable to attack under *Zelman,* especially if *Zelman* were given the narrow interpretation outlined earlier.

Vouchers and the Equal Protection Clause

As noted above, advocates of vouchers like to argue that vouchers serve a principle of educational equality of opportunity. They claim that the kind of voucher scheme involved in *Zelman* helps students who, because of personal poverty, cannot afford tuition to obtain a private school education as middle and upper income families can. But might there be any serious constitutional issue in limiting vouchers to the poor? The short answer is "no."[10] The question I want to raise here is whether a state may institute vouchers in only one part of the state (as Ohio did). May the availability of a voucher depend on where the child lives? This is a challenge that could conceivably be raised by voucher advocates who want to see a voucher plan spread across a state.

Recall that the voucher plan in *Zelman* was available only to parents who resided in school districts that were under direct state supervision because the districts were educationally bankrupt. This category of school district had only a single entry, Cleveland. In effect, a distinction was drawn between students in districts that had been officially desig-nated as particularly bad, i.e., were not delivering a minimally adequate education, and students in districts that were delivering a minimally adequate education. If the classification scheme is defined in this way, there is little chance that any equal protection challenge on behalf of the students in the minimally adequate districts would be successful. The test likely to be used in such a challenge would be the so-called rational basis test, which requires challengers to establish that the policy served an illegitimate interest or was not rationally related to a legiti-mate purpose (*San Antonio Independent School District v. Rodriguez*, 1973). Challengers are not going to be able to meet this burden of proof.

If the Ohio plan were written differently so that it was available only to "poor" children, it is highly probable that the plan would also survive constitutional challenge. Again, the rational basis test would be the likely test, and for the reasons just stated, the challenges would not be able to meet that test (*Dandridge v. Williams*, 1970).

If a different test were applied—the so-called strict scrutiny test—the chances for a successful challenge would be increased. Under the strict scrutiny test it would be the state that would have to establish that its voucher plan (1) was necessary, and (2) served a compelling state interest (*Kramer v. Union Free School District No. 15*, 1969). Few would disagree that the effort to rescue children from, and to improve, a failing school district was a compelling state interest. The real issue in such a hypothetical case would be whether the voucher plan was "necessary" to achieve that end. The state would be hard pressed to make that argument successfully. Thus, if the strict scrutiny test were applied, the voucher plan would probably be found unconstitutional.

But it is highly improbable that a voucher scheme such as Ohio's would trigger the use of the strict scrutiny test. Strict scrutiny is used in cases in which either a "suspect classification" is used, e.g., race, or a fundamental interest is adversely affected. The classification used in the Ohio plan (students in failing schools vs. students in non-failing schools) is not a suspect classification. Thus, the case for use of the strict scrutiny test would rest exclusively on the argument that the plan adversely affected a fundamental interest. Here again, the argument would in all likelihood fail. First, the Supreme Court has refused to recognize education per se as a fundamental interest. It has said that at most only the denial of a minimally adequate education would trigger strict scrutiny or its rough equivalent (*Plyler v. Doe*, 1982). Second, the voucher scheme, far from denying a minimally adequate education, was designed to provide students with such an education.

This line of analysis does not mean that any voucher scheme is automatically immune to successful challenge under the Equal Protection Clause—a voucher scheme limited to minority pupils would face a severe constitutional challenge. In today's Supreme Court even an argument claiming that such a plan was a form of affirmative action would not be successful (*Adarand Constructors, Inc. v. Pena*, 1995). Would it make a difference if, as a practical matter, the voucher plan were used primarily by African American children because the enrollment in the target district was predominantly African American? No, so long as the plan did not intentionally discriminate on the basis of race. The relevant test would be the rational basis test, and, as discussed, the plan would easily survive a challenge based on that test (*Washington v. Davis*, 1976).

Finally, an effort to provide vouchers that could be used only at private nonsectarian schools would raise the same set of issues addressed in *Davey v. Locke* (2002), mentioned earlier.

The Implications for Schools

The Regulation of Participating Voucher Schools

In the future the most divisive and legally complex aspects of vouchers, now that the Court has ruled in *Zelman*, will be the eligibility criteria by which a private school becomes a participating voucher school, and the regulation of those private schools. First Amendment free speech claims and First Amendment free exercise of religion challenges are likely to be involved.

The First Amendment Background

Recall that in the Ohio system a private school wishing to participate in the voucher system had to agree not to discriminate on the basis of race, religion, or ethnic background or to "advocate or foster unlawful behavior or teach hatred of any person or group on the basis of race, ethnicity, national origin, or religion." To understand the significance of this statute, and similar statutes that are going to be part of all voucher schemes, it is important to recognize that private schools today enjoy significant First Amendment protection—in terms of both free speech and the free exercise of religion. For the sake of argument, assume we live in a world without vouchers but one in which the curriculum of the private school is regulated, for example, by prohibiting the school from teaching hatred.

First, any such regulation would be challenged as unconstitutionally "vague" because people of common intelligence must guess at its meaning (*Coates v. Cincinnati*, 1971).

Second, regulation of the private school's curriculum must not be undertaken using laws that are unconstitutionally "overbroad," that is, by laws that suppress not only speech that constitutionally may be suppressed, e.g., "fighting words," but also speech that is constitutionally protected. Several justices found that an ordinance directed at so-called hate speech was "overbroad" because it barred speech that caused "anger, alarm or resentment," and such speech could not be prohibited (*R.A.V. v. City of St. Paul*, 1992, Justice White concurring). In this case, the Ohio law that regulates voucher schools' prohibiting advocacy of unlawful behavior may be "overbroad." It is worth noting that the Supreme Court has said in dictum that "... parents have a First Amendment right to send their children to educational institutions that promote the belief that racial segregation is desirable ..." (*Runyon v. McCrary*, 1976, p. 176). Few would doubt that private schools have the constitutional right to teach the value of segregation and racial discrimination. The Supreme Court has even ruled that government may not single out for suppression hate speech based on race, color, creed, religion, or gender (*R.A.V. v. City of St. Paul*).

Third, it is general First Amendment doctrine that even speech that advocates unlawful behavior such as violence is protected right up to the point that the speech actually involves inciting people to unlawful action and is in fact likely to produce imminent lawless action (*Brandenburg v. Ohio*, 1969). Thus, any challenge to the Ohio law will rest on a strong foundation.

Fourth, government may not allocate its funds in such a way that it discriminates on the basis of viewpoint (*Rosenberger v. Rector and Visitors of the University of Virginia*, 1995). If today a state were to provide money only to schools advocating a pro-Israeli policy and not to schools espousing the Palestinian viewpoint, the First Amendment would be violated.

Fifth, the government may not require organizations not to discriminate in hiring, say, on the basis of sexual preference (*Boy Scouts of America v. Dale*, 2000). If a private school taught that homosexuality was immoral, it could not be required by a state's antidiscrimination law to hire a gay teacher who was an advocate of gay rights, just as the Boy Scouts were not required to hire a gay scoutmaster.

Finally, the private religious school enjoys the protection of the First Amendment's Free Exercise of Religion clause. Therefore, a school that believed that the state was imposing regulations that deeply conflicted with its core beliefs as well as those of its parent population could raise constitutional objections based on the Free Exercise Clause (*State v. Whisner*, 1976).

It is against this constitutional background that we must consider state regulations of private schools participating in a state voucher system. But now the situation is changed because government funding is involved. The question is whether the government's constitutional authority to regulate the private school is enhanced if government money is involved.

Regulated Vouchers and the First Amendment

One could argue that the voucher money involved is money that is going to parents, and therefore there is no public subsidy of the message of the private school. The government gains no constitutional leverage over the private religious school simply because it is funding the parents. When the voucher scheme is looked at in this way, any regulation of the private school must be approached in the same way as outlined above, that is, as if the regulations were simply a direct state regulation of private schools. This kind of regulation would raise the constitutional challenges already discussed. Thus, one could argue that these regulations, even though they are connected to a voucher system, are simply vague and overbroad unconstitutional regulations of the private school.

Advocates of vouchers would find this conclusion *politically* uncomfortable. It would mean that any voucher scheme as a constitutional matter might have to permit students to choose schools that "taught hatred." And if this were the legal reality, it would seem that the political opposition to vouchers would be sufficiently intense and widespread to make it impossible for voucher plans to find their way into law.

To avoid this problem, voucher advocates now have two possible moves, but each one entails problems. One move would be to argue that private schools that receive government money can be made, as a condition of the receipt of that money, to follow regulations such as those adopted by Ohio. The first difficulty with this argument is that it contradicts the position that the voucher advocates and the State of Ohio took before the Supreme Court and contradicts the position adopted by the majority opinion. This argument rests on the assumption that voucher money in fact does subsidize the message of the private school, that this is not money being paid to parents. Suddenly the fact that money first went to the parents would become irrelevant, which was not the argument before the Supreme Court, nor what the majority of the Court said. To try to argue for the legitimacy of the state regulation of the message of the private school in this way pulls the parent out of the equation.

One way around this objection might be to seek to impose the regulations not on the private school itself but on the parents. In other words, the state legislation might be written so that parents who want to participate in the voucher program must agree not to use the voucher at a school that taught hatred or advocated unlawful behavior. In effect, the argument on behalf of the regulations would be that "he who pays the piper can call the tune."

There is precedent that an artful advocate could support this position. In *Rust v. Sullivan* (1991) the Supreme Court upheld a law that prohibited projects that received federal family planning funds from encouraging, promoting, or advocating abortion. The Court ruled that Congress could selectively fund a program to encourage certain activities without at the same time funding an alternative program. This was not discrimination based on viewpoint; it was merely the funding of one activity to the exclusion of another. Family planning projects that did want to advocate abortion simply had to do so using money other than their federal money, which the projects had to keep separate and use separately for the intended federal purpose. The dissenters said this was nothing but viewpoint discrimination. "Whatever may be the Government's power to condition the receipt of its largess upon the relinquishment of constitutional rights, it surely does not extend to a condition that suppresses the recipient's cherished freedom of speech solely upon the content or viewpoint of that speech" (*Rust v. Sullivan*, p. 207). This same advocate might also cite a number of other related Supreme Court opinions giving support to governmental selective funding of speech activities (*National Endowment for the Arts v. Finley*, 1998; *Regan v. Taxation With Representation of Washington*, 1983).

But advocates on the other side of the case have precedent they can use to support the claim that the government may not selectively fund speech. Thus, in *Rosenberger v. Rector and Visitors of the University of Virginia* (1995) the Supreme Court ruled that the University of Virginia discriminated on the basis of viewpoint when it refused to pay the printing costs of a student publication that took a Christian viewpoint, while at the same time the university funded other student-edited publications. These advocates could also use the decisions in *Good News Club v. Milford Central School* (2001) and *Lambs Chapel v. Center Moriches Union Free School District* (1993), in which the Supreme Court ruled that if school districts opened school facilities to other community groups, they could not then discriminate on the basis of religion and exclude religious groups from using the same facilities. Finally, those attacking the controls on parents may cite *Legal Services Corporation v. Velazquez* (2001), in which the Supreme Court struck down a federal law barring the federally funded Legal Services Corporation from funding any organization that represented indigent clients in "an effort to amend or otherwise challenge existing [welfare] law" (p. 537).

This is not the place to resolve the very tangled set of constitutional issues posed by the conflicting lines of precedent. Suffice it to say that efforts to condition the receipt of a voucher raise a set of complex issues, whether the conditions are placed on the parents or on the private school. Governmental efforts to require limits on free speech and on free exercise activities as a condition of receiving governmental money represent an area of constitutional law fraught with conceptual, theoretical, and practical legal difficulties. For example, people working with these lines of cases will precipitate discussions regarding whether the voucher program was designed to facilitate "private speech"—as arguably occurred in *Rosenberger*—or to promote a governmental message—as arguably occurred in *Rust*. The resolution of this discussion holds profound implications for the constitutional status and politics of vouchers. Voucher programs may very well be bogged down in long, expensive, and deeply contentious litigation over these issues for years to come.

Even assuming that conditions such as those imposed by Ohio do survive judicial challenge, implementing those same conditions will unavoidably engender deep and acrimonious political conflict. Justice Breyer's dissent states the problem this way:

> How are state officials to adjudicate claims that one religion or another is advocating, for example, civil disobedience in response to unjust laws, the use of illegal drugs in a religious ceremony, or resort to force to call attention to what it views as an immoral social practice? What kind of public hearing will there be in response to claims that one religion or another is continuing to teach a view of history that casts members of other religions in the worst possible light? How will the public react to government funding for schools that take controversial religious positions on topics that are of current popular interest—say the conflict in the Middle East or the war on terrorism? Yet any major funding program for primary religious education will require criteria. And the selection of those criteria, as well as their application, inevitably pose problems that are divisive (*Zelman v. Simmons-Harris*, 2002, p. 2506, Justice Breyer dissenting).

The only way out of this potential morass is not to impose conditions such as those imposed by Ohio. But it is unlikely that a voucher program without those conditions could garner sufficient political support. Too many taxpayers will object to seeing their money used by parents in schools that teach doctrines that they, the taxpayers, regard as abominable.

Conclusion

Even after *Zelman*, efforts to institute vouchers will face a continuing tangle of legal issues and political conundrums. Precisely what kind of voucher system could survive a constitutional challenge based on the Establishment Clause is not clearly settled. State constitutional provisions analogous to the federal Establishment Clause—Blaine amendments—may or may not still stand as. another obstacle. The design of voucher plans will have to take into account potential challenges based on the Equal Protection Clause. But potentially most significant, efforts to design voucher plans that are politically acceptable by excluding schools that espouse controversial perspectives will encounter severe free speech challenges, which, if successful, will make the voucher plans politically risky. Plans consistent with the Free Speech clause may be politically unacceptable, while any politically acceptable voucher plan may violate the Free Speech Clause.

NOTES

1. The reform program included the establishment of "community schools" funded under state law but run by their own school boards, not by local school districts. These schools enjoyed significant independence regarding hiring and curricular policy. The formation of magnet schools was another feature of the reform package. Thus, Cleveland students, in addition to the voucher plan, had the option of enrolling in a community school or a magnet school.

2. As the Court noted, the 96% figure was calculated by excluding all the students attending community schools, magnet schools, and the tutorial program. If these are included, then 76% of the participating students attended religious schools.

3. Chief Justice Rehnquist and Justices Kennedy, O'Connor, Scalia, and Thomas comprised the majority. Justices O'Connor and Thomas wrote concurring opinions. Justices Breyer, Ginsberg, Souter, and Stevens dissented.

4. Advocates of educational vouchers claim that voucher plans are a way to equalize educational opportunities for poor students attending troubled urban schools, a way of providing those students the opportunity to attend a better school in the same way that the rich can choose to move to a superior suburban school or enroll in a higher quality private school.

5. I am taking no position here on the hotly debated question of whether those plans have led to improved student achievement among the students participating in the voucher plan or in the public schools now facing added competition from the private sector.

6. They will, of course, first of all seek to have the decision in *Zelman* overturned by the Supreme Court itself at a future date.

7. This interpretation of *Zelman* assumes that a public school option is available as required by all state constitutions. As a theoretical matter, under this interpretation of *Zelman* a state could amend its own constitution to drop the self-imposed requirement that there be a public school system and turn to supporting education wholly through a voucher system that involved both religious and nonreligious private schools. Arguably, even this system would be permissible under this interpretation of *Zelman*.

8. We have seen this happen with regard to constitutional challenges to the financial systems supporting the public school systems. In *San Antonio Independent School District v. Rodriguez* (1973) the Supreme Court ruled that it was permissible for a state to fund its public schools in such a way that there were dramatic interdistrict differences in the amounts of money spent per pupil, i.e., so that the amount of money spent on a pupil depended on where the pupil lived. Nevertheless, in approximately 20 states the courts have ruled that such an arrangement violated the relevant state constitution (Michael Imber & Tyll van Geel, *Education Law*, 2000, p. 281).

9. Federal law is, under the U.S. Constitution, superior to state law, even state constitutional provisions. Thus, a federally funded voucher plan could be enacted even if the same plan, if it were to be adopted by a state legislature, were found to be unconstitutional under that state's constitution (Article VI, Section 2, U.S. Constitution.)

10. Equal protection doctrine permits government to draw distinctions based on wealth, especially when a program is designed to assist the less well off. Historically, the wealth discrimination cases that have raised serious constitutional issues are those in which the poor have been discriminated against (*Dandridge v. Williams*, 1970).

REFERENCES

Adarand Constructors, Inc. v. Pena, 515 U.S. 200 (1995).

Boy Scouts of America v. Dale, 530 U.S. 640 (2000).

Brandenburg v. Ohio, 395 U.S. 444 (1969).

Campbell v. Manchester Bd. of School Directors, 641 A.2d 352 (Vt. 1994).

Coates v. Cincinnati, 402 U.S. 611 (1971).

Cord, R.L. (1982). *Separation of church and state: Historical fact and current fiction.* New York: Lambeth Press.

Dandridge v. Williams, 397 U.S. 471 (1970).

Davey v. Locke, 299 F. 3d 748 (9th Cir. 2002).

Good News Club v. Milford Central School, 121 S. Ct. 2093 (2001).

Imber, M., & van Geel, T. (2000). *Education Law*, 2nd ed. Mahwah, NJ: Lawrence Erlbaum Associates.

Kemerer, Frank. (1997). State constitutions and school vouchers. *Education Law Reporter*, 120.

Kramer v. Union Free School District No. 15, 395 U.S. 621 (1969).

Lambs Chapel v. Center Moriches Union Free School District, 508 U.S. 384 (1993).

Legal Services Corporation v. Velasquez, 531 U.S. 533 (2001).

National Endowment for the Arts v. Finley, 524 U.S. 569 (1998).

New York v. United States, 505 U.S. 144 (1992).

Plyler v. Doe, 457 U.S. 202 (1982).

Printz v. United States, 521 U.S. 898 (1997).

R.A.V. v. City of St. Paul, 505 U.S. 377 (1992).

Regan v. Taxation With Representation of Washington, 461 U.S. 540 (1983).

Reno v. Condon, 528 U.S. 141 (2000).

Runyon v. McCrary, 427 U.S. 160 (1976).

Rosenberger v. Rector and Visitors of the University of Virginia, 515 U.S. 819 (1995).

Rust v. Sullivan, 500 U.S. 173 (1991).

San Antonio Independent School District v. Rodriguez, 411 U.S. 1 (1973).

State v. Whisner, 351 N.E. 2d 750 (1976).

Wallace v. Jaffree, 472 U.S. 38 (1985).

Washington v. Davis, 426 U.S. 229 (1976).

Zelman v. Simmons-Harris, 122 S. Ct. 2460 (2002)

Section Three
RETHINKING THE GOVERNANCE
OF SCHOOL DISTRICTS

CHAPTER 8

Governing Learning at the Community Level: Rethinking and Projecting

LUVERN L. CUNNINGHAM

This chapter is developed in two sections. The first section discusses traditional patterns of thinking about the roles and responsibilities of those who take part in the governance of learning. The remaining pages address an emerging community context in which the governing function may occur. In both sections, an assumption is made that improvements in community governance of learning are not only warranted but achievable. It is also assumed that improvements are dependent on processes of community dialogue and reflection. Traditionally, governing has been considered most often in the context of jurisdictions contained within the geographical boundaries of local school districts. This discussion expands the concept of governing, and does not limit itself to the governing parameters of school officials as defined by constitutions and statutes.

Many students of governing argue the importance of context. A brief scenario about Ohio, discussed later, illustrates the political context of education there and introduces the reader to the complexity of the educational environment that citizens encounter. Prior to this discussion, some mention of the work of the late Professor Harold D. Lasswell, a social scientist on the faculty of Yale Law School, provides a richer understanding of the significance of context for education and educational policy.

Luvern L. Cunningham is Professor Emeritus at Ohio State University.

Respect for Context

In 1975, Harold D. Lasswell, perhaps best known as the primary author of the United Nations Declaration of Human Rights, addressed an assembly of educational researchers convened by the Research for Better Schools Education Laboratory. His focus was on political futures and their implications for society and its institutions. He foreshadowed events that became realities a quarter century later, discussing heightened interdependence, the emergence of widespread terrorism, and a world marked by intensifying surveillance and expanding penchants for institutional appraisal at all levels in both the public and private sectors.[1] Lasswell framed his presentation within several conceptual systems that provided the foundation for his address, and his insights were prescient in terms of their implications for education and the governing of learning.

Lasswell's references to interdependence referred to a tightening of the fabric of institutional and individual relationships. Institutionally, local, state, and federal jurisdictions would experience less independence of function and responsibility, both horizontally and vertically. Power sharing would be essential, and collaboration among governments and institutions would become a norm. School districts and their schools would be expected to interact with their communities and local institutions. Professionals—physicians, social workers, lawyers, teachers, principals, and superintendents, among others—would develop collaborative relationships and assume a shared accountability for well being in their communities. New knowledge bases and new skills would be shared.

Terrorism would become more common, affecting economies all over the world, with great significance for budgeting and finance decisions at every level. New provisions for security would be necessary for classrooms, schools, and school districts. Surveillance of increasing sophistication, fostered by advancing technology, would emerge as another consequence of terrorist activity.

Lasswell foresaw rapid expansion of appraisal activity at all levels as well; there would be diverse approaches to assessment and evaluation of performance. Individuals, institutions, and governments would all come under increased scrutiny. In education, other ramifications would include a proliferation of standardized testing, the standards movement, curriculum and fiscal audits, internal and external oversight structures and commissions, and investigative journalism. Those who were the objects of appraisal would develop tools and techniques for counter-appraisal, fostering a climate of suspicion and disrespect for institutions and individuals. Society, Lasswell predicted, would ultimately grapple with the tension over threats to both individual and collective well being.

The future Lasswell foresaw in 1975 is here. Interdependence—desired or not—is more in evidence than it ever has been; demands for intergovernmental, inter-organizational, and interprofessional collaboration are growing. Power sharing and struggles over power are evident. Terrorism is a real threat to our form of democracy. Accountability (the current term for appraisal), often imposed from the top down but coming from all directions, is seen most obviously in the standards movement and the assessment system it has spawned in schools. This movement has become something of a battleground of professional and civic interests. Learning, and the improvement of learning, frequently gets lost in the shouting.

Lasswell's observations are especially striking because of their prominence in life and in the conduct of public affairs in American society today. The idea of interdependence is prominent in thinking about local communities. Terrorism, elevated to the level of war, has left its imprint everywhere; surveillance is now commonplace in the hallways of school buildings and in the aisles of supermarkets. Appraisal of institutions and individuals is ubiquitous. Lasswell commented further about the emergence of "policy clusters" (the "bundling" of issues with common components, e.g., juvenile justice, family support, foster care concerns) as important developments within future political environments. While this prediction has not been realized as fully as others he made, it seems clear that some movement toward policy clustering has begun, at least in terms of education and social service concerns (see Brabeck, Walsh, & Latta, 2003). More is said about policy clusters later, along with the notion of a "social planetarium," another Lasswell concept.

An Intensifying Concentration on Learning

Learning became a national priority in the latter years of the 20th century. Although there was an abundance of rhetoric at all governmental levels about the importance of education, federal legislation underscored its political significance at the national level and called for important changes at the state and local levels through implementation of its requirements. The No Child Left Behind Act of 2001 rearranged the governance of American public education and reduced local control substantially. Future historians will measure the effects of the Act, but of immediate significance is its impact on assessment, accountability, special education, vouchers, charter schools, professional development, and local control. Few institutional cornerstones were left untouched. The act is the embodiment of Lasswell's projections about interdependence, surveillance, and appraisal, as applied to schools and school systems.

The most recent national educational reforms began with the appearance of *A Nation at Risk* (National Commission on Excellence in Education, 1983). This renewed interest continues to drive the discourse of education today. With bipartisan support, the No Child Left Behind legislation and its accompanying rules and regulations became, in the minds of some, the most influential federal legislation to affect schools and classrooms in American history. It places new demands on school officials at state and local levels, including the lower schools, colleges, and universities, as well as on parents and other educational interest groups. The legislation was far-reaching in concept and detail, and given its mandates, was a severe challenge to the concept of local control.

The No Child Left Behind Act was passed during a time of enormous declines in public revenue and budget cuts at all levels of government, uncertain domestic and world economies, devastating scandals rocking large corporations, widespread changes in the demographics and needs of students, and a war on terrorism. In addition, there have been recent struggles for control of education in Chicago, Boston, Cleveland, Hartford, New York, Philadelphia, Los Angeles, Seattle, Baltimore, and Pittsburgh. All of these focused considerable public attention on governance problems.

Governing Learning

The term "governing learning" is a refinement of the more general term "governance of education" and is the focus, at the community level, of this chapter. Much of the historic attention given to governance has addressed structure and policy and has been framed within structural ideas and concepts of government. A distinction is drawn here between the terms government and governance, or governing. *Government* is the constitutional and statutory frame within which institutions develop and pursue their missions. *Governing* is dynamic. In education, it is the work that goes on in communities that enhances learning or limits learning, stimulates achievement or diminishes it, supports optimum conditions for learning or detracts from that objective. For the purpose of this discussion, general governing is defined as *the aggregate of formal and informal influences and decisions that create and sustain society*. The sources of influences and the reasoning behind decisions are multiple, layered, and complex; sometimes they are embedded in law and constitutions, and they are subject to change through processes that are known and exercised.

Educational governing, it follows, is the aggregate of formal and informal influences and decisions that create and sustain the conditions for learning and the consistent focus on learning. The definition of learning utilized in this chapter is simple and direct. Learning is the acquisition of content and belief. Over the decades, many events have affected the roles and the responsibilities of educational governance. Change has often been consequential, rather than intentional, comprehensive, and collaborative.

The Context of Governing Learning in Ohio

To paint a picture of the environment surrounding the governing of learning at the community level, and keeping the notion of interdependence in mind, a brief scenario from Ohio is worth exploring in some detail. Ohio, a populous and at one time heavily industrial state, experienced considerable economic turmoil in the private sector in the 1980s and 1990s, with accompanying turbulence in the public sector. There was a significant decline in support for higher education as the state struggled to resolve a school finance lawsuit filed in 1989. The competition for monies to support K-12 schools versus higher education institutions was intense, even bitter at times. Over 400 of Ohio's 613 K-12 school districts were plaintiffs in a case that challenged the state's method of funding education. Republicans controlled the governor's office and both houses of the General Assembly. Proposals to resolve the dispute emerged from the legislative and executive branches, only to be rejected by the state Supreme Court. Ethical issues, including two successive elections of Justices to the Supreme Court that were extremely politicized and controversial, clouded the climate in which the Court worked.

Urban schools and urban learning attracted little state-level political interest in Ohio, despite the fact that urban schools served 25% of Ohio students in 21 districts. Conservative public officials had, over a half-century, turned a deaf ear to the concerns of overwhelmed urban communities, despite studies that demonstrated the remarkable differences in learning opportunities between Ohio cities and suburbs. A comprehensive 1999 analysis of those differences, sponsored by Phi Delta Kappa International, also received little attention from conservative politicians (Frymier, 1999).

The Ohio General Assembly, partially to soothe plaintiffs in the school finance case, agreed to help local school districts finance school facility construction. This was done through a long-term state bonding process that included a procedure for determining facility needs at the district level, as well as determining the state's share of construction costs. The facility legislation and its implementation prompted considerable activity across the state in districts of all sizes. In November of 2002, for example, school facility levies were on the ballot in several of Ohio's large districts. Akron, Columbus, Dayton, and Toledo passed their levies comfortably, while Cincinnati's levy lost by a narrow margin. Successful passages were attributed to the availability of state matching funds.

There was some concern for learning and educational programs. The Ohio Department of Education implemented proficiency tests for assessment of learning, and, consistent with federal regulations, focused on improving special education. Science and mathematics, literacy, and early childhood education received renewed attention. Vouchers, community schools, and special schools for students who exhibited aggressive behaviors became more available. Debates over the development and design of educational standards consumed a considerable amount of public officials' time, though after more than a decade of work, many curriculum standards were incomplete or unresolved. On the other hand, the regionalization of the work of the Department of Education occurred without much trouble.

All of these efforts, important in their own right, were disconnected from the interests of many teachers and parents. The Ohio Coalition of Board Certified Teachers registered extreme displeasure at state-level policy initiatives in an article in *Phi Delta Kappan* (Rapp, 2002). Their sentiments were captured in its title: "National Board Certified Teachers in Ohio Give State Education Policy, Classroom Climate, and High-Stakes Testing a Grade of F." The Baldridge Criteria for Education Excellence Program and its principles of management were adopted despite an already overloaded educational work environment. Although costly, Baldridge was pushed vigorously by state officials. Little public notice was taken of how heavily its implementation encroached on the work time of education professionals at all levels.

Major changes were made in the governing structure of the Cleveland public schools during a state takeover; a special commission was established by the state legislature in 1997, for example, to oversee a return to fiscal responsibility. When the administration of the system was returned to Cleveland authorities in 1998, the schools were placed in the hands of the mayor, who was given the power to appoint the school board (which had previously been elected) and the superintendent of schools. With these new personnel, a fiscal oversight commission in place, and the withdrawal of supervision of the school system by the federal district court, the Cleveland system was prepared to focus on student achievement. Four years into these new governance and administrative arrangements, student learning began to improve. In the November 2002 election, the citizens of Cleveland voted overwhelmingly to reauthorize mayoral responsibility for the school district, including the right to appoint the school board.

In all these efforts, parent and community involvement in shaping and defining the specifics of school governing was negligible at best, with one or two exceptions. Communities were involved in local planning for school facilities, particularly in building support for passage of local levies to pay for new and improved facilities. Otherwise, education "professionals" and politicians were the major actors in Ohio's drama.

Traditional Thinking About Roles and Responsibilities

Predicting the future governance roles and responsibilities of school personnel, school board members, and other educational stakeholders is a singularly difficult task. It is made more so because of the increasing interdependence among citizens and their institutions, as Lasswell forecast over 25 years ago. Relationships are inherently personal, and marked by varying degrees of allegiance to institutional purposes. Districts acquire reputations over time with respect to the types of roles and relationships they seem to nurture. Healthy, productive relationships with a constructive focus on learning can turn sour with a change in school board composition or the arrival of a new school superintendent, no matter what method of selection is used.

Change over the years has been very slow. What *is* new, however, is the prominence of the notion of educational *leadership* in professional discourse, and its salience in the preservice and inservice professional development of those who govern. Leadership, a term with seemingly unlimited definitions, has displaced 'administration' and 'management' as the focus of professional attention. Traditional understandings of leadership still predominate, though, and generally do not reflect an incorporation of community perspectives and dialogue about learning and its governance.

Governance work in one district often differs markedly from the work in another district, although there are structural similarities and some common usage of position titles. The dynamics described earlier have an impact on day-to-day work as well. What brings coherence to the discussion is the definition of educational governing: governing is *the aggregate of formal and informal influences and decisions that create and sustain the conditions for learning and the consistent focus on learning.* Governing is not synonymous with leading or managing, although both of these are essential for effective governing.

School Boards and Superintendents

Boards have been part of the jurisdictional mix since the mid-1600s (Campbell, Cunningham, Nystrand, & Usdan, 1990). And although there have been proposals to dispose of them from time to time, they are not likely to go away soon, and certainly will not leave of their own volition. Governance discussions of boards over the years have focused on relationships with superintendents, other staff, union leaders, media, legal counsel, and the community (and in Ohio, with treasurers, a constitutional office in each district). Board size, length of terms, methods of selection, micromanagement, and policymaking responsibilities have been topics of debate for years (Land, 2002). Serious dialogue around accountability for learning has been less prominent.

The National School Boards Association and its state affiliates have been considered modest political forces. The mission of the national group, under new leadership beginning in 1999, has included the establishment of a foundation that supports innovative ideas regarding the work of school boards and school board members. A useful survey of boards was completed in 2000 (Hess, 2000). Responses were sought from 2,000 of the nearly 15,000 districts in the country. Funding and student achievement were the two most prominent issues for boards, followed by special education, teacher quality, and the improvement of educational technology. As for board training, respondents to the survey reported satisfaction with training for their roles and responsibilities, but wanted more concentration on student achievement issues, planning and budget allocations, community collaboration/partnerships, and community engagement.

Traditionally, many boards have experienced turbulence in their relationships with superintendents, especially in urban communities. This is not a recent phenomenon. The celebrated 1915 survey of the Cleveland public schools provides testimony to the board-superintendent difficulties in that city and the distractions they bring to the focus on learning, the primary mission of the system (Ayers, 1916). The histories of school districts large and small are filled with descriptions of tensions between the governing bodies and the executives chosen to run school systems. Breakdowns in relationships often result in a loss of capacity to govern learning effectively. Such breakdowns can be triggered by changes in the superintendency, turnover in central office positions, school board elections, or difficult labor negotiations. Energies are diverted from learning to adult issues that exist apart from the classroom, and dollar costs can accrue as well, in the form of personnel searches, buyouts, and lawsuits.

Work on rethinking governing roles and responsibilities that was begun at the University of Akron in 2000 with a group of school board members, superintendents, and treasurers uncovered an increased willingness to be more inclusive and less independent. Focus groups held across Ohio led to a conference devoted to the governing of urban learning. Finding ways for urban districts to work together, as well as finding efficient means for doing so, was an important focus of discussion. Focus group participants were willing to expand their views of who should take part in governance. They were interested in "abandoning tradition," seeing traditional governance at the community level as exclusionary. It must be noted, however, that this chapter's author, in more than 50 years of formal and informal observation of school board/superintendent relationships, has seen little real change. It is unlikely that roles and relationships will become more productive in the absence of local district and community dialogue and reflection on governance.

Central Office

"Central office" is a term that includes a broad range of education workers. The size of the work force and its organization varies substantially from district to district, given variations in enrollments, geography, socioeconomic conditions, and racial and ethnic diversity. The categories often used in the past to label districts—rural, suburban, and urban—are not particularly useful anymore except at the extremes. Districts across the nation are a hodgepodge of organizations caught up in varying stages of growth or decline.

Most districts utilize somewhat similar titles for personnel—assistant, associate, or deputy superintendent, and directors of curriculum, personnel, transportation, budget, facilities, food services, security, public relations, and evaluation, for example. Some positions are directly connected to learning, especially those related to curriculum, instruction, and assessment, and others (for example, those related to security and transportation) are more remote. Some positions are more directly involved in the work of governing than others.

Given the dynamics introduced earlier, the roles and responsibilities of central office personnel are vulnerable to modification and redefinition. New positions are likely to be created around emerging specializations as the governance of learning moves forward. The growing application of technology to governing may lead to changes. The addition of Chief Information Officers (CIOs), commonplace in the private sector and other governmental jurisdictions, began to be considered by a few school districts in the late 1990s. Such appointments would involve membership at the cabinet level and direct reporting to the superintendent regarding the operation and management of information infrastructures. CIOs would also be expected to take the lead in the development of infrastructure and in the coordination of technological resources to support learning and its governance.

Union Leaders

The organized teaching profession plays an important role in the shaping and delivery of learning and the governance of education. Bargained contracts are controlling documents in the determination of the educational well being of learners, and therefore influence the basic mission of schools. Kerchner, Koppich, and Weeres (1997) argue, "… conventional wisdom holds that teachers' contracts are a principal impediment to educational improvement. We agree to a point" (p. 104). They go on to explain, "Yet while we may lament the limiting educational effects of centralized, rule driven contracts, we are also persuaded that the processes and procedures that govern an enterprise's work must be arrived at by means of an orderly and well-understood system" (p. 104). In *The United Mind Workers: Unions and Teaching in the Knowledge Society*, Kerchner et al. spell out how current negotiations in some districts, and in particular the efforts of union leaders in these districts, are leading to promising new educational practices. They argue for the shift of some negotiations to individual schools, especially negotiations around issues such as hiring and evaluation of personnel, curriculum and instruction, and the expenditures of building-level discretionary monies—all basic to the governing of learning.

Significantly, there is more continuity and stability in the ranks of union leadership than among superintendents and school board members. Unions are better custodians of institutional memory, especially in large districts. It will be essential for union leaders and members to be involved in community conversations about governing learning.

Parents and Other Citizens

Parent-teacher organizations grew in importance throughout much of the late 19th and 20th centuries. The National Parent-Teacher Association was founded in 1897. In 2002 it had 6.5 million members, and it remains the largest advocacy group in the country for the educational well being of children and youth, though it has no formal responsibility for the governance of the schools.

Parents have been active in the life of schools in many ways: tutoring, fundraising, parent-teacher conferencing, chaperoning field trips and other events, arranging parties for holidays, volunteering in classrooms, running booster organizations, and serving on committees. Parent involvement has continued to include those traditional activities, but has also begun to extend beyond these boundaries since the 1990s. Parents and community members, for example, hold 8 of 11 positions on Local School Councils in Chicago; these councils have the power to hire and fire principals and to monitor school improvement plans.

Collaborations between parents and teachers do not come easily, though, particularly when it comes to sharing power. Malen's and Ogawa's seminal study (1988) examined whether site-based governance structures actually altered decision making relationships in schools, and if so, how. They found little significant participation in decision making by parents on the Utah public school site councils they studied. Reasons for parental reluctance included a perceived lack of understanding about school operations and activities, a corresponding sense of discomfort with power and its potential, little control over council processes and agendas, and adherence to norms of propriety and civility in interactions that stifled parental input and response. The researchers believed that parents felt that greater participation on their part somehow violated the professional culture of the school and would be seen as an intrusion.

As Mawhinney (1998) comments, part of the problem with coming to collaboration in education is that

Goals, techniques, resources, and sovereignty are uncertain and, thus, disputable. Consider the goals of education. Without clarity of goals, organization of education is difficult. Our history suggests that there are few consensual institutional rules defining what constitutes the goal of schooling. (p. 43)

While some goals may indeed be consensual (all children should be able to read and write), other purposes of schooling—to promote a common or an individual good, for example—remain a subject of debate among parents, community members, and educators.

In addition, the participation of parents and other citizens in community dialogue about learning and its governance has been seriously challenged in districts of all sizes by the influx of immigrants from many parts of the world. The demography of communities has changed dramatically over the last two decades. Incorporating immigrant families in discussions about learning is a serious challenge. In the late 1800s, when the nation experienced waves of new immigrants, settlement houses were able to help cities in the initial assimilation of families. Settlement houses have largely disappeared, moving the burden of assistance to schools.

Fortunately, new sources of help have appeared, some within schools and others in the community. Family resource centers located in schools are often good bridges to non-English speaking families. Not-for-profit initiatives devoted to the needs of newcomer populations and often supported through philanthropy have been developed. The Children's Planning Council of Los Angeles County, California (Dunkle, 2002) is a good example of such an initiative. The County Council and its eight subsidiaries help families obtain assistance from 40 programs with health, safety and survival, economic, social and emotional well being, education, and workforce readiness issues (see also Brabeck, Walsh, & Latta, 2003, for more examples).

Community Accountability for Learning: The Emerging Community Context

Community control. Within the frenzy of searches for accountability, other perspectives began to emerge in the twilight of the 1990s. The accountability spotlight continued to be aimed at school officials, superintendents, principals and school board members, and teachers and teacher organizations. However, a slow understanding—that in the final analysis, *communities* are accountable for the quality of learning occurring in the lives of children and youth—began to surface. Evidence of this shift can be found in the large urban school districts in which mayors began to exercise influence in the 1990s: Chicago, New York, Cleveland, Baltimore, and Detroit. Closer ties with mayors, short of takeovers, developed in most of Ohio's large urban systems, including Columbus, Cleveland, Akron, Dayton, Cincinnati, and Toledo.

Charter schools. The charter school movement picked up momentum in the 1990s, receiving a shot in the arm with an historic decision of the United States Supreme Court on June 27, 2002 (see van Geel, this volume, chapter 7). The Court decided on behalf of plaintiffs who filed a lawsuit against the state of Ohio seeking to sustain Ohio's school voucher law. The decision triggered a national cry of victory from proponents of vouchers and charter schools. Milton Friedman, a Nobel economist and early advocate for vouchers, heralded the decision as removing a major legal impediment that had restrained these alternatives for years (Dewertz, 2002).

Dispersed accountability. In response to turbulent times and widespread dissatisfaction with the performance of schools, shifts began to happen at the community level. "Community accountability" became part of the educational discourse. Evidence of the prominence of the "community accountability" approach was the rapid expansion of collaboratives, compacts, partnerships, consortia, Internet networks, and other forms of grassroots associations aimed at improving learning. Proposals were advanced for leadership development on a community-wide basis rather than via particular institutions, as was traditionally the practice. Centers such as the Institute for Educational Leadership in Washington became a source of new ideas about community cooperation and collaboration, as well as a clearinghouse for the identification and assessment of leadership development programs of all kinds across the nation (Blank et al., 2001).

Important new relationships that featured K-16 initiatives aimed at improved teacher education as well as enhanced training of administrators began to be created between higher education and public schools across the country. Some of the stimulus for these initiatives came from the No Child Left Behind Act; the availability of funds from philanthropies provided further motivation. These developments had a significant impact on the leadership and management of schools and school districts, leading to widespread rearrangements in organizational structure and position descriptions for personnel. This may be the beginning of a new wave of more fundamental changes in local communities involving school districts, city and county governments, higher education, nongovernmental organizations, and professional and interprofessional groups. If it is, the consideration of policy clusters around teaching and learning issues can be more easily incorporated into the education policy discussion.

Technology. Technology in some form or other has been a factor in education longer than may seem obvious. The graphite pencil, chalk and slate, and the hectograph stood tall for their time, but pale in contrast to the printing press, the computer, and the Internet. Technology is a prominent force both in contemporary society and in education, imposing change on institutions and individuals alike.

There are abundant implications for learning and educational policy at all levels to be found in the "e-world." "E-Defining Education" was the theme of the May 9, 2002 issue of *Education Week*, which provided a comprehensive review of the status of electronic education in the United States. The articles covered higher education and the lower schools, issues of policy and practice, and student appraisals of the usefulness of computers and the Internet in education.

For the most part, the educational policy community has not fully utilized the potential of technology for educational governance. It is clear that e-mail has become a powerful instrument for formal and informal communication. The electronic distribution of information and the streamlining of interactions within government and between government and citizens are likely to continue to advance rapidly, and should be exploited in the interest of promoting participation in the educational discourse.

Four short-term projections are drawn from a broad range of literature that relates to the nation's emerging e-experience. They are significant in relation to efforts to distribute governance of education responsibilities more broadly throughout school districts. First, it is likely that there will be an extension of experimentation with online elections, as Arizona undertook in 2000, which in time may include school board member elections. Election-related practices that are currently utilized to poll voters on bond issues and tax matters will be used by school board candidates who have the resources to do so. Second, the politics of running for the board will change over time; for example, candidates will develop web sites to promote their candidacies. Citizen networking will grow as a means of expanding the efforts of campaign workers to solicit support and stimulate voter turnouts. Third, local school officials will develop new skills around packaging information for constituencies, with the goal of enhancing understanding of the district and its services. Over time, it is likely that the information to be shared about schools, districts, and learning itself will become more sophisticated. Fourth, the e-applications rapidly being adopted and perfected within federal and state political domains will become more commonplace in local communities. They are likely to be introduced first in well-off suburban settings, where middle- and upper-class families will be able to interpret and understand the potential (including translating new understandings into local political practices) early. Eventually this utilization of technology for political purposes in wealthier districts will filter down to urban and rural settings, though leaders must remain alert to a possible widening of the "digital divide." More accountable and effective leadership, more effective school board performance, and improved opportunities for public assessment of school performance may lead to improved achievement along with enhanced accountability.

Social planetariums. Bringing the community centrally into dialogue and reflection about learning can be enhanced by another concept developed by Harold Lasswell, that of "social planetariums." When first introduced, this was clearly an idea ahead of its time. A social planetarium framework supports fresh perspectives in thinking about the governing of learning, and is a natural way to address the need for community policy clusters.

The planetarium is represented by eight sides, which correspond to eight value categories that incorporate most of the values and local institutions of the world: power, affection, skill, enlightenment, wealth, preservation, respect, and rectitude. Governmentally, the planetarium could be freestanding or a subsidiary of an existing entity. The work would be organized around these eight sectors and would focus on managing information in forms appropriate to community need. For education, policy scientists would aggregate, organize, and store community data essential to learning and its governance (for a more detailed description, see Lasswell, 1963). The social planetarium is, in essence, a public utility, making information available to individuals, groups, organizations, governments, and planning bodies. A community planetarium lends itself especially to strengthening democracy through provisions for open access for every citizen along with opportunities to dialogue with the assistance of policy scientists on its staff.

It has been noted historically that an informed citizenry is the foundation of democracy. An inclusive approach to involvement in the governing of learning adds strength to the expected outcome of improved achievement. Employing the idea of policy clustering with the enlightening capability of the planetarium provides powerful tools for improving learning and for enhancing the democratic process as well as addressing other community needs. E-technology can, of course, enhance the possibilities of these resources immensely (Muth, 2002).

Democratic considerations. At the community level, the expectation of citizen involvement in the work of the schools has a long history. Parent-teacher organizations, citizen committees of all sorts, booster clubs, parents' nights, and attendance at school-sponsored events remain a significant part of life at schools. More recently, new types of citizen involvement have evolved: site-based management, citizen participation in strategic planning, court ordered desegregation monitoring committees, inter- and intra-district school choice options, charter schools, and citizen involvement in personnel selection (especially superintendents). Nevertheless, the variety of possibilities, and their valuable contribution, cannot disguise the reality that low voter turnout for school board elections, bond issues, and tax increases are serious matters.

Most serious of all, perhaps, is the learning and practice of democracy in the nation's schools. In July 2002, the United Nations Development Program issued a report called "Deepening Democracy in a Fragmented World," an analysis of the status of democracy around the globe (Fukuda-Parr, 2002). This document emphasizes the importance of local communities in ensuring that students learn about the history and status of democracy across America. The report also indicated that a two-decade growth in the adoption of democratic governments had stalled, and that many existing democracies were struggling, sometimes turning to authoritarianism. It called the level of inequality of wealth in the world "grotesque," with the income of the world's richest 5% of countries 114 times higher than that of the world's poorest 5%. The failure to provide education, adequate housing, jobs, and health care for much of the world's population was cited as a major explanation for this decline.

Is democracy in jeopardy in this country? The possibility may seem unlikely, and the question may seem fanciful. Yet there are voices of concern about our democracy, some belonging to educators. This concern is significant to those who govern learning. Keeping in mind the chapter's earlier definition of learning—the acquisition of content and belief—we must be concerned about how democracy is presented and how democratic beliefs are acquired. The Association for Supervision and Curriculum Development (ASCD) announced their "First Amendment Schools" initiative in the summer of 2002. In remarks about the initiative, ASCD's Executive Director challenged educators to think about the strength of our civil communities, and the importance of the experiences students need to prepare for adult lives of productive citizenship (Carter, 2002). Others have urged that educators think seriously about the weaknesses in the fabric of government, citing low participation rates in voting and a decline in ethical behavior at all levels and branches of government as danger signs.

The use of cyber tools in education (Internet learning, chat rooms, networking, social planetaria, e-mail) may expand local discussions of educational issues, influence policy, and in the long run, bring benefits to the learner. The future stewardship of democracy is in the hands of those currently enrolled in schools. This generation, and the one preceding, has the cyber experience necessary to use technology in support of the processes of democracy. It will fall to them to find ways to improve learning and its governance more efficiently.

Policy clusters and learning. Among the events Lasswell projected in 1975 was a shift in how policymakers at all levels would approach issues of well being. Rather than addressing policy matters one by one, and in professional isolation, he saw the need for "bundling" issues of human need into policy clusters. One cluster might have learning as its umbrella, with family development and health care as part of the bundle. Policies affecting education, juvenile justice, physical health, mental health, employment, foster care, and other human services all have bearing on the lives of children and their families. Each of these concerns advances under an independent political banner, and each has its own interest and advocacy groups. There is little integration of purpose and accountability and little understanding of the aggregate impact on community well being.

Public officials devoted to policy clustering would facilitate the pursuit of well being in several ways. Legislative bodies, for example, would develop goals in an integrative fashion, clustering categories of need. Public investments would have more coherence. Accountability would be expected, as all public investments would be projected to support public goals in some way. Coalitions of special interests would form to support broader goals and to reduce the costliness of competitiveness among narrowly defined groups. Lasswell saw the evolution of clustering at federal, state, and local levels, and made the case for widespread public participation in dialogue leading to cluster formation. In his judgment, better, more effective policy would result, and citizens would become more knowledgeable about their communities in the process.

Invoking the Community at the Grassroots

If citizens and institutions are to participate in far-reaching community activity, they need to align their efforts with individual and institutional self-interests. Leadership is essential, and can emerge from many sources. Educators, public and private, preschool through higher education, would have much to contribute, but leadership from other community sectors should not be discouraged. The focus should be on initiatives that are thoughtful, unobtrusive efforts to benefit citizens, and avenues for open participation should be encouraged.

A community initiative to understand learning and its governance will itself be a model of learning. As the process moves forward, there will be insights that can lead to immediate improvements in the work of many institutions—day care centers, hospitals, schools, churches, businesses, professional organizations, families, colleges, sports groups, research centers, media, civil rights organizations, and local governments.

The term "learning community" has been used widely in recent years in diverse settings and situations. It is an appropriate and applicable term when the governance of learning is the subject of discussion. There is a sizable challenge inherent in the expectation that citizens will endorse new ways of thinking about governing, let alone join with others in pursuit of new understandings and improvements. Daniel Yankelovich, in *Coming To Public Judgment* (1991), observes that society should enhance citizens' capacities to come to public judgment. He maintains that an informed public is not enough; rather, it is the *use* of information to arrive at judgment that is important. Understanding this difference is essential when assessing large-scale public dialogue about something as complex as governing. A community focus on governing learning will require committed leadership, with realistic expectations and a strong understanding of the nature of the challenge.

Yankelovich divided public judgment experience into three phases—consciousness raising, working through, and resolution. Lasswell (1971) described something similar; his "decision phase analysis" was made up of seven phases—intelligence, promotion, prescription, invocation, application, termination, and appraisal. These concepts have been widely applied in many contexts for many years and have value for framing community dialogue around the governing of learning. In addition, there are many publications on community building. In 2002 the Aspen Institute released a report filled with ideas and approaches to community building (Kubisch et al., 2002). The report, the product of 5 years of research, describes the foundations for developing Comprehensive Community Initiatives (CCIs). Four levels of action essential to success are identified. They are the actions of community residents, of community organizations, and of support organizations, and broad institutional, policy, or structural reform efforts. The report provides helpful guidelines to those who choose to engage in community dialogue and reflection on the governing of learning.

The concept of *public engagement* advanced recently by the Public Agenda Foundation is based, in its execution, on Yankelovich's (1991) work. Public engagement has been introduced in many school districts in recent years to improve both citizens' understanding of the work of school officials and school officials' awareness of the perspectives of citizens. The Public Agenda Foundation draws a careful distinction between public engagement and public relations, noting

public engagement involves all sectors of a community in ongoing deliberation to build common ground for effective solutions ... 'in schools [this] involves developing collaborations to meet the needs of children and to sustain the serious work of school reform. The former is a governing tool; the later is essentially an information distribution service. Public engagement is a shift in culture from authoritative role to greater self-governance. It is a shift in perspective from seeing the children solely in schools to seeing them as part of the community.'

This clarification can be found in a Danforth Foundation field book (forthcoming) that documents public engagement experiences in several school districts across the country.[2] As a tool, public engagement has been applied to issues of early childhood education, parent involvement, student achievemen, and the school's role in sustaining democracy. It is a promising approach that lends itself to application in communities that wish to learn about the governing of learning.

A Look to the Future

In 2002, the United States and the rest of the world reeled under conditions without precedent in modern times. While a global focus on terrorism predominated, public and private institutions providing K-12 schooling experienced intensive scrutiny and found themselves challenged at every turn by new mandates and new institutional forms. It is within this context that broad community participation in a shared reflection on learning, the governing of learning, and the improvement of learning will go forward.

Commitment to work at community levels is obviously difficult and frequently is an uphill battle. But there are resources; scholars of academe and insightful practitioners of community development in the field record their work for the benefit of others. Daniel Yankelovich and Harold Lasswell typify those whose contributions have stood the test of time. The three phases of coming to public judgment, decision process modeling, and CCIs are noteworthy. Consider too, the powerful potential of a community social planetarium. Technologies, well understood and well managed, may become instruments of success in the search for better learning for citizens of all ages and circumstances

Approaching the invocation of widespread community involvement with a focus on improvement will carry the work forward; launching attacks on community institutions and their practices will not be helpful. Community reflection and dialogue is consistent with democratic principles and values. It is quiet, unobtrusive, and evolutionary. Such activity in community building generates strength and value on many levels, for students and citizens alike.

NOTES

1. The citations here were taken from a tape recording of Lasswell's address.

2. The forthcoming field book referred to here is edited by James Harvey, Nelda Cambron McCabe, and Luvern L. Cunningham. It is a summary of 10 years of work at the Danforth Foundation Forum for School Superintendents. A section of the volume is devoted to the experiences of several superintendents whose districts feature public engagement.

REFERENCES

Ayers, L.P. (1916). *School organization and administration.* Cleveland: The Survey Committee of the Cleveland Foundation.

Blank, M.J., Hale, E.L., Housman, N., Kaufmann, B., Martinez, M., McCloud, B., Samberg, L., Walter, S., & Melaville, A. (2001). *School-community partnerships in support of student learning.* Washington, DC: The Institute for Educational Leadership.

Brabeck, M.M., Walsh, M.E., & Latta, R. (2003). *Meeting at the hyphen: Schools-universities-communities-professions in collaboration for student achievement and well being. The 102nd yearbook of the National Society for the Study of Education,* Part II. Chicago: National Society for the Study of Education.

Campbell, R.F., Cunningham, L.L., Nystrand, R.O., & Usdan, M.D. (1990). *The organization and control of American schools* (6th ed.). Columbus, OH: Merrill.

Carter, G.R. (May 2002). *Laboratories of democracy: The public mission of our nation's schools.* Alexandria, VA: Association for Supervision and Curriculum. Available: www.ascd.org

Dewertz, C. (2002, July 10). A great day, or a dark one, for schools? *Education Week, 21*(42), 19, 21.

Dunkle, M. (2002). *Understanding L.A. systems that affect families.* Los Angeles: Los Angeles County, Children's Planning Council.

E-Defining education. Special Issue. (2002, May 9). *Education Week.*

Fukuda-Parr, S. (2002). *Deepening democracy in a fragmented world.* New York: United Nations Development Program, Human Development Report Office.

Frymier, J. (1999). *Are Ohio's urban youth at risk? Urban and suburban schools in the Buckeye State.* Bloomington, IN: Phi Delta Kappa International.

Hess, F. (2000). *School boards at the dawn of the twenty-first century: Conditions and challenges of district governance.* Alexandria, VA: National School Boards Association.

Kerchner, C.T., Koppich, J.F., & Weeres, J.G. (1997). *The united mind workers: Unions and teaching in the knowledge society.* San Francisco: Jossey-Bass.

Kubisch, A.C., Auspos, P., Brown, P., Chaskin, R., Fullbright-Anderson, K., & Hamilton, R. (2002). *Voices from the field II: Reflections on comprehensive community change.* Washington, DC: The Aspen Institute.

Land, D. (2002). Local school boards under review: Their role and effectiveness in relation to student academic achievement. *Review of Educational Research, 2,* 229-278.

Lasswell, H.D. (1963). *The future of political science.* New York: Atherton Press.

Lasswell, H.D. (1971). *Preview of policy sciences.* New York: American Elsevier.

Lasswell, H.D. (1975). The future of education: Perspectives on tomorrow's schooling. In L. Rubin (Ed.), *The future of government and politics in the United States.* Boston: Allyn & Bacon.

Malen, B., & Ogawa, R. (1988). Professional-patron influence on site-based governance councils: A confounding case study. *Educational Evaluation and Policy Analysis, 10,* 251-270.

Mawhinney, H.B. (1998). School wars or school transformation: Professionalizing teaching and involving communities. *Peabody Journal of Education, 73*(1), 36-55.

Muth, R. (2002). Bringing to life Lasswell's vision of the social planetarium. Paper prepared for the Mary Parker Follett Conversations on Creative Democracy. Boise, ID, October 17-20, 2002.

National Commission on Excellence in Education. (1983). *A nation at risk: The imperative for educational reform.* Washington, DC: U.S. Department of Education.

Rapp, D. (2002). National Board certified teachers in Ohio give state education policy, classroom climate, and high-stakes testing a grade of F. *Phi Delta Kappan, 84*(3), 215-18.

Trenta, L. (2002). *The governance of learning in Ohio's urban school districts.* Unpublished paper. Akron, OH: University of Akron.

van Geel, T. (2003). Vouchers, the Supreme Court, and the next political rounds. In this volume—W.L. Boyd & D. Miretzky (Eds.), *American educational governance on trial: Change and challenges. The 102nd yearbook of the National Society for the Study of Education,* Part I (pp. 136-154). Chicago: National Society for the Study of Education.

Yankelovich, D. (1991). *Coming to public judgment: Making democracy work in a complex world.* Syracuse: Syracuse University Press.

CHAPTER 9

Rethinking the Urban School Superintendency: Nontraditional Leaders and New Models of Leadership

JOSEPH M. CRONIN AND MICHAEL D. USDAN

Major cities in the United States, unhappy with persistent achievement gaps between students of different races and socioeconomic backgrounds, now search for highly effective medicine men who will upgrade urban school productivity. These efforts stand in stark contrast to the first two hundred years of the Republic, when villages relied on local ministers, elders, or farmers with extra time in the winter to visit the schools, many of which operated for only a few months of the year.

Buffalo and St. Louis were the first cities to appoint a superintendent of schools in 1837. Within a dozen years Boston, Chicago, Cleveland, Detroit, New York City, Brooklyn (a separate system), and San Francisco followed suit, and by the 1880s Pittsburgh, Philadelphia, and Los Angeles named superintendents as well. Previously, cities used mayors, school board members, building inspectors, business agents, or treasurers to follow the money and check on the schools, not always wisely or well (Cronin, 1973).

The first assignment given to the new Buffalo city school superintendent was to "ascertain where the schools were situated" (Reller, 1935, p. 29); the new city lacked a complete roster of schools, and the superintendent set out in a horse-drawn buggy to make inquiries. The Buffalo superintendency was an elective post between 1853 and 1916, as was the San Francisco superintendency from 1856 to 1923 (Gilland, 1935).

The Philadelphia Public Education Association, a group of wellborn citizens, explained the early model as they envisioned it: "The Board of Education holds the same relationship to the public schools as a Board of Directors holds to a bank or railroad. It would be as reasonable to argue that the Board of Directors of the Pennsylvania (Railroad) should run the road, and dispense with a President as to argue that the

Joseph M. Cronin is a Senior Fellow at the Nellie Mae Educational Foundation. Michael D. Usdan is a Senior Fellow at the Institute for Educational Leadership.

Board of Education should assume the duties of superintendents" (Cronin, 1973, p. 58).

That was the ideal formulation. However, Reller (1935, pp. 300-301), describing the first hundred years of city superintendents, concluded that the chief executive designation neither guaranteed control over the nomination of teachers nor did it preclude the interference of other executives in the business of the board of education.

Assuming the San Diego superintendency, Ellwood P. Cubberley discovered that his board of sixteen members did most of the work through 16 committees, including the hiring, evaluation, promotion, and dismissal of teachers; selection of textbooks; and handling of business transactions. He gradually persuaded the board to listen to his monthly reports, to act on his recommendations, and to allow his comments on all proposals (Sears & Henderson, 1937).

On the east coast Boston's 24 school committee members each chaired his own small committee in Star Chamber fashion. James Jackson Storrow, a prominent business leader, wrote of Boston in 1905 "even the Superintendent, the actual executive head of the school system, who ought to be held responsible for the efficiency of the school, is for the most part not consulted" (Pearson, 1932, p. 45).

When Storrow, with the support of two former Boston mayors and a Harvard study, persuaded the state legislature to authorize a new five-member city school board, Chairman Storrow encouraged Superintendent Stratton D. Brooks to run the schools like a corporate executive and select teachers by a merit system. Storrow preferred an appointed rather than an elective board for Boston. As of 1900, almost half of the big city boards were appointive, including those of New York, Chicago, Philadelphia, Pittsburgh, and Baltimore. Later, Buffalo and San Francisco switched to appointed boards as well. However, several cities relied on citizen nominating panels to guide the mayor in appointing a mix of business and labor board members and to achieve a balance among the major religious and racial groups.

Fifty years later, Herold C. Hunt, a successful city superintendent who reformed the schools of Kansas City and Chicago, summarized what he saw as the major challenges for education in the 1950s. He saw technology, including automation and atomic energy, hastening a decline in agriculture, heightening the need for specialization in careers, and raising the stakes for education in general. Hunt also saw challenges in increased birth rates, which would force cities to upgrade school buildings and increase teaching staffs, and in urbanization, the growth of cities, resistance to racial integration, and labor management issues.

As late as the 1950s, Hunt felt compelled to argue for board protection of the superintendent from "unfair or excessive criticism" and "excessive work days," and for "independence from factions." He also supported a unit type of organization, with the business manager reporting directly to the superintendent, and accepted the Chicago superintendency conditioned on that change (Hunt & Pierce, 1958, p. 331).

The Uniqueness and Importance of Today's Urban Superintendency

What is so different about the big city superintendency in the 21st century? New York City public schools serve more than one million students—fewer than one third of the states serve that many—and Chicago serves more than 400,000 students. Los Angeles, Philadelphia, and Detroit also have very large school systems. Boston, Baltimore, Cleveland, San Francisco, and other smaller great cities each serve approximately 50,000 students.

In addition, the location of major television stations and metropolitan daily newspapers in cities means detailed coverage of school disturbances, teacher walkouts, citizen accusations against the board or superintendent or teachers, and other controversies. Good news is usually muted, bad news magnified. Citizens in the entire nation judge much of public education by media glimpses of turbulence or problems in the central cities (Cuban, 2001).

Racial minorities, including the latest round of refugees—from Haiti, Somalia, El Salvador, or wherever nations experience revolutions, civil war, or natural disasters—settle most often in the city, lured by cheap housing and the prospect of jobs. Newcomers often arrive without clothing, language skills, jobs, health insurance, or familiarity with American culture. Finally, big cities cope with outmoded housing, poverty, overburdened social services, child asthma and other health problems, vulnerability to drugs and rackets, and evictions from housing. The urban superintendent faces challenges much more complex than those of most suburbs and rural areas, and on a much larger scale.

The superintendency might be considered a minor leadership position in American education were it not for changing populations, high expectations for schools, public perceptions, and tough external demands.

Changing Populations

First, the urban school superintendent bears a major responsibility for helping absorb most immigrants and refugees, the "huddled masses" who come to the United States through the portals of our large cities. Students and their parents learn English and civics, and experience the American way of life in the cities. If they learn well, they contribute to the economy and to the communities they ultimately settle in.

The 2000 U.S. Census shows the extent to which the United States has become increasingly Hispanic over the last decade or two. Peter Drucker some years back described the "reconquesta" of territory once wrenched from Mexico; now the numbers of Mexican Americans in their former territories (California, New Mexico, Arizona and Texas) have increased dramatically. Larger average family sizes will transform many cities in the Southwest, as well as large cities throughout the nation, as adults seek opportunities, especially steady indoor work.

It is clear that immigrants from Latin America, Asia, and elsewhere often bring various problems with them, requiring city agencies involved in preventative health, housing, and social services to work together. Superintendents have not traditionally served on "youth cabinets" in city administrations; they would be well advised to do so in the future.

Expectations for Schools

Urban schools and superintendents staff the front lines in the battles to combat youth gangs, street crimes, and youth unemployment. When youth unrest is rising, and when companies can't find literate help, city schools are blamed and corporate dissatisfaction is widely publicized. City schools represent the bulwark of law and order and social control. They are meant to be the creators of "good citizens" as well as the providers of entry-level manpower for the factories and services that stoke the metropolitan economy.

Public Perceptions

Civic confidence in cities flows from trust that cities are well managed. Every classroom teacher is affected if a superintendent is fired or severely publicly criticized. Without public faith and trust in an urban school superintendent, the reputation of the metropolitan area declines. If a city is perceived as having schools that are improving, corporate and civic leaders are inclined to provide support. The superintendent is a key leader, one of the essential criteria by which a school system and a city are judged.

External Demands

City superintendents must deal with more aggressive, better-staffed, and better-mobilized teacher unions. Superintendents are the agents, the arbiters, and the negotiators in their relationships with teaching staff, although city mayors in recent years have become just as important in bargaining disputes, as will be discussed later in this chapter. Meanwhile, the life span of Americans has lengthened. Many cities will house the very young and the comparatively old, with fewer active parents to vote for resources for schools. This will challenge big city leaders, forcing superintendents, mayors, and other city leaders to collaborate rather than compete for resources.

The Shifting Role and Composition of School Boards

Any efforts to rethink the urban superintendency must be predicated on a concurrent consideration of the changed composition of school boards in many cities. Although their significance is often underestimated, school boards have enormous influence upon the success or failure of the traditional or non-traditional superintendent. The power of the board to hire and fire its chief executive officer ensures its authority and power to influence local governance profoundly. A superintendent's success in an urban district (or in any school system, for that matter) will be largely contingent upon maintaining a close working relationship and mutual trust with the employing board of education.

Many urban school boards until the mid-1960s were composed of successful and visible civic and corporate leaders. These "establishment" bodies emulated a corporate model. They delegated responsibility to the superintendent and his staff and usually did not usurp administrative prerogatives. They acted as "trustees" for the community at large and generally did not perceive themselves as representatives of any special or single interest group or constituency. In many cases, these "establishment" board members' children or grandchildren were not enrolled in the public schools they governed, instead attending private independent or church-related institutions.

The civil rights movement in urban communities changed this arrangement. As efforts to promote racial equality moved from the *de jure* segregated schools in the South to the North, urban school systems found themselves in the eye of the civil rights hurricane. Schools became the focal points of strident and long deferred efforts to achieve equality of educational opportunity. Sit-ins, boycotts, and strikes, with the accompanying media attention, became common occurrences in urban systems throughout the country.

This ferment in the cities intensified as a result of rising teacher militancy, growing opposition to the war in Vietnam, escalating student unrest, and demands from grassroots communities that they have more influence in shaping the institutions (like schools) that so significantly affected their lives. The epic decentralization struggle between the teachers union and the Ocean Hill-Brownsville community in New York City over control of teacher assignments, for example, caused racial and religious tensions that observers say have not yet disappeared 35 years later. The battles over school desegregation and related equity issues raged virtually unabated for years in communities like Chicago, Detroit, Boston, Philadelphia, Cleveland, and Milwaukee. According to the late Stephen Bailey (1976, p. 142), school governance during this time, particularly in urban centers, moved from the "4 b's" (boards, budgets, buildings, and buses) to the "4 r's" (race, resources, relationships, and rule).

The influential civic and business leaders sitting on school boards in more serene environments were less likely to want to serve in politically charged, volatile atmospheres. African Americans and other minorities, neglected by "unresponsive" school boards, demanded access to governing the institutions that played such vital roles in the lives of their children.

These combustible ingredients dramatically reshaped the composition and thus the *modus operandi* of urban school boards. In most urban districts the school boards became much more diverse and representative of the changed demographics. Greater numbers of African Americans and other minority groups served on boards. Unlike their predecessors, new board members were not plugged into the civic and private sector "downtown" establishments. Many of these new board members saw themselves as representative of specific racial, geographic, or educational constituencies that had been bypassed or ignored in the past by unresponsive school systems. Because their own children often attended the public schools, board members were more apt to delve into specific school issues at the regional or building level, and thus "rock the boat," challenging the traditional board-superintendent relationship and its demarcation line between administration and policy. In other words, the old corporate paradigm of school board service was no longer operative in a large majority of urban school systems.

These tensions characterize urban school board-superintendent relationships to this very day. While a compelling case supporting more representative and more demographically diverse boards certainly can be made, these changes have exacted a political price. One of the advantages of the earlier trusteeship boards was their interlocking political and economic connection with the city's power structure. This provided a more direct connection with the civic and private sector elites who so frequently constitute a community's most powerful decision makers. In recent years, great efforts have been made to reconnect the schools with these power brokers, with mixed success.

The New Politics of Education: Implications for Urban School Governance

In the early 1980s, the country's economic weakness and lack of global competitiveness precipitated unprecedented involvement in education by business and political leaders. Concerns about an inadequately trained work force focused on the weaknesses of the schools. Reports such as *A Nation at Risk* (National Commission on Excellence in Education, 1983) criticized the lack of academic vigor and adequacy in an increasingly technological and competitive international economy. In fact, the weakness of our schools was decried as being tantamount to "unilateral disarmament."

Throughout the 1980s and 1990s the nation's business and political leaders coalesced around the need to set explicit achievement goals and higher academic standards in an effort to improve the quality of education. Major business groups like the Business Roundtable, the National Alliance of Business, the U.S. Chamber of Commerce, and the Committee for Economic Development catalyzed influential private sector leaders to push for educational reform at the local, regional, state, and national levels. Elected officials, through the National Governors Association, the National Conference of State Legislatures, and the National League of Cities, likewise focused intensively on school reform.

In 1989, the first President George Bush convened a meeting at the University of Virginia, inviting all 50 governors, to articulate national education goals for the first time in the nation's history. The result was the Goals 2000: Educate America Act of 1994. To reflect the bipartisan nature of this issue, the leader of the governors at the Charlottesville session was a little known young Democrat from Arkansas named Bill Clinton. Business leaders like IBM's CEO Louis Gerstner later convened several summits for the nation's political and corporate leaders in efforts to sustain the momentum for standards-based education reform.

This "new politics of education," in essence, preempted the traditional school leadership. Business and political leaders increasingly pushed for standards and accountability measures in state capitols and nationally. The new secular leaders of school reform largely bypassed school boards, chief state school officers, school superintendents, teacher union leaders, and other professional educators.

These dynamics certainly influenced events in urban school systems, which for decades had been beset by a host of serious problems and mired in an ongoing struggle with low levels of student achievement. Corporate leaders whose firms were headquartered in the urban core were particularly concerned about their ability to attract the desired workforce to communities in which the schools were deemed inferior. Mayors in cities like Baltimore, Boston, and Chicago, having succeeded in rebuilding the physical infrastructure of their central cities, recognized that only good schools could hold or recapture a middle class clientele (see Kirst, this volume, chapter 10, for a more detailed discussion).

Many of these urban business and political leaders became increasingly frustrated with the failure, despite many years of efforts, to improve the school systems in their cities. They became convinced, rightly or wrongly, that dramatic—if not revolutionary—changes would be needed to reform intransigent school bureaucracies that had resisted meaningful change for so long. Understandably, the heightened interest in school governance on the part of both political and business leaders in the cities triggered considerable discussion about the adequacy of the local leadership structure, namely, the city superintendents and the school boards that employed them.

This pervasive discontent with the status quo on the part of practitioners of the "new politics of education" resulted, quite logically, in the evolution of new leadership models, such as stronger mayoral involvement and the employment of non-educators—individuals who had displayed management and political leadership skills in the military, politics, business, and law—as superintendents.

The Urban Superintendency Reconceptualized

Towards the end of the 20th century, expectations about schools escalated as concerns multiplied. The publication of *A Nation at Risk* and the ensuing series of summit conferences featuring governors and corporate leaders led to a new consensus that states must define the standards of literacy for which schools must become accountable. New tests, often required for graduation, reintroduced measurements of learning that only New York State, and to some extent Iowa, had required over the decades.

The nation under Presidents George Bush and Bill Clinton defined goals for the year 2000 and beyond that would place the United

States educational system in the very top tier of nations. International reports that placed the U.S. 15th or 20th in mathematics and science education were viewed as indictments of local control and confirmed widely held notions of school system mediocrity (U.S. Department of Education, 1998).

The urban school superintendent, as the millennium approached and passed, was expected to become a curriculum reformer, an engineer of teacher reeducation, and a guarantor of academic standards substantially higher than had hitherto been expected of urban schools.

Vocal citizen leaders became impatient with bilingual education if it meant that students of other tongues might have an extra year or two to learn English or practice their math in Spanish or Korean. Driver education, art, physical education, and other elective courses would need to be subordinated to English, math, science, history, and technology. Global competitiveness meant that city schools needed to improve right away.

So the urban superintendent would need to become a master of instruction, as well as continuing as the system manager and the administrative leader. He or she would be expected to raise the performance level of every school, even those serving recent immigrants or transient populations. No excuses would be tolerated. Someone else would lead, if the incumbent could not produce by moving schools to a higher academic level.

Frederick Hess (1999), examining the pressure on current urban superintendents, found that "reform" has become the status quo, something of a mantra, expected but often ineffectual. Thousands of innovations have been launched; few survive the "churning" of leaders and their favorite ideas (p. 13). Hess agrees with Harvard's Susan Moore Johnson, who argues that expectations of "heroic leadership" are unrealistic and overestimate the capacity for change. Attempts to modify pedagogy often provoke resistance on the part of those who prefer "the way things have always been done." Increases in school productivity take a steady hand, up to 12 years of reform time, and the lash of publicized test results. This works in other countries, such as Japan, whose student achievement scores exceed those of American students, and it has begun to work in the United States.

Urban Schools and General-Purpose Government

Since the advent of the 20th century, the ethos of the municipal school reform movement has prevailed. This ethos was designed to buffer education from the blatant interference of big city political machines by separating schools from general-purpose government. Until very recently, this pattern of separation has persisted in most urban jurisdictions. The schools had their own governance structure, separate from other governmental services such as the juvenile justice system, social services, recreation, and mental health, which fell under the aegis of mayors, city managers, and bodies such as city councils. School boards are distinct entities often elected on nonpartisan ballots at different times than general elections. Big city school systems are controlled by separate state statutes and have their own discrete fiscal and employment policies and practices.

This culture of isolation of school governance from general-purpose government is being reassessed in a growing number of cities for several reasons. Mayors—who a decade or two ago wanted to avoid entanglement in seemingly no-win school issues such as racial integration, finance, and relations with teacher unions—finally have come to realize that they often are being held accountable for school failures while they lack any authority to confront the issues. The escalating demands for improved student achievement and greater accountability have further reminded mayors of their need to become more involved with school issues.

The most visible way in which mayors have tried to exert leadership is in the school board selection process. Boards are no longer elected but are now appointed by mayors in Boston, Detroit, Cleveland, and other cities. These appointed boards are directly accountable to mayors, who are assuming educational leadership responsibilities that they previously avoided.

Other issues may compel closer relationships between urban school systems and general-purpose government. Our cities are populated by diverse groups, many of limited economic means. Children in these households have multiple social and health needs that profoundly influence their ability to learn. A child who cannot see the blackboard because he has no glasses or who suffers from an untreated toothache will not be able to focus on academics.

The schools have social and grassroots penetration unrivaled by any other institution. Although the undisputed primary mission of schools is to educate, schools are also the most accessible means of reaching needy children and families with essential social, health, and related services. Ways must be found to connect schools with other agencies and institutions without compromising their transcendent academic purposes. It should be easier to compel stronger interagency collaboration if there are organic political links between the schools and the agencies that operate under the greater policy and budgetary authority of mayors and city councils (see Brabeck, Walsh, & Latta, 2003 for further discussion of these possibilities).

The tragic events of September 11, 2001, and the frightening and unpredictable aftermath may create even more compelling reasons for restructuring relationships between schools and the larger society. Fear begets fear. Potentially, violence and biochemical warfare in our uncertain world will compel even closer relationships between schools and a host of agencies, including police and fire departments, public safety systems, and criminal justice and mental health authorities.

Rethinking the Urban School Superintendency: Some Examples

Cities are now rethinking the urban superintendency. These are the major strategies to improve urban school governance: increasing mayoral involvement, altering the selection and composition of school boards, appointing non-traditional superintendents, involving more business leaders, and creating new teaming arrangements.

Increasing mayoral involvement. Mayors have become more aggressively involved in school governance. In addition to appointing boards in cities like Boston, Chicago, Cleveland, and Detroit, in many cities they are leading the school systems in multiple ways. Boston and Chicago provide particularly interesting examples.

In Boston, Mayor Tom Menino has worked closely with the city's highly respected superintendent, Tom Payzant. The popular three-term mayor, in essence, has served as a political buffer for Payzant, handling some sensitive community and union problems and freeing the superintendent to pay attention to educational issues. The two leaders are in fact "joined at the hip"—in Boston, the superintendent serves as a member of the mayor's cabinet—and the arrangement has provided the long troubled school system with stability it has not enjoyed for decades (Usdan & Cuban, 2003).

Mayor Richard Daley literally took over the Chicago school system in 1995. He appointed two of his top staffers as the CEO and the president of the school board, and placed other loyalists in key administrative positions. The school situation in Chicago (as in Boston) is much less volatile than in many other cities, as the mayor wields his leverage and clout to provide political cover for his appointees now running the school system (see Kirst, this volume, chapter 10, for an extended discussion of mayoral involvement in education in Chicago and Boston).

While stronger mayoral involvement has provided school systems with much needed stability, the effect on student achievement remains largely unknown. Some of the preliminary evidence in Boston is promising. It could be argued that the relative political stability provided by increased mayoral involvement in previously turbulent school systems may be a necessary precursor for sustained improvement in student achievement.

Upgrading the composition of boards of education. Should city school board members be appointed? This is a controversial and important question that has significant implications for the urban school superintendency. In assessing the problems of urban schools, many frustrated mayors and civic and business leaders have reached the conclusion that elected boards are an impediment to educational improvement and change. Elected board members too often lack trusteeship perspectives, responding narrowly to single-issue constituencies or to the more parochial needs of their section of the city. Rightly or wrongly, the sense persists that many elected board members lack the requisite managerial and financial backgrounds needed to effectively govern schools, and use their elected school board base as a stepping-stone to higher political office.

As mayors and business leaders become more engaged in school issues, they may find they have little in common with many elected school board members who are indigenous to grassroots communities. The movement toward appointive boards has also been spurred by the concern that many talented people who might be interested in serving on boards simply will not run for elected office; many advocates of appointed urban boards believe that the quality of board members will be improved through the use of an appointive selection process.

Supporters of elected boards, on the other hand, strongly disagree with these arguments. They decry appointive boards as elitist, and believe that in a democracy the people should directly elect the individuals responsible for governing vital public institutions like schools. It is characterized as antidemocratic to take the vote away from citizens. This debate is exacerbated in cities by pervasive class, ethnic, and racial distinctions and divisions. Efforts to shift to appointive boards frequently are viewed by grassroots and community leaders as an effort by the old white establishment—the "downtown" business and political elites—to take back the power it lost to minority communities in recent years.

This debate over board selection processes has raged in cities like Cleveland and Detroit, even as the presence of African American mayors and other minority political and civic leaders has mitigated the racial dimensions of the debate.

A handful of cities are attempting to bridge this gap between proponents of appointive and elected boards. Washington, D.C., for example, recently created a hybrid governance structure in which some board members are elected by districts and others are appointed by the mayor.

Other important examples of growing mayoral involvement (as well as attempts at increased involvement) in board selection procedures can be found in both smaller cities (Oakland, California and Harrisburg, Pennsylvania) and mega-cities like Los Angeles and New York. In Los Angeles, former Mayor Richard Riordan, frustrated with the performance of the school board, financed a successful slate of candidates who replaced a number of incumbents. In New York City, former Mayor Rudolph Giuliani sought unsuccessfully on a number of occasions to obtain greater control of the nation's largest school system. His successor Michael Bloomberg, however, has been successful in gaining control of the city's schools. This trend is likely to continue as mayors seek to expand their influence over one of the most visible areas of the cities they govern—the schools.

Appointing non-traditional superintendents. Perhaps the most visible approach to rethinking the urban school superintendency is the appointment of nontraditional superintendents. While this strategy is viewed positively, particularly by business and political leaders, currently only a small percentage of urban superintendents are nontraditional, meaning non-educators. These few individuals generate tremendous media coverage because their school districts are among the largest and most influential in the country. New York City, Chicago, Los Angeles, Seattle, and San Diego are among the big cities that currently have or have had nontraditional superintendents.

Seattle's schools, for example, employed two nontraditional superintendents in a row. Businessman Joseph Olchefske succeeded the popular and charismatic retired military officer, General John Sanford, whose tragic death cut short a promising career as an educational leader. The huge and long-troubled Los Angeles Unified District attracted national attention with the appointment of former Colorado Governor Roy Romer as its superintendent. Romer, former Chairman of the Democratic National Committee, is a particularly visible individual who in his 70s actively sought this demanding job.

In San Diego, Alan Bersin, a former U.S. Attorney and Los Angeles litigator, is superintendent, and in New York City, Joel Klein, also an attorney, is serving as chancellor. In Chicago, Paul Vallas, Mayor Daley's budget director and political aide, served as superintendent;

when he left that position, he was recruited and hired by Philadelphia's school system.

The employment of former corporate executives, lawyers, and military and political leaders is predicated on the assumption that running large school systems requires a set of financial, organizational, and management skills and political experience that traditional educators often lack. The traits required to run large, complex organizations are presumably generic, and leadership success in other sectors can be transferred into the urban superintendency. However, there are those who do not accept this assessment, and who contend that experience and leadership in the core mission areas of teaching and learning are prerequisites for top-level school executives.

The appointment of nontraditional superintendents is a relatively recent development, and evidence relating to their success is limited. It is too early to tell whether or not these highly visible and well-credentialed administrators will be more successful than traditional educators who ascended to their leadership positions by moving up the ranks in their districts. We do not know whether their tenures will be longer or shorter, or whether their "outsider status" will hinder or enhance the relationships they will need to build. At this point, the long-range significance of this handful of appointments lies in its departure in conceptualizing the urban superintendency—one of the nation's most demanding, least understood, and most important public leadership positions.

The most significant contribution of nontraditional urban superintendents may be their ability to reach key governmental and business leaders in order to convey the complexity of the urban education crisis. Deservedly or not, this small cadre of nontraditional urban superintendents may generate influence in the larger political world that others in education cannot. If they can command additional resources and mobilize additional support to successfully stimulate reform, then nontraditional superintendents may find themselves highly sought-after educational leaders in more cities and districts.

Growing involvement of business leaders. Corporate executives played a very important role in supporting the appointment of nontraditional superintendents Bersin in San Diego, Romer in Los Angeles, Sanford and Olchefske in Seattle, Klein in New York, and Vallas in both Chicago and Philadelphia. Business leaders also have been instrumental in pushing for appointive boards of education in cities like Boston, Cleveland, and Detroit. They have strategically and financially intervened in board elections and referenda. In Boston, for example, in the course of a highly contested referendum, business leaders threw their financial support behind the continuation of an appointive board. This fiscal support was of crucial importance in a very close public vote that barely averted a return to an elected body.

In San Diego, the business community invested heavily in support of the election of board candidates who would endorse Superintendent Bersin's controversial reform plans. Indeed, the very substantial contributions to Bersin's supporters in the school board race generated a strong backlash against San Diego's corporate leaders, who were accused of "overkill" in using their money to blatantly influence school governance. The board in 2002 was divided, which may slow the pace of reform.

The growing involvement of business in education has provoked mixed reactions. While many see clear advantages to this involvement, such as additional funding or greater school/work connections, and suggest that business has a logical interest in "education for economic growth" (Task Force on Education for Economic Growth, 1983), others see such interventions as less about students than about maximizing corporate profits and furthering corporate agendas (Spring, 2002, pp. 17-21).

Creating new teaming arrangements. The manner in which the urban superintendency currently is structured needs to be rethought. The basic managerial, political/community, and instructional leadership responsibilities of the job have simply become too overwhelming for any individual to handle. There is growing recognition of the need to develop team arrangements that increase the chances of success for this demanding public leadership position.

Increasingly in large districts, the multidimensional facets of the urban superintendency are being reconfigured. Growing numbers of districts, including Seattle, Chicago, and San Diego, now have both chief operating officers and chief education officers. This division of responsibility, or what Harvard Professor Richard Elmore (2000) calls "distributive leadership," is making the city superintendency somewhat more manageable and less the "Vietnam of urban politics."

San Diego provides a particularly interesting example of the concept of distributive leadership. Attorney Alan Bersin, a nontraditional superintendent, recognized early in his tenure that he never would have the requisite credibility with teachers and administrators to be the system's educational leader. He hired Tony Alvarado, a respected educator whose successes in raising academic achievement in New York City earned him national renown, as the Chancellor for Instruction (not assistant superintendent). Alvarado is responsible for curriculum, professional development, and other related education issues. While the jury is still out on the Bersin-Alvarado "boom theory of change" in San Diego, and only a tenuous 3-2 school board majority supports Bersin, this team arrangement and its underlying rationale provide an important and visible national prototype for other urban districts to emulate.

Different examples of team arrangements or distributive leadership can be found in cities like Boston and Chicago. In these districts the growing involvement of mayors has also resulted in a team approach. Boston's mayor bears a large burden of the school system's political and community leadership responsibilities, thus freeing the superintendent to focus on the instructional or educational components of the job. The Daley-Vallas tandem in Chicago likewise exemplified Elmore's concept of distributive leadership; Vallas selected a Chief Education Officer to take major responsibility for education issues, and this position continues to be staffed under the new CEO Arne Duncan.

The team concept also may embrace out-of-school agencies. Hill, Campbell, and Harvey (2000), in *It Takes a City*, argue for a strong CEO superintendent working with effective school providers, or a "community partnership" with unconventional partners, such as libraries, arts agencies, churches, and cyber schools. They urge great attention to designing the administrative structures and cultivating parent support and outside investment to make it all work. Staff training, monitoring by an outside entity, and quality teachers are key ingredients. They also recommend a "public real estate trust"—a stock of buildings, which in most cities are in short supply when needed.

They argue, as do Frederick Hess (1999) and others, that superintendents need lengthier tenures, help from the teacher unions, and frequent publicity of gains and reform accomplishments, preferably by civic reformers or watchdog groups—all more likely to happen through partnerships and creative collaborations. In Boston, for example, both the Private Industry Council and the Boston Plan for Excellence in the Public Schools perform the roles of external advocate and watchdog. Team leadership and divisions of responsibility may contribute to more of these partnerships in the future.

The Preparation of Urban Superintendents

Attitudes towards preparing the urban superintendency have gone through three stages over the last century. Joseph Murphy of Vanderbilt University describes these phases:

From *1900 to 1950* technical, mechanical, and business skills were taught to superintendent candidates to meet the expectations of corporate boards. Courses in school plant management, planning, finance, and organization were highly practical and often required by the state for a superintendent's license, with terms often suggested by university professors who taught those courses.

From *1950 to 1985* universities sought to infuse content from the social sciences into the preparation of educational leaders; specifically, sociology, political science, social psychology, and economics were applied to educational thinking. Universities pursued the idea of a "science of administration" to replace technique and skill training. Books on administrative theory and the politics of education became staples of educational leadership doctoral programs.

More recently, superintendents are informed about the instructional and assessment domains in education, and asked to reflect on the intellectual and moral domains. The new breed of superintendent must be humanistic, collaborative, reflective, and ethical. He or she must understand the transformational potential of schools and have the capacity to design and build a more productive and caring human organization (Murphy, 2001).

The Urban Superintendent's Program at the Harvard Graduate School of Education exemplifies this newer orientation. The program accepts eight new school leadership candidates each year, most of them minorities and women. The program emphasizes the politics of local, state, and federal education—how to make politics work for education without formally being a politician. Traditional managerial, finance and budget, legal, and personnel skills continue to be taught. In addition, Robert Peterkin, the former Milwaukee Superintendent of Schools who coordinates the program, encourages attention to teaching and learning and to increasing the focus on student work and classroom performance—the essence of the new and higher expectations of urban school leaders. He places students in carefully supervised internships in cities with effective educational leaders, who increasingly are alumnae of the program. Students then apprentice themselves as associate or deputy superintendents to enhance their leadership skills.

This type of program is an alternative to hiring more lawyers and generals as leaders of school systems. While generals (and many lawyers) are skilled at battle, and certainly some city schools resemble battlefields, a demonstrable talent for figuring out ways to improve classroom and student performance is at the heart of school reform.

Finally, it should also be noted that the Internet and the applications of personal computers will change both the production and consumption of knowledge, and most likely, modes of instruction. It is enough to say now that the urban superintendent must be computer literate, subscribe to online services, check the email each day, and learn how to use technology to educate an urban population as well as to communicate with varied audiences.

An Uncharted Future

We believe that the demographic diversity and the persistent prevalence of poverty among urban youngsters will continue to compel the forging of closer coordination between the schools and general-purpose government. We argue that general-purpose government's elected officials (i.e., mayors, city and county council members, and executives) will gain greater influence over school policy making, not only in large cities but also in inner-ring suburbs and small cities. The central and unique role of the schools will be to fulfill their primary academic mission, but they will also serve as community centers for needed health, social, and related services, and this will force new and closer relationships between educators and general government policymakers. The tragic events of September 11, 2001 make the need for the "community school" even more urgent. The pervasive uncertainty that confronts our society, threats of violence and fears for personal safety, and related mental health concerns loom larger for the immediate future, and possibly for much longer.

These new and unprecedented pressures will further exacerbate the difficulties confronting urban school leaders, as they attempt to juggle the complex managerial, instructional, and community leadership dimensions of their positions. These realities, we contend, will provide a catalyst for the spread of the distributive leadership concept and "teaming" as the only logical ways to handle the diverse components of the urban superintendent's increasingly weighty responsibilities.

These developments, of course, have profound ramifications for the training and overall preparation of urban school leaders. There will be a pressing need to recruit and nurture cohorts of outstanding leaders with superb substantive know-how and the consummate people skills necessary to juggle the multiple demands of school leadership. We will have to cast a wider net to attract such talent from the ranks of both educators and non-educators.

REFERENCES

Bailey, S.K. (1976). The purposes of education. Bloomington, IN: Phi Delta Kappa Foundation.

Brabeck, M.M., Walsh, M.E., & Latta, R. (Eds.). (2003). Meeting at the hyphen: Schools-universities-communities-professions in collaboration for student achievement and well being. The 102nd yearbook of the National Society for the Study of Education, Part II. Chicago: National Society for the Study of Education.

Cronin, J.M. (1973). The control of urban schools. New York: The Free Press.

Cuban, L. (2001). Urban school leadership—Different in kind and degree. Washington, DC: Institute for Educational Leadership.

Elmore, R.F. (2000). Building a new structure for school leadership. New York: The Albert Shanker Institute.

Gilland, T.M. (1935). The origin and development of the powers and duties of the city school superintendent. Chicago: The University of Chicago Press.

Hess, F. (1999). Spinning wheels: The politics of urban school reform. Washington, DC: Brookings Institution.

Hill, P.T., Campbell, C., & Harvey, J. (2000). It takes a city: Getting serious about urban school reform. Washington, DC: Brookings Institution Press.

Hunt, H.C., & Pierce, P.R. (1958). The practice of school administration. Cambridge: Houghton, Mifflin Company.

Kirst, M.W. (2003). Mayoral influence, new regimes, and public school governance. In this volume—W.L. Boyd & D. Miretzky (Eds.), American educational governance on trial: Change and challenges. The 102nd yearbook of the National Society for the Study of Education, Part I (pp. 196-218). Chicago: National Society for the Study of Education.

Murphy, J. (2001). The changing face of leadership preparation. The School Administrator, 10(58), 14-17.

National Commission on Excellence in Education. (1983). A nation at risk: The imperative for educational reform. Washington, DC: U.S. Government Printing Office.

Pearson, H.G. (1932). Son of New England. Boston: Thomas Todd.

Reller, T. (1935). The development of the city superintendency of schools. Philadelphia: The Author.

Sears, J.B., & Henderson, A.D. (1937). Cubberley of Stanford. Stanford, CA: Stanford University Press.

Spring, J. (2002). American education (10th ed.). New York: McGraw-Hill.

Task Force on Education for Economic Growth. (1983). Action for excellence. Denver: Education Commission of the States.

U.S. Department of Education. (1998). Pursuing excellence: A study of U.S. 12th-grade mathematics and science teaching, learning, and achievement in international context. NCES 98-049. Washington, DC: National Center for Education Statistics.

Usdan, M., & Cuban, L. (2003). Powerful reforms with shallow roots. New York: Teachers College Press.

CHAPTER 10

Mayoral Influence, New Regimes, and Public School Governance

MICHAEL W. KIRST

In recent years, a spate of cities—including New York, Boston, Chicago, and Cleveland—have shifted governance structures to give more control of their school systems to mayors. The hope was that such changes would ultimately lead to improved school quality and student achievement, as well as to diminished scandal and turmoil in the school systems. A closer look at these instances, however, shows that these governance changes must be understood within the broader context of a particular city, and the particular frustrations and challenges that led to the willingness to alter the top levels of educational control. The ways in which mayors have become more engaged with schooling have varied, ranging from low involvement (for example, trying to influence traditional school board elections) to high involvement (gaining formal control over the schools or appointment of school board members). Just as each city is different, so are the effects (such as can be determined) of governance changes. While it is difficult to link these governance shifts to improved instructional practices or outcomes, many mayors are forging a new relationship with schools.

Background

Changes in American big-city school governance frequently focus on reform of a prior reform (Tyack & Cuban, 1995). A major "reform" from 1900 to 1920 was the severing of links between city and school governance, in large part because of corruption in city administrations. Tammany Hall's patronage and graft in New York City was the icon of that era. Reformers at the turn of the 20th century wanted to put an end to the excessively decentralized ward-based 50-to-100-member school boards, as well as the corruption of mayoral and city council

Michael W. Kirst is Professor of Education in the School of Education at Stanford University.

influence in teacher hiring. They wanted school boards independent of city government, and touted the seven-member school board as the best vehicle for hiring a professional superintendent, who in turn would hire the teachers. This executive centralization of a small board and certified administrators would make the creation of a uniform citywide curriculum more efficient. Mayors were seen as part of a discredited, inefficient, corrupt regime ill-suited to the more effective industrial model of governance that envisioned the school superintendent as a chief executive officer (Tyack, 1974).

It was not until the 1960s that this 1900-1920 governance pattern was challenged as undemocratic and as insufficiently representative of minority groups. As a result, a partial reversion to the earlier decentralized pattern was instituted. Five- or seven-member school boards were elected from geographic sub-districts of the city and exercised tighter oversight of the superintendent. Unions became widespread and played larger roles in board elections, while voluminous collective bargaining agreements grew annually. Administrative decentralization in the 1970s consisted of area superintendents for each of the five or seven districts in a city. New interest groups created a political pluralism, representing populations such as handicapped, bilingual, disadvantaged, and gifted pupils. Boards responded to these multiple governance pressures, superintendent turnover accelerated, and the era of the superintendent as administrative chief ended (Wirt & Kirst, 2001). Meanwhile, the conditions of many urban children deteriorated into massive poverty, and big-city school bureaucracies grew even more ineffective and inefficient (Kirst & Bulkley, 2000).

From 1960 to 1995, some large cities like Chicago and Philadelphia preserved a role for the mayor in appointing school board members; an exception was Baltimore, where the mayor continued to exert direct policy control over the schools. As the performance of city schools stagnated, various governance prescriptions, including sub-area decentralization and weakly implemented school-based management, failed to improve performance. City school board members increasingly saw their role as redistributing school jobs and contracts to benefit residents in the geographic slice of the city that they represented (Danzberger, Kirst, & Usdan, 1992).

In the late 1960s and early 1970s, mayors like John Lindsay of New York City and Jerome Cavanaugh of Detroit stressed that city economies could not be substantially improved without good schools and middle-class students. But these mayors hesitated to seek operational control of the schools, because they feared that whatever school improvement did occur would be viewed as inadequate to justify their reelection. During the 1980s, African American mayors such as Harold Washington in Chicago and Coleman Young in Detroit focused in part on redistributing school jobs and services to minority communities (Beinart, 1997; Stone, 2001). Los Angeles decentralized central office control to some degree by creating regional superintendents in the 1970s, abolishing them in the 1980s, and then reinstating them in 2000.

The 1990s produced a 180-degree reversal of the Tammany Hall image of corrupt mayoral involvement. Some mayors projected an image of efficient public managers, less interested in redistributing jobs to minorities and more interested in improved services. Mayors argued that City Hall needed to provide more integrated and coherent public services, including services for children. Better schools were essential to attracting the middle class and business back to the central city. Anti-union Republican state legislatures in Illinois, Michigan, and Ohio were ready to reduce the influence of the fractious school boards that faced repeated financial crises, and to reduce the influence of the teacher unions as well. Education reformers stressed that the "churn" of new policies with each new superintendent created lots of wheel-spinning but little educational attainment (Hess, 1999).

The Picture Today

It is too soon to assess whether mayor control in such cities as Chicago, Cleveland, Harrisburg, and Boston will provide more coherent governance and improved pupil performance. But there are some positive signs. According to polls, citizens in Boston and Chicago are more satisfied with mayoral control than they had been with the school boards that were replaced. In 1992, 70% of Cleveland voters voted to preserve mayoral control of schools. Politicians from all over the United States have visited Chicago to see its new governance model, in which former city employees have taken over key bureaucratic operations such as personnel and facilities. But in Baltimore, after years of dismal pupil attainment and public dissatisfaction, Mayor Curt Smoke (who never lost formal power over the schools) had to surrender control to the state in 1997.

In 1999, the author served on Oakland, California Mayor Jerry Brown's commission on education. The commission favored mayoral appointment of all school board members, but not because the commission thought that mayoral control was a panacea. As this chapter demonstrates, new governance decisions depend largely on judgments about conditions in a specific city context at a particular point in time. The Oakland commission believed that mayoral takeover would stimulate more change than electing two school board members from geographic sub-districts every 2 years. Moreover, in the fragmented policy context, with a recent state audit casting Oakland schools in a desperate financial plight, the commission judged that the mayor had a better chance of advancing new coherent policies. Criticism that mayoral appointment of school boards is less democratic than elections has justification, but the mayor is also elected, and is better known by the voters than school board members are. The commission lacked research to support their recommendation of mayoral control, so the appointment issue was subjected to a successful citywide referendum. In 4 years Oakland voters can decide with another referendum whether they want to restore election of all board members.

We are in an era of experimentation with various forms of mayoral influence and control in public education. Operation of the Chicago schools was taken over by former employees of the city, including Paul Vallas, a versatile public administrator, as superintendent. Boston school superintendent Tom Payzant, a former superintendent in three other cities, is a member of the mayor's cabinet. Boston citizens sometimes take their concerns about the schools to the city council because the school board is advisory and does not react to citizen complaints. Under Michigan law, the Detroit superintendent has statutory powers independent of the Detroit school board. Local school board appointees select the Detroit superintendent, but a representative of state government also sits on the school board. Oakland has a mixed 10-member board—seven members elected by sub-districts and three appointed by the mayor. With perhaps the most successful record of change in instructional policy and test scores, Sacramento, California features no formal mayoral appointment power, but the system was galvanized by the election of a mayor-endorsed slate of candidates.

Each new form of governance depends on a specific city context, and the willingness to make significant changes in governance emerges from an intense and long-gestating desire for a major shake-up in school policy and performance (Stone, 2001). Looming in the background in several of these cities is the fear of targeted or massive voucher schemes if mayoral action fails to improve the schools. Vouchers and mayoral control coexist in Cleveland, Ohio, for example, where the long-term governance pattern is in doubt.

Arguments for Mayoral Control

The arguments for mayoral control have strong appeal for some. Proponents justify giving the mayor control of, or an increased role in, the schools because this control provides a single point of electoral accountability and can result in greater integration of children's services with schools and better pupil attainment. Such improvements will spur city economic development, stimulate more middle-class people to live in the city, and forge a closer alliance between city government and businesses. Mayors stress that they are in a better position to integrate citywide services (such as land use, transportation, after-school programs, and children's social services) with the schools. Political losers in this governance shift are district central office professionals and, most important, school board members.

Arguments Against Mayoral Control

Opponents of mayoral control assert that a school board appointed by the mayor will result in less democracy because voters have fewer electoral choices and cannot vote for a board member from their section of the city. An Institute for Educational Leadership study found that electing school boards by sub-districts changed the role and behavior of school board members (Danzberger, Kirst, & Usdan, 1992). Boards became more attentive to the particular needs of certain geographical sections of their cities. The citywide education policy perspective lessened, and board support for geographic redistribution of jobs, contracts, and constituent services grew. Minority representation on school boards, however, increased when citywide selection was changed to geographic districts. Hispanic groups in the West, for example, have strongly supported sub-district board elections in order to increase representation of minority groups on school boards. Whether the alleged policy benefits of mayoral control are worth the loss of better geographic representation cannot be decided by general theories and is a decision better submitted to the local electorate. Theories of governance cannot predict outcomes from mayoral control.

The 1900-1920 movement to centralize school governance was justified in part by a perception that a citywide curriculum was needed to offset multilingual approaches (Tyack, 1974). This perceived need for centralization resurfaced in 1990 when urban reading scores fell dramatically. Proponents of centralization hoped that mayoral appointment would lead to a more intense and coordinated focus on reading in big cities. This shift demonstrates, again, the reform of an earlier reform; it was the alleged excessive centralization of curriculum in city schools that led in part to the call for urban decentralization to better meet the needs of diverse pupils during the 1960s (Hannaway & Carnoy, 1993).

Governance changes, in short, are a way to prioritize certain conflicting values and policies over others. As values and needs change, governance revisions such as mayoral control and decentralization will recycle. Moreover, entirely new governance forms (for example, vouchers and contracting with private firms to run public schools) might be emphasized in the future. Will any of these governance alternatives change classroom instruction, attract quality teachers, and improve pupil performance? And if they do, what is the connection between governance structure and improved classroom instruction? This chapter provides an overview of recent mayoral governance changes as we anticipate these questions coming to the forefront over the next few years.

Every City Is Different

Mayors of many cities are using different approaches to increase their influence over the public schools. Some mayors, such as those in Akron, Ohio and West Sacramento, California, have gone only so far as to threaten takeover unless certain school policies change. Other mayors, as in Chicago and Boston, have in fact taken over their school systems and have gotten involved in major decisions affecting these systems. In cities like San Francisco, the mayor has not sought direct control, but has strengthened the liaison function between the schools and the mayor's office. San Francisco's mayor hired Ramon Cortines, the former superintendent of both New York City and San Francisco, to perform this function.

The striking thing about the growth of mayoral influence over schools is the effect of the unique context of each city on the nature of this influence. A key theme of this chapter is that there are no established patterns; form, function, and operation of mayoral influence are indeed diverse. These differences reflect particular city contexts, local political cultures, interest group structures, state/local relations, the legal basis of city government, historical school governance structures, and other specific city characteristics. The personalities and ambitions of individual mayors also play a role. Mayor Tom Menino of Boston, for example, featured his own school role in his successful reelection campaign, while other mayors, like Michael White in Cleveland, preferred to highlight the superintendent they appointed.

The array of mayoral interventions is presented below, ranging from low to high influence and providing specific examples. At the high end of influence, the mayor makes the schools part of city government, like any other city department. At the low end, the mayor participates only in school board elections. Following presentation of the array, some interesting effects of mayoral influence are examined in greater depth.

Low Mayoral Influence

Mayors have threatened to take over schools, but pulled back when school policy changed in Akron, Ohio and West Sacramento, California. Mayors in Los Angeles and Sacramento, California endorsed slates of school board candidates and provided substantial campaign money and workers for their board choices, but they did not seek to overthrow the school boards' powers or to appoint board members. The mayor of Indianapolis can create five charter schools per year.

Low-Moderate Mayoral Influence

Mayors appoint some school board members, but not a majority of the board. Voters in Oakland, California approved a city charter amendment enlarging the school board from seven to ten members, and allowing Mayor Jerry Brown to appoint three members. The mayor's appointees formed a minority voting bloc that opposed the superintendent more often than the elected members. Brown wanted to appoint the entire school board, but could not obtain city council approval to appoint more than three of the ten members. Of the three candidates endorsed by the mayor, only two were successful.

Until recently, the mayor of Baltimore appointed all school board members because Baltimore never had an elected school board. However, in 1997, because of continued low test scores, the city received $230 million in state aid, and in return, Mayor Curt Smoke lost his prerogative to appoint the members of the board of education. In its place, the mayor and governor jointly appoint a new nine-member board of commissioners, based on a nominating slate provided by the State Board of Education. The board was required to be composed in total of at least four commissioners with a high level of expertise in a large business, nonprofit, or governmental entity; at least three with a high level of knowledge and expertise in education; at least one who was a parent of a student enrolled in the district; and at least one with knowledge or experience in educating children with disabilities. The new board of commissioners (unlike the old board which had been appointed by and controlled by the mayor) is vested with full authority and responsibility for running the school system. The mayor and the

governor have selected people with established education policy credentials to serve on the new board of commissioners, including an education professor, a facilities management expert, and two other academics. In addition, a 14-member parent and community advisory board
was formed to solicit parental input and involvement (Cibulka, 2001).

After Anthony Williams was elected mayor of Washington, D.C. in
1998, he sought more control over school policy by proposing to
appoint all 11 school board members. As in Oakland, the city council
resisted this, arguing in favor of more electoral representation. The
parties compromised by creating a hybrid nine-member board—four
selected by the mayor and four elected from new geographic districts,
with the president elected in a citywide referendum. District voters can
revisit the governance structure through a referendum to be held after
4 years (Cibulka, 2001).

Moderate Mayoral Influence

The Detroit mayor appoints six members and the governor appoints
one member to the city's school board. In some decisions, however, the
governor's choice has veto power over the mayor's six appointees. For
example, in 1999 the governor's representative vetoed the first choice
for superintendent of Mayor Dennis Archer's appointees. But the
Detroit board does little other than choose the superintendent, approve
the superintendent's appointees, and approve the annual school improvement plans. The mayor's deputy press secretary has said, "The
mayor has no direct involvement in the schools ... he has enough on
his plate trying to run the 10th largest city" (Community Renewal
Society, 2001, p. 12). In addition, a Michigan law has terminated the
Detroit principals' union in order to provide the superintendent with
more flexibility.

The Cleveland mayor, under state legislation, appoints the school
board and the district's chief executive officer (CEO). After 30 months,
however, the mayor can fire the CEO, but only with the concurrence
of the board he appointed. Mayor Michael White has chosen not to
get visibly involved in school policy or operations. White's relationship
with CEO Barbara Byrd-Bennett is similar to the relationship between
a non-executive chairman and a CEO in private business (Community
Renewal Society, 2002, p. 6). White has been most active in improving
facilities, and he meets infrequently with the school board. He is kept
informed, but has chosen to let CEO Byrd-Bennett be the public
leader. Both mayoral candidates in the 2001 election supported the
existing mayoral system.

The mayor of Hartford, Connecticut will appoint five members of the school board in 2005, while the voters will elect four. Hartford was taken over by the state government, and has had several forms of local governance over the past decade.

High Mayoral Influence

Philadelphia moved to the high influence category after the voters approved a 2000 charter initiative enabling the mayor to appoint all school board members at one time. Philadelphia's previous mayor, Ed Rendell, could appoint board members in staggered terms, and he chose to defer to his superintendent on matters of education policy and operational decisions. Current Philadelphia Mayor John Street has appointed one person in his office to follow school policy closely and to work with the board-appointed CEO. Street has been able to increase the number of charter schools in Philadelphia (serving 6.5% of total enrollment in 2001) despite resistance from the teachers' union. A huge district deficit in 2001 forced Street to negotiate with the state to provide more aid to Philadelphia schools in exchange for greater state policy control. The governor hired the for-profit Edison Schools to rethink governance and school improvement. *The Philadelphia Inquirer* described the state proposal this way:

Governor Schweiker's Philadelphia plan would transfer control of the school system from local officials to his appointees, who would then put its management in the hands of a private corporation—almost certainly the for-profit Edison. Another seismic proposal: turning over the 60 lowest-achieving schools to partnerships of community groups or universities and private school-management firms.

The governor and other proponents of the plan have cast it as a prototype for urban education reform in the 21st century, one that opens new opportunities for community leadership of the schools. An angry Mayor Street, on the other hand, has called it "fantasyland" and "unacceptable."

If no agreement is reached, a board—with four of five members named by the governor—would control the district for the next five years and impose his original plan. (Lessons from school takeovers, 2001)

In response to Mayor Street's objections, Governor Schweiker agreed to drop Edison's central management of the system, but insisted on district governance by a five-member School Reform Commission, with three members appointed by the governor and two appointed by the mayor. A super majority of four is needed for many key decisions, including selection of the district CEO, adoption of the Commission's by-laws, selection of an independent evaluator, borrowing of money, and appointment of a general counsel. In effect, the mayor's two appointees have veto power over these matters.

The 1995 Chicago governance changes granting an enhanced role to the mayor were layered over reforms instituted in 1988. The earlier reforms, which were supported by state Democrats and civic activists, shifted power from the district to Local School Councils, which were given the authority to appoint principals and to allocate significant discretionary money at each school. The mayor's ability to appoint the city's school board was limited under the 1988 legislation. This impetus for decentralization did not reflect a desire to increase the influence of educators; on the contrary, Shipps (2000) notes, "Educators were blamed for the problems and their discretion curtailed." Rather, the legislation was designed to enhance the influence of parents and community members.

While the 1988 reforms pushed control toward the schools, the 1995 legislation shifted power up the ladder to the mayor. Chicago Mayor Richard M. Daley favored this shift and sought an alliance with a Republican-dominated state legislature. Led and supported by Republican state legislators, the 1995 governance change emphasized centralizing political accountability in the mayor's office, adding the new structure on top of the 1988 reform rather than replacing it.

The 1995 changes gave the Chicago mayor more authority than any mayor since before the Progressive Era, effectively turning the public education system into a department of city government (Shipps, 2000). The legislation eliminated the school board nominating committee, which had effectively minimized the mayor's ability to select school board members, and replaced the traditional board with a corporate-style board. Under the new structure there was a CEO, rather than a school superintendent. The legislation limited the right of unions to strike, and redefined a large number of issues as non-negotiable (for example, class size). The legislation also enabled the Chicago district to contract for many building repairs, services, and purchases, instead of employing numerous union personnel as under the old system.

Mayoral appointment of the school board in Boston began in 1991. In 1996 Mayor Menino made his appointee Tom Payzant, who had previously run the San Diego schools, a member of his cabinet. The school board had been reduced to an advisory role, and the mayor urged voters to hold him accountable for school performance. A 1996 referendum to retain the mayor-appointed board was supported by

70% of Boston's voters, with only African American communities opposed. Board meetings were generally brief and poorly attended, while the superintendent and mayor made the real decisions. The public did want the board to be more effective in transmitting their concerns to the heads of the system. Menino acknowledged that the appointed board had not been accessible to public concerns, but said he and Payzant would attend more to this function (Yee, 2000).

In recent decades the mayor of New York City appointed two members and the city's five borough presidents each appointed one to the citywide school board. In 2002, newly elected Mayor Michael Bloomberg persuaded state legislators to abolish the board and have the schools operated by a commissioner of education, who reports directly to him. Bloomberg appointed Joel Klein, a former U.S. Assistant Attorney General, as Commissioner. A New York School Board exists, but has little influence on major policy. The mayor appoints all members of the New York School Board, and top officials in New York schools were relocated from Brooklyn to an office near the mayor in Manhattan.

The Impact of Mayoral Control

It is possible to link some changes in school policy and practice to changes in governance. Some major trends can be attributed in part to mayoral intervention, although there is no apparent relationship between the level (low, moderate, or high) of mayoral influence and the impact on schools. For example, Mayor Joe Serna of Sacramento (*low influence*) recruited, financed, and supported a slate of school board candidates, but then left them alone to do their jobs. *Education Week* reported the following results:

Many in California's capital city of 369,000 credit Mr. Serna, who died of cancer November 7, 2001, for pushing changes that now have more children reading at earlier ages, more school buildings scheduled for repair, and more politicians and parents backing an urban school system that was once considered a total loss.

In the past year, the 52,000-student district's test scores in elementary-age reading and math have shown dramatic increases that would be the envy of any school system. A focused, determined school board, with a majority of members who were backed and supported by Mayor Serna, has ended the bickering and deadlock that plagued the district's governance for years. The public has shown renewed confidence and interest in the schools by passing, in October, the district's first bond measure for school repairs in more than 20 years.

And despite some criticism of how the changes are being carried out, Sacramento is being looked at nationwide as a model of urban school success. (Sacramento mayor's legacy, 2002)

In addition, the Sacramento school board elevated the deputy superintendent to the top job, and he focused on changing instruction through the Open Court standardized reading program.

Los Angeles Mayor Richard Riordan (*low influence*) used a school board electoral strategy that raised $2 million for the successful election of his candidate slate. The mayor's reform board recruited former Colorado Governor Roy Romer to be superintendent. Romer re-centralized some instructional policy and, like Sacramento, installed Open Court as the standard reading program. The Los Angeles results on the state test (Stanford-9) have not been as impressive as Sacramento's to date, but Superintendent Romer has won the support of the *Los Angeles Times*. Mayor Riordan also used the influence of his office to speed approval of new school construction in this rapidly growing district.

Among the *moderately influential* mayors, Cleveland's Mayor White actively promoted the successful $1.4 billion 2001 referendum to replace aging roofs, faulty wiring, rotted windows, and other chronic school building problems. Cleveland political observers contend that the voter support needed to upgrade the schools (difficult to secure from a middle-aged population) was generated in part by increased public confidence in the new CEO, Barbara Byrd-Bennett. In 1999, Byrd-Bennett announced instructional reforms and accountability changes that centralized the system and de-emphasized past policies in order to provide parents with greater school site influence (Ryan, 2001). The impact of her instructional reforms is unclear, but Byrd-Bennett is so popular that the voters continued mayoral control in November 2002 largely because of her performance (Voters leave Cleveland schools in mayor's hands, 2002). After nearly four years of mayoral control, 58% of teachers polled said schools are "getting better," and 12% said they were always good (Catalyst for Cleveland Schools, 2002).

Mayors have had little impact in cities such as Washington, D.C., Oakland, and Detroit, where the mayor's powers are most ambiguous. In Oakland (*low-moderate influence*), Mayor Jerry Brown has focused more on charter schools; his three appointees have not coalesced with the seven elected board members and their appointed superintendent. The new superintendent in Detroit has a lot of formal power, but has not sought a close relationship with city government, perhaps because the mayor's term expired in January 2002. The Washington, D.C. school system has made progress in restoring public confidence under the leadership of experienced superintendent Paul Vance, who once headed the large nearby suburban system in Montgomery County, Maryland (Cibulka, 2001).

City voters viewed the state-ordered demise of the Detroit school board as usurpation without any local legitimacy (Gewertz, 2000). Despite media support for the new regime (*low-moderate influence*), public opinion polls have indicated that voters, under a referendum allowed by the state law, want to return to an elected board in 2003. The last president of the Detroit school board was indicted on corruption charges. There had been no audit of Detroit budget expenditures in the 12 years prior to the new mayoral regime (Franklin, 2001). The new superintendent has managed to build more schools and make badly needed repairs. In contrast, the elected board could not agree on how much to spend of the $1.3 billion bond approved in 1993. Both 2001 mayoral candidates supported the new superintendent, who has two more years to make a bigger impact (D. Plank, interview, November 2001).

Chicago and Boston—High Influence Changes

The cases of Boston and Chicago (*high influence*) have received the most academic scrutiny. In both cities, the primary movers behind the governance changes granting more power to the mayors were the business community, the mayor himself (especially in Boston), and state legislators. Local groups, such as community activists and minority group representatives, were not directly involved; educator organizations, including the teacher unions, were either peripheral to the debate or opposed to the change.

The proponents of the governance changes in Boston and Chicago had certain similar goals, but goals also differed in some important ways. There was a strong emphasis in Chicago on improving the accountability of the public schools, particularly the fiscal efficiency of the district (Shipps, 2000). This emphasis reflected the interests of the Chicago business community. Improved efficiency was a factor in Boston, but not as central as the issues of standards and curriculum (Yee, 2000).

The role and purpose of the district leader was another difference between the reforms in these two cities. Reflecting the focus on efficiency, the Chicago Public Schools chose one of Daley's financial team, rather than a traditional superintendent. In contrast, the Boston mayor installed a strong educator-leader at the head of the school system. Boston's Menino wanted to be held accountable for the state of the Boston Public Schools, and he wanted to be directly involved in the district's operations. He wanted a strong superintendent who would be a part of the mayor's cabinet, and who would not have to contend with the many demands of an elected school committee.

The intentions of those who initiated the governance changes in Chicago and Boston were reflected in the implementation of these changes, and especially in the differences between the interests and styles of the new leaders.

The governance changes that shifted power toward the Chicago and Boston mayors set the stage for substantial alterations within these two school systems. The mayors and their chosen leaders took advantage of the new structural changes to implement substantive reforms. The selection of Paul Vallas, former Chicago budget director, as CEO of the Chicago Public Schools reflected the business community's interest in a leader from outside traditional public education circles. Vallas believed that clear accountability combined with a district run more like a business would lead to an improved organization. In this top-down change model, management creates the vision and defines clear sanctions for individuals and schools that fail to progress toward that vision (Shipps, 2000).

The selection of Tom Payzant as superintendent of the Boston schools was a far more traditional choice for district leader. His selection reflected Mayor Menino's interest in a professional educator who would avoid, to some extent, the political issues that consumed much of the time of previous superintendents. Payzant's approach reflected the framework of traditional education reform; his primary focus reflected a professional education model involving higher standards and capacity building (Yee, 2000).

The new governance structures in Chicago and Boston, in combination with the mayors' and district leaders' efforts to improve the school systems, resulted in changes that reflected the different intentions of those who sought the new structures. In both cities, there were shifts in the practical operations of the district and in the overall message about teaching and learning being communicated by mayors and education leaders.

Visible changes. Some very visible and practical changes occurred in the first years following the 1995 reform in Chicago. For the first time in years, the school district budget appeared to be in reasonable shape. This change may have been due in part to Mayor Daley's willingness to support the schools through property tax increases and funds diverted from other parts of the city budget. In addition, there was relative labor peace in the Chicago Public Schools. There has not been a teacher strike since the governance changes took place.

Some major changes occurred following Vallas' installation as CEO. Roughly 100 former City Hall employees came to work in the central office, displacing more traditional education staff. The leadership of the Chicago school district was now drawn largely from the business sector, rather than from education. Local School Councils still exist at all Chicago public schools, but their influence has been reduced; new central office leaders have increased their role in the operation of the schools. The combination of no budget crises, no strikes, and generally positive public opinion of the reforms instituted by Vallas improved the legitimacy of the school system over the last several years (Shipps, 2000). Mayor Daley replaced Vallas in 2001 with Arne Duncan, who has focused upon new reading and math initiatives, 24 new area instructional officers, and better designed staff development in an attempt to improve test scores that had leveled off.

The direct impact of the changes in the governance structure of the Boston Public Schools has not been as marked as in Chicago. The most notable change was the elimination of the bitter battles within the school committee and between the committee and the mayor—a logical outcome of having a committee appointed by the mayor rather than elected. The committee included allies, first of the previous mayor, Raymond Flynn, and then of Mayor Menino. Many committee members had close ties to the business community. As in Chicago, labor relations, particularly with the teachers' union, improved in the years following the governance change, and some of the district's most blatant budget problems disappeared. The Boston mayor has always influenced *how much* money is spent by the public school system, but the new governance changes allowed the mayor also to influence *how* the funds were spent. Unlike Chicago, however, Boston saw no dramatic changes in the structure or staffing of the district's central office, and no transfer of city employees to key positions in the district's central office (Yee, 2000). But Mayor Menino has provided a clear focus for public accountability by saying to the electorate that he wants to be judged for election by school improvement (Yee).

Teaching and learning. The style and substance of the Chicago and Boston education reforms are quite different. The overall focus in Chicago has shifted to academic accountability, defined largely by test scores and accompanying action where schools and students do not meet predefined goals for these scores. The emphasis has been on strong and immediate sanctions for schools that did not meet performance goals set by CEO Vallas. This was especially true for schools whose students fell into the bottom 25% of test scores in the district;

these schools faced high-stakes consequences such as probation and reconstitution. For students, there were new and high-stakes repercussions for low test scores as well; for example, Vallas' call to end social promotion, which was supported by Mayor Daley. Students who did not meet required performance levels at certain grades faced mandatory summer school, and generally would not be promoted if their test scores did not rise adequately by the end of the summer session.

These accountability measures focused mostly on minimal standards and on improving the educational outcomes of low-performing students in Chicago's schools, but there were also changes affecting students at the upper end of the performance spectrum. For example, Vallas supported the creation and expansion of alternatives including magnet schools, charter schools, and accelerated programs such as International Baccalaureate options. In addition to efforts removing "troublesome or slow-learning students" from regular public schools to other settings, such as transition centers and alternative high schools, there was a push for more "upper-end" options linked to the goal of attracting middle-class families back to the Chicago Public Schools.

Overall, Vallas based his efforts on two assumptions. First, he assumed that much of the capacity needed to improve performance was already available within the public school system, but that incentives and sanctions were necessary to elicit this preexisting capacity. As a result, there has been less emphasis on building additional capacity in Chicago than in other districts, such as Boston. The second assumption was that test scores, while not a perfect measure, were the most logical means of assessing progress in pursuit of quality education. However, when test scores reached a plateau in 2001, Mayor Daley decided that Vallas had done all he could do to improve scores, and forced him and the board president out. Accountable to the electorate for major changes in policy and personnel, the mayor thought the district needed to supplement its get-tough accountability policy; accordingly, the new Chicago superintendent is focused on promoting more effective instructional strategies.

In November 2001, the Illinois State Board of Education included three fourths of the state's elementary schools on its academic Early Warning List, based on state assessment scores. A majority of students in 67 of Chicago's 76 high schools failed the Eleventh Grade Prairie State Achievement Exam. Still, while statewide scores remained flat, Chicago's overall state test scores rose slightly, and Mayor Daley's new magnet schools had some of the highest scores in the state. Five of the state's top 10 elementary schools were in Chicago, but so were 21 of the state's bottom 25 schools. Chicago's chief accountability officer defended the magnet schools, saying, "If we did not have these programs, we would probably lose these kids to private and parochial schools" (Banchero, Olszewski, & Dougherty, 2001).

The style of the education reforms undertaken in Boston is quite different from those in Chicago. Former Mayor Flynn and Superintendent Lois Harrison-Jones were the first leaders to experience the mayorally-appointed school committee, but the significant changes resulted largely from the actions of Mayor Menino and Superintendent Payzant. In contrast to Vallas, who was an education outsider, Payzant was very much the professional superintendent who sought to work primarily within existing structures. Vallas relied heavily on the existing capacity within the school system; Payzant focused on increasing capacity. According to Yee (2000), "Payzant emphasized his long-term commitment to steady, resolute progress through staff training, new materials, and high standards" (p. 24).

Improvement strategies employed by Payzant included raising standards, leadership development, whole-school change, and developing a reorganization plan focused on student performance. His focus on teaching and learning tended to rely on professional norms, rather than sanctions, as a means of improving performance. Unlike Chicago under Vallas, there has been little change in the tenure of administrators or teachers in Boston, and no talk of school-site reconstitution. Payzant replaced the district's standardized test with the Stanford-9 because he believed it better reflected new standards that emphasized higher-order skills, and he included results on school report cards.[1]

The new governance frameworks in Boston and Chicago set similar stages for educational reform, but the leaders in these two cities used the expanded role of the mayor to make quite different changes. Both cities had strong mayors, and both had school districts troubled enough that the state legislatures (and the individual voters in Boston) were motivated to enact major structural changes. The actual regime change occurred, however, when the mayors, school leaders, and others used the governance changes to significantly alter the administrative and educational practices of the district leadership and change the practices of educators in the schools.

The different directions taken by Boston and by Chicago leaders were not just whims of the individual mayors and school district chiefs. To some extent, they reflected the historical political culture and the desires of powerful constituencies within these cities and states. The regime changes particularly reflected the different emphases of the business communities in Boston and Chicago. Selection of a business-style leader like Vallas to lead the Chicago school system was not surprising, given the role of the business community and the Republican legislative leaders in initiating the 1995 reform. The focus on management issues in Chicago is consistent with the interests of its business community. The Boston business community, however, tended to focus more on issues of school quality, so an experienced educational leader was a more acceptable choice.

The regime changes in both cities are still relatively new. But there is little indication that there will be a return, at least in the near future, to the previous governance structures. Since Menino and Daley have been reelected and face little serious opposition, it is more likely there will be ongoing tinkering within the present regimes than any more major structural changes.

Mayoral Control Vis-à-Vis State Takeovers

As mayoral control has become more common as a major governance reform, so, too, has state takeover of schools and districts. Wong and Shen (2001) compared the effects of mayoral takeover in Boston and Chicago with state takeover in Lawrence, Massachusetts and Compton, California. They concluded that mayoral takeover had a positive impact on pupil achievement:

First, mayoral takeover is linked to increases in student achievement at the elementary grades. Second, gains in achievement are especially large for the lowest performing schools, suggesting that mayoral takeovers involve a special focus on these failing schools. Third, mayoral takeover seems less effective for the upper grades, where the cumulative effects of many years of poor schooling are not easily reversible. Fourth, when state takeovers produce administrative and political turmoil, student achievement suffers. After a period of adjustment, however, state takeovers may also be able to produce positive achievement gains. (p. 14)

Wong and Shen (2001) write that mayoral control had other attributes:

Our analysis of city and state takeovers suggests the following conclusions. First, there are significant differences between mayoral takeovers and state takeovers, and mayoral takeovers appear to be more productive in terms of academic improvement. Mayoral takeovers may make a significant impact on the lowest-performing schools. Second, takeovers may also produce more efficient financial and administrative management, and in the case of mayoral takeover, lead to a broadening of management expertise. Third, both city and state takeovers bring with them a heavy emphasis on academic accountability, and mayoral takeovers are more likely to utilize additional tests beyond state-mandated exams. (p. 20)

The Six-City Study

Researchers have conducted case studies of six cities[2] that function under mayoral control or have school boards that appointed unconventional superintendents who had no prior experience in education administration (Cuban & Usdan, 2002). In general, under mayoral control they found improvement over the previous regime of school boards, but little evidence of reaching higher goals such as widespread instructional improvement in classrooms. The researchers did find "partial evidence of increased city and school coordination," but not at the level that mayoral-control advocates hoped would take place. An overview of the findings for the three mayor-controlled cities is presented in Table 1.

TABLE 1
OUTCOMES IN MAYOR-CONTROLLED SCHOOL DISTRICTS

Outcome	Boston	Chicago	Philadelphia
Aligned curriculum, tests, professional development, and rewards/penalties	Moderate	Low	Low
Political support of district reforms	High	High	Low
Improved coordination of city and school services	Slight	Slight	None
Increased turnover among:			
Teachers	Moderate	Moderate	High
Principals	High	High	High
Improved test scores:			
Elementary	Slight	Moderate	Moderate
Secondary	No	No	No
Reduced gap between white and minority scores	No	No	No

Source: Cuban, L. & Usdan, M. (2002). *Powerful reforms with shallow roots: Getting good schools in six cities* (p. 154). New York: Teachers College Press.

The six-city study found that Boston was making progress in aligning the various elements of its systemic strategy to support principals and teachers in helping students to improve academic performance, but Chicago and Philadelphia were not. Support of mayoral actions by business, media, and elites was strongly favorable in Boston and Chicago. But, as Cuban and Usdan (2002) note:

Although the Chicago case offers an instance of a CEO decisively acting in determining budgets, waiving rules, and slicing through bureaucratic layers, the accumulated evidence counters civic and business leaders' deep wish to connect governance changes and better management to improved student outcomes. (p. 157)

Cuban and Usdan applaud Boston for its leadership stability in extending Superintendent Payzant's contract from 1996 to 2005. They contend that a school without broader linkages to city, community, and private out-of-school services has little chance of success. Mayoral control is one means to enhance these linkages.

Conclusion

There is no political majority urging return to school board-dominated regimes in any of the cities that moved toward greater mayoral influence over the schools. Boston voters have reauthorized mayoral control in Boston, and the Illinois legislature extended the Chicago mayor's regime for another three years. Sacramento does not regret former Mayor Serna's campaign for a new board. Detroit has seen the president of its prior school board indicted for corruption, as well as bookkeepers and principals fired for misappropriating funds (Franklin, 2001). Still, the impact of enhanced mayoral influence on instruction remains tenuous and unclear (Rich, 1996). Mayors are able to help balance the budget, improve the condition of buildings, and increase school resources, but intervention in the classroom is more difficult. The most notable trend in these cities, however, is the diversity of the governance arrangements, and how local context and civic culture influence outcomes (Stone, 1998). While some mayors got involved in the details of school management, others gave their appointed superintendents wide discretion in running the schools. Increased centralized control of education policy was a consistent trend among these districts; there was no district where mayoral influence was primarily oriented to decentralizing policymaking to the schools.

Mayor Menino of Boston and Mayor Daley of Chicago sought to become the central symbol of school accountability in their cities, while Detroit Mayor Archer and Cleveland Mayor White preferred to stay behind the scenes and defer to the superintendent as the focus of accountability. Several mayoral regimes need to be reauthorized by the voters in the next 5 years. These elections will determine in large part whether 1995-2001 was just another quick cycle of mayoral influence, or a more lasting governance change (Boyd & Cibulka, 2002). Even if these new regimes are extended, there are limits to mayoral influence and control:

In other words, mayoral control of urban schools is merely one reform strategy. Changing governance arrangements clearly can make a difference in the way urban public school systems function, but such a strategy requires the right combination of ingredients—committed and skilled leadership by the mayor, willingness to use scarce resources, a stable coalition of supporters, appropriate education policies, and a cadre of competent, committed professionals to implement the reforms. (Cibulka, 2001, p. 35)

State domination of governance, where mayors play a secondary role to the state (as in Philadelphia and Baltimore), is one possibility for more urban districts. Mayors may have to demonstrate increases in pupil attainment and financial stability in order to ward off state intervention. The mayors of Baltimore and Philadelphia traded increased state aid for increased state control, so city economic growth may be a crucial factor. Slow-growing city economies will reduce local tax revenues and lead to calls for financial bailouts by the states. States, however, seem less inclined to provide more money without a greater governance role, including state appointment of board members. More mayors are becoming active in schools without seeking direct control of board appointments. At an October 2002 meeting, the National Conference of Mayors discussed numerous ways in which mayors can improve schools, including help with recruiting teachers, greater investment in preschool and after-school programs, new charter schools, improvement of school facilities, and recognition of schools that demonstrate improvement. A new relationship between schools and city government is evolving, diminishing the separation that was apparent between the two from 1900 to 1920. Mayoral control and mayoral influence on schools will be major components of this new relationship.

This paper was originally published as a Consortium for Policy Research in Education report in May, 2002.

NOTES

1. Boston and Massachusetts are phasing in a new statewide test called the Massachusetts Comprehensive Assessment System (MCAS), so test results at the time of our study were unclear.

2. These cities were Chicago, Boston, San Diego, Seattle, Philadelphia, and Baltimore.

REFERENCES

Banchero, S., Olszewski, L., & Dougherty, G. (2001, November 15). Seventy-five percent of city's grade schools on warning list. *Chicago Tribune*, p. 1.

Beinart, P. (1997, June 30). The pride of the cities. *New Republic*, 16-24.

Boyd, W., & Cibulka, J. (2002). *Reforming urban school governance*. Westport, CT: Ablex/Greenwood.

Cibulka, J. (2001). Old wine, new bottles. *Education Next, 1*(4), 28-35.

Community Renewal Society. (2001). *Catalyst: For Cleveland Schools, 2*(5), 6, 12.

Community Renewal Society. (2002). *Catalyst*, November 2002, p. 1.

Cuban, L., & Usdan, M. (2002). *Powerful reforms with shallow roots: Getting good schools in six cities*. New York: Teachers College Press.

Danzberger, J., Kirst, M., & Usdan, M. (1992). *Governing public schools*. Washington, DC: Institute for Educational Leadership.

Franklin, Barry (2001). Race, restructuring, and educational reform: The mayoral takeover of the Detroit Public Schools. In L. Miron and E. St. John (Eds.), *Reinterpreting urban school reform*. Albany, NY: SUNY.

Gewertz, C. (2000, January 26). Detroit board splits over superintendent choice. *Education Week*, p. 5.

Hannaway, J., & Carnoy, M. (Eds.). (1993). *Decentralization and school improvement*. San Francisco: Jossey-Bass.

Hess, F. (1999). *Spinning wheels: The politics of urban school reform*. Washington, DC: Brookings Institution.

Kirst, M., & Bulkley, K. (2000). New improved mayors take over schools. *Phi Delta Kappan, 82*, 538-546.

Lessons from school takeovers: Big change at districts, less so in classrooms. (2001, November 4). *The Philadelphia Inquirer*, p. 1.

Rich, W. (1996). *Black mayors and schools*. New York: Garland.

Ryan, P. (2001). Can't let go. *Education Next, 1*(4), 36-41.

Sacramento mayor's legacy: Improved schools. (2002, February 2). Retrieved December 13, 2001 from www.educationweek.org

Shipps, D. (2000). *Regime change: Mayoral takeover of Chicago Public Schools*. Unpublished manuscript, Consortium for Policy Research in Education, University of Pennsylvania.

Stone, C. (1998). *Changing urban education*. Lawrence, KS: University of Kansas.

Stone, C. (2001). *Building civic capacity*. Lawrence, KS: University of Kansas.

Tyack, D. (1974). *The one best system*. Cambridge, MA: Harvard University Press.

Tyack, D., & Cuban, L. (1995). *Tinkering toward utopia: A century of public school reform*. Cambridge, MA: Harvard University Press.

Voters leave Cleveland schools in mayor's hands. (2002, November 6). *Cleveland Plain Dealer*, p. 1.

Wirt, F., & Kirst, M. (2001). *Political dynamics of American education*. Berkeley, CA: McCutchan.

Wong, K., & Shen, F. (2001). *Does school district takeover work? Assessing the effectiveness of city and state takeover as a school reform strategy*. Paper presented at the annual meeting of the American Political Science Association, San Francisco, CA.

Yee, G. (2000). *From Court Street to City Hall: Governance change in Boston Public Schools*. Unpublished manuscript, Consortium for Policy Research in Education, University of Pennsylvania.

CHAPTER 11

"Ravening Tigers" Under Siege: Teacher Union Legitimacy and Institutional Turmoil

CHARLES TAYLOR KERCHNER AND BRUCE S. COOPER

Teachers—their work, their contributions to society, and their associations—should be easily recognized and legitimated, since teachers are fundamental contributors to the learning of students and act as direct, personal links between children and society. They toil in the field for the benefit of the next generation. Yet teachers' occupational legitimacy has always been shadowed (Lortie, 1975). While teachers are praised and recognized for their key role in schooling, they and their unions are often blamed for failing to produce acceptable academic and social results. As Finn (2001, p. 127) explained, "American teachers do not get the respect, the freedom, the compensation, or the rewards that many of them deserve. At the same time, U.S. schools are not producing satisfactory results, a problem that is not likely to be solved until our classrooms are filled with excellent teachers." Legitimacy for teachers—and their work—is now inextricably linked with the actions of their unions.

While the advent of collective bargaining for teachers has been described as one of the most potent public policy changes in the last half-century, the unionization of teachers is often cited as a source of rigidity and resistance to change. Organized teachers have gained a powerful voice in their schools and districts, and their unions have become major forces in state and national politics. Teacher unions have moved from the periphery of the institution of public education to its center. Wirt and Kirst (1997) write that no other group has had "... increased influence on education policy in recent decades as much as have teachers. The timid rabbits of 30 years ago are today's ravening tigers in the jungle of public school systems" (p. 181).

Charles Taylor Kerchner is professor of education at the Claremont Graduate University and author of many books and articles on teacher unionization. Bruce S. Cooper is professor and vice chair, Department of Educational Leadership, Administration and Policy at Fordham University's Graduate School of Education.

Still, teacher unions remain highly vulnerable, more so than they would admit. It is true, as their enemies maintain, that the National Education Association (NEA) and the American Federation of Teachers (AFT) are formidable opponents, and that they often successfully oppose the market-based reforms that are the Holy Grail of libertarians. But it is also true that the unions' prominence in the existing structure of public education has increased their vulnerability to attack. To challenge teacher unions, it is not necessary to attack them directly; one need only challenge the institution of public education as currently organized.

Teacher unions, which gained legitimacy as a critical voice for teachers in their struggle for dignity, respect, and a little money, now find themselves the prime defenders of the institution they sought to criticize. This irony has both ideological and political aspects. Teacher union leaders, and most teachers, believe that the institution of public education as currently constituted—state-owned schools, districts with defined boundaries, and public employees—has served the nation well, and that sustaining this mode of organization is necessary to produce the best possible outcomes.

At the same time, unionists know that every shred of economic benefit and occupational status that their members possess is tied to what former Labor Secretary John Dunlop (1993 [1958]) called the "web of rules," an interlocking set of laws, contracts, and policies that define public schooling. Arching over this institutional plumbing is an ideology, "or a set of beliefs held by the actors that helps to bind or to integrate the system together as an entity." Situations in which actors do not provide a legitimate role for others "would be regarded as volatile and no stability would likely be achieved" (p. 53).

Public education as an institution has become unstable. Political forces, unleashed by axial changes in the economy and in society, are attacking public education as we know it. The words "failing public schools" can be used in a presidential campaign without amplification and without challenge. In 26 states, unions face Republican governors, many raised in a political culture in which very little good was said about public education, and nothing at all positive was said about labor unions. Unlike Republican office holders in the post-World War II generation, contemporary Republican incumbents do not see organized labor as serving an institutional function for either the country or for their states.

Some recent governors, such as Tommy Thompson in Wisconsin, John Engler in Michigan, and Tom Ridge in Pennsylvania, have pointedly positioned themselves as opponents of teacher unions (Boyd, Plank, & Sykes, 2000). Big city mayors have become educational activists;

some, like John O. Norquist of Milwaukee, who organized charter schools under city rather than school district control, explicitly state that they cannot lure the middle class back to the city unless the schools improve. "People were leaving for the suburbs because of the quality of public schools, and that's not acceptable" (White, 1999, p. 34). African American politicians, traditionally supporters of public school reforms, have become doubtful of the system's ability to right itself, and are increasingly inclined to consider quasi-market alternatives. Libertarian think tanks present glowing visions of the schools the market might create, comparing them with the dreary reality of the public schools today.

In this context, unions have simply lost the momentum of reform. One of the great change forces in public education over the past half-century, teacher unions are largely reduced to fighting changes supported by others, rather than advocating for and organizing around a new set of educational ideas of their own. The legitimacy of teacher unions is being challenged, both directly as unions and indirectly as a result of their association with the existing public schooling structure. Four challenges to union legitimacy are explored in this chapter:

1. *Challenges to the legitimacy of teaching as a profession.* Unions struggle to decide whether entry to teaching should be highly regulated with specialized training or regulated primarily through market forces. This challenge raises the question of an appropriate role for unions in shaping the training, licensing, and tenuring of teachers and in supporting teaching as a profession (see Etzioni, 1969; Lortie, 1969, 1975).

2. *Challenges to the legitimacy of unions as school reformers.* If teaching is not to be organized as a profession, then unions have only a modest role in education reform. Many of the same voices that argue that unions cannot transcend narrow self-interest to endorse professional standards of conduct also believe that they should not (Moe, 2001).

3. *Challenges to the legitimacy and adequacy of unions as political forces.* The substantial political power of teacher unions brings challenges particularly, but not exclusively, to Republicans, who rarely get union electoral support. Elected officials in several states have found attacking teacher unions to be good politics.

4. *The legitimacy of unions in attracting the next generation of teachers.* Unions as mature organizations (Cooper & Liotta, 2001) now face the difficulty of passing the torch to younger, newer teachers,

most of whom were not part of the struggle for recognition and the fight for the right to bargain collectively under state law. How can unions continue to protect their members while inducting a new generation into the fold?

Challenging Teaching As a Profession

The most profound challenge to teacher unions comes not from the attack on unions themselves but from the attack on the profession of teaching. An increasingly raw political discourse rages between advocates of a more explicit professionalization of teaching and those who see benefits in deregulating the teacher marketplace (Cochran-Smith & Fries, 2001). Partisans pointedly discount their opponents as ideologues, challenging each other's evidence and questioning their accountability and motivations on behalf of the public good versus private interests.

Unlike many educational policy fights, this fight is substantive and revolutionary. Long before it embraced collective bargaining, the NEA was part of the reform establishment that sought higher standards for teachers and more rigorous teacher education. For all of the 20th century, increased professionalization was an avowed goal of educational reformers, and the history of education over the century reflects this position (Tyack, 1974). The attack on teacher professionalism, then, is not conservative at all—it is truly radical.

Arrayed against teacher unions, most federal and state government officials, and a host of foundations are the voices of deregulation, especially those of the Thomas B. Fordham Foundation and its president, Chester Finn; the Heritage Foundation; and the Manhattan Institute. The signatories of a Fordham Foundation manifesto on teaching, including William Bennett, E.D. Hirsch, and Diane Ravitch, argue against professionalization achieved through traditional university preparation and state licensure:

A better solution to the teacher quality problem is to simplify the entry and hiring process. Get rid of most hoops and hurdles. Instead of requiring a long list of courses and degrees, test the future teachers for their knowledge and skills. Allow principals to hire the teachers they need. Focus relentlessly on results, on whether students are learning. (Thomas B. Fordham Foundation, 1999, p. 1-2)

Linda Darling-Hammond and the National Commission on Teaching and America's Future (NCTAF) have been the most visible advocates of a stronger professionalization agenda. The heated debate between Darling-Hammond (2000) and Dale Ballou and Michael Podgursky (2000) in the *Teachers College Record* exemplifies the intensity of the arguments, featuring attacks on one another's evidentiary base and the labeling of opponents as ideologues. The most important institutional support for professionalization has come from the National Council for the Accreditation of Teacher Education (NCATE), headed by Arthur Wise; the Interstate New Teacher Assessment Consortium (INTASC); and the National Board for Professional Teaching Standards (NBPTS). Teacher unions support all three. NEA and AFT officers and members serve on these organizations' governing boards; union lobbyists advocate for government support for new regulations and financial support for creating and monitoring such regulations; and collective bargaining agreements reward teachers who seek and gain professional standing as outlined by INTASC and NBPTS.

The importance of this debate has to do with the occupational identification of teaching. There are four basic ways to organize work, each distinguished by the expectations of the workers and legitimized by institutional and organizational rules. Any worker can be identified as 1) an industrial laborer, 2) a craft worker, 3) an artist, or 4) a professional (Kerchner & Mitchell, 1988). Unions can organize around any of these four types, but the resulting unions emphasize different aspects of work. For example, artists unionize around control over the work as well as its financial rewards. Entertainment industry negotiations over who gets the "final cut" of a movie or the control over the playlist of a radio station are as hard fought as negotiations over compensation.

Likewise, professionals organize over the question of who sets and controls standards: witness the current struggle of physicians against health maintenance organizations (Kerchner & Abbott, 1999). Craft unions join economic concerns with an emphasis on skills. They wield control through apprenticeship and job placement programs. As Cobble (1991) reports in the case of a now-disbanded waitress union, the women assumed responsibility for management tasks such as the hiring and discharge of employees, mediation of on-the-job disputes, and the assurance of fair supervision. He concludes, "In a sense workers in the culinary industry had instituted a form of self-management" (p. 426).

However, by the 1960s and 1970s, when the majority of teachers in the United States unionized, the word "unionism" largely meant industrial unionism. Older forms of worker organization—guilds, artisan associations, and craft unions—had been supplanted by a form of unionism designed to function within large hierarchies featuring an atomistic division of labor. In public education, industrial unionism was labor's answer to an education system constructed on the principles of scientific management, a system in which the content and pacing of work were not designed by teachers themselves, but by school administrators. As the history of education in the 20th century clearly shows, schools were bureaucratized long before they were unionized (Tyack, 1974; Tyack & Hansot, 1982).

Strictly interpreted, industrial-style organization would hold teachers responsible for the faithful reproduction of curricula, lesson plans, and classroom routines developed elsewhere. The main obligation and the main responsibility would be to follow directions. Invention, creativity, and spontaneity would not be required or expected (Kerchner & Mitchell, 1988). The rigidity of school systems has been part of teacher lore for decades, inspiring minor classics such as Bel Kaufman's (1964) *Up the Down Staircase* and fueling teacher unionization efforts. But, ironically, teacher unions have become one of the strongest advocates for this system, whose managerial excesses and rigid rules they sought to tame with collective bargaining. And some would claim that the system's rigidity is actually reinforced by teachers' contracts, "work rules," narrow interpretations of regulations, and inflexibility regarding rules (Moe, 2001).

Part of the irony can be explained by the fact that schools, despite heavy borrowing from the scientific management movement, never were factories. Despite their bell schedules and thick policy documents, there is more than a little truth to the teacher refrain "I'm in charge when the classroom door is closed." In the industrial sense, schools were always incomplete bureaucracies, incapable of operating on a literal command and control basis. Still, the logic of industrial organization created a clear division between work design and control and task execution. Under industrial bureaucracy, codified into industrial labor relations, managers asserted control over the content and design of teaching.

In labor relations terms, these were management's reserved rights and not mandatory subjects of bargaining, and frequently law and custom excluded the content of teaching from the bargaining process altogether. The idea of organizing teachers around the craft, artistic, and professional dimensions of their jobs is tied primarily to the legitimacy of organizing teaching as a profession, precisely the effort now being questioned by libertarians and conservatives.

At the core, this debate affects unions in their role as labor market intermediaries. All unions, and particularly craft, artistic, and professional unions, operate to shape the marketplace in which their members trade (bargain) training, time, and commitment for wages, benefits, and social status. Teacher unions have weighed in heavily on the side of teacher professionalism.

Professional Certification

By reinforcing the industrial work paradigm, opponents of teacher professionalism also resist or find little value in the initiatives unions use to advance their professionalization agenda. The National Board for Professional Teaching Standards (NBPTS) has become a favorite target. Ballou and Podgursky (1999), for example, argue that teachers who enter education through alternative certification routes seem to do as well as those who are fully credentialed, and that concentrations of National Board-certified teachers seem to make little difference in student outcomes. (For its part, the NBPTS is actively seeking inquiry into the effects of its program, which has now certified more than 16,000 teachers.)

Unions, for their part, support the professionalism agenda. They find that teachers respond to incentives for additional certification, and that universities respond to state pressure for NCATE certification of their teacher training programs. Numerous states and localities—often with private foundation support—have adopted fee supports, created salary supplements, allowed license portability, or made provision for board certification to count toward license renewal or continuing education units.

Collective bargaining pressures school districts to link monetary incentives to National Board certification and other forms of continued education. In the Los Angeles Unified School District, a board-certified teacher receives a 15% salary differential; this is in addition to a $20,000 one-time bonus statutorily provided all teachers when they achieve National Board certification. United Teachers Los Angeles also runs a program for teachers preparing to take National Board exams, one of the few programs in the country in which teachers of color score as well as white teachers. In New York City, a board-certified teacher qualifies for a salary differential of approximately $3,700, in Cincinnati $1,000, and in Rochester, New York $1,500. Minneapolis, Hammond, Indiana, and other cities advance board certified teachers in the regular salary schedule. In Chicago, the union supports training for and subsidizes the fees of many candidates for board certification. The Chicago Teachers Union has also announced the formation of the nation's first union-run program in teacher leadership aimed at making the schools' best teachers, in its words, "agents of change rather than targets of it" (Rossi, 2002).

Union Involvement in Teacher Education

Almost all unions involve themselves in some kind of teacher professional development, some modest, some substantially integrated into the district's programs. Interestingly, the union, rather than the school district leader, often provides the continuity to keep a professional development project alive. For example, during the late 1980s and early 1990s, Miami-Dade County (Florida) Public Schools witnessed five changes of superintendents, along with rapid demographic shifts in its student body, a recession, and a devastating hurricane. The staff development programs that had been negotiated with the United Teachers of Dade survived these tough times (some with substantial modification), and continue today, because the programs have an anchor in negotiated agreements and benefit from continuing union leadership (Phillips, 1993).

In New York City, the United Federation of Teachers (UFT) and the school system collaborate in creating staff development that is embedded in the schools and in the workdays of teachers. More than 220 teacher specialists operate professional development teacher centers in schools. Through the centers, these teacher-mentors deliver classroom coaching and direct assistance with school-adopted interventions, such as Success for All, a highly structured "whole school reform" program. A substantial number of the teacher specialists have received intensive workshop training in the New Standards Project, whose work has been adopted by the school district, and they have become the means for turning New Standards rhetoric into reality.

Embedded staff development has been spurred by the increased attention given to standards and accountability. Some 97 New York City schools are on the state commissioner's failure list, called the Schools Under Registration Review (SURR), on statewide academic probation. Both the union and the district needed to respond to schools already on the list, as well as those in danger of being listed. Providing high quality professional development in schools was one of the responses that the UFT endorsed and provided. Embedded staff development is particularly well established in Community School District 2, which includes an economically diverse swath on the East Side of Manhattan (Elmore, 1997; Koppich, 2002a).

Every state in the union has teacher certification standards and university degree programs that are charged with preparing novices to teach. However, big city districts in particular face a chronic undersupply of teachers and experience difficulty in holding onto the teachers they attract. The issuing of emergency credentials is endemic in cities such as New York and Los Angeles. Teacher turnover strains efforts to improve schools, and the lack of institutional memory or organizational culture dries up the social glue that holds schools together.

The professionalizers (including teacher unionists) and the libertarians have different views of how the labor market will work in this situation. Advocates of professionalism believe that a tighter labor market will result in higher quality teacher candidates and will eventually contribute to increasing the attractiveness of the occupation and raising the salaries of teachers. Free market advocates believe that a relatively unrestricted market will attract talented individuals who have little appetite for the tedium of teacher education and who will perform as well as those with professional degrees and licenses.

Challenging the Union Reform Role

If teaching is not to be organized as a profession, then what might be called the "reform wing" of the teacher unions cannot have legitimacy, either politically or among teachers themselves. Newly established reform practices such as teacher peer review, union involvement in professional development, union/university collaboration in teacher training, site-based management, and shared decision making are improper to union critics. These practices are viewed as union power grabs, an encroachment on management's rights, or just wrongheaded. Consider Myron Lieberman's (1998) commentary that calls professionalization "a step backward" in public policy:

> In some respects, the basic issue in peer review appears to be whether it is possible to reconcile the concept of a union, legally and practically responsible for promoting the interests of its members, with the concept of a professional organization. This depends on how we define "professional organization." If it is defined as an organization to protect the public, as NEA publications imply, we must bear in mind that "professional" organizations eventually become as self-serving as unions. (p. 44)

This depiction of reform clashes with the reality that a minority of unions and school districts has begun creating labor-management relations that target school quality (for a description of these relationships, see Kerchner & Koppich 1993, 2000; Kerchner, Koppich, & Weeres, 1997). Under various names—professional unionism, new unionism, or reform unionism—school districts and local union leaders have begun to expand their dialogue to include questions of educational quality and how quality is created in schools and classrooms. In Lieberman's (1998) view, these activities are a costly usurpation of management rights (p. 33); they take senior teachers from the classroom and are of dubious effectiveness (p. 95). For the teachers who do the work, however, changing unionism means expanding the focus of the work to include legitimate concerns with *content* as well as ongoing concerns with *conditions*. For school districts, it means that the union becomes a partner in reform, albeit sometimes a contentious one.

Many reform experiments, adopted during periods of collaborative labor relations or flush budgets, have atrophied or evaporated when personalities changed or budgets tightened. The most durable reforms use the *contract as the anchor for a new relationship*. It is important to remember that the collective bargaining contract is only the tip of the labor relations iceberg. It reveals a little of what is underneath, but only a little. In a reform union relationship, labor and management sometimes invent ways of working together to solve educational problems. Sometimes they change what they fight about and how they fight. But the object of the expanded labor-management relationship is to focus labor relations on the problems of reforming schools and raising student achievement.

In the most sophisticated applications—Minneapolis, Minnesota, and Columbus, Ohio, are good examples—unions and districts have created a cluster of interactions that tend to reinforce one another. The first element in this relationship is an agreement about educational quality: what it is, and how it shows itself in classrooms, most frequently described in academic standards. This agreement is not part of the bargaining contract; rather, it is an accord that describes what students should know and be able to do and what teachers should be able to teach, and it becomes the heart of the relationship between labor and management.

Working through such an agreement can be accomplished in a number of ways, some of them quite conventional. The Minneapolis process illustrates the effects of gradually building and deepening the relationship between management and labor. Begun in 1984 with a joint Labor/Management Task Force on Teacher Professionalism, the process spawned a mentor teacher program, and in 1989, a new teacher evaluation procedure. The professional development program, which is administered by a joint district-union panel, links professional education to tenure, salary, and teacher support and evaluation (Berggren, 1999; Blair, 2002b; Koppich, 2002b; Nordgren & Smith, 1997).

The union becomes an active recruiter and educator of new teachers. In both Minneapolis and Columbus the union and schools have cooperative arrangements with a local college or university. In Minneapolis, where the Minneapolis Federation of Teachers (AFT) represents teachers, the union has partnered with the University of St. Thomas to offer a master's degree program taught at union headquarters, and it has developed professional development programs offered online. In Columbus, where the Columbus Teachers Association (NEA) represents teachers, an arrangement with Ohio State University provides both initial teacher training and continuing staff development.

Peer Review

New teacher programs are enhanced by peer review, by which teachers take responsibility for supporting new teachers and for firing those who cannot teach. Peer review began in 1981, when the Toledo, Ohio schools and the Toledo Federation of Teachers added a one-sentence clause to their contract outlining teachers' agreement to police their veterans in return for the right to review new teachers. Since then, peer review has spread among progressive districts, and both the AFT and the NEA now support it, the NEA having shifted its position in 1997. Districts with active peer review programs include Seattle; Columbus, Ohio; Rochester, New York; Minneapolis; Hammond, Indiana; and Poway, California. Interest is increasing in the wake of the NEA's policy change. In May 1998, a peer review conference sponsored by the Columbus, Ohio union local drew more than 500 participants from 30 states (Bradley, 1998).

While detractors view peer review as ineffective and as a power grab for new jobs, proponents assert that it provides schools with a demonstrably better evaluation system than that provided by school administrators in the decades when they had sole responsibility for evaluating teachers. A complete peer review program operates at three levels. First, novices receive formative help during their initial years of teaching; then a panel of teachers and administrators makes a summative judgment about teacher performance and recommends retention or dismissal to the superintendent and school board. Second, experienced teachers whose teaching is satisfactory—the vast majority of teachers—are expected to improve their practice based on benchmarks such as the California Standards for the Teaching Profession. These are more stringent requirements than those represented in the conventional yearly principal's observation in the classroom. Finally, experienced teachers who are performing poorly are judged to need intervention. Although intervention plans vary in detail, they all call for the assignment of a supervising teacher, who works with the struggling veteran to remedy problems. If the intervention is unsuccessful, dismissal proceedings are initiated.

Detractors say that the system is not tough enough, but in every district, the numbers of dismissals and referrals to intervention have been substantially higher than they were during the previous era of administratively driven evaluations. In Toledo, in the 5 years before peer review, not one experienced teacher was fired. Since peer review, 52 experienced teachers out of a pool of about 2,600 have been placed on intervention over 16 years. All but 10 have left the classroom. About 10% of Toledo's intern teachers are not rehired for a second year of teaching.

In Columbus, 178 teachers have entered the district's intervention program during the last 12 years, out of a teaching force of 4,800. Over 40% returned to teaching in what is called "good standing." The others resigned, retired, or were terminated. During the same period, 3,312 new teachers participated in the Columbus intern program. Seven percent received unsatisfactory ratings (Bradley, 1998). In Poway, California, a 20,000-student suburban district north of San Diego, relatively rapid growth has created a situation in which a majority of the teachers in the district have gone through the peer review program during the last 12 years.

Pay For Performance

Only a few districts have begun to experiment with the final element in the quality cluster: changing teachers' reward and incentive structures. What is called "the standard single salary schedule" is one of the nearly ubiquitous organizational characteristics of public schools. Both in the 41 states where teachers are allowed to bargain contracts and in the nine where they are not, teachers are paid according to the amount of education they have and their number of years of service in the district (Odden & Kelley, 1997).

Although unions are frequently credited or blamed for the disconnect between pay and performance, the salary schedule traces its origins to civil service and its universal application during the post-World War II enrollment boom. It became necessary for school districts to attract women by paying them as much as male teachers, who had previously made higher salaries. While education and years of service may in some rough way equate to expertise, the system ignores any relationship between salary and effectiveness.

Nonetheless, departures from the standard single salary schedule have remained on the "non-discussable" list for most unions and indeed for most schools. In 2000, against the advice of its leadership, the NEA convention adopted a strong resolution rejecting any form of merit pay either to attract or to reward teachers: "The Association opposes providing additional compensation to attract and/or retain education employees in hard-to-recruit positions. ... The Association also believes that performance pay, such as merit pay, or any other system of compensation based on evaluation of an education employee's performance, are inappropriate" (Editorial, 2000). Only a few unions have adopted alternatives to the single salary schedule. In Cincinnati, Ohio, a salary schedule tied to five career skill and responsibility levels has proven extremely controversial, and its implementation has been slow following a pilot run in 1999-2000 (Blair, 2000).

More recently, the Denver Public Schools and the Denver Teachers Association have captured public attention by agreeing to a two-year pilot program that ties a small amount of salary to student performance for teachers in participating schools. Each teacher in the 12 pilot schools will receive $500 for participating, and up to $1,000 more if the majority of a teacher's students improve academically (Janofsky, 1999). Evaluations of the project point to its complexity and suggest that changing the salary schedule takes in much more than simply how, and how much, a teacher is being paid and what incentives are offered. Evaluators found that the district's data system was not sufficient to provide teachers timely information on student achievement, and that the student assessment system was not sophisticated enough to provide multiple measures of achievement. The findings suggest that merely paying teachers for student performance did not strongly affect test scores. At the same time, the pilot program seemed not to devastate working relations between teachers; on the contrary, teachers seemed to cooperate more (Community Assistance and Training Center, 2001).

Internal and External Legitimacy

Opposition to reform unionism does not come solely from non-teachers, and this opposition is seized upon by critics to bolster their argument that unions continue to be barriers to change in schools. In a Hoover Institution publication, Terry Moe (2001) writes:

In recent years, certain scholars [including a co-author of this chapter] and even a few union leaders have argued the need for "reform unionism" and claimed that, with enough enlightened thinking, the unions can voluntarily dedicate themselves to education reforms that promote the greater good. This is a fanciful notion, based on a fatal misconception: that the unions can be counted on not to pursue their own interests. No such thing is going to happen. (p. 40)

Indeed, grassroots unionists are leery of abandoning the organizing principles that brought them to power. In the small city of Mattoon, Illinois, Bill Harshbarger, a leader in the local NEA affiliate, sees the educational quality agenda as deflecting attention away from traditional issues. "Instead of fighting for members' concerns about wages, hours, and working conditions, they collaborate with reformers on quality, professional development and improvement of schools" (Blair, 2002a, p. 1). These beliefs drift upward in the NEA, where teachers from small towns and comfortable suburbs outvote colleagues from the cities and poverty belts where public education faces its most visible challenges.

Other unionists see reform as close to treasonable. They argue that, at root, market-based reforms are aimed at eliminating public education, not strengthening it, and that systemic reformers generally mean to hurt the system. In response to NEA President Bob Chase's advocacy of a "New Unionism," the leaders of Wisconsin's largest affiliates wrote: "Your remarks are not only appalling, they ignore the fundamental strength of a union. ... We are union and we are proud; we stand in solidarity to defend against those who are attempting to destroy us" (Quoted in Fuller, Mitchell, & Hartman, 2000, pp. 114-115).

In rough terms, union ideology cleaves along three fault lines. *Traditional industrial unionism* believes the union's role is to protect teachers, and that fixing schools should never be allowed to compromise this goal. *Professional unionism* tends both to honor unionism's past and to be self-critical about its present and future. These unionists believe that teachers should assume joint ownership of reform, and that both school districts and unions need to undergo substantial change. *Social justice unionism* "is grounded in the need to advocate for all students which in turn leads directly to confronting issues of race and class" (Peterson, 1999, p. 11). The boundary lines separating these three types of unionism are highly permeable. Most union leaders espouse all three beliefs, but a defining battle between them has yet to be joined.

More than a decade ago Kerchner and Mitchell (1988) observed what they called *generational* behavior in teachers' unions, describing different eras of ideological belief, each separated by revolutionary struggles for control of teacher union locals and corresponding turn-overs in school administrators. Teacher union officers and staff who advocate for change often face substantial opposition from their own members, some of whom are contenders for their positions. Union staffs are divided between those who support a new identity and those who oppose it. At issue are changes in both unionism (a belief system) and unionization (a way of getting organized). Embrace of the educational quality agenda represents a generational change that has not yet played out as either belief or organizational reality.

Challenging Political Legitimacy

Unions always have struggled for political legitimacy and influence. At first, teacher unions were seen as a threat to the rights of managers and school boards and to the professionalism of education. Union revolutionaries had to fight in state legislatures, in school districts, and even on the picket lines (taking strike action and occasionally going to jail) to earn union recognition and the right to co-determine with school districts their pay, fringe benefits, and conditions of employment. Once established, however, teacher unions became joined at the hip—or at least at the billfold—to the public school institution, defending the status quo as a means of keeping their jobs. Currently, teacher unions are fighting a four-front *political* war, against incredible odds, to retain political legitimacy and power.

A Loss of Union Size and Solidarity

As labor union size and influence has diminished in the U.S. (with private sector union membership down from 38% to 11% of the workforce), teacher unions—along with other public sector employee groups—found themselves becoming the torchbearers for the legacy of industrial unionism that began as a proletarian class battle of blue-collar employees against corporations. In fact, union membership data show that while the private sector unions have remained static or have shrunk, the NEA reported growth in membership from 2.2 million to 2.6 million members between 1996 and 2001, while the AFT claims a jump from about 900,000 to 1.2 million teacher members—strong increases of a total of 23% in 5 years. It is ironic that public school teachers—the nation's largest group of educated, middle-class, licensed professionals—should become the largest segment of the work force organized along industrial lines.

The drop in private sector union membership and the decline in the visibility and clout of the national AFL-CIO unions have had a subtle effect on teacher unions. Thirty years ago, when parents (and even school board members) in many communities were members of unions themselves, the residual sympathy for teachers to begin collective bargaining and even to strike was strong enough to urge teachers along. Now, however, with so few workers in unions, and with both mother and father working in many families, the idea of a teachers' strike attracts little sympathy or support. Who's going to mind the children if the teachers "close our schools"?

Moreover, the connections between teacher unions and the house of labor have grown more tenuous. The AFT was always affiliated with the AFL-CIO, and Albert Shanker served as Vice President of the Public Employees Division of the national union. But the great growth in teacher unionism occurred in the NEA, which for years would not even call itself a union, and which despite recent overtures remains opposed to AFL-CIO affiliation. This occurs at a time when the unionization of physicians, nurses, artists, high tech workers, and other highly skilled workers appears on the upswing.

An Awkward Union Structure

Teacher unions look to suffer from gigantism. Indeed, both unions have a hierarchical structure that makes them appear highly united and centralized. But this is deceptive. The union "boss" allegation, if probed very deeply, often reveals people with highly limited individual power. The NEA Representative Assembly frequently turns down the leadership's reform ideas, sometimes in unspoken coalition with lower level staff members. "We trained them too well in old-style unionism," a national staff member recently mused (personal communication with the authors, 2001). The AFT has the appearance of being a national union, but the power lies in the locals, whose leaders are not restricted by term limits and which therefore often retain their positions for more than two decades. A close look at either union reveals fractures and cleavages that make it almost impossible for the unions to speak for teachers with a unified voice.

Teachers themselves also exhibit wide political divides. It is often noted that union leadership tends to lean farther to the left than the membership, and this is probably true. About 40% of teachers are Republicans, while few union leaders are. Teachers, by their nature, are conservative gradualists when it comes to changing their jobs and affiliations. John Goodlad (1990), studying the socialization of teachers, noted just how traditional the job has become, observing, "And if the final socialization process is largely in the hands of practitioners in regulated, relatively conservative school districts, we can hardly expect novices to challenge the conventional wisdom from alternative, contradictory perspectives" (p. 210).

The typical American teacher is still a 47-year-old woman, with a husband and children, who prefers to see things happen slowly and carefully, with ample opportunities to test and check. Jumping from a comfortable, local, and secure situation to being a contributor to a national mega-union is foreign and risky for some, irrelevant and unimportant for others. Sustaining its Southern locals, where the members are more conservative, is a major concern for the NEA (personal communication with author).

There are also enormous workplace differences. The U.S. public education system is divided among 13,600 local school districts in 50 states, all with different public employment labor laws, separate and distinct union contracts, and very disparate employee-employer traditions. These school districts look similar, patterned by law and tradition now nearly a century old, but they create highly different workplaces. Many of the critiques of public education concern the 50 to 100 largest school districts, which enroll about one third of the nation's children of poverty and children of color. The national debates over vouchers, standards, testing, restructuring, and accountability are often meaningless to teachers in the other 99% of school districts. The urgency of the urban school crisis, which drives education policy and policymakers, seems a distant concern for many.

These workplace differences reflect differences in labor law. Forty-one states allow collective bargaining, either by statute or practice. In some states, and in the nine states that prohibit bargaining, teachers have gravitated to so-called independent associations. About 250,000 teachers in 14 states belong to these organizations. In Georgia, Missouri, and Texas the independent associations have more members than the state NEA affiliates. Most are ideologically conservative and part company with the AFT and the NEA over the unions' liberal bent in politics and their participation in presidential and other elections (Kirkpatrick, 1999). Most, but not all, believe that collective bargaining in general and strikes in particular are wrong. However, some local teacher unions not affiliated with either national union do fulfill traditional union roles. The largest is the Akron (Ohio) Education Association, with more than 2,000 members (Kirkpatrick).

The national unions have responded to being attacked and to the fractures in their structure by proposing merger. Bob Chase (1999), president of the NEA, and Sandra Feldman, president of the AFT, have both strongly supported this option. The 10,000 delegates of the NEA's Representative Assembly, the largest democratic deliberative body in the world, voted against this initiative on July 4, 1998, falling far short of the 67% pro-merger vote needed. Two weeks later, however, 97% of the AFT delegates voted *for* merger. Limited, gradual efforts are now underway to merge state organizations and to develop common national agendas between the organizations. Florida, Minnesota, and Montana are in the process of statewide merging; other states are talking about it.

The dilemma, then, is how to create a powerful force for teachers nationally, most likely through a merger of the NEA and AFT, while remaining responsive to the bargaining and political needs of teachers who work for local school districts. That the NEA delegates voted resoundingly against a national merger testifies to the trade-off between localism and national power—a willingness to give up "big union" power for local needs and concerns. The big urban unions, mostly AFT affiliates, saw the advantages of exchanging local autonomy for a stronger national presence. The majority of NEA representatives reflected the opposite perspective, which is logical given that their membership is concentrated outside the central cities. Other forces were at work as well. Under the merger terms, large city locals—including NEA affiliates such as Seattle, Denver, and Columbus, Ohio—would gain substantial autonomy from their state organizations, which made existing state organizations and their staffs nervous. In addition, uncertainty about job security among union staff, awareness of major procedural differences, and a long-standing animosity between the two unions were formidable obstacles and were not likely to be easily dismissed.

One important reason for the failure of the merger proposal lay in the characteristics of the two unions themselves—their origins, histories, cultures, and structure. While the NEA is much older, begun in 1857 as a broad-based professional education association that included superintendents, principals, and teachers, the AFT was founded in 1916 by urban, ethnic-Jewish, left wing, pro-democratic activists with ties to the organized labor movement. As a union, the AFT advocated strikes, while until the 1960s the NEA traditionally opposed work stoppages as unprofessional for education.

Teachers, too, find it hard to accept a national approach. After all, for many, the genius of American education has always been its local roots, local support, and local commitment. The concept of an enormous "big brother" (or "big sister") union is alien. Furthermore, teachers in many states and communities have little or no experience with the labor movement or the AFT. The very idea of the AFL-CIO is foreign to them.

A Workable Political Affiliation and Common Ideology

Unions in the U.S. are not explicitly ideological, nor are they formally affiliated with a political party. Thus, unlike many European unions, U.S. teachers have no explicit socialist connection and no identification with a "working class" party and its politics (Cooper, 1992). Critics will say that a connection that is not explicit does not gainsay its existence. Indeed, the connection between organized labor and the Democratic Party is clear. The NEA has always supported Democratic candidates for president. In the 1996 congressional election, it supported 250 Democrats and one Republican. At the Democratic National Convention that year, 405 NEA members were delegates, an aggregation larger than the delegation from any state except California (Lieberman, 1997, p. 66).

While members may be of every political stripe, the roots of the labor movement in the U.S. are in the Left. That movement peaked during the New Deal, when the Wagner Act (National Labor Relations Act of 1935) was passed to grant workers in the private sector the right to seek union recognition by management and to bargain collectively as a means of co-determination. In the 1960s and 1970s, public employees received some of the same rights under various state public employment relations laws and acts (e.g., New York's Taylor Law) in a movement largely supported by the wave of political liberalism associated with the Vietnam era and the disastrous 1964 Goldwater presidential campaign. Thus, teacher unions owe their very existence to the left wing of the Democratic Party.

This unacknowledged relationship, however, creates difficulties for unions. The same exclusive representation mechanism that feeds unions new members with relatively little difficulty also supplies a membership that has only loose connections with union belief systems or history of political behavior. The relationship to a political party creates a disadvantageous relationship, in that the Democratic Party often takes teacher unions for granted, while the Republican Party shuns them. Democratic strategists know that the worst unions can do during campaigns is sit on their hands, resulting in electoral victories for Republicans. Republicans know that many teachers will vote for

Republican candidates despite union opposition. As Bob Dole found out in 1996, however, explicit criticism of unionized teachers—even though he attempted to distinguish between "teachers" and "unions"—is highly detrimental and causes teachers as voters to shift to the opponent.

Certainly, teacher unions have fared better under Democratic presidents than Republicans. But the educational policy and positional payoffs have not been huge. With the exception of Sharon Robinson, who moved from the NEA staff to become assistant secretary of the U.S. Department of Education in charge of the Office of Educational Research and Improvement, teacher unions were not conspicuous in the Clinton Administration. In the 2000 election campaign, the educational platforms of candidates Gore and Bush had more similarities than differences. Bush showed a willingness to toy more with privatization, although it was nowhere near the centerpiece of his campaign; however, both candidates endorsed similar testing, accountability, and educational reform measures.

Thus, regardless of which party is in power, the unions are at some distance from the center of power. The real distancing comes at the intellectual or policy initiating level. Conservative and libertarian think tanks have made teacher unions a special target, and the unions have not responded effectively. A key challenge to the future of teacher unions and their legitimate role in public education is the current absence of a strong, rooted belief in unionism, in the collective rights of workers, and in the role of teacher unions in securing the future of public schooling.

Against a Sense of Union Recalcitrance

Perhaps the greatest threat to the political legitimacy of teacher unions is the perception that they stand in the way of real school reform. While teachers are the largest, best organized, and most vocal boosters of public education, they often find themselves wedded to the status quo and taking the brunt of criticism for being obstructionist, narrow-minded, and "political." These claims are not new—managers in the private sector frequently assert that unions resist change, make restructuring difficult, and block efforts to increase efficiency and productivity. The most obvious examples in education are the recent efforts of unions to block or cripple privatization, outsourcing, and vouchers; these are perceived as political actions that hinder change and de-legitimate the unions' claims to care about children and school improvement. As Terry Moe (2001) explains,

The bottom line, then, is that teachers unions' greatest power is not the ability to get what they want, but rather the ability to *block* what they don't want—and thus to stifle all education reforms that are somehow threatening to their interests. Union interests are deeply rooted in the status quo, and most changes of any consequence are likely to create problems for them and to be opposed as well. (p. 181)

Besides the challenges to union legitimacy brought on by their political standing, unions are also losing the battle to socialize new members into the union fold. The next section discusses this problem as a stumbling block to the legitimacy of public school unionism in particular and to the public school enterprise in general.

Teacher Unions As Socializers of New Teachers

Organizations are reborn with each new generation of members, and so it is with teacher unions. It is estimated that a demographic bulge of retiring teachers along with public schools' inability to keep younger ones from quitting will require the hiring of 2.2 million schoolteachers over the next decade (Recruiting New Teachers, 2001; Viadero, 2002). As legions of new teachers begin work, their unions struggle to re-legitimate themselves, not only in the larger society but also with their own future members. Today's aging union leaders face the challenges that Erik Erikson (1968) associated with the last stages of human development: *generativity* (the passing of culture and meaning to the next generation) and *integrity* (the ability to give meaning and wholeness to a life's work). Facing these challenges is not an easy task.

The Generation X (Gen-X) teachers—born between about 1964 and 1978—do not remember days when teachers were fired for getting married, for becoming pregnant, or for demanding to be treated as professionals—and of course for fighting for their right to be unionized. They do not remember 1968, when the teachers in New York staged a first great urban strike, the first salvo in the *Great School Wars* (Ravitch, 1974). This lack of historical perspective challenges the legitimacy of the union for younger teachers who came into the fold after the big "unionization movement" of the 1970s (see Cooper, 1982; Kerchner & Mitchell, 1988; Lieberman & Moskow, 1972).

The Lack of a Union Saga

The labor movement has a rich and interesting history, embedded in the Industrial Revolution and the rise of capitalism and replete with examples of union leaders who gave up their freedom and even their lives in the struggle for decent pay, benefits, and improved working conditions. This historical saga of sweatshops, the six- or even seven-day work week, and child labor in mines and factories is seldom part of the cultural makeup of new teachers. They do not understand, as Wayne Urban put it, that "Unions were part of the daily life for many families and were perceived as valued partners that helped common folks win the right to a fair wage and better working conditions" (Blair, 2002a, p. 16). With union membership in the general work force having declined to 10% from nearly 40% in peak years, it may well be possible for a young college-educated worker to have had no formative experience with a union or a union member.

The lack of a union saga may lead to a lack of union commitment, even if one pays dues. Historically, teachers often struck in the face of what they knew would be harsh penalties against them. In 1990, for example, teachers in Yonkers, New York, walked out in spite of a restraining order warning the union against "engaging in a strike, causing or instigating, encouraging or condoning a strike"; against "interfering with the orderly continuance of the function of the School District"; and against "inducing, persuading, or intimidating any person to fail to perform services for the School District" (Liotta, 2002, p. 129). Teachers were out for 12 days just before Christmas. They paid heavy fines and, under the terms of the state labor law, lost two days' pay for every day they were on strike.

The incoming generation of teachers will come to schools at a time when unions are seen as part of the institution rather than as a social movement organized against the ills of the system. Progressive unionists see the situation in do-or-die terms, with unions needing to embrace educational quality, instructional issues, and particularly the mentoring and socialization of new teachers as priorities (Blair, 2002a). But this is often a hard sell to older teachers, the ones most likely to serve in union executive councils (Blair, 2002a). And these older teachers do not consider it the job of their unions to solve problems in school operations. After reading a book on union reform (Kerchner, Koppich, & Weeres, 1998) a 30-year veteran teacher wrote, "I do not want to pay union dues to an organization that does anything but help me in defense, income, benefits. Do you understand?" (Personal communication, April 4, 2002).

Younger teachers tend to see the union as irrelevant (Blair 2002a; Peske et al., 2000). We are told that polls conducted by the unions themselves show that teachers want help with problems concerning student achievement but do not particularly associate their unions with this function. Indeed, teachers who work at charter schools seem disassociated from the union and from public education altogether (Koppich, Holmes, & Plecki, 1998). Newer teachers who see a need for unions to be more involved in education reform often do not associate their unions with such reform. These beliefs percolate upwards in the unions. The emotional pull—the elemental anger—that allowed teachers to organize against school administrators is harder to tap when trying to motivate teachers to organize around quality. But sometimes, voices for change are heard. In 2001 the incumbent president of the Chicago Teachers Union was unseated by a challenger who promised to form a "true partnership" with the school district, and in particular to support new teachers (Blair, 2002a). The union has since designed its own graduate school, a union program in teacher leadership (Rossi, 2002).

Dues Paying and Union Activism

Under state public employment laws in most jurisdictions, it is fairly easy to get new teachers to pay dues or "agency shop fees" to the union. The argument for *mandatory support* is simple: by law, unions are required to represent *all* teachers in a particular bargaining unit, whether or not they are members. Unions bargain for them and represent them in disciplinary actions or other grievance matters, whether they join the organization or not; and teachers should be required, so the rationale goes, to pay for these union services.

So, as the number of teachers increases, so, too, do the union coffers. The NEA has about 2.6 million members, an increase of more than 400,000 since 1996. The AFT claims 1.2 million members in 2002, up about 300,000 over 5 years (Blair, 2002a). Activating new members is different from merely collecting dues. The lack of a fiscal emergency makes it more difficult to recognize that younger teachers are not automatically enthusiastic about the union. Sometimes, they can be members without even knowing they *are* members. Holly Kaye, a recently hired Chicago Public Schools teacher, said: "The union? I don't even think I'm a member. I've heard that they are a good thing, but I don't know much about them" (Blair, 2002a, p. 1). Yet, this new teacher is paying union fees as required by state labor laws.

Activating a New Generation of Teachers

Some unions have figured out how to activate younger members, however. Louise Sundin, president of the Minneapolis Federation of Teachers, has consciously attempted to make her organization more attractive to Gen-X teachers, who comprise 50% of the Minneapolis teacher work force. Overall, 85% of MFT teachers have been hired since 1990 (Blair 2002b).

Minneapolis witnessed a systemic effort to link professional development and school improvement, using the teachers' collective bargaining contract as one of the primary vehicles of this effort. The contracts and the programs that resulted reflected the newer teachers' desires to improve their teaching practice. The connection seems logical to Sundin: "Teachers pay attention to the contract. Policy manuals and guides are never consulted by either teachers or managers. The contract is" (interview with author). As a result, the contract combines traditional subjects of bargaining—wages and work rules—with long sections on professional development and school improvement. It includes a preamble that joins the union to the school district's adopted mission statement: "We exist to ensure that all students learn" (Minneapolis Public Schools and Minneapolis Federation of Teachers, 1997, p. 2). And it also pledges union support for a unified effort to overcome "the seemingly overwhelming factors of poverty, racism, and disillusionment, to arrive at an environment where teachers can teach successfully," concluding, "Therefore, we cannot afford to waste energy or resources distracting ourselves with petty power struggles" (p. 4; see also Minneapolis Public Schools and Minneapolis Federation of Teachers, 1996). The professional partnership with the district and some unusual contract provisions, such as the ability to cash in unused sick leave days for gym or health club membership fees, has had an effect on the numbers of younger teachers participating in union activities and the percentage staying in teaching. Approximately 10%-15% of Minneapolis teachers leave during their first five years of teaching, compared to about 50% nationally (Blair, 2002b).

Activating new teachers as unionists requires understanding them politically, professionally, and economically and being willing to build a union that they perceive as speaking to their needs—or at least as necessary to their socialization. It is essential to create a union that is less institutional and more individual. A sampling of surveys and participation records shows Gen-Xers are "less politically engaged, exhibit less social trust or confidence in government, have a weaker allegiance to their country or either political party, and are more materialistic than their predecessors" (Halstead, 1999). But part of what is seen as materialism is actually a keen understanding of social and economic position. While wages for older Americans have mostly stagnated in the last quarter century, the real median income of men aged 20 to 30 has fallen by almost one third, making them the first generation whose lifetime earnings will be less than their parents'. Gen-Xers who go to college carry a legacy of debt into the workplace. Sixty percent have credit card balances, and the average student loan has jumped from $2,000 to $15,000 (Halstead). Not surprisingly, recent studies of novice teachers reveal less attachment to the occupation, or less intention to remain in teaching, than was the case with previous generations (Peske, 2000). The failure to understand younger teachers' general lack of belief in institutions, their sense of economic instability, and the tentativeness of their job choices preserves the unions' momentary prosperity, but fails to foster and take advantage of the youthful energy of "converts" who see unionism as a part of a civil religion—the type of individuals who organized teachers in the first place (Murphy, 1990).

Conclusion: The Blob Moves

Legitimacy for teacher unions is trickier than it appears. Not only must unions be perceived as rightful agents for teachers by the polity at large, they must also work to retain legitimacy *within* the teacher work force, convincing their ever changing, ever younger membership that union affiliation is worth the time and (dues) money. Thus, the challenge to union legitimacy comes from the union's standing in the community and society, as well as from its own members, who frequently have little knowledge, sympathy, or loyalty to the union as a concept or as a political entity.

Unions are becoming aware of this crisis. They are forming coalitions around teaching quality, such as the partnership formed in Massachusetts that includes teacher unions working alongside state associations representing superintendents, parents, school boards, and principals to strengthen teacher evaluation (MassPartners for Public Schools, 2002). Shoots of reform unionism continue to sprout, even in places where it had been declared dead, such as Rochester, New York (Boo, 1992; Murray, 1999). For example, we found the Rochester career-in-teaching program, which combines mentoring, teacher professional development, and peer review, alive and well in the face of administrations that have provided little support (Koppich, Asher, & Kerchner, 2002).

In other places unions are offering new courses for teachers and new programs for prospective teachers. The Oregon Education Association (OEA) organized three chapters on college campuses, which had the dual effect of recruiting undergraduates into teaching as an occupation and of making these college students more aware of the history and role of unions in American life. As an officer of the OEA explained in an interview, "We are offering workshops to those interested, on everything from classroom management—a big interest—to how to interview. They come into the profession understanding what the organization can provide for them, and feeling some commitment" (Blair, 2002b, p. 17).

Some believe that "reform unionism" will carry the day. As Johnson and Kardos (2001) explain,

Changing central office procedures, building capacity for decision making in schools, preparing expert teachers to assume advisory roles, and developing principals' confidence as educational leaders all take time, a tolerance for failure, and a determination to get things right. The work is sure hard, but the stakes are high, and reform bargaining still holds the best promise for success. (p. 44)

It is certain that the legitimacy of unions in education will face continuing challenges in the future. If schools are fundamentally restructured following the decision by the U.S. Supreme Court in the Cleveland voucher *Zelman* case (June, 2002; see van Geel, this volume, chapter 7), or if the current federal tax credit policy being debated in Congress passes, then the large, hegemonic public school system could begin to become private, small, and diverse. In this case, teacher unions will face the same problem that private-sector unions are confronting—how to unionize a restructured, entrepreneurial economy in which more and more companies are small and technology- and/or service-oriented.

Critics of public education, such as Jeanne Allen, liken the existing education institution to a "blob" with quicksand-like qualities, "where ideas sink slowly leaving everything just as it had been before" (Center for Education Reform, 2000, p. 2). Unions, too, have been depicted as a phlegmatic and stable target, vulnerable to collapse if vouchers become widespread, if an education market is created, or if the current situation of education is changed in any important way.

These critics fail to read history. In the 1920s, the AFT was declared dead—except for its failure to fall down (Murphy, 1990). Organized labor was also at a low ebb, as the economy boomed and corporate paternalism and work participation schemes flourished (Geoghegan, 1991; Lichtenstein, 2002). The next two decades produced the largest boom in union membership the nation has ever seen, and created a watershed in American politics. Depression-driven discontent and the passage of the National Labor Relations Act in 1935 made the rise of widespread industrial organizing and the rise of Big Labor possible.

It is true that the national unions have been slow to change, sometimes maddeningly so. But historically, unions have been very good at organizing teachers—better than government agencies, better than colleges and universities, and better than school districts. Even as this is written, unions are already actively reorganizing, merging, and refocusing themselves in several states where they have taken a drubbing. No one knows how the current struggle between teacher unions and their environment will turn out. But the settings to watch are places where the unions have been involved in a substantial struggle, have come under real political pressure, and perhaps have lost important battles. The form that these wounded unions take as they rebuild will provide us with important clues about the future face of teacher unionism.

REFERENCES

Ballou, D., & Podgursky, M. (1999). Teacher training and licensure: A layman's guide. In M. Kanstoroom & C. Finn (Eds.), *Better teachers, better schools* (pp. 31-82). Washington, DC: Thomas P. Fordham Foundation.

Ballou, D., & Podgursky, M. (2000). Reforming teacher education and licensing: What is the evidence? *Teachers College Record, 102*(1), 5-27.

Berggren, K. (1999). Professionalism in Minneapolis: A new view. In B. Peterson & M. Charney (Eds.), *Transforming teacher unions: Fighting for better schools and social justice* (pp. 40-44). Milwaukee, WI: Rethinking Schools.

Blair, J. (2000, Sept. 27). Cincinnati teachers to be judged, paid on performance. *Education Week*, 1.

Blair, J. (2002a, January 30). Gen-Xers apathetic about union label. *Education Week*, 1.

Blair, J. (2002b, January 30). Minneapolis labor leaders mold a different kind of union. *Education Week*, 17.

Boo, K. (1992, October). Reform school confidential. *The Washington Monthly*, 17-24.

Boyd, W.L., Plank, D.N., & Sykes, G. (2000). Teachers unions in hard times. In T. Loveless (Ed.), *Conflicting missions? Teachers unions and educational reform* (pp. 174-210). Washington, DC: Brookings Institution Press.

Bridges, E. (1986). *The incompetent teacher*. Philadelphia and London: Falmer Press.

Center for Educational Reform. (2000). Why we call it the BLOB. Retrieved January 13, 2002 from http://edreform.com/info/blob.htm

Chase, B. (1999). *Lead, follow, and get out of the way*. Washington, DC: National Education Association.

Cobble, D.S. (1991). Organizing the postindustrial work force: Lessons from the history of waitress unionism. *Industrial and Labor Relations Review, 44*(3), 419-436.

Cochran-Smith, M., & Fries, M.K. (2001). Sticks, stones, and ideology: The discourse of reform in teacher education. *Educational Researcher, 30*(8), 3-15.

Community Assistance and Training Center. (2001). *Pathway to results: Pay for performance in Denver*. Boston: Author.

Cooper, B.S. (1982). *Collective bargaining, strikes and related costs in education*. Eugene, OR: ERIC Center for Educational Management.

Cooper, B.S. (1998, March 11). Commentary: Merging the teachers' unions: Opportunity amid complexity. *Education Week, 52*, 34.

Cooper, B.S. (Ed.). (1992). *Labor relations in education—International perspectives*. Westport, CT: Greenwood Press.

Cooper, B.S., & Liotta, M.E. (2001). Urban teachers face their future. *Education and Urban Society, 34*(1), 101-118.

Cremin, L.A. (1988). *American education: The metropolitan experience, 1876-1980*. New York: Harper & Row.

Darling-Hammond, L. (2000). Reforming teacher education and licensing: Debating the evidence. *Teachers College Record, 102*(1), 28-56.

Dunlop, J.T. (1993[1958]). *Industrial relations systems*. New York: Holt.

Editorial. (2000, July 10). Without merit. *Wall Street Journal*, A34.

Elmore, R.F., & Burney, D. (1997). *School variation and systemic instructional improvement in Community School District #2, New York City*. New York: National Commission on Teaching and America's Future and the Consortium for Policy Research in Education.

Erikson, E.H. (1968). *Identity: Youth and crisis*. New York: Norton.

Etzioni, A. (Ed.). (1969). *The semi-professions and their organization*. New York: The Free Press.

Finn, C.E. (2001). Getting better teachers—and treating them right. In T.M. Moe (Ed.), *A primer on America's schools* (pp. 127-150). Stanford, CA: Hoover Institution Press.

Fuller, H.L., Mitchell, G.A., & Hartmann, M.E. (2000). Collective bargaining in Milwaukee public schools. In T. Loveless (Ed.), *Conflicting missions: Teachers unions and educational reform* (pp. 110-149). Washington, DC: Brookings Institution Press.

Geoghegan, T. (1991). *Which side are you on: Trying to be for labor when it's flat on its back.* New York: Farrar, Strauss & Giroux.

Goodlad, J.I. (1990). *Teachers for our nation's schools.* San Francisco: Jossey-Bass.

Halstead, T. (1999). A politics for Generation X. *The Atlantic* [Electronic Edition]. Retrieved November 30, 2001 from www.theatlantic.com/issues/99aug/9908genx.htm

Janofsky, M. (1999, Sept. 10). For Denver teachers, a pay-for-performance plan. *The New York Times*, A19.

Johnson, S.M., & Kardos, S.M. (2001). Reform bargaining and its promises for school improvement. In T. Loveless (Ed.), *Conflicting missions? Teachers unions and educational reform* (pp. 17-46). Washington, DC: Brookings Institution Press.

Kaufman, B. (1964). *Up the down staircase.* Englewood Cliffs, NJ: Prentice-Hall.

Kerchner, C.T., & Abbott, J. (1999). *The implications of the health care revolution for the organization of school teachers.* Paper presented at the NEA Conference on Frontiers of Unionism.

Kerchner, C.T., & Abbott, J. (2001). *The implications of the health care revolution for the organization of public education.* Unpublished manuscript.

Kerchner, C.T., & Koppich, J.E. (2000). Organizing around quality: The frontiers of teacher unionism. In T. Loveless (Ed.), *Conflicting missions? Teachers unions and educational reform* (pp. 281-316). Washington, DC: Brookings Institution Press.

Kerchner, C.T., Koppich, J.E., & Weeres, J.G. (1997). *United mind workers: Unions and teaching in the knowledge society.* San Francisco: Jossey-Bass.

Kerchner, C.T., & Mitchell, D.E. (1988). *The changing idea of a teachers' union.* New York and London: Falmer Press.

Kirkpatrick, D. (1999). Teachers find alternatives to national unions. School reform news [On Line]. Retrieved December 13, 2001 from: http://www.heartland.org/education/ jul99/alternatives.htm

Koppich, J.E. (2002a). Focusing on low-performing schools: The chancellor's district in New York City. Unpublished manuscript.

Koppich, J.E. (2002b). Distributing the pie: Allocating resources through labor-management agreements. Unpublished manuscript.

Koppich, J., Asher, C., & Kerchner, C.T. (2002). *Developing careers, building a profession: The Rochester career in teaching plan.* New York: National Commission on Teaching and America's Future.

Koppich, J.E., Holmes, P., & Plecki, M. (1998). *New rules, new roles? The professional work lives of charter school teachers.* Washington, DC: National Education Association.

Lichtenstein, N. (2002). *State of the union: A century of American labor.* Princeton, NJ: Princeton University Press.

Lieberman, M. (1997). *The teacher unions: How the NEA and AFT sabotage reform and hold students, parents, teachers, and taxpayers hostage to reform.* New York: Free Press.

Lieberman, M. (1998). *Teachers evaluating teachers: Peer review and the new unionism.* New Brunswick, NJ: Transaction Publishers.

Lieberman, M., & Moskow, M. (1996). *Collective negotiations for teachers: An approach to school administration.* Chicago: Rand McNally.

Liotta, M.E. (2002). *The four great strikes of Yonkers teachers: Historical analysis of conflict and change in urban education.* Unpublished dissertation, Fordham University, New York.

Lortie, D.C. (1969). The balance of control and autonomy in elementary school teaching. In A. Etzioni (Ed.), *The semiprofessions and their organization* (pp. 1-53). New York: Free Press.

Lortie, D.C. (1975). *Schoolteacher: A sociological study.* Chicago: University of Chicago Press.

Loveless, T. (2000). Introduction. In T. Loveless (Ed.), *Conflicting missions? Teachers unions and educational reform* (pp. 1-6). Washington, DC: Brookings Institution Press.

MassPartners for Public Schools (2002). *Teaching matters: Strengthening teacher evaluation in Massachusetts*. Monson, MA: Author.

Minneapolis Public Schools and Minneapolis Federation of Teachers. (1997). *Teacher contract, agreements and policies, June 1997-June 30, 1999*. Minneapolis, MN: Minneapolis Public Schools.

Minneapolis Public Schools and Minneapolis Federation of Teachers Local 59. (1996). *Assuring professional excellence: Professional development process for increased student achievement* (Career in Teaching handbook for teachers). Minneapolis Public Schools.

Moe, T.M. (2001). A union by any other name. *Education Next, 1*(3), 40-45.

Murphy, M. (1990). *Blackboard unions: The AFT and the NEA, 1900-1980*. Ithaca, NY: Cornell University Press.

Murray, C.E. (1999). Rochester teachers struggle to take charge. In B. Peterson & M. Charney (Eds.), *Transforming teacher unions: Fighting for better schools and social justice* (pp. 46-49). Milwaukee, WI: Rethinking Schools.

Nordgren, L., & Smith, B. (1997). Professional development process (Progress Report). Minneapolis, MN: Minneapolis Public Schools.

Odden, A., & Kelley, C. (1997). *Paying teachers for what they know and do: New and smarter compensation strategies to improve schools*. Thousand Oaks, CA: Corwin Press.

Peske, H.G., Liu, E., Kardos, S.M., Kauffman, D., & Johnson, S.M. (2000, April). *Envisioning "something different": New teachers' conceptions of a career in teaching*. Paper presented at the American Educational Research Association annual meeting, New Orleans.

Peterson, B. (1999). Survival and justice: Rethinking teacher union strategy. In B. Peterson & M. Charney (Eds.), *Transforming teacher unions: Fighting for better schools and social justice* (pp. 11-19). Milwaukee, WI: Rethinking Schools.

Phillips, L. (1993). Miami: After the hype. In C.T. Kerchner & J.E. Koppich (Eds.), *A union of professionals: Labor relations and educational reform* (pp. 116-135). New York: Teachers College Press.

Ravitch, D. (1974). *The great school wars*. New York: Basic Books.

Rossi, R. (2002, March 29). Teachers union launches unique graduate school. *Chicago Sun-Times* [Electronic Edition]. Retrieved April 4, 2002 from www.suntimes.com/output/news/cst-nws-ctu29.html

Thomas B. Fordham Foundation (1999). The teachers we need and how to get more of them: Manifesto. In M. Kanstoroom & C. Finn (Eds.), *Better teachers, better schools* (pp. 1-18). Washington, DC: Author.

Tyack, D.B. (1974). *The one best system: A history of American urban education*. Cambridge, MA: Harvard University Press.

Tyack, D., & Hansot, E. (1982). *Managers of virtue: Public school leadership in America, 1820-1980*. New York: Basic Books, Inc.

Urban, W. (1982). *Why teachers organize*. Detroit, MI: Wayne State University Press.

van Geel, T. (2003). Vouchers, the Supreme Court, and the next political rounds. In this volume—W.L. Boyd, & D. Miretzky (Eds.), *American educational governance on trial: Change and challenges. The 102nd yearbook of the National Society for the Study of Education*, Part I (pp. 136-154). Chicago: National Society for the Study of Education.

Viadero, D. (2002, April 10). Researcher skewers explanations behind teacher shortage. *Education Week*, 7.

White, K.A. (1999, January 13). Ahead of the curve. *Education Week*, 32-35.

CHAPTER 12

Educational Bankruptcy, Takeovers, and Reconstitution of Failing Schools

JAMES G. CIBULKA

Accountability As a Principle of Democratic Governance

It is a basic tenet of democratic thought that governments are accountable to the sovereign people. According to the Random House Dictionary (1968), accountability entails the obligation to report, explain, or justify something, to be "responsible" and "answerable." Thus, in the United States accountability is incorporated in many aspects of the constitutional framework and in the legal traditions of the nation, including elections, division of powers, and federalism. At the most basic level, elected officials are responsible to the voters. The framers' fear of concentrated power led them to divide authority among the executive, legislative, and judicial branches, with each branch being accountable to the others in certain respects. Furthermore, in our federal framework, specific powers are reserved to the federal, state, and local governments, and while accountability flows upward through the federal structure, there is significant autonomy at each level. In other words, the principle of accountability is highly institutionalized in our political system.

Accountability can be viewed both as a prevention for abuses of power and as a corrective device once those abuses occur. Hence, higher levels of government can intervene with lower levels when there is evidence that corrective action is needed. This corrective dimension of accountability tends to lead to policy approaches that are highly directive and top-down. The implicit assumption in such approaches is that unacceptable behavior can be eliminated only through the use of regulatory sanctions. Depending on the nature of the violation and the remedy sought, a theory of motivation that relies heavily on compliance may or may not be appropriate for bringing about wanted changes.

James G. Cibulka is Dean of the College of Education and Professor in the Department of Administration and Supervision and in the Department of Educational Policy Studies and Evaluation at the University of Kentucky.

Until recently, most accountability policies were directed toward government failures requiring a straightforward response. For example, if enough voters are dissatisfied with the performance of an elected official, they can replace him or her at the next election with someone more likely to represent their preferences. If they are very dissatisfied and seek prompt action, they can recall the elected official. Members of the U.S. Congress have the authority to discipline their own members, and to impeach the President of the United States. In the case of abuses of administrative power, higher-level governments can step in and remove the offending official(s) and take steps to restore appropriate performance and normal democratic processes. These offending behaviors normally are characterized by a clear violation that can be remedied by a proximate, short-term response of a directive nature.

As we shall discuss, recently accountability policies have been extended to a more complex task: reversing performance failures of entire units of government. Focusing on performance failures raises a host of complex issues: what is the appropriate performance sought, what are the causes of the failure, and what should be the nature of the intervention? These questions often lack clear answers. Moreover, a highly prescriptive, top-down approach may be counterproductive if it generates resentment and only routine compliance. To be sure, this is another version of the old "carrot or stick" argument, but in this case one with severe negative consequences if the government's approach relies on the stick (threats and sanctions) largely to the exclusion of other approaches to motivating and changing the behavior of individuals working in "failing" organizations.

Accountability is only one of many values in our political system. The multiplicity of values leads to institutional arrangements that are, at best, compromises among competing principles. The value of efficiency, for example, often is associated with efforts to centralize administrative power, but these efforts can be taken to the point where the executive agency's accountability to the public is compromised. In contrast, those who favor competence as an overriding principle for organizing government tend to favor institutional arrangements that grant significant autonomy to professionals. In the 1960s and 1970s, when urban school boards and educators were under attack by civil rights reformers, a popular solution was to increase lay participation through administrative and political decentralization. The argument for lay participation is that it strengthens representation by encouraging the development of policies reflecting the needs and values of local communities. However, political systems that are highly representative of local interests strengthen legislative power, weaken judicial power, and restrict opportunities for executive leadership, particularly at state and federal levels. In other words, the principle of accountability must operate alongside many other governance values, often in tension with them.

Institutional arrangements carry value biases. The governance of K-12 education in the United States, for example, was designed by political progressives early in the 20th century to give professional educators authority and to insulate them from political abuses (see Kirst, this volume, chapter 10). Mayors and other local elected politicians, as well as laypeople, lost significant authority and influence. The independent school district, at-large election of smaller school boards, nonpartisan tickets, appointment by merit, and a host of other institutional reforms were intended to create an institution that in many respects would be *less* accountable to the public than the system it replaced. The current attack on many of these earlier reforms is based on the perception by many critics of K-12 education that the reforms were all too effective in reducing accountability to the public. Many of today's debates over institutional reforms are about how important a role accountability should play, and what kind of accountability will be in place. As is well known, the resurgence of neo-classical economics and enthusiasm for markets has led some to argue that markets are more accountable to the public than educators are (Chubb & Moe, 1990).

The emphasis on accountability in our political system ebbs and flows. It tends to receive attention whenever there has been an abuse of power, or where government is perceived to have failed in carrying out its mission. Politicians hurriedly investigate the breach, create new laws or regulations to address the problem, or invoke laws already on the books in order to restore public confidence. In the aftermath of the Watergate scandal in the Nixon administration, Congress authorized special prosecutors with broad powers to investigate presidential wrongdoing. The Presidential Commission that published *A Nation at Risk* was appointed to address what many regarded as a crisis in public school performance, and its findings ushered in an era of increasing accountability. The Enron scandal and related corporate abuses in 2001 and 2002 led to a host of proposals, and some new policies, intended to make corporations and Wall Street more accountable.

At least in part, all accountability policies are symbolic efforts (Edelman, 1967) intended to give the public the impression that politicians are truly concerned and committed to uprooting the problem, regardless of whether or not the policies are likely to be successful. When public attention fades, government performance may well return to business as usual. Thus, accountability becomes institutionalized, regardless of its actual success in improving government performance.

We should keep these observations about accountability policy in mind when we turn to a discussion of accountability policies in education. We can summarize these generalizations as follows:

- Accountability is only one of various values that compete for dominance in our political system.

- While accountability is embedded in our democratic political institutions in diverse ways, often it is seen as a palliative for performance failures within existing institutions.

- This reactive impulse gives accountability policies a strong tendency toward punitive and sanction-oriented approaches to correcting institutional performance.

- The demands being made on accountability policies to solve complex performance problems are growing. How these policies can be augmented or coordinated with other policies to improve school performance is a central issue.

These observations help explain some of the characteristics, as well as limitations, of educational bankruptcy, takeovers, and reconstitution of failing schools as policy instruments for change.

Educational Bankruptcy, Takeovers, and Reconstitution As Accountability Policies

Particularly since the publication of *A Nation at Risk* in 1983, policymakers at state, local, and federal levels have enacted a variety of policies to improve the quality of the nation's public school system. These policies have evolved through various stages, initially focusing on increasing graduation requirements, lengthening the school day and school year, and other efforts to intensify the educational program. By the late 1980s continuing dissatisfaction with the improvement efforts that had been made led policymakers to emphasize school restructuring, with particular attention to making instruction more challenging. By the early 1990s states such as Kentucky and Maryland, followed by others, adopted what came to be known as "high-stakes" accountability policies. As these policies evolved, they included content and performance standards for students, state assessments aligned to the standards, public reporting of district and school performance, and rewards and sanctions for students, educators, and schools, among other things. In this chapter the focus is on one subset of these policies—educational bankruptcy, takeovers, and reconstitution.

At the start it is useful to distinguish these policy approaches very briefly. *Educational bankruptcy* refers to state laws or regulations (sometimes both) that permit the state to intervene in a school district for a variety of reasons. As the term bankruptcy implies, fiscal mismanagement may be a cause. However, bankruptcy can also refer to allegations or findings of corruption, incompetent governance and/or management, unsafe or substandard infrastructure, or academic failure (sometimes referred to as "academic bankruptcy"). Not all state interventions have used the term bankruptcy specifically, even though their intent is similar. Some state laws have been directed at a single troubled school district (for example, Baltimore, Chicago, and Detroit).

State intervention to address bankruptcy problems often includes a range of possible successive sanctions that can be invoked over time if the school district's performance is not remedied. *Takeover* is the common term used to refer to one remedy or sanction, although in practice takeover can mean different things. It may involve varying degrees of state oversight and management of the district, depending on the violation, and the duration may be indefinite or time-specific, with more severe sanctions imposed over time.

Takeover may also involve changing governance to empower new authorities such as a mayor. In this case, the intervention may be understood as a "mayoral takeover" rather than a state takeover. In reality, however, state takeovers and mayoral takeovers are two different approaches to reform, because the first relies primarily on external intervention, while the second seeks to replace one form of local governance with another.

Given the overlapping and confusing nature of these terms, in the following analysis we shall not use the general term "educational bankruptcy" to denote state action to deal with perceived performance problems. Instead, we will distinguish between *state takeovers* and *mayoral takeovers*.

Reconstitution refers to state or local policies for intervention in "failing" schools (rather than entire school districts). Reconstitution can include creating a new school philosophy and a new curriculum and replacing staff. This focus on school performance reflects policymakers' growing concern about academic failure, beyond financial or administrative failings. This policy approach actually began in San Francisco in 1983, as part of a desegregation case involving the San

Francisco Unified School District. Since then many local school districts have adopted reconstitution policies, and a growing number of states have followed the lead of Kentucky and Maryland (discussed later in the chapter). Like some state takeover policies, reconstitution policies often include a succession of sanctions that may be invoked. In Maryland, a school that has been labeled low-performing on a state index for 3 consecutive years can be placed under "local reconstitution" (formerly known as "reconstitution-eligible"). If the school fails to improve, the state board of education can reconstitute it. The state has a number of options, such as closing the school or reopening it under private contract.

Policy Examples and Trends

State Takeovers

Despite two decades of reform, dissatisfaction with public schools and distrust of educators has persisted. Under these circumstances, one common trend has been a more or less steady strengthening of state (and now federal) control. Despite much rhetoric about relaxation of state policies in exchange for greater accountability for results, there has been a steady growth in state regulation, which increased significantly in the 1980s with the first efforts to improve public school quality. By the 1990s, the stronger focus on accountability had caused many states to focus their regulation on the high-stakes approaches discussed above. Part of this development has been an increase in state-led takeovers of local school systems. Most states had education bankruptcy laws on the books for many years, but few exercised them until recently (Cibulka, 1999). Presently, 24 states have such authorizing policies. According to Ziebarth (2002), 18 states and the District of Columbia have exercised this authority in 49 school districts. Wong and Shen (2001) found 40 examples of city (mayoral) and state takeovers between 1988 and 2000.

This does not necessarily mean that the incidence of takeovers is growing. Wong and Shen (2001) indicate that the peak years for takeovers were 1995-97, when 16 occurred. Between 1998 and 2000, only 9 occurred. This may reflect the heightened concern about public school quality in earlier years, which has abated moderately.[1]

The reasons for state intervention have varied. In some places, financial ineptness or corruption was the focus, with attendant managerial problems. This was true of many of the earliest state takeovers in California (1991, 1992, 1993), Connecticut (1988, 1992), Illinois

(1994), Kentucky (1988, 1989, 1992, 1994), Mississippi (1996), New Mexico (1999), Pennsylvania (1994), and Rhode Island (1991).[2]

More recent takeovers in these and other states have tended to invoke a broader scope of state action and are more likely to address breaches of academic accountability. This no doubt reflects the recognition that a school district demonstrating significant breaches of performance in its governance and management may be failing academically as well. Where low achievement is an issue, state authorities tend to scrutinize a range of possible causes, such as poor governance, management, and financing. In some places this has led to a "comprehensive strategy" focusing on multiple issues and including financial, managerial, and academic components (Wong & Shen, 2001).

The governance strategy used in the takeovers also has varied. In some cases, the state has actually run the school district. New Jersey took over the schools of Jersey City 13 years ago, and subsequently took over Newark and Paterson. School board members and high-level administrators in these districts were replaced (Ziebarth, 2002). Connecticut took over the town and school district of Bridgeport (1988) and West Haven (1992) and eventually returned power to local authorities. The state also assumed control of Hartford's schools 5 years ago, with a governor-appointed board of trustees replacing the local school board. The State of California took over the Compton Unified School District in 1993 by removing the administrator and appointing a trustee to oversee the academic and financial performance of the school district. In May 2002 New York State's Commissioner of Education dissolved the Roosevelt, Long Island school board and subsequently took over the school district (Powell, 2002). All of these cases are examples of highly centralized approaches to state intervention, in that the state typically replaced the local school board and assumed either direct management of the school system or close oversight.

Frequently, this approach has resulted in tension between state officials and the local community. There was an acrimonious relationship between California state officials and members of the local community in Compton, California, after the state stepped in to address a $20 million debt in 1993. The takeover was characterized by protests, attempted violence against one of the state-appointed administrators, a class action lawsuit against the state in 1997 brought by the American Civil Liberties Union with a resulting consent decree, a lack of cooperation by the local school board, and an initial high turnover of state-appointed administrators. The Compton mayor resented the state's role in the school district so much that he campaigned successfully against a school bond issue.

The state-appointed administrator had sole control of the district, with the school board serving in an advisory role. In addition, to comply with the 2000 consent decree mandating performance improvements in five areas, the State of California appointed a Fiscal Crisis and Management Assistance Team (2002). Each Team is an arm of the state legislature that assists and evaluates struggling school districts. In 2001 the state returned the Compton district to local control, subject to continued state oversight, after a state review showed that Compton had met its goals in the five areas and had become solvent with repayment of a $19.6 million state loan (Reid, 2001, September 19). Some members of the new school board, however, continued to be highly critical of the state. Given the troubled history of the state takeover, it is not surprising that improvements in student achievement have been modest.

Compton is not an isolated case. Among others, New Jersey's top-down approach to takeovers also has encountered significant local resistance (Seder, 2000).[3] Sometimes local resistance to state intervention has been so strong that less than a total state takeover resulted. In Lawrence, Massachusetts the state reached a compromise with local officials that narrowly averted a complete takeover. A new nine-member school committee was jointly appointed by the existing school committee and by state officials, with the state retaining veto powers over key administrative appointment and financial decisions (Wong, Shen, Jain, & Novacek, 2000).

Another compromise occurred in 2001 when the State of Pennsylvania took over control of the Philadelphia schools. After much conflict between state officials favoring a takeover (the governor, state commissioner, and key legislative leaders) and Philadelphia's mayor, the teachers' union, and various local groups, the state created a School Reform Commission with authority to place low-performing schools under alternative governing models, including privatization. The mayor sought, largely unsuccessfully, to expand his authority to run the city school system. However, as part of the compromise settlement that emerged eventually from this turmoil, the mayor gained the right to appoint two of the five members of the Commission, with the others appointed by the governor (Boyd & Christman, 2003).

States have not always taken such a top-down approach to interventions, or at least their actions have not always been resisted as strongly as was the case in Compton. The state takeover of Logan County, West Virginia frequently is cited as a success story (Bushweller, 1998; Seder, 2000; Wong & Shen, 2001). In 1992 the state of West Virginia stepped in after years of poor financial management and cronyism in personnel practices, as well as low student achievement. The state appointed an administrator and retained the school board in an advisory role. Despite strong initial resentment, local and state authorities began to work collaboratively. A barometer of this good will was the local school board's willingness to hire John Myers, the state-appointed superintendent, to run the district for another year when the state returned local control in 1996. On the eve of the takeover, 71% of elementary schools and 55% of secondary schools scored below the 50th percentile on state standardized tests. School attendance had fallen in many schools, and the dropout rate at Logan High School was 24%. When the state returned the district to local control 4 years later, all of the schools were scoring above the 50th percentile and had attendance rates of 90% or better. Some improvements occurred in dropout rates (Bushweller, 1998; Hoff, 1996, September 18).

The state of Maryland chose a City-State Partnership approach as an alternative to a state takeover when it intervened in Baltimore City to reverse academic failure and a host of management problems. The partnership pledged new state revenues in exchange for reducing mayoral authority over the schools and instituting a new reform board and a corporate-style administrative structure (Cibulka, 2003). Initially, the Partnership was resisted vigorously by many in Baltimore. However, city school officials subsequently developed a strongly collaborative working relationship with the state, as the state had originally envisioned in undertaking a partnership approach.

While the Logan County case was relatively amicable, and Baltimore's partnership has evolved similarly, many state takeovers have involved bitter clashes (Hendrie, 1996). This raises questions about the political problems that state takeovers tend to engender. On the positive side, external intervention may be necessary to create institutional disequilibrium and change organizational culture. A policy focus on incentives and sanctions can alter behavior, as can clear performance targets linked to consequences. However, the potential negatives are substantial. External intervention may be resented, or resisted as unnecessary, because of its tendency to rely on punitive sanctions as a motivator of change (Cibulka & Boyd, 2003).[4]

Mayoral Takeovers

Mayoral takeovers generally involve some kind of state intervention, because states have constitutional responsibility for public education and therefore must authorize any change of governance arrangements. At the same time, after the initial involvement in authorizing a change, the state typically turns over fiscal control and political authority to the mayor, who is expected to be the "change agent" who will turn around a failing school system.

Mayoral takeovers are almost entirely an urban strategy that has emerged to address the substantial performance problems of urban school systems. Undeniably, urban schooling in the United States is in a crisis. Staggering dropout rates and abysmally poor student achievement have become indicators of an institution that is failing. During most of the post-World War II period and until recently, the nation's mayors sought to distance themselves from the public school systems in their cities. Progressive-era reforms had sharply limited the amount of control mayors could exercise, and "good government" reformers, as well as many school system leaders, often sought to protect schools from the mayor's political influence. Furthermore, given the mounting political and fiscal problems of these school systems from the 1950s onward, it was seen as risky for a mayor to invest too much political capital in them.

By the late 1980s, however, a "new breed" of urban mayors (Kirst & Bulkley, in press) began to see their public school systems as part of an urban development strategy to rebuild the middle-class base and the economic viability of cities (Peterson, 1981; Wong & Shen, 2000). From a resource perspective, public schools are one of the largest public employers and a major recipient of tax dollars. As public dissatisfaction with public schools has mounted, elected officials such as mayors have attempted to respond to expectations for improved productivity and efficiency. Hence, for a number of convergent reasons, the 1990s were characterized by a major policy effort, initiated either by mayors or by the state, to have mayors "take over" their city's public school systems. In some cases, mayors have merely sought greater influence over school board appointments or some other aspect of education policy, not total control of the schools.[5]

There are compelling reasons why mayors might be able to improve public school performance. As the chief executive of the city, a mayor can build a broad citywide coalition of stakeholders as an antidote to the highly fragmented politics of urban education, where many interest groups compete for dominance but few have the resources and support to build a durable coalition. Stone (1999) argues that this "civic capacity" has been the key to reform success in some cities, such as Pittsburgh.

Mayors also can leverage other city services to assist schools. In addition, because the average tenure for mayors is much longer than that of urban superintendents, they have the potential to bring leadership stability to the governance and management of the school system (Cibulka & Boyd, 2003).

One limitation of this approach, however, is that school district boundaries and municipal boundaries are not always coterminous. The Los Angeles Unified School District serves more than 20 municipalities. Thus, placing the mayor of Los Angeles in control would diminish local control for some of these jurisdictions (Seder, 2000).

Normally, state officials have responded affirmatively to requests from the mayors for more authority over the school system. In Boston (1992), Chicago (1995), and New York City (2002) the state gave mayors complete control over the appointment of the school board. In Chicago, the Illinois legislature gave operational authority to Mayor Richard M. Daley, who in turn was authorized to appoint not only the five-member board but also a chief executive officer for the school district.

In seeking this authority, mayors may encounter significant resistance from some stakeholder groups. Detroit is a good example. Originally, Detroit's mayor Dennis Archer proposed mayoral control as an alternative to state takeover, but his 1999 agreement with state officials, while supported by local business leaders, engendered strong opposition by the teachers' union and a split in the black community (Wong, Shen, Jain, & Novacek, 2000). Many felt that they had been disenfranchised by the change from an elected to an appointed school board. Archer ultimately left much of the governing of the schools to Detroit's superintendent.

In some cities the state role in reforming governance has been more indirect, as where the state has authorized local voter referenda in which mayors have gained the right to appoint some members of the local school board. This occurred in Oakland, California, where Mayor Jerry Brown won the right in 2000 to appoint three members of a new 10-member board. In Washington, D.C., Mayor Anthony Williams narrowly won the right in 2000 to appoint four members of a nine-member board. His efforts were resented by many poor African Americans as an attack on local control of schools and on African American influence (Cibulka, 2003).

Indeed, each city presents a somewhat different scenario. In 1995 a federal district court in Cleveland removed the powers of the local board of education and handed authority to the state. When the federal court returned local administrative authority in 1998, the mayor was given control. In Hartford, Connecticut years of state oversight preceded mayoral control of the public school system. In these situations, when the state restored local administrative powers to the mayor, its action was seen as a reward for improved performance rather than a punishment for failure.

Reconstitution of Failing Schools

Most school reconstitution efforts have been undertaken by local school districts. In 1997 Chicago's chief executive officer Paul Vallas reconstituted seven poorly performing high schools. Locally initiated reconstitutions also have occurred in Cleveland, Denver, Houston, New York City, San Antonio, and other cities. Typically, these policies require replacement of the principal and staff, although these personnel are not necessarily dismissed. Reconstitution usually involves redesign of the school as well. Currently, 19 states have enacted policies that allow them to reconstitute schools (Ziebarth, 2002).

Frequently, there are several stages or levels of state or local intervention, beginning with monitoring and/or support but eventually leading to reconstitution of a school if it fails to improve. In Maryland, for example, when a school is placed under local reconstitution, it must develop a plan for improvement that is approved by the state board of education. In 2000, the state for the first time invoked the more severe sanction reserved for schools that fail to improve under local reconstitution. The state reconstituted three such schools in Baltimore City and hired Edison, Inc., a private for-profit firm, to operate them. In the following year (2001) it reconstituted a fourth Baltimore City school but delegated to Baltimore's Chief Education Officer Carmen Russo the authority to hire a private contractor for the failing school. Philadelphia's state takeover of the school district has led to a similar approach; many poorly performing schools will be operated under contractual arrangements with for-profit firms, universities, and community organizations (Boyd & Christman, 2003).

The amount of state (or school district) support provided for low-performing schools, in contrast to mere monitoring of school compliance and performance, varies greatly. In the early years of Maryland's reconstitution policy, the state department of education's role was to monitor compliance with the plan, on the assumption that improvements are the responsibility of the local board of education. However, not every school district was equally willing or able to assist the failing school(s). This strategy was particularly faulty in the case of Baltimore City, where state officials concluded that a school-by-school reform strategy would not remedy the city's systemic failures. This recognition was one reason the state intervened in the school system in 1997.

The City-State Partnership not only mandated a number of improvements in the school system's capacity but also expanded state responsibility for helping Baltimore's public schools turn around. Similarly, in its reconstitution policy the state began to augment its monitoring approach with more assistance to schools that had been placed under local reconstitution. Thus, Maryland has gradually adapted its high-stakes accountability policies to strike a better balance between monitoring and support.

Kentucky's high-stakes accountability policy provides an example of an approach more oriented to helping schools improve than to imposing sanctions. Under the Kentucky Education Reform Act (KERA) of 1990, the state targeted any school that failed to improve adequately from its baseline (using an accountability index). While a school could be labeled as in decline or in crisis, there never was an ultimate sanction for failing to improve, such as provided in Maryland's policy. A much larger number of schools become eligible for state intervention than in Maryland because Kentucky's approach to low performance identifies any school that does not meet its target, not simply the schools with the lowest student performance levels. The state's "distinguished educator" program[6] places a state-designated and state-trained expert in the school to provide assistance, along with additional resources. That provision subsequently was altered to make the choice of state assistance voluntary for schools. In 1998 the state passed legislation that provided for scholastic audits as part of assessing whether a school should be designated as in crisis or in decline, thereby deemphasizing reliance on student achievement results in the accountability index. This has narrowed state attention to improving student achievement in the lowest performing schools of the state, because many other schools are able to demonstrate that they are performing well on "input" measures of performance (Lusi & Goldberg, 2000).

A small number of other states strongly emphasize capacity building for schools in their high-stakes accountability system. Like Kentucky's program, North Carolina's ABC accountability program also includes a strong focus on helping low-performing schools to improve. The state provides school assistance teams, but the state also has the authority to dismiss principals and teachers in these schools.

The federal reauthorization of the Elementary and Secondary Education Act, known as the No Child Left Behind Act, in December 2001 greatly expanded federal efforts to make *all* public schools accountable for bringing *all* their students to an achievement level deemed "proficient" by the state. While the policy applies even to non-federally funded schools, for the 50% of the nation's schools that receive Title I aid the penalties are more severe, up to and including restructuring (what has been referred to here as reconstitution) (Cowan, Manasevit, Edwards, & Slater, 2002). The law provides escalating sanctions for schools with low performance.[7] Building on a performance reporting system pioneered in Texas, the law requires the reporting of test scores for all student subgroups, by poverty, racial and ethnic group, students with disabilities, and those with limited English proficiency. All are expected to perform adequately on state assessments or the school's performance will be designated for state intervention. The new federal law attaches sanctions for low performance. A local education agency (LEA) must identify a school for improvement if the school has failed to make "adequate yearly progress" (AYP) for two consecutive years. Students have the right to transfer to another public school in the LEA that has not been identified for improvement. If the school fails to make AYP for three consecutive years, low-income eligible students must receive supplementary services. After the fourth year, if the AYP goal still is not met, the LEA must impose one or more "corrective actions" enumerated in the statute. After a fifth year, the school will develop a restructuring plan, which will be implemented in the following year if AYP is still not attained. The law also requires local education agencies and states to meet AYP provisions, and states must take corrective action against LEAs that are not improving sufficiently.

Because it applies to all states, the No Child Left Behind Act in effect "nationalized" the concept of reconstitution, potentially altering the way existing state policies operate and also extending the policy to new states.[8] The policy also broke new ground by incorporating elements of Florida's accountability policy for low-performing schools. While President Bush and conservative Republicans in the U.S. Congress had favored giving vouchers to parents of children in failing schools, the law represented a compromise that included the right of students to transfer to other *public* schools and the provision of supplementary education services, as described above.

Effectiveness of Takeover and Reconstitution Policies

Research on the effectiveness of state takeovers, mayoral takeovers, or reconstitution of low-performing schools is limited, and it does not explicitly address all aspects of effectiveness. We can think of these policies as having potential benefits in the following main areas:

1. Improving management and financial practices, including eliminating cronyism;
2. Improving the quality of the physical plant and physical condition of buildings;
3. Improving instructional practices, educational programs, and student achievement;
4. Increasing political support for school improvement efforts.

Two reviews of the evidence (Wong & Shen, 2001; Ziebarth, 2002) indicate that the gains are most consistent in the first two areas. Not surprisingly, it is easier to achieve improvements in administration and resource allocation than in core educational functions. In the case of funding improvements, the reason is straightforward: states typically provide new revenues to the school system as part of the intervention settlement. However, this additional revenue does not necessarily rectify fundamental inequities and inadequacies in the system of state financing, because the monies provided to low-performing schools in an accountability scheme typically are short-term outlays for school improvements at the low-performing school. Generally, it takes a court decision or legislative action beyond the specifics of the accountability system to address equity or adequacy issues. In the case of Kentucky, the court required an entirely new funding system to accompany KERA. In New Jersey, funding adequacy for the so-called "Abbott" districts came later than the state's takeover law, and outside its framework. In Maryland, legislative action to improve state funding for schools, including greater equity in the school funding system, came in 2002, well after the passage of the 1997 City-State Partnership.

If most takeover and reconstitution policies have been successful mainly in creating changes above the level of the classroom, even these administrative and funding reforms have not been achieved in all cases. Newark's state-appointed administrators accumulated a $70 million deficit. Detroit suffered a costly 10-day teachers strike in 1999, shortly after the state handed authority to Mayor Dennis Archer. The results of the New Jersey takeover program have been so insubstantial that New Jersey's education commissioner called the 14-year-old state legislation to take over and reform public schools "ill-conceived and poorly executed" and recommended ceding control back to Newark, Paterson, and Jersey City (Jones, June 19, 2002; New Jersey Department of Education, 2002). Among other things, the state's burden was greatly complicated by the continuing obligation to meet court mandates associated with improving low-spending, poor school districts under *Abbott v.*

Burke, because Newark, Paterson, and Jersey City are included among these districts.

There often has been an increased focus on student achievement during state takeovers, even where the initial purpose of state efforts was to address managerial problems. This has been the case in Newark (Frahm, 2002, June 3) and Jersey City (Seder, 2000). However, dramatic and sustained improvements in student achievement have proven elusive in the vast majority of state takeovers.

Although more research is needed, there are a cluster of potential reasons why managerial, funding, and building improvements are easier to achieve than improving instructional practices, educational programs, and student achievement. To begin with, principles of sound administration are relatively well understood and agreed upon, compared with curricular, instructional, and student assessment requirements. In these core educational domains, a variety of perspectives tend to cloud the development of a clear set of priorities, even though there may be general agreement on setting goals for student achievement. Second, teachers enjoy great discretion in their work; their work is not easily monitored, despite calls for greater accountability. For a combination of reasons, even school principals have difficulty providing the instructional leadership to change instructional practices. When the target of improvement is a whole school system, not just individual schools, bureaucratic impediments can block or dilute change efforts. These two constraints—lack of consensus on educational "best practices" and the weak chain of accountability in K-12 education—tend to weaken efforts of reformers at the top of the organization to redirect performance of a school system or individual schools.

Another reason that student achievement gains do not flow automatically from takeovers and reconstitution is that low-performing schools, which disproportionately serve economically poor students, tend to have the least qualified teachers. Yet, research establishes that providing students with access to qualified teachers with strong content knowledge and an ability to work with students who come from different backgrounds or who have special needs is a more powerful predictor of *individual* student achievement than poverty, ethnicity, or other factors (e.g., Darling-Hammond, 2000; Haycock, 2000; Sanders & Rivers, 1996; Wenglinsky, 2000). It is very difficult to reverse the damage done to a student who has poor teachers for two consecutive years. Given this body of literature, the failure to provide students in low-performing schools with qualified teachers may be a powerful explanation for the limited impact of many takeover and reconstitution policies.

Why do students in poorly performing schools have a greater likelihood of being taught by an inexperienced, unqualified, or otherwise inadequate teacher? There are numerous factors at play: teacher shortages; inadequate resources to compete with wealthier school districts for qualified teachers; teacher transfer policies that allow experienced teachers to leave impoverished schools for more attractive teaching assignments; rigid, undifferentiated pay schedules that inhibit recruiting teachers in critical shortage areas such as math, science, and special education; and others. Many of these inadequacies are deeply embedded in the policies and practices of school systems. Therefore, the degree to which takeover and reconstitution policies are successful may turn on whether these policies explicitly seek to provide students in low-performing schools with qualified teachers. To accomplish this, officials must be willing to deal with substantial political obstacles and vested interests.

As we have noted, there are a few examples of takeovers and reconstitutions that have led to actual student achievement gains. Looking at these cases, we may be able to identify some characteristics of successful efforts. West Virginia state officials attributed the improvements in standardized test scores in Logan County to the fact that the state did not dissolve the school board and worked to win local support for the reforms (Seder, 2000).

In a similar vein, Chicago's mayoral takeover led to improved student achievement, particularly at the elementary level (Wong & Shen, 2001). However, mayoral interventions are not a panacea. The mayoral takeover in Detroit was controversial. Also, mayors do not always choose to exercise the authority they are given. The mayoral reform model is basically a restructuring scheme, nothing more, and this is one of its limitations. While the formal features of the policy settlement can be important, so is the approach the mayor decides to take. In Detroit, Mayor Archer gained only limited powers to appoint the school board. Perhaps as a result, and because of the controversy that surrounded his initial role in reforming the governance of the city's schools, Mayor Archer has shown little further interest in exercising leadership on school issues (Russo, 2001). In Cleveland, Mayor Michael R. White, despite significant (but still shared) authority over the schools, also has taken a hands-off approach (Van Lier, 2001). By contrast, Boston's Mayor Tom Menino has forged a close partnership with Superintendent Tom Payzant and staked his reputation as mayor on improving Boston's public schools (Yee, 2003). Chicago's reforms gave clear accountability to Mayor Richard Daley, and he responded with strong leadership. Chicago's former school CEO Paul Vallas (1999, quoted in Seder, 2000) argued that the mayoral takeover per se was only one of numerous factors leading to improved student achievement; others were more spending flexibility in state funds, the setting of high standards and expectations, increased systemwide accountability, and special assistance to students, principals, and teachers to achieve the standards. In short, the potential benefits of mayoral leadership are shaped by a combination of formal legal authority and the mayor's personal disposition toward devoting time and political resources to school reform.

Results of reconstitution policies offer no conclusive effects. Only a small number of Maryland's schools under local reconstitution have improved enough (attaining the state average on MSPAP) to be removed from the state list. Kentucky's program, on the other hand, moved the vast majority of schools designated for state assistance off the state list. The apparent differences in the success of the two states' policies may stem from the fact that Kentucky took a local capacity building approach from the inception of the policy, whereas Maryland moved in this direction later. However, differences in the characteristics of the schools that were targeted for intervention in the two states make it difficult to draw conclusions about which policy has been more effective. Mintrop, Curtis, King, Plut-Pregelj, and Quintero (2001) concluded that the modest result of the reconstitution policies in the Maryland schools they examined resulted from the inability of the policies to change principals' management styles, which focus on compliance rather than organizational learning and professional development for teachers. Instructional practices of many teachers remain unchanged because of their routine compliance with their principal's expectations.

Conclusion

The slow pace of school reform, particularly in American cities, has made politicians impatient to find an approach that will achieve demonstrable and dramatic improvements. The popularity of accountability policies is a response to this frustration. State takeovers, mayoral takeovers, and reconstitution of failing schools are part of the impulse to get results today, or if not today, soon. So far, however, the outcomes of such approaches have been mixed at best. Some successes can be found, but counterexamples are evident as well.

The reasons for this modest record no doubt inhere partly in the fact that takeovers and reconstitution deal for the most part with districts and schools that are at the low end of the scale in terms of performance.[9]

These are the most intractable cases, and they would provide a challenge for any policy design. Indeed, the modest achievements of these policies in many jurisdictions have led to more policy experimentation. The incorporation of elements of school choice in Florida's accountability policy and in No Child Left Behind are examples of this experimentation. While this choice dimension of the new federal law fell far short of what President George W. Bush had asked for initially, it nonetheless illustrated a willingness to innovate in shaping school reconstitution policies. Some local school districts have moved to incorporate charter schools and contracts. Even state takeovers of school districts, which have been prone to rely heavily on traditional regulatory approaches to intervention, have been evolving in innovative ways.

Unfortunately, much of this experimentation is ideologically driven and built on acts of faith; policymakers are designing policies without solid evidence that any of these approaches to reversing failing schools (and school systems) will be successful. There is a paucity of research, and there are too few policymakers who believe research should inform their work. There must be more emphasis on "policy learning" if these policies are to have their intended effects.

If the "second generation" of these policies is to be any more effective than the first, some of the basic assumptions of their "theory of action" need to be rethought. Perhaps the biggest challenge is to determine how to create the right combination of *incentives* for stakeholders (teachers, administrators, students, and parents) to improve outcomes, how to provide meaningful *consequences* (sanctions) for performance failure, and how to increase the *capacity* of the educational system to improve. This, it turns out, is a more complicated challenge than the motivational assumptions embedded in the first generation of takeover and reconstitution policies.

Moreover, accountability policies have become more complex, incorporating standards for students, complex student assessments, standards for teachers and administrators, and myriad other requirements. All these pieces must be coordinated in a meaningful manner.

Finally, sustaining the *political* commitment to reverse a legacy of failure in some school districts and schools is just as important as the technical features of a policy's design. Accountability policies must operate within a fragmented political system driven by shallow and fickle public interest, short-term pressures, the self-interests of elected officials, leadership turnover, and responsiveness to vested interests.

Therefore, making accountability policies such as takeovers and reconstitution a genuine tool for school reform is a formidable challenge.

The task of reshaping these policies so that they are more effective, as well as building political support for the changes, is work that has only begun.

NOTES

1. For the first time in the 33-year history of the Phi Delta Kappa/Gallup poll of public attitudes toward the public schools, a majority of respondents (51%) gave the public schools in their community an A or B grade. In 1998, for example, the percentage was only 46%. However, there continued to be a significant difference when respondents rated the *nation's* schools; only 23% gave them an A or B (Rose & Gallup, 2000, 2001). This was still an increase from 1998, when only 18% assigned the nation's schools an A or B.

2. Specifics of these cases can be found in Ziebarth (2002), Appendix B.

3. The state law authorizes the state to step in to operate the district when the district does not meet state standards and when local officials "do not demonstrate a willingness to improve their performance" (quoted in Wong, Shen, Jain, & Novacek, 2000). It is not surprising that this pejorative tone stirs local resistance.

4. Another unintended consequence that has arisen in several states, including Texas, is the potential violation of the federal Voting Rights Act of 1965 (Ziebarth, 2002).

5. In this chapter I do not try to make sharp distinctions among degrees of mayoral influence. Chicago represents the purest case, with total mayoral control. In some cities, such as Washington, D.C., even modest efforts by mayors to assert more influence over school board appointments have been resisted as though they are tantamount to an external takeover. Thus, the local political context is key to understanding how mayoral influence will be perceived.

6. These state-appointed officials have been renamed "highly-qualified educators."

7. The basis for determining low performance builds on and extends policies enacted in Texas while George W. Bush was governor of that state.

8. After the law was passed, states with accountability systems already in place began to lobby the Congress and officials at the U.S. Department of Education for assurances that their existing systems would not be disrupted by the new federal requirements. This issue has not been resolved as of this writing, because the U.S. Department of Education has not clarified many points in the lengthy law.

9. Kentucky's accountability program can be described as a continuous improvement model that targets a wider range of schools for voluntary participation in the "highly qualified educator" program than a model that focuses only on the lowest performing schools in the state.

REFERENCES

Boyd, W.L., & Christman, J.B. (2003). A tall order for Philadelphia's new approach to school governance: Heal the political rifts, close the budget gap, and improve the schools. In L. Cuban & M. Usdan (Eds.), *Powerful reforms with shallow roots*. New York: Teachers College Press.

Bushweller, K. (1998, August). Do state takeovers work? *American School Board Journal*. Retrieved March 13, 2002 from http://www.asbj.com/199808/0898coverstory.html

Chubb, J.E., & Moe, T.M. (1990). *Politics, markets, & America's schools*. Washington, DC: The Brookings Institution.

Cibulka, J.G. (1999). Moving toward an accountable system of K-12 education: Alternative approaches and challenges. In G. Cizek (Ed.), *Handbook of educational policy* (pp. 184-210). San Diego, CA: Academic Press.

Cibulka, J.G. (2003). External intervention to improve Baltimore and Washington, D.C.'s public schools. In J.G. Cibulka & W.L. Boyd (Eds.), *A race against time: Responses to the crisis in urban schooling*. Westport, CT: Greenwood Publishing Group.

Cibulka, J.G., & Boyd, W.L. (2003). Urban education reform strategies: Comparative analysis and conclusions. In J.G. Cibulka & W.L. Boyd (Eds.), *A race against time: Responses to the crisis in urban schooling*. Westport, CT: Greenwood Publishing Group.

Cowan, K.T., Manasevit, L.M., Edwards, C.J., & Sattler, C.L. (2002). *The new Title I: Balancing flexibility with accountability*. Washington, DC: Thompson Publishing Group, Inc.

Darling-Hammond, L. (2000). Teacher quality and student achievement: A review of state policy evidence. *Education Policy Analysis Archives 8(1)*. Available: http://olam.ed.asu.edu/epaa/v8n1/

Edelman, M. (1967). *The symbolic uses of politics*. Urbana: University of Illinois Press.

Financial Crisis and Management Assistance Team. (2002). Compton Unified School District, *Serna v. Easton* Consent Decree. Six-month progress report (February). Available: http://www.fcmat.org

Frahm, R.A. (2002, June 3). Across nation, mixed results. *The Hartford Courant*, A1.

Haycock, K. (2000). No more settling for less. *Thinking K-16, 4(1)*: 3-8, 4-12.

Hendrie, C. (1996, June 12). Ill will comes with territory in takeovers. *Education Week on the Web*. Retrieved March 1, 2002 from http://www.edweek.org/ew/vol-15/38contro.h15

Hoff, D.J. (1996, September 18). West Virginia leaves district better than it found it. *Education Week on the Web*. Retrieved March 1, 2002 from http://www.edweek.org/ew/1996/03wva.h16

Jones, R.L. (2002, June 19). Education chief urges restoring local school control in Newark, Paterson, and Jersey City. *The New York Times*. Retrieved July 3, 2002 from www.nytimes.com. Document 143.

Kirst, M.W. (2003). Mayoral influence, new regimes, and public school governance. In this volume—W.L. Boyd & D. Miretzky (Eds.), *American educational governance on trial: Change and challenges. The 102nd yearbook of the National Society for the Study of Education*, Part I (pp. 196-218). Chicago: National Society for the Study of Education.

Kirst, M.W., & Bulkley, K. (in press). Mayoral takeover: The different direction taken in different cities. In J.G. Cibulka & W.L. Boyd (Eds.), *A race against time: Responses to the crisis in urban schooling*. Westport, CT: Greenwood Publishing Group.

Lusi, S.F., & Goldberg, P.D. (2000). A new mission for the Department of Education. In R.S. Pancratz & J.M. Petrosko (Eds.), *All children can learn: Lessons from the Kentucky reform experience* (pp. 225-243). San Francisco: Jossey-Bass.

Mintrop, H., Curtis, K., King, B., Plut-Pregelj, L., & Quintero, M. (2001, April). *The effect of probation on school improvement, Part II: Organizational responses to probation in high-stakes accountability systems*. Paper delivered at the annual meeting of the American Educational Research Association, Seattle, WA.

New Jersey Department of Education. (2002). Developing a plan for reestablishing local control in the state-operated school districts: A final report to the New Jersey Department of Education. Available: http://www.state.nj.us/njded/schools/sosd/local2.pdf

Peterson, P.E. (1981). *City limits*. Chicago: University of Chicago Press.

Powell, M. (2002, April 21). Separate and unequal in Roosevelt, Long Island: A New York town's struggle against the toll of segregation. *The Washington Post*, A3, A13.

Random House. (1968). *College dictionary: Revised edition*. New York: Random House, Inc.

Reid, K.S. (2001, September 19). California returns Compton district to local control. *Education Week (21)*3, 3.

Rose, L.C., & Gallup, A.M. (2000, September). The 32nd annual Phi Delta Kappa/Gallup poll of the public's attitudes toward the public schools. *Phi Delta Kappan 82*, 41-56.

Rose, L.C., & Gallup, A.M. (2001, September). The 33rd annual Phi Delta Kappa/Gallup poll of the public's attitudes toward the public schools. *Phi Delta Kappan 83*, 41-58.

Russo, A. (2001). Detroit's Archer keeps distance from schools. Cleveland: Catalyst for Cleveland Schools. Retrieved February 26, 2002 from http://www.catalyst-cleveland.org/05-01/0501story5.htm

Sanders, W.L., & Rivers, J.C. (1996). Cumulative and residual effects of teachers on future student academic achievement. Knoxville: University of Tennessee, Tennessee Value Added Assessment System.

Seder, R.C. (2000). Balancing accountability and local control: State intervention for financial and academic stability. Policy Study No. 268. Los Angeles: Reason Public Policy Institute.

Stone, C.N. (1999). Civic capacity and urban school reform. In C. Stone (Ed.), *Changing urban education* (pp. 250-276). Lawrence, KS: University of Kansas Press.

Van Lier, P. (2001). Cleveland's White wields power, limits public role. Cleveland: Catalyst for Cleveland's Schools. Retrieved February 26, 2002 from http://www.catalyst-cleveland.org/05-01/0501story2.htm

Wenglinsky, H. (2000). How teaching matters. Bringing the classroom back into discussions of teacher quality. A policy information center report. Princeton, NJ: The Milken Family Foundation and Educational Testing Service.

WESTAT. (2002). Report on the final evaluation of the City-State Partnership. Baltimore City Public School System. Retrieved May 18, 2002 from http://www.bcps.k12.md.us/admin/westat/index.html

Wong, K.K., & Shen, F.X. (2001). Does school district takeover work? Assessing the effectiveness of city and state takeover as a school reform strategy. Paper prepared for delivery at the 2001 Annual Meeting of the American Political Science Association.

Wong, K.K., Shen, F.X., Jain, P., & Novacek, G. (2000). City and state takeover as a school reform strategy. Paper prepared for delivery at the 2000 research conference of the Association for Public Policy Analysis and Management.

Yee, G. (2003). From Court Street to city hall: Governance change in the Boston Public Schools. In J.G. Cibulka & W.L. Boyd (Eds.), *A race against time: Responses to the crisis in urban schooling*. Westport, CT: Greenwood Publishing Group.

Ziebarth, T. (2002). State takeovers and reconstitutions. *Policy brief: Accountability— Rewards and sanctions*. Denver: Author.

Section Four
RETHINKING THE STATE AND FEDERAL ROLE IN EDUCATIONAL GOVERNANCE

CHAPTER 13

Rethinking the Role of States and Educational Governance

CAROLYN HERRINGTON AND FRANCES FOWLER

The State and Educational Governance

State governments are stronger today than ever before in history. Their most important responsibility, public education, has come under renewed scrutiny and benefited from this renewed strength. As a 1999 *Education Week* occasional series tellingly titled "Power Play" put it, "These days, state officials are exerting unprecedented influence over public school classrooms" (Johnston & Sandham, 1999, p. 1). At the same time, heightened political unrest around public education and state policies demonstrates how far state governments are from consistently exploiting their strength for effective policymaking.

Derided in the past as "that sick old man of the federal system" (Reichley, 1974, p. 11), state government has traditionally lacked both the will and the capacity to exercise vigorous leadership in education. School districts, though structurally creations of the state, were routinely permitted considerable autonomy in the name of local control. It is the purpose of this chapter to explore this phenomenon in some

Carolyn Herrington is Professor and Chair of the Department of Educational Leadership and Policy Studies at Florida State University and currently serves as the Associate Dean for Graduate Studies and Research. Frances Fowler is Professor of Educational Leadership at Miami University, Ohio.

271

depth. In doing so, we will present the historic function of state government in education and the emergence of a "special governance structure" for public education, which both protected and isolated public schooling from other state political arenas. The chapter will then detail the dramatic transformation state governments and policymakers have undergone over the last few decades, and describe how this change has emboldened and empowered state public school policymaking.

The chapter will then discuss two core policy areas—funding and academic standards—and how newly empowered state governments have tried to conceptualize their roles in these key areas. The chapter will finish with an analysis of the use by state governments of the most fundamental and risky of reform options—governance changes—to promote reforms that have eluded them through more conventional channels. We will cautiously suggest that another approach—that of state investment in research and development—may hold more promise as an engine for reform than governance does.

Historical Overview of State Educational Governance

During the colonial period, schools were generally under local governmental or private (usually religious) authority. Soon after the Revolution began, however, the founders began to consider state systems of education. In 1779 Thomas Jefferson made the earliest such proposal in *A Bill for the More General Diffusion of Knowledge*, which he introduced into the Virginia Assembly. This bill failed, and a similar one introduced 38 years later did not meet with success either. However, Jefferson and others had sowed fruitful seed; by 1820 thirteen of the 20 states had included provisions for education in their constitutions. At first, education was controlled by general government, that is, by the governor and state legislature, but by the middle of the 19th century so-called "special education governance" was becoming common at the state level. By 1870 thirty-six states had chief state school officers (CSSOs). The first permanent state board of education (SBE) was established by North Carolina in 1825, and others soon followed. Thus, in the early 1900s, almost all states had in place the special education governance structure taken for granted today—a chief state school officer and a state board of education (Campbell, Cunningham, McPhee, & Nystrand, 1970).

This structure would remain unchallenged for the better part of the century. It is enlightening to read what Campbell et al. had to say about educational governance in 1970, when the second edition of their widely used textbook, *The Organization and Control of American Schools*, was published. They devoted a mere page and a half to the role of the state legislature, conceding that it "has plenary power in making basic policy decisions regarding the schools" (p. 56). Governors did not even rate a special section in the chapter on state governance; the authors told their readers in the single paragraph about governors that they influenced education through "messages ... to the legislature" and "provisions ... in budget" (p. 56) as well as through their veto power. Campbell et al. devoted far more space (22 pages) to special education governance than to general state government, meaning the CSSO, the SBE, and the state education agency (SEA). They described the CSSO as having "considerable influence" (p. 57) over education policy, yet lamented the fact that in many states CSSOs earned less than principals, making it difficult to attract able people to the position. They indicated that SBEs "are limited to rather routine school operation problems and have little influence on educational policy making" (p. 58). As for the SEAs, the authors depicted them as understaffed and overworked, and asserted that "local school districts often build more effective administrative staffs than do state departments of education" (p. 59). It is small wonder, then, that with such a vacuum at the state level, they also stated that "responsibility for the actual operation of most of our schools has been delegated to district boards of education" (p. 60) and that "the courts have consistently held that delegation ... to district boards of education is 'appropriate'" (p. 60). Nor is it surprising that they described a state educational governance system that primarily set minimum standards in such areas as the instructional program, certification for teachers, and requirements for school buildings.

To read their description of state educational governance is to realize how much the politics of education has changed in just three decades. We live today in a period of "education governors"; assertive state legislatures; CCSSOs, SBEs, and SEAs that interact at the state and national level through intergovernmental lobbying organizations; a business establishment that aggressively seeks to influence education policy; and a governance system that has set its sights much higher than minimum standards. What happened? This is the question we seek to answer in the next section.

The Recent Emergence of the State as a Strong Political Player

It is in the immediate aftermath of World War II that one can find the roots of the state's growing interest in public schooling and its capacity to act on that interest. The demographic surge after World War II required a vast expansion of the state's public school systems, and the economic expansion provided the resources. Local school districts needed and received aid from the state in building new schools, hiring teachers, and modernizing the curriculum. The large number of adults who furthered their education after World War II, along with an economy requiring higher levels of academic skills from its employees, fueled the demand that more students stay in school longer. In effect, the 1950s and 1960s saw the formation of a very large, politically active middle class who wanted more and better schooling for their children. The local school districts attempted to respond to these demands, but needed help from the state to do so.

At the same time, the state's capacity to respond was improving. Two events in particular accelerated the strengthening of state influence. First, the one-man, one-vote judicial reforms of the late 1960s significantly shifted power in state legislatures from rural to urban areas, where interest in education and a willingness to levy the taxes to pay for education were greater. Second, the Great Society federal programs of the 1960s charged state governments with oversight and administrative responsibilities for these programs, creating the need for larger state agencies and providing the resources for staffing them.

Responses to the pressure from these broad demographic, economic, and political changes were well underway when an additional set of pressures was added. Huge increases in oil prices as a result of the formation of the Organization of Petroleum Exporting Countries (OPEC), the subsequent recession of the early 1980s, and the decline in the manufacturing sector challenged the United States' economic hegemony and gave voice to charges that a mediocre educational system was the soft underbelly of our economic system. The belief that an educational deficiency was compromising the country's global economic standing added to existing pressures stemming from demographic growth and from states' increasing capacity as a governmental force.

New Roles and New Actors

The focus and rationale for this increased state presence and capacity simultaneously altered the numbers and the types of players in state educational circles. Over the last few decades, veteran policy actors have gained new power and roles, and new policy actors have come on stage. These changes have strongly shaped the dynamics of state education governance.

It is fair to say that most of the actors identified in 1970 by Campbell et al. have increased their power and, as a result, have taken on new roles. There is a truism in political science that the American governorship has been "presidentialized." Until recently, most American governors were weak and ineffectual political players, but today they serve longer terms, have larger staffs, and have been granted more constitutional authority than was the case 30 years ago (Fowler, 2000a). As a result, they have begun to exert greater influence in education and other policy domains. The economic crisis of the early 1980s led to the emergence of "education governors," activists like Bill Clinton, Lamar Alexander, and Richard Riley, who built political careers by pushing for education reforms in their states (Stricherz, 2001). And if the governorship has been "presidentialized," state legislatures have been "congressionalized." Once amateurish bodies that lacked both the will and the capacity to assume genuine political leadership, they are much more professional today because of a series of reforms in the 1970s. They meet for longer sessions, have larger staffs, and are paid better than earlier state legislatures. Legislatures, too, have become more assertive in their attempts to reform education (Fowler, 2000a).

The special education governance structure set up in the 19th century has also gained power. For example, CSSOs are no longer the underpaid workhorses described by Campbell et al. (1970). CSSOs have increased their power by way of their national organization, the Council of Chief State School Officers. As recently as 15 years ago, the Council was merely a professional organization; today it directs more than 30 research projects and employs a large staff. It provides networking and training opportunities for CSSOs as well as up-to-date information on education issues (Richard, 2001). SEAs have also become more effective and more powerful. They, too, were reformed in the 1960s and 1970s in order to more efficiently implement federally funded education programs. As a result, their staffs grew significantly (Fowler, 2000a; State agencies take hands-on role in reform, 1999). A 1994 study found that SEAs were the second most influential education group at the state level (Questionable clout, 1994).

Not surprisingly, as these policy actors have gained authority and assumed new roles, power struggles have broken out among them. One struggle pits the general state government (the governor and legislature) against the special governance structure of education (the CSSO, SEA, and SBE). Governors in particular have tried, often successfully, to increase their control over education governance by gaining the power to appoint both CSSOs and SBEs. Occasionally, power struggles have led to lawsuits (Johnston, 1999). Governors and legislators do not always get along, especially when they are of different parties.

Nothing is more striking to veterans of state educational politics than the increasingly partisan nature of the educational debate. One long-time observer of state education politics commented, "When I came to work in the 1970s, the politics really focused on labor relations. Nobody ever thought of education in a partisan way other than that. Now, how to teach reading has become a partisan issue" (Sandham, 1999, p. 3). In 1996, a conservative splinter group, the Education Leaders Council, broke away from the older Council of Chief State School Officers. Very influential within the second Bush Administration, it offers CSSOs another arena in which to influence education policy; some CSSOs belong to both groups (Sack, 2001). Partisan battles have broken out across different state political arenas. For example, between 1995 and 1999, former Pennsylvania Governor Tom Ridge and the legislature repeatedly locked horns over vouchers, while in 1999 the Arizona legislature quarreled for months over stricter regulations for charter schools (Sandham, 1999).

In addition to shifting power, politics, and roles among the traditional actors, two powerful new actors have emerged at the state level in the last three decades. The first is teacher unions; the state affiliates of the American Federation of Teachers and the National Education Association are often the most powerful education groups in state politics (Questionable clout, 1994). Their power grew in the 1960s and 1970s, when they moved first into collective bargaining and then into endorsing political candidates (Fowler, 2000b). The second group is business, which has become increasingly aggressive in its attempts to influence state education policy. The National Alliance of Business, for example, with 5,000 member companies and CEOs, works exclusively "to improve student performance at all levels" (National Alliance of Business, 2001). It works collaboratively with the Business Roundtable to influence policy at the state level. Other business groups active in shaping education policy include the state affiliates of the U.S. Chamber of Commerce, the National Association of Manufacturers, and the Farm Bureau.

State politics of education has changed dramatically since 1970. Today, the political process is more partisan and more unpredictable, often producing unexpected policy surprises.

The next section of this chapter addresses the substance of educational policy at the state level. How have newly empowered and newly ambitious state players come together around core reform issues in an increasingly partisan atmosphere? We look at state initiatives in two core areas: school finance and standards and assessments. In each case, we find the state is using its newly found strength to push aggressively for reform, while finding its capacity still sorely strained and its legitimacy challenged at every move.

School Finance: Challenges to State Policymakers and State Capacity

No responsibility for state governments is clearer than the responsibility to assure adequate and equitable funding for public schooling. Almost every state constitution speaks to that responsibility in some form. And the last 30 years have shown that states are increasingly stepping up to the responsibility. The percentage of total funding for public schools borne by the state increased from 38.3% in 1971-72 to 46.8% in 1994-95 (National Center for Education Statistics, November 1998).

The state's conventional role has been to build upon local funding, with the state's addition adjusting for variation in levying capacity at the local level. Through this supportive role, many states have been able to achieve substantial increases in both the level and the equity of funding for education (Murray, Evans, & Schwab, 1998). Newly empowered state policy actors have gone even further. They have devised numerous strategies to increase funding for schools as well as to increase funding equity among schools, to tie substantive reforms to funding policies, and to attempt to link funding with performance. However, despite considerable progress in these areas over the last few decades, and an explosion of novel and promising new policy structures, most commentators and policy analysts find that states are still far from achieving either equity or adequacy in school funding.

Virtually all analyses of interdistrict funding demonstrate that large inequities still exist (National Center for Education Statistics, 2001; Wong, 1999). Even the heavy hand of judicial scrutiny has not been sufficient to create the support that would be necessary to achieve a radical redistribution of state resources (State Policy Reports, August 2002; Wong, 1999). Nowhere is this clearer than in the case of *Abbott v. Burke* (1990), where the New Jersey Supreme Court unanimously ruled the state's finance formula unconstitutional as applied to poorer urban school districts. Despite the clear ruling, more than a decade later, gross inequities continue (Wong, 1999). In Illinois, where minority children make up 26 percent of the enrollment, the gap in funding between rich and poor districts is 3.1 to 1 in elementary schools (Wong, 1999).

While under any circumstance the political will to redistribute resources from the well-off to the less well-off is hard to come by, the other approach—raising poorer districts to the level of better off ones—is rendered virtually impossible in an era of no new taxes and frequent tax relief (National Education Association, 2001). In fact, one of the mechanisms by which the state assumes an even larger role in the funding of public education is not the increase of overall state taxes, but the replacement of largely unpopular local property taxes with state-based taxes. (Currently there are 9 states that do not rely on local property taxes to fund schools.) Several states, led by Illinois, rely on local property taxes for more than 40% of education revenues. As reported in State Policy Reports, these states are likely to be under the most pressure to relieve the local property tax burden, and possibly address equity considerations, through a greater state role in education finance.

As states struggle, often unsuccessfully, to deal with equity issues between districts, adequacy issues are moving to the foreground as well, often propelled by state court rulings. Adequacy as a concept relates funding to sufficiency, i.e., it raises the question of whether or not available funding is adequate for what the state is trying to achieve. As courts have shown more willingness to force states to face up to the obligations in their constitutions guaranteeing a certain level of education for all children, states are being forced to calculate the related costs (Guthrie & Rothstein, 1999). Here, too, both political will and technical knowledge lag far behind. While there are a number of theories on how one might pin down the costs necessary to achieve a certain level of educational attainment for children in a state, only a few states have begun to apply related models, and their technical efficacy is far from assured. (See Odden et al., this volume, chapter 5, for a review of the different approaches and an argument for the efficacy of one particular approach.)

The inability to realize financial equity and adequacy undermines progress in the other areas of state reform interest—standards and governance (discussed below). State attempts to hold schools and districts responsible for student performance is compromised if variation in performance can be plausibly attributed to variation in resources.

The Standards Movement and Challenges
to State Policymakers and State Capacity

Standards-based reform has been the focus of educational reform in almost every state. It may best be described as the establishment of curricular standards at the state level and the assessment of student performance against these standards. Today, nearly every state has established standards in at least some subjects, and 44 states have completed standards in English, mathematics, social studies, and science (Education Commission of the States, 2002).

While concern for student performance at the state level can be traced as far back as the 1950s, it was the 1983 release of the now legendary report of President Reagan's National Commission on Educational Excellence, *A Nation At Risk*, that clearly defined the challenge facing the public school system as a crisis of low academic standards. Pointing in particular to the small number of high school students pursing demanding courses in math and science, to declining performance on the SAT, and to the large numbers of students needing remediation at the postsecondary level, the Commission sounded the alarms to which states have been responding ever since.

The aftermath of the report saw a good deal of experimentation with reform strategies, such as increased teacher pay, class size reduction, increased use of technology, and improved early childhood services. The 1980s and 1990s saw a flood of other single-issue reforms. The development of curriculum standards and accompanying assessments, a more focused and centralizing strategy, grew in no small part from frustration with the inefficacy of such incremental and unrelated reforms. Standards-based reform thus emerged by the end of the century as a premier state reform strategy (Fuhrman, 2001). Its emergence was also legitimated by an early 1990s economic recession, which suggested that poor educational performance was jeopardizing the country's economic and political presence on the world stage. Finally, support came from agency staff at the U.S. Department of Education who argued for a national (if not federal) role in defining academic standards (Ravitch, 1995), and from the models of potential standards offered by discipline-based groups such as the National Council on Mathematics Education. The simplest reason, however, may be the most important: it was inevitable that as education became more prominent as a public issue, more attention would be directed toward defining standards and measuring attainment.

The quick acceptance of this focus by states threatens to mask how truly dramatic a change it is. In one fell swoop, states have positioned themselves as primary actors in the educational enterprise, challenging school boards as the key political actor at the local level and challenging educators as the authority on academic content and instructional strategy.

Both of these challenges require further examination. American federalism, in theory, and federal and state constitutional precepts never supported the arrangements that operated prior to this reemergence of states as educational actors. Both clearly assign responsibility for public education to states, not to the local or to the federal government. Likewise, the principle that professional educators should control the public school curriculum has never been legitimated, except in popular myth. It has, in fact, been tradition and myth that have supported the presumption that control of education should be locally based, and that politics should stay out of education. States are facing an impasse, caught between the logic of the political foundations of the intergovernmental system and long-standing and powerful citizen and professional norms. This conflict of beliefs and traditions remains unresolved, as both sides press the legitimacy of their claims of control.

The challenges to states brought about by the standards-based reform thrust differ somewhat in intensity in this reform's four most common components—standards, assessment, public information, and consequences. By far the most widely acceptable component has been the adoption of state standards. The second component, state assessment of these standards, has been more controversial, with many arguing that state assessments by definition are too narrow an instrument to measure what children are learning or what they should be learning. Even more controversial have been the operational details of virtually every state assessment system. The remaining two components—public reporting and every aspect of linking performance results to consequences—have been extremely contentious among educators and also among parents and the public at large, though sometimes for different reasons.

The intensity of the criticism is deep, in particular from professional educators and their representatives. These education critics argue that the assessments measure only limited educational outcomes and may not measure the most important outcomes. They assert that the focus on testing outcomes creates a set of unintended consequences that reverberate throughout school systems, disrupting the overall curriculum, classroom practice, and instructional strategies, as well as depressing teacher morale and undermining commitment to teaching (Kohn, 2000; Ohanian, 1999). States have countered, not without some success, that in fact some curricular objectives *are* more important than others, and that the neglect of students who are difficult to educate, rampant in the public school system, could not be allowed to continue.

The criticisms emanating from educators have been echoed by local school board members and district administrators and by many parents. In the name of local control, they have argued that local school officials, those closest to and most responsive to the community, should determine what kind of curriculum is valued and how it should be assessed. Following this line of argument, state accountability systems impose a blunt, if not brutal, instrument—such as a standardized test—as a barrier between schools and the communities they serve, distorting schools' sense of community and their ability to respond to constituents.

Clearly, states have a legitimate interest in educational outcomes. Equally clearly, performance must be measured in order to be assessed and supported. To date, however, attempts to do that have plunged states into a thicket of design details and implementation consequences. Neither side shows any indication of backing off. The state interest in students' academic performance has plunged it into a whorl of controversy, in which the legitimacy of its means, if not its ends, is under persistent and continuous challenges.

An absence of consensus about assessment among state actors, local actors, and professional educators might be less important if there were evidence that the dominant state strategy of testing was at least effective in improving student performance. However, states have scant evidence to support this strategy. The publication of conflicting reports on reform in Texas shows how far we are methodologically from having the tools to know whether accountability and assessment reforms work, and if they do work, why. These two reports, both released by the research corporation RAND in 2000, offered differing conclusions about whether the Texas accountability system had significantly improved student achievement (relative to other states), as well as about whether it had closed the gap between white students and students of color (Grissmer, Flanagan, Kawata, & Williamson, 2000; Klein, Hamilton, McCaffrey, & Stecher, 2000). Similarly, a 30-year review of Florida's reliance on accountability systems and state assessments as a dominant reform strategy produced little evidence that accountability systems per se were sufficient to produce significant improvements in student learning. The historically weak performance of Florida's students did not improve relative to other states' performance over this same time period (Herrington and MacDonald, 2001).

Reform Through Governance

The most dramatic efforts on the part of state governments to improve schooling are based on challenging prior governance arrangements and attempting new ones. These are among the most radical strategies that state governments have employed, as well as the most controversial. They clearly demonstrate the state's frustration with more traditional reform routes, and indicate both the state's awareness of its new strength and its willingness to use this strength.

Three reforms will be discussed in this section: state takeovers of local schools and school districts; school choice; and site-based management.

State Takeovers

The state takeover is a governance reform that intentionally strengthens state power at the expense of school boards. About half of the nation's state legislatures have enacted laws that permit them to "take over" districts that are guilty of serious financial mismanagement or districts in which student achievement is unacceptable. Several states also have statutes that permit the takeover of individual schools. New Jersey has acted the most aggressively in this area, taking over the operations of three districts—Jersey City, Paterson, and Newark—between 1989 and 1995. But New Jersey is by no means alone. Other states that have intervened in local districts and made sweeping changes in them are Ohio (which took over both the Cleveland and Youngstown districts), Alabama, California, Maryland, and Illinois. Moreover, the federal government has intervened in the schools of the District of Columbia. Sometimes state governments fire school boards and the superintendent when such a move is made. More commonly, however, they work behind the scenes to accomplish change. Even when states take power from school boards, they often try to work collaboratively with other local leaders, especially mayors. When the Michigan legislature decided to take over the Detroit system, for example, it gave power over the schools to Mayor Dennis Archer, although the governor retained an important role in the process. Similarly, Maryland's Governor Parris Glendening established a partnership with city officials when the state took over Baltimore's schools system (Johnston & Sandham, 1999; Race and takeovers, 1998; Reinhard, 1998).

The effectiveness of state takeovers as an education reform measure has been questioned. New Jersey's experience in Paterson, Newark, and Jersey City suggests that it is easier to improve the financial management and general administration of a district than it is to improve student achievement. As a result, state legislatures have begun to move rather cautiously with takeover plans, especially when dealing with large urban districts. Many of the states with takeover laws on the books have never applied them; instead, they often choose less heavy-handed methods, including the allocation of money for staff development for district administrators or the use of intervention teams to work with schools. Nonetheless, even these gentler approaches represent a substantial increase in state activity at the local level (Sandham, 1999).

Needless to say, state takeovers of local districts are controversial. The local officials and administrators who are involved feel considerable anger and resentment when state officials come in to run things, feelings that are likely to be widespread in the community. Moreover, takeovers often lead to charges of racism, since in the typical takeover scenario a cadre of largely white state officials takes charge of a largely minority urban district. A 1998 *Education Week* analysis of actual and proposed takeovers revealed that in 24 of 29 districts, the majority of the students were members of racial minority groups. Three of the five remaining districts—Logan County, West Virginia, and Letcher and Floyd Counties in Kentucky—were located in rural Appalachia. Thus, almost all of the actual and proposed takeovers during the 1990s involved districts in which the majority of students were members of populations that historically have experienced considerable discrimination (Race and takeovers, 1998). Because of this, a number of takeovers have been challenged in court. For example, when Texas officials took control of the Somerset district near San Antonio, where more than 75% of students are Hispanic, a group of citizens sued, alleging that the state's override of a valid school board election was in violation of the federal Voting Rights Act. This suit led the Texas legislature to amend its takeover law. Several other state takeover laws have been legally challenged (Reinhard, 1998).

School Choice

Another governance reform that is more widespread than state takeovers is school choice. Proponents of this reform often frame school choice as allowing greater freedom for parents, allowing poor families to have the same right to choose schools that middle- and upper-class families already enjoy, and highlighting the power of competition to improve public schools (Chubb & Moe, 1990; Morken & Formicola, 1999; Viteritti, 1999). However, many forms of school choice are, in effect, an expression of states' willingness to assert themselves at the expense of school boards; they shift the power to choose schools from the boards to parents, but at the same time they establish new departments in the State Department of Education to implement school choice programs. Most public voucher proposals call for the state to give money, in the form of a voucher, directly to parents to use to pay for their child's education either at a private school or at a public school outside the family's district of residence. In essence such policies liberate parents from local school districts, turning them into relatively free agents who can "shop" for the school that seems best for their child.

However, it is naive to assume that states will simply provide vouchers to parents and do nothing more. Even Chubb's and Moe's (1990) proposed "scholarship" (i.e., voucher) program called for the establishment of an agency that would oversee the program, approve schools for participation, and help parents through the application process, leading to charges that yet another government bureaucracy would be created. Even if a state passed legislation that did not originally include setting up such an agency, it is likely that after a few years the public would insist on closer regulation of voucher programs, leading to the creation of an office to provide program oversight. Moreover, many critics argue that in order for voucher programs to be equitable, parents must be provided with extensive information about schools and given assistance in evaluating them. After inevitable complaints about unfairness, pressures would build to give voucher oversight offices authority over the preparation and dissemination of this information as well.

As of this writing, only three public voucher programs exist in the United States: voucher programs limited to poor children are operating in Milwaukee and Cleveland, and Florida has adopted legislation that would give vouchers to the parents of children in "failing schools." The state government has been intimately involved in setting up and operating these programs. Interdistrict open enrollment, which allows children to move from one public school district to another, requires similar administration by the state. In Ohio, the state department of education required school boards to register their open enrollment policies, to prepare booklets explaining the program to local school officials and parents, to send state funds for each transfer student to the receiving districts, and to monitor and evaluate the program (Fowler, 1996).

Charter schools, another form of school choice, do not necessarily increase state power over public education. Some charter school laws restrict authority for chartering of schools to local school boards; most, however, do not. State boards of education, state departments of education, special chartering agencies set up by state law, and higher education institutions are among the entities that have been given the authority to approve charters (Hassel, 1999). Clearly, several of these options enhance state power; all reduce the power of local school boards. After several years of experience with charter schools, states are likely to tighten their oversight of them because of public concerns about financial accountability (see, for example, Ohlemacher & Stephens, 2001). Indeed, lawsuits have already been filed in some parts of the country, charging that state governments are not adequately monitoring the use of funds in charter schools. As with vouchers and interdistrict open enrollment, we can expect that charter schools will gradually increase the power of state government at the expense of local authority. Although charter schools are "sold" to parents with the claim that they are more autonomous than traditional public schools, scholars should be aware of the likelihood that, over time, they will actually enhance the power of the state at the expense of local authority.

Site-Based Management.

Another governance reform that can increase the power of the state is site-based management (SBM). Not every version of SBM has this effect. When a local school board votes to implement SBM within the borders of its own district, the power of the central office may be weakened, but the power of the state is not enhanced. However, in many instances state government itself mandates SBM, strengthening the building administration and council at the expense of the school board, superintendent, and district office staff. The Kentucky Education Reform Act (KERA), for example, required many schools in the state to engage in SBM. In a study of SBM in two high schools in Northern Kentucky, Goode (1994) found that the state government was actively engaged in training leaders as they implemented this new governance system. The SEA provided training sessions in Frankfort for principals and their school councils. Professional development plans initiated at the school level had to be approved by the SEA, not by the local board of education. Under KERA it was even possible for principals to apply to the state attorney general's office to obtain waivers releasing their schools from school board rules. Thus, in Kentucky and elsewhere, SBM, like state takeovers and school choice, has had the significant effect of strengthening the state governance structure vis-à-vis the local governance structure. There is still little evidence, however, that this strength has translated into improved student learning.

What Can States Do?

Over the last three decades, state governments have reasserted themselves, as the structures, the actors, and the roles of state government have come of age. States' commitment to educational reform has been continuous and persistent and shows no signs of abating. The fiscal and governance reforms that have been proposed and implemented have significantly strengthened the control of state governments over public education. In spite of this, state reform efforts have fallen far short of their goals. States have endured increasing pressures for fiscal equity and adequacy, for standards-based reforms, and for governance reforms, but for the most part the responses to these pressures have been incremental and ineffective.

Traditional and easily understood changes have been advocated by education reform commissions, school improvement plans, and the popular press, and have been seized upon by state governments. These have included smaller class sizes, longer school years, changes in teacher pay, higher standards, national certification, vouchers, and many other initiatives. The failure of these efforts to improve educational results effectively continues to frustrate policymakers who seek broad solutions. Even increasing teacher pay appears to produce few improvements (Ballou & Podgursky, 1997). Data published by Berliner and Biddle (1995) and Bracey (1991) have provided compelling evidence that student performance remained unchanged for the previous 20 years.

Educational researchers have always argued that robust and sustained improvement in student achievement can be attained only through the application of valid knowledge. Branson (2001) argues that substantial gains have been realized in other economic and social sectors through systematic research and development, and that there is no reason to believe that the educational sector would not see similar gains from such investment. State governments have by and large avoided funding or managing research and development in general, particularly in education. Arguably, states will never push past the political impasses of modest reform efforts, and the even more modest gains in student achievement, in the absence of a serious, sustained effort to develop a foundation of valid knowledge, to identify causes and effects, and to incorporate knowledge and theory in a learnable technology disseminated to practitioners for implementation (see Perelman, 1989).

Successful sectors of the American society and economy, including information technology, medicine, agriculture, and the military, have shown that substantial investment in research and development provides a large return on investment. State funding supports only a minute percentage of the education sector's total expenditures on research and development. And even when good research is available, implementation mechanisms are frequently absent and no benefit is realized. It is difficult to believe that states will ever improve student outcomes without doing the difficult and deliberate research and development work all advancing sectors are required to undertake. Whether or not a technical approach like systematic research and development can break through the political and professional struggles for control at the state level remains to be seen; for example, despite the evidence that smaller class sizes produce only modest advantages for particular students, class size reduction remains a popular reform goal among teachers, parents, and politicians.

The Impact of the Events of September 11, 2001

Undoubtedly, terrorism and the related problems of public safety and security have already significantly altered the state policy agenda. Education and education reform will cease to be the priorities they have been in national and state policy agendas over the last two decades, taking a back seat to security issues and budget concerns. There is almost certain to be a decline in funds available for schools from state governments. Although the federal government will have to assume much of the cost of the war against terrorism, a heavy financial burden will fall on states, as they take on new tasks related to security and public health while coping with a reactive and uncertain economy (Sandham, October 2001). Much of the money that becomes available for schools may end up allocated to improving security in them, leaving increased class sizes and decreased spending on areas such as professional development and instructional technology as likely outcomes.

In this changed policy environment, there may be little impetus for the state to pursue power and authority at the expense of local school boards. Some reforms, such as state takeovers, may become singularly unappealing to government officials who are struggling to meet more immediate challenges. It is possible that the shift of power from the local to the state level will slow or even stop. Nonetheless, we do not anticipate that the states will give their newly acquired power back to local school districts. As history has shown, once institutions gain power, they are loath to part with it. Despite these unprecedented events, we do not expect state governments to be an exception to this rule.

REFERENCES

Abbott v. Burke, 119 N.J. 287, 575 A.2d 359 (1990).

Ballou, D., & Podgursky, M. (1997). *Teacher pay and teacher quality*. Kalamazoo, MI: W.E. Upjohn Institute.

Berliner, D., & Biddle, B. (1995). *The manufactured crisis*. Boston, MA: Addison-Wesley.

Bracey, G.W. (1991). Why can't they be like we were? *Phi Delta Kappan, 73*, 104-117.

Branson, R.K. (2001). The untapped promise of educational research and development. In C.D. Herrington & K. Kasten (Eds.), *Florida 2001: Educational policy alternatives* (pp. 191-223). Jacksonville, FL: Florida Institute of Education, University of North Florida.

Campbell, R.F., Cunningham, L.L., McPhee, R.F., & Nystrand, R.O. (1970). *The organization and control of American schools*. 2nd edition. Columbus, OH: Charles E. Merrill Publishing Company.

Chubb, J., & Moe, T. (1990). *Politics, markets & America's schools*. Washington, DC: Brookings Institution.

Education Commission of the States. (2002). *No state left behind: The challenges and opportunities of the ESEA 2001*. Denver, CO: Author. Available at www.ecs.org

Fowler, F.C. (1996). Participation in Ohio's interdistrict open enrollment option. *Educational Policy, 10*, 518-536.

Fowler, F.C. (2000a). Converging forces: Understanding the growth of state authority over education. In N.D. Theobald & B. Malen (Eds.), *Balancing local control and state responsibility for K-12 education* (pp. 124-146). Larchmont, NY: Eye on Education.

Fowler, F.C. (2000b). *Policy studies for educational leaders*. Upper Saddle River, NJ: Merrill/Prentice Hall.

Fuhrman, S. (2001). *From the capitol to the classroom: Standards-based reform in the states. The 101st yearbook of the National Society for the Study of Education*, Part II. Chicago: National Society for the Study of Education.

Goode, E. (1994). Site-based management in public education: A challenge for critical pragmatism. Unpublished doctoral dissertation, Miami University, Oxford, Ohio.

Grissmer, D.W., Flanagan, A., Kawata, J., & Williamson, S. (2000). Improving student achievement: What NAEP state test scores tell us. RAND: Santa Monica, CA. Available: http://www.rand.org/education/pubs/assess.account.html

Guthrie, J.W., & Rothstein, R. (1999). Enabling 'adequacy' to achieve reality. In H.F. Ladd, R. Chalk, & J.S. Hansen (Eds.), *Education finance: Issues in equity and adequacy* (pp. 209-59). National Academy Press, National Research Council.

Hassel, B.C. (1999). *The charter school challenge: Avoiding the pitfalls, fulfilling the promise*. Washington, DC: Brookings Institution.

Herrington, C., & MacDonald, V. (2001). A thirty-year history of accountability legislation in Florida. In C. Herrington & K. Kasten (Eds.), *Educational policy alternatives: 2001* (pp. 7-34). Jacksonville, FL: Florida Institute of Education, University of North Florida.

Hoff, D.J. (2001, October 17). States urged to keep eyes on education. *Education Week on the Web*. Retrieved December 12, 2001 from http://www.educationweek.org/ew/ewstory.cfm?slug=07summit.h21&keywords=Hoff

Johnston, R.C. (1999, May 12). Governors vie with chiefs on policy, politics. *Education Week on the Web*. Retrieved December 17, 2001 from http://www.edweek.org/ew/ewstory.cfm?slug...of%20Chief%20State%20School%20ficers%20

Johnston, R.C., & Sandham, J.L. (1999, April 14). States increasingly flexing their policy muscle. *Education Week on the Web*. Retrieved December 17, 2001 from http://www.edweek.org/ew/vol-18/31/contro.h18

Klein, S.P., Hamilton, L.S., McCaffrey, D.F., & Stecher, B.M. (2000). *What do test scores in Texas tell us?* RAND: Santa Monica, CA. Available: http://www.rand.org/education/pubs/assess.account.html

Kohn, A. (2000). *The case against standardized testing: Raising the scores, ruining the schools*. Portsmith, NH: Heinemann.

Morken, H., & Formicola, J.R. (1999). *The politics of school choice.* Lanham, MD: Rowman & Littlefield.

Murray, S.E., Evans, W.N., & Schwab, R.M. (1998). Education finance reform and the distribution of education resources. *American Economic Review, 88*(4), 789-811.

National Alliance of Business. (2001). Web site. Available at: http://www.nab.com

National Center for Education Statistics. (November 1998). *Digest of Education Statistics.* Washington, DC: U.S. Department of Education.

National Center for Education Statistics. (2001). Cost adjustments in education. (Editors, William Fowler and David Monk). Washington, DC: U.S. Department of Education.

National Education Association. (2001). *Higher education and the states.* Washington, DC: National Education Association.

Odden, A., Archibald, S., & Fermanich, M. (2003). Rethinking the finance system for improved student achievement. In this volume—W.L. Boyd & D. Miretzky (Eds.), *American educational governance on trial: Change and challenges. The 102nd yearbook of the National Society for the Study of Education,* Part I (pp. 82-113). Chicago: National Society for the Study of Education.

Ohanian, S. (1999). *One size fits few: The folly of educational standards.* Portsmith, NH: Heinemann.

Ohlemacher, S., & Stephens, S. (2001, May 15). Charter school opponents drag Ohio into court. [Cleveland] *Plain Dealer,* 4B.

Perelman, L.J. (1989). *Closing education's technology gap.* Briefing Paper No. 111. Indianapolis: Hudson Institute.

Questionable clout. (1994, September 28). *Education Week,* 30.

Race and takeovers. (1998, January 14). *Education Week on the Web.* Retrieved December 8, 2001 from http://www.edweek.org/ew/vol-17/18mins1.h17

Ravitch, D. (1995). *National standards in American education: A citizens' guide.* Washington, DC: Brookings Institution.

Reichley, A.J. (1974). The states hold the keys to the cities. In W.P. Collins (Ed.), *Perspectives on state and local politics* (pp. 11-26). Englewood Cliffs, NJ: Prentice-Hall.

Reinhard, B. (1998, January 14). Racial issues cloud state takeovers. *Education Week on the Web.* Retrieved January 3, 2002 from http://www.edweek.org/ew/vol-17/18minor.h17

Richard, A. (2001, November 21). State chiefs' group readies for new direction. *Education Week on the Web.* Retrieved November 30, 2001 from http://www.edweek.org/ew/newstory.cfm

Sack, J.L. (2001, October 10). No longer a "splinter," ELC flexes new political muscle. *Education Week on the Web.* Retrieved December 21, 2001 from www.edweek.org/ew/newstory.cfm

Sandham, J.L. (1999, April 14). Despite takeover laws, states moving cautiously on interventions. *Education Week on the Web.* Retrieved January 8, 2002 from http://www.edweek.org/ew/vol-18/31local..h18

Sandham, J.L. (1999, June 9). Partisan politics lend new twist to state debates. *Education Week on the Web.* Retrieved January 3, 2002 from http://www.edweek.org/ew/vol-18/39legis.h18

Sandham, J.L. (2001, October 31). States' wallets grow thinner after Sept. 11. *Education Week on the Web.* Retrieved February 3, 2002 from http://www.edweek.org

Sandham, J.L. (2001, December 12). Budget problems force big layoffs in Buffalo schools. *Education Week on the Web.* Retrieved February 3, 2002 from http://www.edweek.org

Standards–Overview (2002, January 10). Available: http://www.ecs.org/ecs

State agencies take hands-on role in reform. (1999, June 23). *Education Week on the Web.* Retrieved December 29, 2001 from http://www.edweek.org/ew/newstory.cfm slug...ords=state%20departments%20of%20education)

State Policy Reports. (August 2002). *Education shares and shifts.* Alexandria, VA: Federal Funds Information for the States.

Stricherz, M. (2001, March 28). Governors seeking levers to improve education. *Education Week on the Web*. Retrieved December 27, 2001 from http://www.edweek.org/ew/ewstory.cfm?slug...of%20chief%20State%20School%20Officers%20

Viteritti, J.P. (1999). *Choosing equality: School choice, the Constitution, and civil society*. Washington, DC: Brookings Institution.

Wong, K.K. (1999). *Funding public schools: Politics and policies*. Lawrence, KS: University Press of Kansas.

CHAPTER 14

From the White House to the Schoolhouse: Greater Demands and New Roles

JACK JENNINGS

On January 8, 2002, President George W. Bush signed the No Child Left Behind Act, a bill that had been a major priority for passage during his first year in office. At the events surrounding this enactment, the President and congressional supporters hailed this legislation as the most important federal action to improve public education in many years. News reports described the legislation as heralding a much stronger federal role in education.

What should be made of this Act? Is it really that important? Is it truly calling for a different federal role in elementary and secondary education, or were all those speeches political hyperbole? If this is a change, what does it mean for traditional federal-state-local relationships? Most importantly, will school children learn more as a result, or are these just adults making speeches promising more than can be delivered?

The new legislation does indeed represent a broader and stronger federal role in elementary and secondary education. The federal government is putting more pressure on states and local school districts to raise student academic achievement, especially as measured by test scores. It is also increasing the pressure to reduce the achievement gaps between different racial, ethnic, and income groups of students. It has begun requiring states and school districts to upgrade the qualifications of teachers in all schools.

Rather than signaling an abrupt departure from the past, however, this expanded federal role is the culmination of a major change in federal aid to education that began in the late 1980s.

Furthermore, a more active federal role in education does not mean a diminished state or local role—to the contrary, states and local school districts are taking on more responsibilities than ever before. In

Jack Jennings is the Director of the Center on Education Policy in Washington, D.C.

short, changes in the governance of education are coming up and down the line, from the schoolhouse to the White House.

This chapter analyzes the significance of the No Child Left Behind Act from both a historical and a governance perspective. The chapter briefly reviews the early and recent history of the federal role in education, as a context for understanding how the new legislation builds on past precedents and where it is breaking new ground. It also looks at the political dynamics that led to the enactment of the Bush education bill. It next describes in detail the provisions of the new law and discusses their significance. Finally, the chapter examines five broad themes that underlie the changes in the federal role and in state and local responsibilities.

The Early Federal Role

The American national government has been involved in supporting education since the very first days of the Republic. In 1787, the Northwest Ordinance, one of the first laws enacted by the newly created federal government, encouraged the new territories of the country to establish schools by setting aside public land for that purpose. This national policy eventually led to the use of 77 million acres of land for the support of public education. Another significant step occurred after the Civil War, when the federal government required all new states admitted to the Union to provide free, nonsectarian public schools, thus furthering the spread of publicly supported education throughout the nation. That policy continued through the 19th century as many new states were admitted to the union (Rentner, 1998).

During the first half of the 20th century, national policies supported elementary and secondary education in several ways: through provisions in the federal tax code that permitted deductions for state and local taxes for education; through laws establishing vocational education programs in the schools; and through enactment of the National School Lunch Act of 1946, which led to the creation of feeding programs in most public schools. In 1954, the U.S. Supreme Court greatly affected public schools by its ruling in *Brown v. Board of Education*, which banned legal segregation by race in public institutions, including schools (Rentner, 1998).

Although these national policies had a significant impact on the schools, the traditional federal role was still ancillary to the much more visible role of local school boards and state governments. The Constitution implicitly vests the states with responsibility for public elementary and secondary education, but even the state governments played a limited role in education during much of the nation's history. Instead, they allowed local school districts—their legal creations—to exercise control over most of the fundamental issues affecting public education. Consequently, the concept of "local control of education" is deeply ingrained in the American consciousness, along with its traditional corollary of a limited role for both the federal and state governments.

The Modern Federal Role

The role of the federal government in elementary and secondary education began to change in the late 1950s. In 1957, the Soviet Union successfully launched a satellite that circled the globe, setting off alarm bells in the United States that the Communists were beating the West in the race for military dominance. One product of this anxiety was the National Defense Education Act of 1958, a federal law that provided funds to improve teaching in mathematics, science, and foreign languages. This legislation marked the beginning of a new era in educational governance, in which the federal government would play a more visible role.

In the early 1960s, Presidents John Kennedy and Lyndon Johnson helped bring about an overall expansion of federal aid for education. A prime motivation of these leaders was to address issues of poverty and racial discrimination, two themes that became part and parcel of the Great Society programs of the mid-to-late 1960s. President Johnson felt strongly that improving education was a critical way to address these social problems, and the depth of his feeling is evident in his comments as he signed into law the Elementary and Secondary Education Act of 1965. He said then: "I will never do anything in my entire life, now or in the future, that excites me more, or benefits the Nation I serve more ... than what we have done with this education bill" (Public papers of the presidents, 1966, p. 1).

The burst of national legislation in education and social welfare that occurred from the mid-1960s through the mid-1970s had a strong equity theme, in that it sought to address the causes of poverty and racial and social inequalities. Programs were created for poor children, disabled children, migrant children, children in institutions for the neglected and delinquent, and children who were limited English-speaking. Even those education programs that were created to address other issues or problems often had an equity orientation—for example, in their poverty-based funding formulas.

During the early 1980s, President Ronald Reagan strongly assailed all these programs, and was successful in trimming back some of the education and social welfare programs of the preceding era. However, he was unsuccessful in eliminating the new, more prominent federal role in education. In fact, *A Nation at Risk* (National Commission on Excellence in Education, 1983), a report that Reagan released at the White House, created such concern about the conditions of the public schools that it initiated a burst of education reform activity that continued through the late 1980s and early 1990s. These reforms strengthened both the federal and state roles in education.

The first indication of this strengthening at the federal level came in 1988, when the U.S. Congress amended the Elementary and Secondary Education (ESEA) Act of 1965 (Public Law 100-297, 1988) to require states to establish benchmarks for the academic progress of disadvantaged children; to use these benchmarks to measure the progress of disadvantaged children in schools receiving aid under Title I of the Act; and to assist schools that showed little or no progress in raising achievement for these students. These amendments came about because of criticism that the test scores of disadvantaged children were not rising even though schools were receiving significant amounts of federal aid to help in their education. During the next several years, the state departments of education began to implement these changes, but their progress was uneven. Some states identified many schools for assistance, while others named very few. Even so, these provisions of law had created the first links between the receipt of federal aid and the need to raise academic achievement, especially in schools that had persistently failed at that task.

Standards-Based Reform

In 1989, President George H.W. Bush convened the first national summit on education, with the active involvement of the governors of the states. The summit created a political dynamic that eventually encouraged the states, for the first time, to establish academic standards for students, design testing systems tied to these standards, and develop accountability measures based on test results. These three elements—standards, tests, and accountability systems—form the tripod of standards-based reform.

The path to these developments began when the nation's governors, in their follow-up deliberations to the 1989 summit, endorsed the concept of national goals for education. The path was further marked in the early 1990s when the administration of the elder Bush advocated for national academic standards and national tests and funded the development of such national standards. Bush had not asked Congress to endorse his push for national standards and tests, because he was afraid of becoming embroiled in political controversy about this idea. Instead, he asked for a new program to fund experimental schools, arguing that as part of a comprehensive school reform effort, schools had to change the way that they had been doing business. Congress, though, rejected this modest legislation, with the most intense objections coming from Republican conservatives who opposed even this slight enlargement of federal funding for education (Jennings, 1998).

In 1992, Bill Clinton defeated George Bush and changed the nation's course on many issues, but not on education. In fact, as one of his first priorities, President Clinton continued the efforts begun under Bush to advance standards-based reform from the national level. In 1994, after an intense struggle in the Congress, he achieved enactment of two significant laws that placed the federal government squarely behind standards-based reform: the Goals 2000: Educate America Act and the Improving America's Schools Act.

The Clinton legislation of the mid-1990s brought about a major shift in the expectations associated with federal aid for education. The Great Society programs had sought to focus additional federal funding on children with special needs, so those students would receive extra attention and thereby do better in school. Poor children and others with special needs were the recipients of targeted financial assistance from the federal government. Although the goal was to improve teaching and learning for these children, there were no serious consequences for school districts or states that failed to raise academic achievement among the targeted groups. As mentioned above, the 1988 amendments to the Title I program sought to tighten up accountability for districts and schools that received federal funds, but these changes were implemented timidly by the federal government and the states.

The Goals 2000: Educate America Act was based on a different concept. This law made federal assistance available to states that agreed to establish high academic standards for *all* students in their public schools and to implement state assessment systems that would measure the academic attainment of all students (Public Law 103-227, 1994). Although several states expressed some initial misgivings about these policies, eventually 48 states accepted the federal aid and began to implement these changes.

The other noteworthy law supported by Clinton was the Improving America's Schools Act, a 1994 set of amendments to the Elementary and Secondary Education Act. These changes required states to put into place academic standards in reading/language arts and mathematics for children receiving Title I assistance. It further required these Title I standards to be the same as the state's standards for all children, in states that had general standards. Paralleling Goals 2000, the ESEA amendments required states to have assessments that measured how well children were learning the content of the state standards. The legislation also required states to "disaggregate," or break out, test score data for children by major racial, ethnic, and income groups, and to set timetables for dealing with schools that failed to raise test scores for Title I children (Public Law 103-382). Although these ESEA amendments were focused on disadvantaged children, they also reinforced the broader expectations of higher academic achievement for all children contained in Goals 2000.

Thus, in the mid-1990s the federal government deepened its interest in education by incorporating into the equity purpose of earlier decades an explicit requirement to raise the academic achievement of disadvantaged children. At the same time, the federal government broadened its role in education by adding the purpose of raising the academic achievement of all students. The means to accomplish these ends was standards-based reform.

By putting the federal government solidly behind standards-based reform through these two complementary federal laws, the Clinton administration goaded the states into establishing academic standards, creating or expanding their assessment programs to measure students' progress in attaining those standards, and establishing systems of dealing with failing schools. It would take the states many years to accomplish those tasks, with some moving more slowly than others, but the direction was clearly set. While the federal government was considering this new policy, many states had already started to implement these kinds of changes on their own, with prodding from their governors, business leaders and others. In those states, the federal legislation served as an additional impetus to change.

Reaction and Recommitment

When the Republicans took control of both houses of Congress in 1995, it was the first time in 40 years that they had such power. Their enthusiasm to implement their positions was similar to the pent-up pressure from a lake rupturing a dam. Federal aid to education was one of the first targets of their political energy, as the Republican leadership took steps not only to reverse the expanded role brought about by Clinton, but also to eliminate or at least cut back sharply on the 35-year-old equity role fashioned by Lyndon Johnson (Jennings, 1998).

In 1995 and 1996, the new Republican Congress tried to repeal a number of education programs, attempted to consolidate others into block grants, and voted for cuts in education funding. The tenor of these efforts is illustrated by a remark made by Representative Charles Joseph Scarborough (R-Florida) when he introduced a proposal to repeal or consolidate most federal programs. "The great federal experiment in education is over," said Scarborough. "It failed. It is time to move on" (Sanchez, 1995, p. A-19).

Despite the ardor of the Republican majority, none of the party's proposals for block grants and education repeals had been enacted by the end of that Congress, and education funding was increased, not decreased. Clinton and the congressional Democrats, with help from some Senate Republicans and education and business leaders, beat back attempts to circumscribe the federal role in education.

In 1996, President Clinton was reelected, decisively defeating Senator Robert Dole (R-Kansas), who campaigned on a platform highly critical of public education and supportive of shifting federal funds from public schools to private schools through tuition vouchers. Clinton campaigned on a platform of raising academic standards in public schools and opposing vouchers. Immediately after the 1996 election, Texas Governor George W. Bush opined that Clinton had won because he had been able to win the women's vote, in part because of his stance on education (Balz, 1996).

When the younger Bush decided to run for president in 2000, he remembered that political lesson and made education a centerpiece of his campaign. He advocated higher standards for public schools, more testing for students, and a strict timetable to deal with failing schools. He proposed private school vouchers as a last resort for children in persistently failing public schools. He also called for a modest increase in federal education spending. Clearly, Bush was attempting to position himself as primarily interested in the improvement of public schools. Al Gore, his Democratic rival for the presidency, announced a much broader program of public school improvement that would raise teacher salaries, help schools with construction costs, and expand preschool programs. Gore's proposals would have increased education spending more than three times as much as Bush's.

As governor of Texas, Bush was already familiar with standards-based reform; his state had been an early leader in the standards movement. During the 1980s, Ross Perot, as head of a statewide committee, had proposed reforms to the public schools that eventually led Texas to define academic standards and implement a standards-based testing program. A noteworthy feature of those reforms was that each school had to raise the academic achievement of every major racial, ethnic, and income group of students in its building in order to be deemed successful. A school could not hide behind an overall increase in student performance while a major group of students, such as Hispanic or low-income students, was doing poorly. Two Democratic governors and Republican and Democratic state legislators supported these reforms before Bush became governor. Once elected, Bush continued gubernatorial support for standards-based reform through his appointments to the state board of education.

Consequently, when Bush became President he was comfortable in advocating national support of standards-based reform. His experiences in Texas reinforced his political judgment about the need to be identified with improving public schools. It was not as comfortable a position for many Republicans in Congress, however, who had just spent 5 years trying to undo Clinton's legislation. These conservatives were being asked by Bush not only to support the reforms they had opposed, but also to increase federal requirements on states and local school districts. Specifically, Bush proposed mandatory state tests for all students in grades 3 through 8; stronger accountability for raising academic performance among students in all major racial, ethnic, and income groups; and compliance with a precise timetable for improving schools with lagging achievement.

Bush proposed two elements as part of his school improvement package to help persuade Republican conservatives that he had heard their messages of more competition and less federal control: the offer of private school tuition vouchers as a last resort for students in failing public schools, and a legislative experiment called "Straight A's," which would allow several states to block grant federal programs and distribute the funds as they wished. When the Congress considered Bush's legislation in 2001, the Democrats succeeded in stopping both the proposal for private school vouchers and amendments for any large-scale block grants. Thus, the conservatives lost both ideas as major components of reform, but they did succeed in retaining vestiges of those concepts, in the form of a provision allowing parents to use a portion of federal funds for after-school tutoring provided by public or private

entities for students in persistently failing schools, and a very circumscribed experiment for a few states and districts to blend a few federal
programs.

No Child Left Behind Act

In January 2002, President Bush signed into law the No Child Left
Behind Act. The central feature of this law requires the states to adopt
a specific approach to testing and accountability, intended to lead to
higher achievement for all children. The legislation sends the message
that the federal government will be assuming a more forceful role in
elementary and secondary education, one that makes unprecedented
demands on states and local school districts to raise academic achievement, to take direct action to improve poorly performing schools, to
close the achievement gaps between various student groups, and to
raise the qualifications of teachers.

Regular testing in key subjects. Under the 1994 federal legislation,
states had to administer annual exams in reading/language arts and
mathematics at least once during grades 3 to 5, grades 6 to 9, and
grades 10 to 12. The 2002 law requires states to test students in more
grades, using assessments developed or chosen by each state. Since
these testing requirements will entail additional costs, they are contingent on the federal government's providing a set amount of funding
each year to help states cover these costs.

To be specific, by school year 2005-06, states must administer
statewide tests in mathematics and reading/language arts annually to
all children in grades 3 through 8, and at least once during grades 10 to
12, and must provide individual student test scores. By school year
2007-08, students must be tested in science at certain grade levels.
Starting in school year 2002-03, states must annually assess the English
proficiency of students who are learning the English language.

Every other year, states must administer the mathematics and reading exams of the National Assessment of Educational Progress (NAEP)
to a sample of their students in grades 4 and 8, with the federal government paying for the costs. This requirement is meant to serve as an
independent check on the accuracy of the scores from the states' own
tests.

Test design and use. The new law also requires state tests to be
aligned with the state's academic standards and to produce results that
are comparable from year to year. State tests must yield results that can
be used to determine whether students are meeting the state standards

and to help teachers diagnose and address students' specific academic needs. States must promptly provide test scores to local school districts by no later than the beginning of the school year after the test is given.

Disaggregated test results. Every school, school district, and state must disaggregate the average test results for certain groups of students, including major racial and ethnic groups, major income groups, students with a disability, and students with limited English proficiency.

Closing the achievement gap. Using disaggregated test information, states are required to follow a precise timeline to close achievement gaps between different racial, ethnic, and income groups, and other groups noted above. Beginning in school year 2002-03, states have 12 years to move all groups of students to the benchmark set by the state for proficiency in mathematics and reading. States must set regular targets for increasing achievement throughout the 12-year period, using as a starting level the average achievement of the lowest performing group of students or schools in the state.

Failing schools. Each school in the nation must test at least 95% of its students, and each group of students in a school must meet or exceed the annual objectives set for them. Schools that do not reach state performance objectives will be notified, and those that receive Title I aid will be subject to various forms of technical assistance, intervention, and other actions, depending on how long the failure persists.

- If a Title I school fails to meet performance objectives for *two consecutive years*, then it must receive technical assistance from the district to help it improve, and its students will have the option to transfer to another public school in the district.
- In the *third consecutive year* of failure, technical assistance to the school and options for public school choice will continue. In addition, students will have the option of using their share of Title I funds to pay for tutoring and other supplemental educational services either from their own school or from a state-approved outside group, such as a for-profit company, religious institution, or other private nonprofit entity.
- In the *fourth consecutive year*, technical assistance, public school choice, and supplemental services will continue, but the failing school must also change its staffing or make some other fundamental change.
- In the *fifth consecutive year*, the governance of the failing school must be changed—for example, by converting it to a charter school,

turning it over to a private management company, or having the state take it over.

Report cards and parents' right to know. Each school district must issue a report card to parents and the public that includes certain information about the school's achievement level, and parents are given the right to request information on the qualifications of teachers in a school.

Teacher qualifications. By 2005-06, states must have highly qualified teachers in all public school classrooms where core academic subjects are taught. "Highly qualified" means that a teacher must be fully certified or licensed, have a bachelor's degree, and show competence in subject knowledge and teaching skills (generally demonstrated by passing a rigorous state test). The requirements differ somewhat for new and already-hired teachers, and for elementary, middle, and high school teachers. New paraprofessionals hired with Title I funds must have at least 2 years of postsecondary education or pass a rigorous state test if they are involved in instruction, and current paraprofessionals must meet these requirements within a few years.

Flexibility. In exchange for meeting these federal demands, the new law gives educators more flexibility in the use of federal money. The main flexibility provisions allow districts to shift half of the funds in four federal programs among those various programs as they see fit, and to use Title I funds more loosely in any school with at least 40% poor children (currently that eligibility criterion is 50%).

More funds for the poorest districts. The new statute makes several changes for distributing Title I funds in order to direct additional funding to the poorest school districts. Even more significantly, the actual dollars to carry out this increase for low-income areas were appropriated by the fiscal year 2002 appropriations bill.

Other programs. The new legislation revises and extends many other federal aid programs for elementary and secondary education, and creates two noteworthy new programs—the "Teacher Quality" initiative to help school districts to recruit and retain teachers and principals and provide them with professional development, and the "Reading First" program to help districts carry out comprehensive programs to improve reading instruction.

Immediate action for students in failing schools. To underscore the urgency of the new federal demands for accountability, the law included some important changes that were effective in the school year that began eight months after the President signed the bill into law:

- In fall 2002, new teachers hired with Title I funds had to be highly qualified.

- In fall 2002, students in schools that had failed for a *second year* to meet the improvement provisions of the prior law had the option of leaving the failing school and enrolling in a different public school in the district. According to an early estimate from the U.S. Department of Education, students in an estimated 6,729 schools will have qualified for this option in fall 2002. The local school board had to pay for some or all of these students' transportation expenses.

- In fall 2002, students in an estimated 3,000 schools had to be offered two options: enrolling in a different public school or transferring their per-pupil share of Title I funding (between $300 and $1,000 per child) from the public school system to an outside provider of tutoring or supplemental services. This latter option applied to students in schools that had already been labeled as failing for *three years* under the previous federal law.

A More Demanding Federal Role

The No Child Left Behind Act of 2001 marks a significant shift in governance of elementary and secondary education in the United States. As is obvious from the detailed description above, the federal government is assuming a larger role in elementary and secondary education and making great demands on states and local school districts. Five major themes underlie this expansion of the federal role and of state and local responsibilities.

First, the federal role in education is now meant to affect every student and every school in the United States. Gone are the intents of past legislation to limit the requirements of federal aid to defined classes of children.

The equity-oriented programs of the 1960s and the 1970s provided financial assistance for certain groups of children, and the requirements of these laws were generally limited to ensuring that funds reached the targeted children and provided them with extra services. The most detailed example is the Individuals with Disabilities Education Act, the federal law that seeks to ensure that children with disabilities receive a free and appropriate public education. Although this law applies to all school districts and in some ways affects the education of other children, its clear focus is on children with disabilities.

The elder Bush's campaign for national academic standards and assessments during the early 1990s opened the door at the national level for a different federal role than a limited, equity-oriented one. During the mid-to-late 1990s, President Clinton pushed harder on that door with laws that aimed to raise academic achievement not only for disadvantaged children, but for all children in public elementary and secondary schools.

The younger Bush's No Child Left Behind Act opens that door wide. There is no doubt now that the federal government is in the business of improving the education of all public school students. Students in grades 3 through 8 will have to be tested in three subject areas, regardless of whether their schools receive federal funds. The achievement gap will have to be closed for specified groups of children, regardless of whether they are the beneficiaries of additional federal aid. Schools that do not raise academic achievement for all students, as well as for specified groups of students, will be labeled as failing, although mandated corrective action will have to occur only in those schools receiving Title I dollars. All teachers in every school will have to be highly qualified according to the federal definition.

Clearly, the federal government is now involved in elementary and secondary education on a broad scale. In a way, this is a reversion to the role the national government had in elementary and secondary education in the late 18th century and the 19th century, when it helped to lay the foundations of public education through its land and statehood policies. The public school systems that resulted now cover every community in the nation and serve nearly 90% of American children. A noteworthy difference today is the degree of specificity of the federal requirements being placed on the states and school districts to broadly improve education.

Second, the principal reason for the federal government's involvement in elementary and secondary education has been clearly declared to be raising students' academic achievement. This sharpness of purpose is a new development, as are the detailed consequences for not measuring up to that purpose.

During the 18th and 19th centuries, the federal government worked to expand public schooling, and during the early 20th century, it indirectly supported education through the tax code and through ancillary services. During the latter part of the 20th century, the federal purpose was to expand educational opportunity by providing funds for additional services for specified subgroups of children. Underlying all this activity was the premise that expanding public schooling or providing additional services was good enough. If there were more public schools, and if these schools focused more services on certain children, it was assumed that students would learn and the country would benefit from a more educated citizenry.

The elder Bush's push for change, Clinton's landmark legislation, and now the younger Bush's law make clear that the purpose of national support for education has been changed, and the bar has been raised. Merely providing for public education or paying for additional services is no longer good enough.

The new criterion for success is higher academic achievement, as measured by student test scores, the proxy for improved learning. States and school districts must raise test scores overall and for various ethnic, racial, income, and disability groups. Accountability now means higher test scores, and there are clear consequences for states and school districts whose students do not perform well. Schools receiving federal funds are put into a 5-year schedule of changes, leading to eventual reconstitution or state takeover, unless their test scores go up in the aggregate *and* for all major subgroups.

Third, the insistence on raising test scores for specific subgroups of children shows that the equity purpose of the 1960s and 1970s has been retained and sharpened. Precise goals are set to improve the education of disadvantaged children, and detailed timelines are established for achieving these goals.

States have 12 years to bring major subgroups to the achievement level specified by the state as proficient, based on its academic standards. Every school, even one that does not receive a dollar of Title I aid, is held to this same requirement and has to disaggregate its test scores by group. The school district must release to the public the test scores of students in the aggregate, of all major groups, and of each school. Schools that receive Title I funds but do not raise scores for each major group are held to the accountability measures described above. Last, every school, including the poorest, will have to have highly qualified teachers in every classroom.

Fourth, the federal government is demanding major improvements in the qualifications of teachers and paraprofessionals. This demand is worthy of special note because it has very broad implications. The field of elementary and secondary education is very labor-intensive, with approximately 80% of the current expenditures salary-related. Therefore, the new federal requirements to raise the qualifications of teachers and paraprofessionals will have a major budgetary impact.

By fall 2002, all new teachers and paraprofessionals hired with Title I funds had to meet the qualifications spelled out in the new law. By school year 2005-06, all teachers in the country have to be fully qualified, regardless of whether or not their salaries are from federal funds.

The congressional proponents of this provision argued that the quality of the teaching force had to be raised if children were to show greater academic achievement. They pointed to the Tennessee STAR experiment (Finn & Achilles, 1990), which was a longitudinal study tracking the effects of various factors on students' success, and other studies showing the great impact that teaching can have on youngsters. They further argued that schools having concentrations of poor students and children from minority groups also had high concentrations of uncertified teachers and teachers teaching outside the field for which they were trained. These factors make it difficult to close the achievement gap between the various racial, ethnic, and income groups.

These arguments were persuasive enough to garner support for the teacher quality provisions in the new federal law. The impact of these requirements will be enormous. In California, for instance, a large percentage of teachers are not certified, and the greatest concentrations of these teachers are in the state's poorest schools. Due to the immensity of the problem, California is unlikely to comply with this requirement by the deadline specified in the law.

Many supporters of standards-based reform had argued that the emphasis ought to be on the outcomes or results, and that it did not matter how states and school districts attained those results. These supporters argued that the inputs of education, such as per-pupil spending, class size, and teacher qualifications, could not be proven to result in higher test scores for students, and therefore there was no need to attend to the inputs. Obviously, this argument has not fully carried the day in debates at the national level. After being told that the new law permits a more flexible approach toward program requirements, states and school districts may find it ironic that they must comply with much more difficult and expensive provisions dealing with salaries and remediation.

Fifth, the larger federal role also means a larger role for states and school districts. It is not a zero-sum game, where state and local responsibilities shrink as the federal role expands. Rather, standards-based reform as embodied in this federal legislation means that all three levels of school governance—federal, state, and local—must assume responsibilities they have not previously had or have not fully embraced.

In creating a larger federal role as outlined above, the president and congressional leaders are expecting much more of state governments and local school districts. States must expand their assessment programs and provide individual student scores that can be used to diagnose student needs. States must provide technical assistance to local school districts that are not raising their test scores. States must show gradual progress toward closing the achievement gap. States must take steps toward having highly qualified teaching forces.

Local school districts must provide technical assistance to persistently failing schools that receive Title I funds. They must show progress toward reducing the achievement gap. They must respond to parental requests about the qualifications of teachers and must issue report cards showing the achievement levels of students in each school. Local school boards and superintendents will also have to find highly qualified teachers for every classroom.

Although some states and school districts are already providing technical assistance to failing districts and schools, very few are doing so on the scale envisioned by this Act. Some states offer small incentives to teachers to work in the poorest schools in the state, but none is offering the higher salaries and other benefits that are likely to be needed to fill every classroom in the most challenged schools with highly qualified teachers.

It is a legitimate question to ask whether the federal government, in urging these expanded responsibilities up and down the line, is paying its fair share of the costs of these additional duties. To accompany his education proposal, President Bush had wanted a modest increase in federal spending on education. The Democratic congressional leaders successfully insisted on a larger increase of 17% for the first year of the new law, in order to justify its demands. The president has asked for an even smaller increase for the second year of the new law than he had asked for the first year. It is an open question whether the federal government will match its increased demands with additional assistance to meet them.

Conclusion

The federal role in elementary and secondary education is expanding. The No Child Left Behind Act of 2001 embodies a very ambitious set of goals for improving public schools and increasing academic achievement among all students. Carrying out these goals will be enormously difficult.

In terms of federal enforcement, the U.S. Department of Education can cut some state administrative funds supplied by the federal government if a state does not comply with various provisions of the new law. But that amount is not significant in the overall scheme of state and local funding of education. The Department can resort to a broader cutoff of a state's federal funding if it is not in compliance with the requirements of the law. Traditionally, however, the Department has taken the approach of prodding states to comply, rather than withholding major funding. A strong deterrent to broadly denying funds is that most financial assistance from the Department to the states is for the benefit of disadvantaged and disabled children. Therefore, cutting funds means fewer services for these children—a chilling factor when any such threat is considered.

In prodding states to comply with federal laws, the Department encounters serious difficulties. For example, when President Bush signed the new law, a minority of states was in compliance with the changes enacted 8 years earlier under President Clinton. As of March 2002, only 17 states had fully approved standards and assessment systems as required by the 1994 education amendments. U.S. Secretary of Education Rod Paige has said that states must comply with the 1994 law, even as he faces the more difficult task of getting the states to conform with the far more demanding requirements of the 2002 law (Weinstein, 2002).

The states face their own difficulties in changing their educational systems to incorporate standards-based reform. For instance, state departments of education often do not have many experts in assessment or in providing technical assistance to persistently failing schools. Inadequate funding of state agencies is also a common problem, since several states have severely cut the budgets of state education departments within the last decade. Last, state legislators may resent providing state appropriations for activities that are mandated by federal law but not fully funded by the federal government. Currently, the federal share of total contributions for elementary and secondary education is about 7%, far less than will be needed to fulfill the goals of the new law.

Local school districts share some of these same problems. Frequently, they do not have sufficient expertise on staff to deal with assessment, curriculum, and technical assistance matters. Many school districts also lack the financial resources that will be needed to hire more qualified teachers and to provide extra time and effort to help students whose achievement is lagging.

This new federal role calls for the nation's schools to fulfill some very worthy and ambitious goals. Yet, the federal government currently lacks the capacity to carry out those goals, as do states and local school districts. The next several years will show whether this new federal role is trimmed back because its promises are difficult to fulfill, or whether all levels of government will rise to the challenge of making American public schools better for all children.

NOTES

A shortened version of the part of this chapter dealing with a more demanding federal role (pp. 302-306) appeared as an article in the *American School Board Journal*, September 2002, pp. 25-27, © National School Boards Association.

REFERENCES

The Augustus F. Hawkins-Robert T. Stafford Elementary and Secondary School Improvement Amendments of 1988. Public Law 100-297, April 28, 1988.

Balz, D. (1996, November 27). Stands on education cost GOP among women, governors told. *Washington Post*, A-6.

Finn, J.D., & Achilles, C.M. (1990). Answers and questions about class size: A statewide experiment. *American Educational Research Journal*, 27(3), 557-577.

Goals 2000: Educate America Act. (1994). Public Law 103-227, March 31, 1994.

Improving America's Schools Act. (1994). Public Law 103-382, October 20, 1994.

Jennings, J.F. (1998). *Why national standards and tests? Politics and the quest for better schools*. Thousand Oaks, CA: Sage Publications.

National Commission on Excellence in Education. (1983). *A nation at risk: The imperative for educational reform*. Washington, DC: U.S. Government Printing Office.

Public papers of the presidents of the United States: Lyndon Johnson, Book 1, January 1 to May 31, 1965, 2 vols. (1966). Washington, DC: U.S. Government Printing Office.

Rentner, D. (1998). *A brief history of the federal role in education*. Washington, DC: Center on Education Policy.

Sanchez, R. (1995, May 25). House Republicans' proposal would end much of federal role in education. *Washington Post*, A-19.

Weinstein, M. (2002, May 1). Making the grade. *Government Executive Magazine*.

Name Index

Note: This index includes names associated with a theory, concept, program, experiment or other work with a substantive description. It does not include names given in examples or passing references.

Subject Index

313

RECENT PUBLICATIONS OF THE SOCIETY

1. The Yearbooks

102:1 (2003) *American Educational Governance on Trial: Change and Challenges.* William Lowe Boyd and Debra Miretzky, editors. Cloth.

102:2 (2003) *Meeting at the Hyphen: Schools-Universities-Communities-Professions in Collaboration for Student Achievement and Well Being.* Mary M. Brabeck, Mary E. Walsh, and Rachel E. Latta, editors. Cloth.

101:1 (2002) *The Educational Leadership Challenge: Redefining Leadership for the 21st Century.* Joseph Murphy, editor. Cloth.

101:2 (2002) *Educating At-Risk Students.* Sam Stringfield and Deborah Land, editors. Cloth.

100:1 (2001) *Education Across a Century: The Centennial Volume.* Lyn Corno, editor. Cloth.

100:2 (2001) *From Capitol to the Cloakroom: Standards-based Reform in the States.* Susan H. Fuhrman, editor. Cloth.

99:1 (2000) *Constructivism in Education.* D. C. Phillips, editor. Cloth.

99:2 (2000) *American Education: Yesterday, Today, and Tomorrow.* Thomas L. Good, editor. Cloth.

98:1 (1999) *The Education of Teachers*, Gary A. Griffin, editor. Paper.

98:2 (1999) *Issues in Curriculum*, Margaret J. Early and Kenneth J. Rehage, editors. Cloth.

97:1 (1998) *The Adolescent Years: Social Influences and Educational Challenges.* Kathryn Borman and Barbara Schneider, editors. Cloth.

96:1 (1997) *Service Learning.* Joan Schine, editor. Cloth.

96:2 (1997) *The Construction of Children's Character.* Alex Molnar, editor. Cloth.

95:1 (1996) *Performance-Based Student Assessment: Challenges and Possibilities.* Joan B. Baron and Dennie P. Wolf, editors. Cloth.

94:1 (1995) *Creating New Educational Communities.* Jeannie Oakes and Karen Hunter Quartz, editors. Cloth.

94:2 (1995) *Changing Populations/Changing Schools.* Erwin Flaxman and A. Harry Passow, editors. Cloth.

93:1 (1994) *Teacher Research and Educational Reform.* Sandra Hollingsworth and Hugh Sockett, editors. Cloth.

93:2 (1994) *Bloom's Taxonomy: A Forty-year Retrospective.* Lorin W. Anderson and Lauren A. Sosniak, editors. Cloth.

92:1 (1993) *Gender and Education.* Sari Knopp Biklen and Diane Pollard, editors. Cloth.

92:2 (1993) *Bilingual Education: Politics, Practice, and Research.* M. Beatriz Arias and Ursula Casanova, editors. Cloth.

91:1 (1992) *The Changing Contexts of Teaching.* Ann Lieberman, editor. Cloth.

91:2 (1992) *The Arts, Education, and Aesthetic Knowing.* Bennett Reimer and Ralph A. Smith, editors. Cloth.

Order the above titles from the University of Chicago Press, 11030 S. Langley Ave., Chicago, IL 60628. For a list of earlier Yearbooks still available, consult the University of Chicago Press website: www.press.uchicago.edu

2. The Series on Contemporary Educational Issues

This series has been discontinued.

The following volumes in the series may be ordered from the McCutchan Publishing Corporation, 3220 Blume Drive, Suite 197, Richmond, CA 94806. Local phone: (510)758-5510, Toll free: 1-800-227-1540, Fax: (510)758-6078, e-mail: mccutchanpublish@aol

Academic Work and Educational Excellence: Raising Student Productivity (1986). Edited by Tommy M. Tomlinson and Herbert J. Walberg.
Adapting Instruction to Student Differences (1985). Edited by Margaret C. Wang and Herbert J. Walberg.
Choice in Education (1990). Edited by William Lowe Boyd and Herbert J. Walberg.
Colleges of Education: Perspectives on Their Future (1985). Edited by Charles W. Case and William A. Matthes.
Contributing to Educational Change: Perspectives on Research and Practice (1988). Edited by Philip W. Jackson.
Effective Teaching: Current Research (1991). Edited by Hersholt C. Waxman and Herbert J. Walberg.
Moral Development and Character Education (1989). Edited by Larry P. Nucci.
Motivating Students to Learn: Overcoming Barriers to High Achievement (1993). Edited by Tommy M. Tomlinson.
Radical Proposals for Educational Change (1994). Edited by Chester E. Finn, Jr. and Herbert J. Walberg.
Reaching Marginal Students: A Prime Concern for School Renewal (1987). Edited by Robert L. Sinclair and Ward Ghory.
Restructuring the Schools: Problems and Prospects (1992). Edited by John J. Lane and Edgar G. Epps.
Rethinking Policy for At-risk Students (1994). Edited by Kenneth K. Wong and Margaret C. Wang.
School Boards: Changing Local Control (1992). Edited by Patricia F. First and Herbert J. Walberg.

The two final volumes in this series were:

Improving Science Education (1995). Edited by Barry J. Fraser and Herbert J. Walberg.
Ferment in Education: A Look Abroad (1995). Edited by John J. Lane.

These two volumes may be ordered from the Book Order Department, University of Chicago Press, 11030 S. Langley Ave., Chicago, IL 60628. Phone: 1-800-621-2736; Fax: 1-800-621-8476.